NONLINEAR PRICING

NONLINEAR PRICING

Theory & Applications

Christopher T. May

JOHN WILEY & SONS, INC.
New York • Chichester • Weinheim • Brisbane • Singapore • Toronto

Library of Congress Cataloging-in-Publication Data:
May, Christopher T., 1961–
    Nonlinear pricing : theory & applications / Christopher T. May.
      p.   cm.—(Wiley trading advantage)
    Includes bibliographical references and index.
    ISBN 0-471-24551-8 (cloth : alk. paper)
    1. Pricing.   I. Title.   II. Title: Nonlinear pricing.
    III. Series.
    HF5416.5.M39   1999
    658.8'16—dc21   98-37590

To my parents, who taught me that public service is the price you pay for occupying your space on Earth.

I am also graced in that God gave me not only sight but vision as well. I share this vision with you through this book. I cannot share sight, but I can contribute to it.

Part of the proceeds of this book are donated to the most Venerable Order of The Hospital of St. John of Jerusalem which runs an eye hospital there.

CONTENTS

Preface   ix

Acknowledgments   xix

1 A Toy Story for Wall Street   1

2 Nonlinearity: A Retrospective   29

3 Nonlinearity: A Prospective   68

4 Fractal Analysis   111

5 Results of the Hurst Exponent   149

6 Nonlinear Technology   173

7 Biology and the S&P   197

8 Father Time   209

9 Nonlinear Pricing—Advanced Concepts   229

10 The Last Word—Resonance   288

Appendix   Survey of Nonlinear Thinking in Financial Economics   303

Glossary   323

Bibliography   333

Index   353

PREFACE

Part of the difficulty in reaching an understanding of nonlinear pricing is that we must see three major trends simultaneously. First are the assumptions and the mathematical constructs that embody those assumptions at various levels of resolution in economics. For example, levels of resolution are illustrated in the difference between micro- and macroeconomics. Second, we must see the conceptual links, again expressed in mathematics, between other disciplines and economics. For example, later we will introduce genetic algorithms, a mathematical technique based on the principles of evolution and founded by a computer scientist. Third is the environment of faster clock speeds of microchips and greater bandwidth in which the change in financial economics takes place—that is, cyberspace. We must also take a step back and see how and why we got to where we are now. One cannot trade or value financial instruments without understanding. We also have to discuss some aspects of science and the accepted rules of logic. This may be considered by some to be a digression. Maybe it is, but on the other hand maybe companies that lost a lot of money on derivatives wished they had better understood the nature of the beast. Skip this at your own peril.

With such a broad purview, perhaps beginning with an executive summary may focus thoughts and attentiveness. What is the conclusion of *Nonlinear Pricing*? In general, we are at the beginning of an age where the role of the computer is maturing from an enabler of mere clerical functions to a creator of computer-based valuation techniques, like nonlinear pricing, that either rival or augment traditional investment methodologies. Specifically, by "nonlinear" we mean disproportionate, and "pricing" signifies that we are attempting the imperfect art of placing a number or value on some type of information.

Why is this happening? For two simple reasons: (1) Nonlinear pricing is the small but logical next step of cost cutting by the finance, high-tech, and telecommunications industries to improve efficiencies, and (2) the influence of the high-tech and telecommunications industries in finance is increasing. True, my computer may never get the tip on the golf course, but the amount of computational horsepower that can be marshaled and thrown at a problem doubles every 18 months and the price of this capability is dropping asymptotically to zero. And it can be done consistently. By putting finance on-line—from trading brokerage accounts to eliminating paper checks—the finance industry, perhaps unwittingly, is rapidly creating the conditions to make nonlinear pricing a common reality. Bandwidth is also becoming more available and cheaper at an unprecedented rate of growth that exceeds that of microprocessor clock speed. The rationale of cost cutting follows closely on the heels of a rate of technological innovation that is happening at warp speed.

At present nonlinear pricing is qualitatively a different sort of information than investors are used to viewing. That is, characterizing periods of partial predictability does not seem to jibe with concepts such as earnings and market share. In time these types of information will converge. Nonlinear pricing will become another arrow in the quiver of analytical techniques. In a June 8, 1998, *Fortune* interview with Arno Penzias, Nobel laureate and recently retired chief scientist of AT&T and Lucent, Dr. Penzias gave this answer to a query on networking: "Owning a telephone network is a license to learn about customers. The important thing is the management of the information rather than the movement of the bits. Walter Wriston once said something like this: 'The time will come when the information derived from a financial transaction will be more valuable than the execution of the transaction itself.' " Both Penzias's and Wriston's purview as network administrators is broader than that of the analyst using nonlinear pricing. They sought to learn about customers and we seek to learn about financial time series. However, the essence of both messages is identical. Nonlinear pricing and knowledge of customers' transactions both say something new. And what makes that new message possible is the medium of cyberspace in which the transaction occurs. What must be kept in mind is that disclosures of company financials mandated by the Securities and Exchange Commission continue to migrate further into cyberspace: from analysts' spreadsheets to company web sites. It is not unreasonable to expect that the SEC will require an online posting by public companies for reasons of economy and fairness, so that everyone will have access at the same time. As this happens, nonlinear pricing will extend its reach because at that point relationships between sales, earnings, and so forth—the traditional purview of the fundamental analysts—will be married to other variables such as subjective descriptors and price action—the traditional purview of technical analysts. The relationships between and among all these different kinds of variables will be subject to interpretation—either verification or falsification—by nonlinear means in cyberspace. Why? The reason is simple: Much of the linear- or equilibrium-based theory we now use to explain relationships in financial economics exists because the computational horsepower to execute nonlinear/nonequilibrium analysis did not exist or was too expensive. With the barriers to feasibility and cost-effectiveness effectively removed and the operational reality of an electronic environment, why perpetuate the already compromised assumptions of randomness and equilibrium—the linear technology—to interpret those relationships?

From changing the physical execution of a transaction to an electronic means for cost reasons, it follows that the new electronic environment or cyberspace allows us to challenge some old assumptions about how instruments are valued and to quantify aspects previously unseen. After all, the business reason of cost cutting is well comprehended and the same technological infrastructure that allows us to change the way we trade also introduces new types of information we can extract to value the trade—or the customer. Information is the lifeblood of Wall Street. It is in every participant's financial self-interest to extract as much information as cheaply as possible. Broadly speaking, this is how you will make money. As an emergent methodology of interpreting relationships in financial economics, nonlinear pricing presents as big an opportunity—or threat—to traditional views as did Copernicus's symbolic (i.e., mathematical) interpretation of the universe, which rivaled the Church's method of interpretation based on divinity. So radical a paradigm shift was Copernicus's book *The Revolutions of the Spheres* that our modern-day use of the word "revolution" in a political context commemorates this fact. In sum, the applied science of information technology is good business.

In examining all the component technologies (e.g., Hurst, genetic algorithms, fuzzy logic, abductive logic, etc.) of nonlinear pricing or the possibilities of combinations of those technologies (e.g., fuzzy GAs), this book presents only two—the Hurst exponent as displayed on Bloomberg and a genetic algorithms analysis. Had more been presented, this volume would be unwieldly. The Hurst exponent is applied to a variety of financial instruments and the GA analysis is applied to component indexes of the S&P. Of all the nonlinear technologies in nonlinear pricing, the Hurst exponent is the most accessible, broadly speaking, in that it is on a private network—Bloomberg. The Hurst exponent is the most important technology of nonlinear pricing to be disseminated at this nascent stage because it refutes the 25-year-old assumption of Brownian motion—a central tenant of the Capital Asset Pricing Model and the Black-Scholes option pricing model and equilibrium. Having disproved this central tenent begs the question, and in light of a cyber environment with superior mathematics and computational ability, what other assumptions in the realm of financial economics are in need of substantive revision?

So the Hurst exponent is only the tip of the iceberg. To attack the larger assumptions of equilibrium upon which macro- and microeconomics rest requires deeper thought and more powerful—or exotic—techniques. It also requires conceptualization on a level of abstraction to which the nominative user of software in financial economics is probably not accustomed. It is true that the various nonlinear technologies may not be familiar; however, they only produce output on a screen. What may be challenging is cognizing what the output really means. Most people have to begin by interpreting a nonlinear output within their traditional linear framework. Only after some work will the more realistic nonlinear framework emerge. For example, the methodological approach to problems in nonlinear pricing is qualitatively different than it is in the naive world that assumes linearity. This is not a trivial hurdle because computational rather than analytic solutions are used. That is, we use multiple iterations to evolve a solution rather than just throwing a formula at the problem. Formulas tend to be static, whereas iterative techniques, like evolution, are dynamic. Thus, the vital but often overlooked dimension of time is included in the analysis. This is a subtle point but a major stumbling block for most people because they have been trained to believe that most—if not all—relationships in financial economics can be characterized by a simple formula. Of course, what makes computational proofs possible is more microprocessor clock speed and bandwidth.

Thus, to understand the techniques of nonlinear pricing requires an understanding of the tools that make it possible. This is also a subtle point and a major stumbling block. Too often a basic understanding of (1) science (e.g., biology, mathematics, physics, etc.), (2) technology (e.g., PCs, networking, software, etc.), (3) asset valuation techniques (e.g., fundamental analysis, CAPM, Black-Scholes, etc.) and (4) styles of money management (e.g., distressed securities, arbitrage, currency/commodity trading, emerging markets, etc.) are not found in the same body. Geeksters have a natural advantage on numbers 1 and 2 and traditional Wall Street types have the advantage on numbers 3 & 4. Although the cyber environment and the analysis and underwriting of technology stocks have brought these two groups together, their direct interface occurs only in well-choreographed spots such as the technology support role or the high-tech analyst or banker or the odd physicist in the derivatives department. However, the critical mass of integration has been achieved so that technology can progress up the financial value-added chain from changing how we trade to changing how we *value* what we trade. Although their integration is far from complete, nonlinear pricing is the next chapter. Thus, evolutionary techniques are not news to computer scientists; however, to most of Wall Street they are news.

As can be see in Table P.1, there is a definite relationship between micro- and macroeconomics and the assumptions of linearity and equilibrium. These assumptions find their roots in physics. More realistically and as a direct con-

Table P.1   Financial Economics: Old Theory and New Reality

		Old Theory (Physics-based)	New Reality (Biology-based)
Financial economics	Macroeconomics (economics)	Equilibrium (Newtonian-based physics)	Nonequilibrium (complexity theory)
	Microeconomics (finance)	Linear (randomness or Brownian motion)	Nonlinear (fractional Brownian motion as measured by the Hurst exponent)

sequence of the computing power, a rival interpretation has emerged based largely on the concept of evolution in biology. The term *financial economics* is preferred because the subject of nonlinear pricing touches both finance and economics. Finance is really microeconomics as opposed to macroeconomics, which is usually just called economics. The distinction between micro- and macroeconomics is not precisely defined, but microeconomics as it is generally accepted applies to a narrower definition of phenomena such as a company rather than a country. This narrowness also implies a shorter time horizon of days, weeks, and months rather than months and years. A further implication exists as a result of both a narrower definition of phenomena and a shorter time horizon, and that is a stronger causal relationship—that is, a more direct relationship between cause and effect.

The differences between economists, analysts, investment bankers, and traders have more to do with their level of resolution or generality at which they view phenomena than the tools they use to characterize financial and economic relationships. Much of the information used by these various parties in practice is informal in the sense that much is not bound in theory. Of course, with time, as greater amounts of knowledge are codified, progress is measured. It is the hope of theory to better explain reality and likewise that much of what is successful will find its expression in more rigorous terms.

However, when we do look at the assumptions and the mathematical constructs used to give rigor to those assumptions we see that in finance there is an assumption of randomness of the movement of a time series. As we shall later see, when the late Fischer Black, coauthor of the famous Black-Scholes option pricing model, designed the model, he did so with the express concept of equilibrium in mind. Neoclassical economics, the stuff 99.9% of you studied in high school, college, and graduate school, had influenced him. The link to be made here is that it is impossible to have nonlinearity in finance and equilibrium in economics. They are mutually exclusive. Put another way, once we destroy linearity in finance, the concept of equilibrium in economics must also fall, and vice versa.

The Hurst exponent, which is subsequently discussed, is prima facie evidence that a time series in finance is not random and nonlinear. The Hurst exponent is sort of like the proverbial loose thread of the sweater, which when pulled unravels the whole garment. In our case that garment is the financial economic theory and the mathematical constructs used to express that theory. Thus, even though the most likely audiences of this book are microeconomic practitioners or financiers of some sort, for thoroughness we present a complete background to avoid potential confusion.

Seeing the whole, we may be able more clearly to see how the contributions of others fit in. For example, Benoit Mandelbrot is a mathematician and father of the fractal. This concept ties in more easily to finance rather than economics per se. Conversely, at the macro level, economists such as Paul Romer have dealt with increasing returns; John Holland, a computer scientist, is father of genetic algorithms; Stuart Kauffman, a mathematical biologist, has worked with complexity theory and self-organization. All of these scholars have dealt with nonequilibrium concepts. Some are borne in economics proper and some are not, but that does not make them any less worthy of our attention—or any less applicable.

To see across disciplines we need a common denominator. That common denominator is science, primarily physics for historical reasons and biology for contemporary reasons. Sometimes we will have to revert to the language of objectivity to express those concepts called mathematics. This may seem like a circuitous route but it is not since most of the underpinnings of financial economics are restated physics: the concept of equilibrium for macroeconomics and the gas-diffusion equation for Black-Scholes.

Our vision across disciplines must also have depth. We spoke earlier of the concept of resolution between micro- and macroeconomics. The same holds true of the sciences, with physics considered the most fundamental. Despite physics's primacy, its explanatory power is limited with respect to more derivative phenomena such as biology or economics. True, animals may be comprised of atoms, but the weak force attraction of atomic nuclei do not shed much light on how or why we buy and sell. Someday it may but for the present the phenomena of economics are too sophisticated for explanations based on first principles. Thus, sciences like biology and economics that cannot solely be explained by physics are higher-level sciences.

The difficulty is in having (1) a depth of view in terms of resolution and explanatory power, (2) breadth across disciplines, and (3) knowledge of the information age which is making these changes possible. This interdisciplinary approach is the shape of things to come.

PREPARATION

Chapter 1, "A Toy Story for Wall Street," prepares the reader for the impact of technology on Wall Street with three examples: from Hollywood, clothing, and the oil business. The relationship between the technology and information manipulation is made and the concept is extended to show that finance is information management. Because much of the technology and its related terminology may be foreign to the financial practitioner, we aim for the professional without a background in nonlinear concepts. Being clear is important, because in the information age, where the pace of new technology is relentless, it is unreasonable to assume that everyone can keep up. For example, as Keith Devlin tells us in 1994 in *Mathematics: The Science of Patterns*, "In 1900 all the world's mathematical knowledge would have fitted into about eighty books. Today it would take maybe 100,000 volumes to contain all known mathematics. . . . At the turn of the century, mathematics could reasonably be regarded as twelve distinct subjects. . . . Today, between sixty and seventy distinct categories would be a reasonable figure."

With this plethora of knowledge, the technique of progress in the 21st century involves straddling viewpoints. One foot is a specialist in your own specific discipline where the problem is identified. The other foot is a generalist scouting about to see if concepts from other fields can be reconfigured and applied to your own problem. Armed with new knowledge, one can and formulate a solution. This practice, known generally as the *interdisciplinary* approach, is in its infancy but gaining momentum as it is realized that it is more efficient to see what is available than it is to reinvent the wheel everytime a new challenge occurs. Moreover, in relating new techniques, often pictures are more effective than words, just as map is better than text when depicting terrain.

If you have ever struggled with putting your feelings to a loved one into words, or chuckled at the adjectival pirouettes of a dithyrambic wine writer, then you have my empathy. For what emotion is to the lover and taste is to the enologist, three- and four-dimensional visualization is to the practitioner of nonlinear techniques in financial economics. Cost factors prevent the display of 3D graphics, which provide a real bridge of intuition to the novitiate for the various invisible logic processes such as genetic algorithms and fuzzy logic. Cumbersome words will have to suffice.

ABOUT THIS BOOK AND BLOOMBERG

Some may inadvertently assume that this book is an advertisement for Bloomberg. That is not *Nonlinear Pricing*'s primary purpose, though some

positive effects may accrue to them. Thanks to the good offices of
Bloomberg's people: namely, Messrs. Dave Bortnichak, Derrick Harrison,
Sanjiv Gupta, "Equity" Joe Schmitz, and Tom Secunda, they have helped
make the beginnings of *Nonlinear Pricing* accessible via the KAOS function. Why they agreed to post KAOS is easy to discern—to improve content, be there first, and sell more terminals. What made them receptive to the
idea of *Nonlinear Pricing* in the first place is even more important: They are
cutting-edge in their mentality.

As a result, Bloomberg is the first of the major financial service
providers, including Reuters and Bridge, to offer any nonlinear techniques
in finance whatsoever. I am convinced that a cutting-edge mentality is fos-
tered because they occupy a desirable space at the intersection of real-time
applied technology and finance. This cutting-edge state of mind will be a
prerequisite for anyone wishing to progress in the understanding of or implementation of *Nonlinear Pricing*. In return for the technology transfer, I
am aided in spreading the gospel of *Nonlinear Pricing* to an upscale audi-
ence in a manner that demonstrates the underlying concept of nonlinearity
to you on a real-time basis.

One day Dave called and said, "We are going to call it KAOS." I replied,
"It is not really chaos but nonlinearity." Dave's reply was pure Wall Street:
"KAOS sounds catchier, and besides, particle physicists are not our clientele."

A facet of *Nonlinear Pricing* came to the world via Bloomberg on January 9, 1997. *Nonlinear Pricing* is here and now.

Throughout this work, nonlinear standards are constantly compared with
the financial theory of the 1970s, including the Capital Asset Pricing Model,
the Efficient Markets Hypothesis, and the Black-Scholes option pricing
model. Collectively they are known as Modern Portfolio Theory. However,
I do not refer to Modern Portfolio Theory as modern because it no longer is.

BACKGROUND

"All men dream: but not equally. Those who dream by night in the dusty re-
cesses of their minds wake in the day to find that it was vanity: but the
dreamers of the day are dangerous men, for they may act out their dream
with open eyes, to make it possible." So wrote T. E. Lawrence, better known
as Lawrence of Arabia, in *Seven Pillars of Wisdom* in 1920. I dream by day
and this book is but another part of my dream-puzzle being articulated for
the outside world. It is the American dream.

My spiritual antecedents are my fellow Texans, typically oilmen, who despite great odds and frequent misfortune built their dream—men John Bain-
bridge wrote about in *The Super Americans*. Michael Halbouty's biography

Wildcatter indelibly impressed me as I read it during my college days at our alma mater, Texas A&M. I grew up with stories of and infrequently even meeting the likes of Amon Carter, Howard Marshall, John Oxley, D. H. Byrd, Sid Richardson, the Bass family, the Walters, the McBees, Richard Rainwater, the Beals, the Bivins, the Murchisons, and Boone Pickens—heroes of the Industrial Age. The legendary oilman H. L. Hunt once said, "I'd rather be lucky than smart." So would I.

Today the independents, as they are called, trade producing wells and deal with issues like tertiary recovery. It is profitable to be sure, but the opportunities for my generation at the tail end of the baby boom to explore and discover a gusher and thus to experience the excitement are not what they were 60 years ago in grandfather's time. MBAs from the best schools seem as common as petroleum engineering degrees from Texas A&M. I believe that, were these heroes of the industrial era to begin anew today in the information age, they would apply new configurations of information directly to money. But then maybe this is redundant, for what information does not find its ultimate application in terms of dollars and cents?

Although I grew up with wildcatter folklore, I was never a part of it because we are atypical of the traditional source of Texas wealth, we are not oil people, we are finance people. My only investment in oil is framed and hangs on a wall. The subtle mental shift that must be made is the realization that in 1998, we are in the digital age not the industrial era and because of that, we are not in the money management business in the traditional sense of the term anymore, either, we are in the *information* business as it applies to buying and selling liquid financial instruments. Ideas are the true stock-in-trade of the money manager. Money is only the commodity. Ideas are limited by creativity and the ability to execute them. The information age has radically altered the ability to execute ideas by allowing information to be reconfigured. The creativity to see profit and risk management applications in these new information configurations is my *métier*.

In the digital age, I also believe that the next source of great wealth for America specifically and the world in general will combine the best of the entrepreneurial spirit with the know-how from the leading research universities. As for my beloved Texas, the wildcatters have endowed us with a rich heritage for entrepreneurialism and the research hotbeds of Texas A&M University and the University of Texas have ensured that there is action here. With no foreseeable abatement in Moore's Law—which holds that the processing capacity of semiconductors doubles every 18 months—or available bandwidth or investors' appetites for returns, it is an exciting time to be building a dream.

In 1992, Ed Peters's *Chaos and Order in the Capital Markets* launched me into this line of inquiry. In 1996, the second edition listed me as one of its few practitioners. Today, as I drill for patterns in data (data mining, as it is sometimes called) with technology that advances so quickly that it boggles the mind of all but the best of dreamers, I am an "old man" of a discipline that has come out of applied research in other disciplines—the proverbial nowhere—which thrives on technological advancement and which, at present, is so obscure that few outside my circle of acquaintances are even aware that it exists.

The ideas behind *Nonlinear Pricing* are locked with microprocessor advancement, available bandwidth, and mathematics in a symbiotic dance of evolution. It is a dance marked less by the fluidity of the ballroom than by the shimmying of youthful energy and the frequent nonlinear lurch to a new standard. From my perch on the planet, it is like being in the eye of a great storm.

CHRISTOPHER T. MAY

Manhattan, Vail, and Texas

ACKNOWLEDGMENTS

I always thought this space was wasted in a book until I wrote one myself. My deep appreciation of the fact that the work you now hold in your hands is really the collective efforts of many—both living and deceased—who were instrumental in shaping my thoughts and making this project a reality, is robust.

Many of the ideas expressed herein are lineal descendants from Edgar Peters. If research is stealing from many, then I must admit to plagiarism because in many respects Ed's work is seminal. His contribution to this evolving field cannot be underestimated. There was no other practitioner who published. Ed has shared and continues to share many interesting thoughts with me. Fortunately, though, the next practitioner who publishes can do research.

I first met Michael J. Harkins, a lowland Scot, with his lovely English wife Michele, many years ago at a dinner party and we have been friends ever since. He and his partner, Edwin Levy, agreed to let me use the space for a nominal charge and then largely left me to my task. The net effect was that the relationship was a sort of incubator; not only was the telecoms room warm but there were those very important occasional words of encouragement. I am fortunate to be able to count Ed and Mike among my friends.

And to those dull gray souls—the touchy timeservers—who are the bane of innovation everywhere; and those niggardly and miserly people who are more concerned with divvying up the economic pie rather than growing it—may the devil take the hindmost. Do your best. You may be big like Goliath, and we all know what happened to him. To the problem solvers and the innovators—*Cheers!* May the good Lord love us all, and call for us none too soon.

God bless Vinnie Ronnacher, co-owner of Imperial Pizza, New York's finest, near the corner of 35th Street and Third Avenue. In my earliest days, the practical goal of my high thinking was mere subsistence. In

Texas we euphemistically say that "He was so poor, he could barely afford to pay attention." This was tested during my morning meditation; when I came to the part about ". . . give us this day our daily bread . . ." it was no idle prayer. To this day, I cannot eat a slice of pizza without thinking of Vinnie. Next time you are in the neighborhood, stop by and visit him; you'll be glad you did. I would also like to thank Kevin Kallaugher for providing the illustrations.

NONLINEAR PRICING

1

A Toy Story for Wall Street

Las ideas no se matan!
Don't kill the ideas!
— Don Domingo Faustino Sarmiento,
President of Argentina, 1875

Almost everything you believe about characterizing financial-economic relationships is wrong. Explaining this statement would fill many books. It has
already filled a few; it filled this one and it will fill others. Most MBAs and
CFOs (chief financial officers) are trained to believe, not to know. Belief can
be manipulated. Knowledge, on the other hand, is dangerous. This book is
about knowledge of how the real world works and not how theoretical constructs assume it to be. We will examine how we got to this point where theory and reality do not mesh, what the differences are between old and new
interpretations, and how we can better explain the real world. In the final
analysis, it does not matter whether one believes a thing is true. The only
thing that matters is whether a thing *is* true. That is all.

The journey to the new explanation is arduous, and not everyone will
make it. The challenge is not physical; it is mental because we need new
technology to help us—technology with which many may not be familiar.
Complacency and the inability to make up one's own mind will be the
biggest hindrances. Mirrors can be painful instruments of introspection. But
persevere, because great advantage awaits those who reach the other side.

There is a central concept that will help you on your journey: In the digital age, we are no longer in the financial business as we know it traditionally. We are in the *information* business. Money is only a commodity.

Characterize financial relationships that have yet to be articulated and you
will change information. Change information and you change the business.

To win, investors have to see things from a different perspective. John
Maynard Keynes in his *General Theory of Employment, Interest and Money*

observed that this kind of independence is seen as "eccentric, unconventional and rash in the eyes of average opinion. . . . Worldly wisdom teaches that it is better for reputation to fail conventionally than to succeed unconventionally." Mindful of Warren Buffett's admonition not to confuse conventionality with conservatism, the present text argues that a more realistic—that is, nonlinear—picture of reality, is conservative, while extant beliefs in the form of linear constructs, though widely held, are merely conventional.

DRUCKER AND CONCEPTS

Articulating this change in perspective is Peter Drucker who is credited with founding management and who penned a prescient article, "The Next Information Revolution," in the 28 August 1998 *Forbes ASAP*. The introductory paragraph reads:

> The next information revolution is well underway. But it is not happening where information scientists, information executives, and the information industry in general is looking for it, it is not a revolution in techology, machinery, techniques, software, or speed, it is a revolution in CONCEPTS.

Nonlinear pricing is a revolution in concepts. Drucker goes on to say that mensuration or what we can measure influences if not soley determines how we think about something. In financial-economics measurement is called accounting. Although double entry booking dates from the Fibonacci's *Liber Abaci* in 1305, Generally Accepted Accounting Principles and economic theory are industrial era legacies of the 1930s. GAAP was created by the Securities and Exchange Act of 1933 in response to a need for better information by investors following the great depression. Neoclassical economic theory is the result of an attempt to make economics more rigorous by quantifying it. To do this, economics purloined the concept of equilibrium from physics. As the "what is measured" and "how it is thought about" of the 1930s, GAAP accounting and equilibrium theory are related. In the information age, they do not go away, but become specialized subsets of a broader nonlinear interpretation of reality. Improvements in traditional measurements, like yield-management for airlines and new measurements, like the Hurst exponent or nonlinear simulations build this new interpretation. Measure a nonlinear time-series and you change derivative pricing, hedging, portfolio and risk management. Better measurement puts us at increasing odds with extant theory and compels us to find new explanations. If that is not a change in CONCEPT, I do not know what is.

In financial-economics, transitioning to the electronic medium has highlighted the concept of discounting as in the case of Amazon.com for books and on-line stock trading for commissions. Optimark extends discounting to liquidity in the markets, by the clandestine matching of buyers and sellers. It began operation on the Pacific Stock Exchange in the Autumn of 1998 and is scheduled to take effect in the over-the-counter market a year later. But the question has not been asked, what happens next? It is like asking what happens when emerging markets "emerge"? At some point discounting must become passé. After discounting, the next conceptual leap will be to leverage the electronic infrastructure and the advances in science and mathematics to give us insight into pricing financial assets.

With new nonlinear assumptions in place we can now move beyond discounting to "pricing." Pricing includes the concept of valuation—which holds that any financial instrument's value is tied to some aspect of economic performance. Nonlinear pricing has a role to play here by discovering metrics which are more indicative of performance by information era companies than the industrial era legacies which now exist. The real question is to what sort of metric is value tied?

Beyond valuation however is the inclusion of dynamics of markets themselves. As we know it valuation is a static concept that occurs in a dynamic environment which is highly nonlinear—that is the cause—effect relationship is disporportional. Because of this deterministic formulas *per se* do not apply. In lieu of formulas is simulation. The goal of nonlinear pricing is the continuous running in real-time of "what if" scenarios to capture the dynamics of the interaction between values and the market. The inherent assumption is that valuation and dynamics are "reflexive," that is, they can affect each other although most of the time the effect of valuation is more pronounced on dynamics than vice versa. A good though unfortunate parallel of the latter is politicians who "lead" by first taking a poll and then follow the poll's findings.

Nonlinear pricing is a more realistic and thus more complex view of reality. Simulating results for the purpose of making investment decisions is a more sophisticated concept than discounting. The concept of discounting is analogous to an example discussed in greater detail later where non-English speaking employees in the early days of the semiconductor business sought a mechanistic interpretation of chip making. that is, sort of intuitive approach that required no special education. However, the information age is driven by CONCEPTS. Like our counterparts in engineering there is nothing intuitive about how electrons or the pricing mechanisms in markets sometime behave. Without the background in financial-economics and the sciences there is little in this book that will appeal to a simplistic or mechanistic interpretation and the scientific legacy of Newtonian determinism which it represents. Without the background you cannot participate.

Blame it on Sir Isaac Newton, the first fellow to be knighted for scientific achievement. He is the primary reason we need so much science in this text on financial economics. You see, after the apple dropped on his head and he discovered gravity, Newton then codeveloped the calculus in 1686. He did this by making a basic assumption about the world. That is, that we can make an observation if all points in the universe are fixed. This came to be known as determinism, because if all points are fixed and a few are known, then we can determine all the others. After Cambridge "Adam Smith" (George J. W. Goodman) wrote in 1981 in *Paper Money,* the government gave Newton a sinecure post called Master of the Mint, which roughly corresponds to Chancellor of the Exchequer, or Secretary of the Treasury in the United States today. The same mind using the same guiding philosophy that fixed physical relationships in science fixed or pegged the currency in 1717! Goodman tells us, "One guinea, that is, 21 shillings, would be worth 129.4 grams of gold, and thereby he [Newton] said, *We intend this currency to hold its value*." Newton also lost a fortune in the South Sea Bubble.

This was to hold until 1931, when Britain let the pound "float" because of a world crisis. In 1944, in an attempt to reestablish order, the Bretton Woods conference fixed world currencies and specifically the new reserve currency, the dollar, at $35 per ounce of gold. Later, in August 1971, because of the oil crisis or the unsustainable demand for gold, President Richard Nixon took the dollar off the gold standard. Newtonian determinism became discredited in the scientific world in 1926 with quantum physics. Sadly, in financial economics we have been trying to interpret the relativistic and relational world with the wrong set of assumptions.

Goodman saw the future in *Paper Money*, but the collateral concepts were not sufficiently developed to dismount the status quo. Listen to his words, now 17 years old, and hear their prescience.

When the atomic physicists began to describe the subparticle universe of quantum mechanics, they needed a description of the existing world as a base reference. They called it "Newtonian": classical, balanced, fixed. . . . Index funds, and beta and Modern Portfolio Theory—and three more computer-derived techniques now a-borning—are all quests for certainty, for orientation, for classical science, for the lost Newtonian universe. . . . The Newtonian universe is gone.

The mere floating of currencies and introduction of quantum physics have eroded the fringes of Newton's overly successful legacy, but they have not been enough to expunge its tattered remnants. It is to be hoped that non-linear pricing is the final nail in the coffin of Newton's legacy in financial economics. To get to the heart of our argument we have to undo three centuries of complacency.

Once upon a time Newtonian determinism was both conventional and conservative, but now, with the advent of superior technology, it is only conventional. As the nonlinear paradigm begins to permeate the practitioner's world, keeping the old paradigm will ensure that you are with the herd. But you can no longer be considered conservative.

Finance, at both the corporate and market levels, is a complex adaptive process. Ever-increasing amounts of computational horsepower and scientific development allow us to characterize relationships of which we were previously ignorant or that we suspected and ignored because direct proof and practical application were neither feasible nor possible. This results in:

- A fundamental change in measuring and illustrating the risk-reward relationship;

- Increased use of sophisticated information management

- Adaptation of advanced techniques, common in other industries to finance

- Updated skills for people in the finance industry who wish to stay competitive

We are not concerned with investing in technology stocks, how computerization will improve your billing system, or other mundane tasks. Our inquiry is more fundamental.

SIMPLE FINANCE

John Holland, father of the genetic algorithm, once said, "It is little known outside the world of mathematics that most of our mathematical tools, from simple arithmetic through differential calculus to algebraic topology, rely on the assumption of linearity." The change to nonlinearity requires a restatement of the traditional way we think about and express some common concepts.

Think of two simple examples in finance: correlation and volatility. In English, correlation expresses the concept of how much something goes up and down vis-à-vis something else. For example, futures on the S&P index are highly positively (near perfectly) correlated with that basket of stocks which comprise the S&P index. If the stocks go up, the futures very quickly go up by an almost identical amount, and if stocks go down futures go down as well. The linear mathematical measurement of this correlation in statistics is known as regression and is called R^2. If R^2 is 1.00 then the movement of the S&P index or the dependent variable, perfectly accounts for the movement of the independent variable or the basket of stocks. If R^2 is only 0.87 then only 87% of the movement of the S&P index is described by the stocks and something else accounts for the other 13%. Conceptually characterizing the movement of one variable with another variable or group of variables is a good idea. The problem is with the assumptions of the math itself. R^2 assumes that the underlying distribution, which describes the futures contract and the basket of stocks in the S&P index, is Gaussian. The assumption is wrong. It was proved wrong as far back as 1964. Conceptually we are like the tailor who assumes that one size fits all. So why do financiers use R^2? Out of habit perhaps, but not out of reason.

A more accurate and nonlinear measure uses "fuzzy logic." Why? Fuzzy logic does not make an assumption about the underlying distribution of the things being measured. It does not try to fit reality into a presized suit or defined mathematical framework. The simple definition of fuzzy logic is that it is a "universal approximator." In Chapter 6 we will cover it more in depth. But fuzzy logic is not new; it was invented in 1965.

Nonlinearity does not mean the futures contract and the underlying basket do not rise and fall in synchronicity. They most certainly do. The relationship is what it is. Nonlinearity merely allows us to characterize more accurately all the disproportionate influences or "noise" in the market to help reduce that 13% difference, or what the index arbitrageurs call "tracking error."

Volatility is another popular concept in finance and it expresses the degree to which something goes up and down vis-à-vis itself. For example, a stock with 50% volatility, which may be considered high, is indicative that this stock has higher risk and therefore supposedly a higher potential reward. Like the previous example, volatility is expressed mathematically by a Gaussian probability distribution. Distributions are described by "moments." The first moment is the well-known mean or average. The second moment is called variance and expresses the concept of how often an observation deviates from the mean—hence the term *standard deviation*. The linear measurement of volatility is defined in mathematical terms as variance or standard deviation squared.

Thus, variance is the second moment of a distribution. If we assume a normal distribution, then the second moment is finite; in other words, it exists. If we actually measure the returns of the stock, like Eugene Fama did in 1963, we discover that returns of a stock are not normally distributed, and that the tails of the distribution do not touch the horizontal axis, and therefore variance is infinite. In other words, it does not exist. Poof! There goes volatility as we know it.

Nonlinearity does not say that stocks do not go up and down. They most assuredly do. Nor does it deny that risk may be generally commensurate with reward. However, nonlinearity suggests that using a stable distribution—or "fractal" distribution as it is sometimes called—that better describes reality is a superior economic model.

Both correlation and volatility are good descriptive concepts. But as they are present at defined, both assume a normal distribution. That assumption is wrong. It is the imposition of a linear ruler to measure a nonlinear world and, therefore, not very good science. To reiterate what Holland said, "It is little known outside the world of mathematics that most of our mathematical tools, from simple arithmetic through differential calculus to algebraic topology, rely on the assumption of linearity." He went on to say, "Polls, project trends, or industrial statistics, all of which employ summation, are only useful if they describe linear properties of the underlying systems. It is so much easier to use mathematics when systems have linear properties that we often expend considerable efforts to justify the assumption of linearity." The previous examples illustrate Holland's point exactly.

Unfortunately, the markets are not a linear system; they are a complex adaptive system, meaning that they adapt and change slightly with time. Businesses measure the degree to which they interpret and satisfy client needs with sales. Clients respond or give feedback by purchasing the product or service or not. Sales are the clearest example of a feedback mechanism in an economy. Viewed generically, an economy is an adaptive system and the concepts developed from other adaptive systems in other disciplines may have merit in financial economics.

Yet, we continue to attempt to justify using linear concepts to describe a nonlinear system. A scientist would probably say, if the theory does not fit

the facts, change the theory. An enlightened student of the markets should ask, how do I make money exploiting a more accurate measurement of the risk-reward relationship while my competitors sleep?

A MILD CRISIS IN ECONOMICS

There is a mild crisis boiling in financial economics, which is the underpinning of virtually all investment strategy. It ought to be a major crisis but it is not one yet. Many recent (and not so recent) developments in other disciplines suggest that the field of financial economics is long overdue for some major revisions, not only in the way we conceptualize theory but also—and more importantly—in the way the financial business operates. Whether financiers will be ahead of the crisis or behind it depends on whether, and how, we interpret these developments and put them into practical application.

With an unprecedented flow of money being put into mutual funds by the investing public, good corporate earnings, and the Dow high, one might well ask, "What crisis?" The upshot is, as Will Rogers so aptly put it, "So much of what we know, just ain't so." This is an unsettling admission, because finance, for all its supposed dynamism, is really quite a staid field when it comes to new ideas. Financial economics has done a good job in providing new products; however, the mathematical assumptions—the technology—which often underpins those products is 25 years old, or older.

The fact is that many of the underlying assumptions we use to construct our explanations of the financial economics world are beginning to look highly questionable—and most certainly, severely limited—in light of developments in other fields, particularly computer science and mathematics. Probably the two biggest sacred cows are: (1) The distributions of any financial asset are a normal or Gaussian distribution or the familiar bell-shaped curve. All three terms mean the same thing. Further, the Gaussian distribution is the limit of a Brownian motion the mathematical name for the randomness we assume applies to financial time series. (2) Markets exist *only* in equilibrium. The concepts of equilibrium and randomness are part of linear mathematics.

In financial economics, the only time the precision of linear mathematics accurately reflects reality is when the discount rate is fixed and applied to government debt. And then the math is applicable only if we, like Walter Wriston, the former chairman of Citibank, assume that countries do not go bankrupt. And even then, the assessments are far different for a banana republic or a developing nation than they are for the world's policeman and lender of last resort. In all other instances of applying linear mathematics to characterize relationships in financial economics, Einstein's famous quote applies: "So far as the laws of mathematics refer to reality, they are not certain. And so far as they are certain, they do not refer to reality." The certitudes expressed by linear math do not apply to the nonlinear and nonequilibrium reality of financial economics.

NONLINEAR PRICING

Nonlinear pricing is defined as any technological trading aid that acknowledges the nonlinearities exhibited by markets to more accurately characterize the patterns exhibited by traded assets. Nonlinear pricing comprises new technologies such as complexity theory, fuzzy logic, abductive logic, genetic algorithms, and loosely coupled sets to model the new paradigm of evolution or adaptation.

One possible opportunity to profit is the arbitrage between the pattern depicted by nonlinear pricing and the market's inability to detect the pattern as accurately. Moreover, it is an efficiency unlikely to be arbitraged away because of the number of variables involved, the varying investment horizons, and the technology gap among market participants.

Nonlinear pricing is based on the fact that markets are adaptive; that is, they change with time. Possible trades are run in hypertime—quicker than real time, like the fast-forward button on your VCR—to get an idea of how a pattern may evolve. The goal of nonlinear pricing is to quantify the relationship in time between multiple variables and their movements to gain some degree of predictability over probable future prices. This is the goal of any and all analysis in financial economics. The primary distinction between nonlinear pricing and prevailing views is the underlying nonlinear technologies used and the understanding that goes with them. The Hurst exponent is but a single statistic; thus it is only a small part, but the most visible mathematical tool of all the tools available in nonlinear pricing.

In many important respects, nonlinear pricing is a practical implementation of George Soros's theory of reflexivity, which he first wrote about in 1987. The theory of reflexivity holds that equilibrium—the assumed norm in classical economics—is but a special case of the more common disequilibrium state in markets and the more infrequent far-from-equilibrium state (e.g., market swings and crashes).

Reflexivity goes one step further in describing the warp and woof of market activity. It states that practitioners' expectations can actually influence the markets themselves. Nonlinear pricing can take many variables and aggregate them into a nonlinear framework so that the concerted effect of those variables renders a stronger statement than any single metric can make individually or that myriad individual metrics can make in a linear analysis. There is a strong basis for the principle of reflexivity in Heisenberg's uncertainly principle, which holds that either the momentum or the position of a molecule can be known but not both simultaneously. The logical upshot is that subject and object are linked. To observe a molecule requires bouncing a photon of light off of it. At the quantum level, the light is strong enough to alter the molecule's trajectory. The real problem probably lies in the separation of subject and object. This is also a problem in financial economics.

The concept of reflexivity can be partially visualized within the microcosm of trading an S&P futures contract of an index versus the basket of underlying equities that the S&P index represents. The futures and the index are equivalent, though not identical. When the target spread is reached, a buy/sell or sell/buy signal is triggered. However, executing the trade will narrow the gross spread. The net spread will be affected by liquidity and execution delay and will not be known until all the prices at which stocks in the basket were executed are received. Moreover, the fact that your competitors have the same information at the same time means that you have to *anticipate*. If several firms do large trades, their collective views and resultant action will have a real but temporary effect on the markets. Views of the spread affect the markets, and views of the markets affect the spread. Thus, reflexivity is easily demonstrated. It is a recursive or reflexive relationship.

Paradigm shifts are typically recognized by disparate parties nearly simultaneously, each formulating to the best of their understanding a brick on the path to progress. Ed Peters and Tonis Vaga wrote *Fractal Market Hypothesis* and *Coherent Market Hypothesis*, respectively. The differences between these gentlemen's views and Soros's are primarily generational. Whereas Soros cast his theory of reflexivity in terms of classical economics, Peters and Vaga, as befits the schooling of their generation, have cast their theories in terms of the Modern Portfolio Theory of the 1970s. The terms to describe nonlinear relationships have grown up and become formalized within the hard sciences in the last two decades, and Peters and Vaga are facile in using them to describe market realities. Although each of the three theories has a specific thrust, their underlying commonalities are greater than their differences, and their collective effort to shift equilibrium-based economics toward a new nonlinear and nonequilibrium paradigm is undeniable.

Academician-based economics has moved much more slowly, although it has recently offered the concept of increasing returns. This is the opposite of diminishing returns and holds that something gets easier to sell the larger the installed base. A good example is the fax machine, which is not worth very much if you are the only person on the planet to have one. Conversely, the more profligate the fax machine, the more of a necessity it becomes. Other recent examples are the VHF-Betamax war, the QWERTY keyboard layout, and technology standards like Windows NT and Netscape browsers. The concept of increasing returns is a very nonlinear phenomenon.

The paradigm shift to evolution or adaptation is not limited to financial economics. In fact, much is derived from the microprocessor, which has evolved from the stand-alone personal computer (PC) to the network and now to the dynamics of networks. The dynamics of networks, where thousands of autonomous entities clandestinely interact, are remarkably similar to those of financial markets. Kevin Kelly provides a thought-provoking account in *Out of Control: The Rise of the Neo-Biological Civilization*. Since biology has been our traditional source of evolutionary study, it would seem that biology then would be a more powerful paradigm than physics for finance and be in keeping with Philip Anderson's funnel remark (Anderson, who received the 1977 Nobel Prize in physics, said that no amount of studying water molecules will help you in learning about the *emergent property* like a funnel formed by draining water).

Nonlinear pricing totally refutes the theory that a financial time series will be random 100% of the time—a tenet of both the Capital Asset and Black-Scholes option pricing models. The theory is directly disproved via the KAOS screen in Chapter 3. But this proof, which illustrates the Hurst exponent, is only one of many technologies that can be used to characterize data. *Nonlinear* means that the input-output of a relationship is disproportionate. If three hours of studying results in a B grade on an exam, it does not follow that four hours will result in an A. A linear relationship, in contrast, is proportional. As a simple robot, a Coke machine is proportional in that three quarters go in and one Coke comes out every time. Stated differently, if relationships are nonlinear some of the time, they are also partially predictable. Exploiting this partial predictability is a central concept of nonlinear pricing.

Much of what nonlinear pricing has to say modifies extant financial theory because theory is the gestalt, weltanschauung, or *über*-view of how things are supposed to work. Unfortunately, the modifications are incomplete in the sense of being the final answer to everything, or what physicists call "the theory of everything." To understand market or physical behavior we have concepts and theory from which predictions are derived.

For example, Einstein's general theory of relativity published in 1916, and quantum theory in final form replaced Newton's theory of motion, which ceased to be credible in 1926. Relativity does give superior predictions; however, that is not the primary basis for its value. Similarly, in finance we have the Black-Scholes option pricing model, which assumes that the movement in time of a financial time series is totally random. The primary basis for the value of both theories is the depth of understanding that each gives us about reality, a reality which we do not necessarily experience directly.

To wit, Galileo was challenged by the Inquisition for his heliocentric theory of planetary motion, in which he claimed that the Earth and the other planets moved around the Sun. His theory replaced the Copernican view that the Earth was the center of the universe. The questions he reportedly received were: "How do you know the Earth moves? Can you feel the Earth move?" No. No one can feel the Earth move, and it is relativity that tells us why. His answer, which he was forced to recant, was based on the fact that we could interpret reality symbolically and that observations can be reduced to an understanding or theory. In modern terms, those symbols are mathematics processed by computers in cyberspace. The Roman Catholic Church did not care about the planets; it rightly perceived a rival interpretation of reality based on mathematics versus its own of divinity.

This discovery may be said to be the birth of modern science. Although it took Galileo three hundred years to win the argument, with the Vatican finally admitting its error in 1992, his is the understanding we have today. We accept Galileo's interpretation because it is the most plausible explanation that we have. To understand why, we have to take a step back and look at the most modern interpretations of reality. What gives theory its validity over mere fact memorization or prediction is the understanding derived from it.

Yet many in financial economics are concerned only with short-term predictions. In the scientific world these people are called *instrumentalists*. Instrumentalists do not care for theory or understanding, only for correct predictions. In a very limited sense this view may seem appealing. However, taken to its logical conclusion it leads us in the wrong direction. The logical conclusion would be predicting at the turn of the 20th century that man would walk on the moon, or that interconnected computers all over the world called the Internet would exist. In 1900, computers and rockets did not exist. Without the requisite understanding—which is the scientific and financial ideal—correct predictions cannot lead very far, because there is no basis to interpret them.

The misunderstanding of the role of predictions may arise from the fact that subjecting a theory to an experimental test is part of the scientific process. That is, two theories are subjected to the same test and the theory with the affirmed result is adopted. Some theories without any logic of explanatory power, are rejected outright without testing because there is no thread of logic running through them—for example, the theory that jumping up and down will improve the performance of your portfolio.

As knowledge proliferates, better theories that provide a broader and deeper understanding of the world are constantly evolving. Often, the new theory that replaces the old augments our understanding of the reality that we inhabit and seek to master. Financial economics, as a derivative phenomenon, is quite far removed from first principles. First principles are the statements that can be made about the most fundamental constituents of matter or particles. The implicit hope was that once these first principles were understood, the rest of the universe could be explained in terms of them. Practitioners have, to their great credit, achieved some success in managing risk and return. Unfortunately, they cannot express much of their knowledge in terms of extant financial theory or mathematics. It is a hodgepodge of habits, rules of thumb, superstitions, instinct, and other attributes garnered from the master-apprentice relationship and experience. The explanatory gap between the economics professor and the bond trader is a chasm. Nonetheless, that operational hodgepodge is, or contains, some form of mental framework we call financial-economics theory. Progress ensures that the knowledge is deeper and structurally different.

A century ago, we did not have as firm a grasp of fiscal or monetary policy as we do now. Nor did we have equilibrium-based economics until 1930s, fundamental analysis until the 1930s, or knowledge of derivatives until 1972. To make better theories of financial economics requires a firm understanding of the reality it inhabits. Financial theory stands to benefit greatly from the explanatory power of the theories of reality, which has improved dramatically in recent years. One of the problems in creating a superior theory is the philosophical approach taken when formulating it. The most popular approach for the past 350 years is the *reductionist* approach. Inspired by Newton, reductionism attempts to reduce things into ever finer parts. It has met with great success. For example, we can explain the physical constitution of an inanimate object by going from piece to molecule, to atom, to particle, to subatomic particle. The success has not extended to animate objects, typically the subject of organic chemistry—better known as life. The reason is knowledge of atomic behavior occurs at too fundamental a level to be applicable in describing a more complex interaction of atoms in the animate form of an animal. For example, knowing the weight of the carbon molecules that make up a goodly part of bears and humans will not help you if the bear decides to chase you. The philosophical conundrum is this: Reductionism has always said to tear the thing to be studied into finer parts. When that approach fails, what is the beginning point? Is it the bear, the ecosystem, or human interaction with bears? Similarly, in financial-economic analysis we start with the world and then focus on the national economy, the sector, the industry, the company, the division, and finally the product. We rip it into even finer pieces. Real analysis, though, involves the mental abstraction to see how an increase in employment numbers and an increase in sales may bode for the price of a stock. In other words, sometimes stocks go up or dow on good news, and sometimes they go down or up on bad news, but the analysis needs to address highly nonlinear relationships across varying levels of resolution. However, reductionism solves only part of the problem.

The other part of the problem in recent years, in both financial economics and physics was well stated by Philip Anderson. Anderson gave the example of the funnel that forms in bathtub water when the plug is pulled. The funnel that spontaneously forms is an *emergent phenomenon*. Emergence is high-level simplicity from low-level complexity. Emergence is an example of dynamics that is too complex to derive from first principles or extant physical or economic knowledge, but which nevertheless occurs. The emergence results in a state of *self-organized criticality* or SOC. SOC reflects the simple rules that generate complex behavior in nature to evolve into a poised or critical state. The change to a state of SOC is mathematically catastrophic in that the changes are discrete rather than smoothly continuous.

It is the movement in discrete units or quanta that lends strength to our later use of the concept of quantum physics in the markets. The evolution to SOC is autonomous. It requires neither a design nor an outside agent; hence it is self-organized. SOC exists as a result of the dynamical interactions within a system. SOC is the only known general mechanism to generate complexity, and the most robust paradigm we have to explain this complexity is biological evolution.

The classic example of SOC in financial economics is Adam Smith's pin factory, where performance dramatically increased with specialization. One man drew the wire, another clipped, another formed the head, and so on, rather than each man performing all steps. Henry Ford would rediscover a similar benefit over a century later with the assembly line.

However, no amount of reductionist thinking, like counting water molecules, determining their mass, measuring the shape of the bathtub, and so forth, will help you to understand an emergent phenomenon like a funnel of water. Similarly, no amount of reductionism in the form of reiterating the fact that XYZ Corporation just got a big order and can anticipate an increase in earnings per share will help you to understand the dynamics of the market. This is of concern to you because your client wants to know why the stock is dropping. It is a common rut in finance.

At the reductive level of knowledge, science and mathematics form a bedrock—whether it is counting water molecules or earnings per share. People cling to this bedrock, however useless it may be in the face of a different class or level of problem. The rut is to assume that all you wish to know and understand can be reduced to this sort of reductive thinking—the sort that is intuitive and easy to explain in a sound bite to a client who would rather be playing golf. It is not to be. Since reality is complex, we will need more advanced explanations to describe it. Money and information flows of an economy or a company may indeed be a reductionist concept in that dollars or bytes are concrete and discrete units. Unfortunately, flows, whether in the context of physics or finance, are dynamic. Moreover, these dynamics are nonlinear or disproportionate more often than they are linear or proportionate—if they are ever linear at all.

The second problem with reductionism is that it accepts explanations only in terms of cause and effect. This is a chicken-and-egg problem, which implies that an earlier cause is superior to a recent one—for instance, the trite "butterfly effect" in chaos theory in classical physics, where a butterfly in one part of the world causes a storm in another part because the weather is highly sensitive to initial conditions. Since you can never go back to the beginning of time and know the initial states with infinite precision, this avenue does not seem very fruitful. The reductionist cause-and-effect approach does not lead to any theory, either. To be an explanation or a theory means to be falsifiable. Since "the tape" of history or the stock market cannot be replayed, we are left with only a historical narrative or, worse, a justification for an ill-posed course of action. Higher-level or derivative sciences like evolution, financial economics, politics, and psychology cannot be treated in such a manner.

Perhaps of greatest importance in the type of thinking needed to fully embrace nonlinear pricing is the realization that the power to model is the power to experiment. And the power to experiment is the power to move from the retrospective of a historical narrative to a prospective or forward-looking analysis. By simulating scenarios and testing the effects, their intervention regulators and investors can better tailor their impact.

In fact, the purpose of higher-level phenomena may enable us to understand emergent phenomena, of which the most important are life, thought, and computation. All three will have a role in the restated physics we need in order to begin to address financial economics in the nonequilibrium and nonlinear reality which it inhabits.

There is a counterpart to reductionism called *holism*. Holism would have us look at only the whole and not the parts. That is okay, but if we can reduce anything to its most fundamental constituent parts we can learn something and are thus obliged to do so, if only to form a substrate of knowledge. The danger is the extreme approach in which observations about properties of a system, exhibited at the most fundamental level or a higher level, are excluded in favor of convenience. In sum, if it happens, there must be a reason and that reason has to be explained.

At this point we will need to explore a little more about the links between neoclassical economic theory and physics. There are two direct links between financial economics and the space-time physics of Einstein. Space-time is the three dimensions of space and one of time. In reality, it is the same stuff. The introduction of space-time here is important since financial-economics occurs strictly in the temporal realm. Later we will need to build on this concept to create a time-dependent arbitrage.

First is the concept of equilibrium, which is the basis for neoclassical economics. In physics, equilibrium refers to a stasis or period of stability. In financial economics, equilibrium says that for every buyer there is a seller. That is, the change in price is assumed to be smooth and continuous. Opening a market limit down, "trading limits" such as those on the New York Stock Exchange, and discontinuous prices such as those that go from $48\frac{1}{2}$ to $41\frac{1}{4}$ for example, do not exist. Equilibrium also makes no allowance for markets that can and do occasionally crash or more often exist in the far-from-equilibrium state.

Second is the concept of diffusion, as in a gas diffusing randomly and evenly throughout a room, or milk in your coffee. Stocks are assumed to follow this diffusion in one dimension (because they move up and down) or two if time is included rather than three for gas (length, width, and height). The mathematical term for randomness is *Brownian motion*.

The third link is so obvious that it is usually never stated. It is the limits of classical physics and not mathematics that determine what we can compute. The most evident example of this to date in conventional computing is the original Moore's Law, which states that the density of semiconductors will double every 18 months. Moore subsequently amended this in 1997 to increase its potency.

We will see that all three are wrong. Quantum physics, even though it has not yet encompassed gravity, is a more powerful paradigm than classical physics. In financial economics, equilibrium and randomness do not exist 100% of the time. Physics has a direct effect on Wall Street because of quantum computation. That is, quantum computers are more efficient than normal computers, which means that numbers can be factorized quickly. This lack of efficiency means that none of the *encrypted* transactions that are based on factorization, such as those provided by the industry leader RSA Security Inc., are as secure as one might have previously thought. Factorization is the opposite of multiplication. It is trivial to multiply two large numbers together, but it is hard to find two unique primes. It is possible to factorize a 125-number key. They already exist and are classified by the U.S. government as "munitions" and forbidden for export, which is why you have to attest to Netscape that you are a U.S. citizen before you can download that functionality. With the addition of every number, the difficulty increases by a factor of three. Thus, a 126-digit key takes triple the time of a 125-digit key to factorize. It is the unique factorization of two primes that enables the cryptographic key to work. It is not trivial to factor a 250-digit number. This problem is computable in that a solution exists. However, it is not tractable with normal computers since it would take roughly a million years using a network of a million computers, or so estimated the computer scientist, Donald Knuth. In the example above, computing is given a very specific meaning. If the term *compute* can be interpreted more liberally, then it can also include the last major economic expansion caused by the steam engine in the mid 19th century, which is literally, thermodynamics in motion. From this example we can see that in general, as technology progresses, physical laws and theories become more relevant not only to the development of technology itself but also to the realm of financial economics, where those physical laws find their expression in the form of pricing goods and services in the free market.

A financial industry that is increasingly moving on-line for cost reasons and which needs security versus the reality of quantum physics, pits two huge forces against each other. Moreover, this example highlights the mismatch of the two ways of looking at something: Wall Street, which is comprised of reductionists who want to tear things into little parts, instrumentalists, who want only predictions, or a group that wants only simple explanations for nontrivial problems versus the counterintuitiveness of quantum reality. To be more precise, we have accepted quantum reality in limited applications such as lasers and microprocessors. What we have not done is logically conclude what those isolated instances mean for a broader view of reality. Extending existing facts to a logical conclusion may give us some crucial insight.

Ultimately, financial necessity will mandate an improved understanding, although I cannot say when, anymore than I can say when quantum computing will become a commercial reality. The fact that quantum computing exists, though, means that the threat to encryption exists. If experience is any guide, then the understanding in financial economics will also be very uneven. We see the effects of this understanding take place in terms of Intel's early experience in hiring people. Gordon Moore said something like, "When we first started out, we hired non-English speakers because of the simplicity of what we were doing. It was intuitive—you could sort of figure it out, like automobile parts. We can no longer do that because the technology has become too sophisticated." The implication is clear. There is nothing intuitive about how electrons behave. You cannot see them with the naked eye. It is concept-driven and therefore intellectual. It is the province of the knowledge worker rather than the laborer. He concluded, "Without the background you cannot participate." The same is true in financial economics. In terms of nonlinear techniques, at our current stage of development, we are like the non-English speakers without formal education. We are trying, understandably but incorrectly, to deal with very complex phenomena in terms that are intuitive. After all, the linear approach, which is simple and intuitive, has gotten us this far.

It is rarely stated but trust is also an essential element in progress. It is impossible in terms of time or money to verify every body of knowledge that affects us in modern life. For economic reasons alone, we simply trust knowledgeable people by their reputation, credentials, and previous successes, and believe that they will do their best on our behalf. Of course, assessing levels of trust is highly subjective. We implicitly rely on experts. The reality is like medicine, or any specialized body of knowledge—when you go for a checkup, you don't want to know all that the doctor knows, if you did, you would have gone to medical school, too. All you want to know is whether the doctor knows what he or she is supposed to know. It usually happens over time that we come to trust the people who are supposed to know. After all, you have never felt the Earth move.

Some of the concepts in this book may be far removed from the experience of daily life, yet they are logically constructed. They are no more visible to the naked senses than is an electron, but they are real and a contributory part of their acceptance will be based on trust. Refusing to understand and even accept is not a successful long-term strategy. To the client it means poor financial products, or as the late Emile Peynaud, professor at

the Bordeaux Institute, said, "You drink the wine you deserve." The implication is chillingly clear. The client of financial products and services who
wants superior results will have to demand them, but first will have to understand them. The free market works for the entire spectrum of quality.
Bad wine and bad financial products exist only for buyers of inferior goods
and services. The professional who admits ignorance and is no more capable
than the client, leads the client to wonder, "What am I paying you for?"
From a competitive point of view, if your competitor understands and you
do not, what does that say about you?

A NEW UNDERSTANDING

Theories that apply to fundamental or emergent phenomena may thus be
said to be low-level like physics or high-level like biology and economics,
respectively. But that does not imply a privilege in the sense of hierarchy.
Rank is based solely on explanatory power. It is not a reductive "theory of
everything" that we will find, but one taken from David Deutch's, *The Fabric of Reality*, that is quantum-based. More specifically, Deutch combines
three other theories, which are high-level in relation to quantum physics.
They are:

1. The theory of evolution as articulated by Darwin and Dawkins

2. Epistemology (the theory of knowledge) as articulated by Popper

3. The theory of computation as set forth by Turing

4. Quantum physics as set forth by Bohr

Deutch's view may not be right in the sense of being final, but it is cogent
and contains all the elements we need to look at economics for the 21st century. It also performs a great service in attempting to unify some seemingly
disparate bodies of knowledge. His *Fabric of Reality* is far richer than boring old Newtonian physics.

Financial economics, as a complex adaptive process exists in a web of all
four theories. Historically, financial economics has been cast in terms of
Newtonian physics. That explanation was right for its era. Science dropped
the Newtonian paradigm in 1926, yet financial economics still clings to it. It
is time to move on. Thus, to look at financial economics again, we first have
to look at a modern interpretation of the world, and much has changed. It
must also be noted that while each of the four theories has been accepted in
part, their full ramifications have never been embraced, probably because
the change would be too big. Moreover, a combination of the four theories

of reality as set forth by Deutch, is by no means accepted at the household level, either. However, they made sense to me, which of course does not necessarily make them right. The conclusions drawn from them for financial economics are supported, but they are by no means generally accepted in the broad sense, either.

There is an important point to be made here. In the previous paragraph I said that economics was cast in terms of Newtonian physics. This is true specifically, since economics borrows equilibrium and diffusion, and it is true in general in the sense that we look at something by itself. It is as if we can step outside reality and examine it to the exclusion of everything else. Can we view the vital organ of a body independent of the body? This sentiment was humorously expressed by a mechanic who said to the doctor, "You know, doc, we really do the same thing." "Yes," the doctor replied, "but try it while the engine is running."

We need to be less like the mechanic and more like the doctor in our views. The markets are an extraordinarily complex phenomenon. No theory of financial economics exists independent of the physical laws of the universe or of the biological laws to which humans are subject. There is no fixed backdrop to view something because one cannot arbitrarily step outside of existence and acquire it like a target. Once we accept that we cannot do this, our Newtonian explanation of things, however comforting, crumbles. The view becomes more relational and we have to view things in terms of each other, not just as an extracted entity. Simply put, one does not get to stand on the bottom of the pool; one gets to tread water. The relational world foregoes the anchor of a Newtonian fixed backdrop that the mechanic enjoyed.

Fortunately, there is a sort of renaissance going on now and it is thought by many leading scientists that complexity in nature is the next big challenge. Complexity is the variety in a system, which in financial economics is sometimes called bounded rationality. Since financial economics does not exist independent of the world, it therefore seems natural and appropriate to introduce concepts from other disciplines that may help us understand our discipline better. Among the sciences, physics has done the best job of this, probably because physicists perceive everything as their subject. Perhaps we should be affronted by an intrusion, but personally I welcome a catholic taste in problem solving, regardless of its source. I once deadpanned to a scientist friend that just as astronomy became astrophysics in my lifetime, we will see economics become "ecophysics." He did not get the joke but after a solemn moment, nodded his head in agreement.

Our quest means we have to encompass some broad fields of knowledge and ask some big questions. Given an interdisciplinary approach in an attempt to formally describe the world, every reference is fair game. Remember, in choosing the nonlinear path, we are deviating from the linear path set into motion by Newton 350 years ago and the Western academic tradition, built upon it. The panoramic nature of such an inquiry typically makes it remote from those people with a narrow or simplistic interpretation and those who tend to be on the consuming side of knowledge rather than on the producing side. One of the subjects raised will be religion. The link between the measurement of financial instruments and religion is trivial. The mathematics used to characterize relationships in financial economics is linear, in equilibrium, and based on the absolute view of Newton rather than the relative view of Leibniz, the other founder of the calculus. This absolute view has a parallel in Christianity and Judaism, where the Ten Commandments are absolute laws rather than relative in that "Thou shalt not steal" makes no reference to situational ethics. By contrast, Eastern thought and religion tends be more relational rather than absolute. We need to know more about the relational.

The errant thrust of many of these sorts of books is that in the supreme effort to "just tell the reader how to make money" and thus sell books, the scaffolding of understanding that goes with that moneymaking process tends to be omitted. Moneymaking without understanding is a dangerous business, as the contemporary examples of large derivatives losses attest. The other crutch is to throw a bunch of formulas at the reader, thus satisfying everyone. The editor, reader, and teacher all agree on formulas like recipes in a cookbook. Unfortunately, nonlinear techniques are computational rather than analytic. There are no formulas to memorize. There are techniques like genetic logarithms, and there are relationships, like the price of a bond to an index. In illustrating the interplay between techniques and relationships, often the written word does better than mathematical symbols but not as well as three-dimensional graphics. If one wishes to extend the analogy of cookery, then real cookery is not about following any recipe; real cookery is about cognizing the relationships between ingredients, texture, portions, temperature, flavor, and so on for yourself.

This lack of formulas is one of the largest hurdles for most people in cognizing nonlinear pricing. Three hundred and fifty years of intellectual tradition has led them to expect that a formula always exists. In a larger sense, it has led them to expect that the nonlinear approach, is sort of like the linear approach, with just a tweak here or there. It is more involved than that. Upon receiving notification of the Nobel Prize, Richard Feynman was asked by a *Time* reporter, "Can you tell us in a minute what you got the Nobel Prize for?" Feynman retorted, "Buddy, if I could tell you in a minute, it wouldn't be worth the Nobel Prize." Yes, you can try to "just make money" by pulling up a software program on your screen, but with nonlinear techniques, the better you want to be, the better your understanding will need to be.

SACRED COWS

It seems customary for the writers of popular books on science to put their cards on the table so you know their assumptions. One of the most fundamental subjects is God. Since we will slaughter a few sacred cows in this book, in the interests of full disclosure we need to look at all assumptions. Religion is often the first arena in a young person's life where the really big questions are addressed and encouraged. To a Westerner's eyes, I am an Episcopalian although my religious studies are influenced by having lived in the Far East and on the subcontinent for several years. The lesson is that science and religion are not mutually exclusive. In fact, spiritual achievement is gained by inquest and doubt as achievement is in science as well as by practice, as in any other discipline, like jogging. John Polkinghorne, a former particle physicist cum Anglican priest and president of Queen's College, Cambridge, makes this point in his book *The Faith of a Physicist*. It is a revealing and erudite account of a man who exists at the rare intersection of science and religion. Frank Tipler's *The Physics of Immortality* is also a thought-provoking account for readers who want to deal with high levels of abstraction.

From Hinduism, I commend *Vedic Mathematics* by Jagadguru Swami Sri Bharati Krishna Tirthaji Marahaja, the late Sankaracharya of Govardhana Math, Puri, India. This little gem reinforces the underlying unity of science and religion by deriving mathematics from Vedic scripture—certainly an alien intersection of subjects to most Westerners. *Vedic Mathematics* is interesting because it deals with the patterns of numbers. In nonlinear pricing we also detect patterns. However, since the subjects we are addressing of risk and return and time that are borderless, perhaps the origin of *any* knowledge should not be viewed with undue prejudice. Further study here may provide some insight to Ramanajun's thinking. Ramanjun was an early-20th-century savant who kept finding patterns in numbers, particularly the number 24. Ramanajun's work in the mathematics of renormalization group theory plays an important part in another advanced description of reality called *string theory*. Many such numbers exist, such as 8 and 18 in electron shells; 1/137, known as the fine structure constant in quantum physics; or, from chaos, Feigenbaum's constant, 4.669. More approachable for the Westerner are the slim but potent volumes, *The Holy Science* by Swami Sri Yukteswar and *The Science of Religion* by Paramahansa Yogananda. In sum, I do not accept the answer "because that is the way God made it" as a substitute for scientific understanding. Nor do I see a conflict. There is a God. I believe in Him. There you have it.

The previous paragraphs are important for two reasons: first, because in the face of great uncertainty we, as a discipline, are bound socially to a common view, and second, to highlight the stance of the author on the anthropic principle. We will address them sequentially. Per Bak, the physicist who pioneered self-organized criticality, once queried geophysicists on the first point:

> "Why is it that you guys are so conservative in your views, in the face of the almost complete lack of understanding of what is going on in your field?" I asked. The answer was as simple as it was surprising. "If we don't accept some common picture of the universe, however unsupported by the facts, there would be nothing to bind us together as a scientific community. Since it is unlikely that any picture of reality we use will be falsified in our lifetime, one theory is as good as any other." The explanation was social, not scientific.

Of course, there is a difference between earthquake prediction and financial economics, but the fact remains that financial economics and thus trade, by definition, are a form of social intercourse. While parochialism in interpreting phenomena in the information age is not our friend, woe to the person who dismisses commonly held social beliefs like the assumptions of linear mathematics in financial economics now held as articles of faith by a couple of generations of MBAs. That person's pronouncements may be met with a social response which in effect says, "You are cast out because you are not like us," rather than a scientific one.

Regarding the second point: The anthropic principle is the first of the three major lines of reasoning that can be pursued in attempting to explain something as broad and deep as nonlinear pricing. The anthropic principle reasons from man's existence that something exists. Examples include "because that is the way God made it" and guilt experienced by survivors of a devastating experience such as war. The anthropic principle is illustrated because had they not survived, they would not be able to question why they did. This is not our path. The second line of reasoning is that the laws of the universe are fixed. The failure of deterministic Newtonian physics highlights this problem. If laws are fixed for all time, how does anything evolve? If everything is fixed, how do we explain change? The third line of reasoning, that the laws of the universe actually evolve, is posited by Lee Smolin in *The Life of the Cosmos*. This avenue seems to be the most promising because economies and markets are complex adaptive processes and those processes are not static. They evolve. True, all time scales of change may not be that of an investment horizon, but that is beside the point. What is true of any scale must be true of all scales. And we do know that stars have a beginning, a middle, and an end.

By definition, all intellectual inquiry is a work in progress, whether scientific, mathematical, or financial. Every so often, knowledge plateaus to form a generally recognized standard that is workable but has a few "workarounds" for the unanswered questions. Time goes by, and those niggling questions are challenged and either supported or refuted. This is the

Kuhnian method articulated by Thomas Kuhn in *The Structure of Scientific Revolutions*. Usually by increments, but sometimes overnight, a new paradigm emerges. At each step, a theory's acceptance is governed as much by its ability to improve over previous explanations as it is by the tenacity of its proponents to explain and defend it. So radical a change was relativity that Einstein often mused privately that relativity would not have been accepted at all had he not lived so long, after articulating it, to defend it. Of course, Einstein's general relativity preceded the ability to test it by several years. Gamow's theory of the age of the universe preceeded the ability to test it by decades. Both theories were subsequently proved correct. This text endeavors to introduce and demonstrate a few of the nonlinear building blocks in the context of a theoretical framework with some practical examples. Presumably, nonlinear pricing will not shake the world as did relativity, but it may prove more profitable to those who can understand it and apply it.

It would be safer, but much less interesting, if nonlinear pricing was retrospective in nature; instead, it is a travel guide and thus prospective—even speculative. If someday we are to know how "it is," then we must begin today by constructing ideas based on what we know of how "it might be." There is inherent risk in doing such work. If the theory is wrong, it will be refuted, but at least it stimulates inquiry. However, if the theory or aspects of it are correct, that theory's explanation of reality leads to a superior understanding, then much less remains to be explained. Such is the struggle of all human understanding.

I cannot tell you what the end picture looks like, because I do not know myself. It would be the height of arrogance and also wrong to claim that I did. However, I can show some points of interest along the way that will give you an informed idea of the shape of things to come. Thus, I undertake this task with a great deal of humility. Fortunately, humility is no stranger to anyone who has invested in the markets, and therefore, perhaps, I can expect a small degree of empathy. I take great solace in the fact that there is no progress without effort and no effort without failure.

As we shall subsequently see from Kelly's laws, failure in the information age is guaranteed. You just have to shake it off like a bad trade. Technological advancement is very rapid and my learning curve, like yours must seem to be, is often so steep that it seems vertical. The mild crisis boiling in financial economics is, of course, only for the thinking, because ignorance is bliss.

TOY STORY

The financial benefits of nonlinear pricing to Wall Street will occur in the form of new mathematical descriptions of financial behavior that will replace 25-year-old technology. They are also more accurate, which will yield an improved risk-reward performance. To visualize these new products for finance, we need to take three steps:

1. Use dynamic rather than static analysis.

2. Change old assumptions about how mathematics characterizes relationships.

3. Graphically illustrate changes in time with existing technology (e.g., 3D and 4D).

These points correspond approximately to the following three illustrations: One, a dynamic analysis will change Wall Street's end product of the risk-reward relationship just as Disney did with *Toy Story*. Two, advanced math will allow us to take more accurate measurements just as Levi Strauss did when it used lasers to measure jeans for women. Three, graphics is a more sophisticated interface and will show temporal relationships in finance just like it does for Landmark Graphics in oil exploration.

In 1995, Disney created a movie called *Toy Story*. But "A Toy Story for Wall Street" is not really a toy story in the traditional sense. It is instead a plan for how cutting-edge technology, like nonlinear mathematics and graphics, can change finance at its most basic level—analysis of return and risk.

Wall Street and Hollywood have long used computers to automate existing administrative tasks, like payroll and accounting. Hollywood also uses computers in editing and postproduction. Wall Street uses them for news and stock-quote delivery systems like Bloomberg, Reuters, and Bridge—which are mostly basic analytical programs using old assumptions and ancient formats such as rows and columns of numbers, rather than graphics. But Wall Street has not yet harnessed the true power of cyberspace for changing its end product—specifically the analysis of return and risk. Hollywood has. So has the clothing business with lasers and so has the oil patch with three-dimensional seismic imaging. *Toy Story* was the first movie created totally on computers or "in cyberspace." Although the traditional landscape of Hollywood has not changed overnight, it has changed, nevertheless, in a very important way.

The real lesson of *Toy Story* is that creative tools from cyberspace—namely advanced mathematics and four-dimensional visualization—are entirely applicable on Wall Street. Rather than wearing full body armor from Brooks Brothers like their Wall Street colleagues—the "suits," as Hollywood calls them—programmers are disguised in khakis and polo shirts. And they are here for a long stay.

In Hollywood, programmers of all stripes, especially computer animators, are transcending their traditional role as technical enablers of existing functions by transforming their medium into a creative force in its own right. In *Toy Story*, computers brought toys to life. If history is any guide, heroes, villains, and starlets will follow and programmers in khakis, not just directors in berets and producers in double-breasted designer suits, will grow rich on royalties. Of course, the analogy is imperfect. Animation is not new. Bugs Bunny was created on a draftsman's table. But that is precisely the difference. Today, computers extend that creative force in ways unimaginable to the pencil-and-paintbrush animator of decades past.

Mastering the expanding knowledge of cyber-infrastructure becomes more important and less noteworthy every day—it is simply necessary, like using the telephone. Oddly, those indisposed to learn these skills often are those who have the most substantial financial stake in their outcome. *Toy Story* is a cutting-edge product and 3D is a cool technology. But Hollywood did not make *Toy Story* primarily as a demonstration of technical prowess; Hollywood made *Toy Story* to make money. Wall Street is no different. No doubt, the movie pitch included something to the effect that, "If *Toy Story* is a hit, we can license the characters forever without the possibility of death, days off, disagreements, or devastatingly expensive compensation packages." In short, the movie would suffer fewer of those expensive things which affect humans, particularly stars.

THE QUEEN'S NEW JEANS

You do not have to understand any mathematical arguments in this book. Common sense dictates that if you want a well-fitting suit, get the tailor to take your measurements first and the suit will fit your shape. It is a straightforward concept. Likewise, if you want superior risk-reward descriptions, first take the measurements. Forget the intimidating buzzwords like nonlinear, fuzzy logic, and genetic algorithms. They are just fancy tape measures. However, they do a better job that the old ones. And that is where the new technology coupled with some new thinking comes into the picture.

Think for a moment; would your tailor stock only one size suit? No, of course not. The idea seems preposterous on its face. Why? Because one size does not accurately fit or describe everyone! Of course it is easy to reorder, but those "efficiencies" would scarcely save the business from failing. Why then do financial managers stock only one mathematical distribution theory in their software to measure the return and risk of all financial products under every possible market condition? Why doesn't this strike us as equally preposterous?

The new nonlinear tape measures do a better job, because they don't assume everyone wears the same size (i.e., that all financial time series can be characterized by a single Gaussian distribution) 100% of the time. To press the analogy, we want our technology to be able to fit whatever type of financial physique walks through our front door on any given day of the year, and to sell a tailored suit to every customer.

Not surprisingly, at least one forward-looking company has capitalized on this concept. Levi Strauss now fits women for blue jeans using templates and computers. Lasers are on the way as is expanding the program to men. The very successful brand called Personal Pair costs $65, takes about three weeks, and gives women a better fit in myriad combinations of waist, rise, and hip measurements. If clothiers can use high-tech tape measures like lasers, then we, as financiers, ought to be able to handle our new tape measures, too.

OIL LOOKS SLICKER IN 3D

Hollywood, the jeans business, and even the oil patch are making use of graphic displays and new tools. The guys who used to find oil with divining rods, like tailors with tape measures or animators with a draftsman's table, have also updated their tool kits. The oilman's business problem is basically this: He has to keep finding more of the stuff; however, punching holes in the ground is very expensive. Someone came up with the idea to model the layers of earth, known in the trade as geophysical strata, in 3D. This entailed exploding a charge deep underground and recording the degree to which different levels of strata resonate with the frequency created by the blast. Since granite, cretaceous rock, porous rock, and oil have different densities, they each will produce a unique "signature." Advanced mathematical techniques, such as wavelet analysis, are used to interpret the rebounding signals. A computer assigns different colors to the strata and soon a whole map is filled. The result is a sort of geophysical snapshot in 3D. Obviously, if we test the same location over successive points in time, we see motion, a geophysical movie, also called 4D. This may sound a bit daft, but it is quite real—and profitable. Robert Peebler, CEO of Landmark Graphics in Houston, does this for the oil industry, and quite successfully.

Apply these skills to the financial world and risk managers, bankers, analysts, traders, salespeople, and clients will be able to see finance in motion: real-time changes in risk and reward distilled into intuitive, straightforward 3D graphics.

CONCLUSION

By now, some readers are no doubt wondering if the booksellers mistakenly put a physics text in a jacket for financial economics. They did not. It may be worth noting that when Black-Scholes first submitted their paper on options pricing to an academic journal for publication it was rejected *twice* because it wasn't considered financial economics. Subsequent intervention by the Nobel laureate Merton Miller got it through. Similarly, Bak's work on self-organizing criticality was rejected twice because it wasn't considered geophysics. How trivial this looks in retrospect 25 and 10 years later, respectively. But it was not simplistic at the time. Now it is our turn and it is not simple now. I do empathize.

But I must emphasize that this is not the first time in history that difficult or unusual concepts and facts have been presented, and it certainly will not be the last. There is little consolation to be offered to those who take the ostrich approach and pretend that a new idea does not exist or cling to the past. Any professionals who suddenly finds their gods smashed and their idols false and are looking for comfort may draw it from those who have been there before. Richard Feynman, the late Nobel laureate in physics, once said, "Do not keep saying to yourself, if you can possibly avoid it, 'But how can it be like that?' because you will get 'down the drain,' into a blind alley from which nobody has yet escaped. Nobody knows how it can be like that." In literature the same sentiment was aptly reflected by Sir Arthur Conan Doyle's Sherlock Holmes in *The Sign of Four* when he remarked to Watson: "How often have I said to you that when you have eliminated the impossible, whatever remains, *however improbable*, must be the truth."

In the face of nonlinearity supported by superior technology, the facts have changed. The "aha"—or the bright light at the end of the tunnel—is remembering Lord Keynes, who said, "When the facts change, I change my mind. What do you do, sir?"

2

Nonlinearity: A Retrospective

History does not repeat itself, but it rhymes.
—MARK TWAIN

MEMORY BUILDERS

About once a year or so, my friends, Richard Otter and his wife, Ann, take what our mutual friends Jim and Bobbi Vaugn call a "memory builder"—a trip that will give them a smile as they recollect their years. In 1981, in association with the University of California at Berkeley, Dick's alma mater, they went to Greece on an archaeological dig at Nemea. Here they were told about Kruegas and Damoxenus: two Greek wrestlers, thought to be only a legend, who are famous for a particular bout around 250 B.C. The fight had taken so long that to end it the judges let each deliver a punch until the fellow who remained standing won. Damoxenus wrapped his flat hand and thrust it knife-like into the gut of Kruegas, killing him. Ironically, Kruegas was declared the winner and Damoxenus disqualified because his knife-hand was judged not to be a fist.

It is also Dick's custom, when the stock market closes at 1 P.M., to leave his San Francisco office for lunch. One day after returning from Greece, and just prior to rounding the corner of a well-trod path, he noticed two statues partially obscured by columns in front of the Olympic Club on Sutter Street. They were, of course, Kruegas and Damoxenus poised for their historic fight.

Digging for and finding the remains of two Greek statues is an interesting story, one made more so by the subsequent personal experience of finding them so close to home. It does not matter whether one finds meaning in this because one believes "there are no accidents in the universe" or no meaning because one believes it is merely coincidence. The point is that a heightened awareness of Greek statues from Dick's dig allowed him to notice something which had always been there and which he had undoubtedly seen, if only peripherally, on his walk to lunch, but had never really taken note of. His life, and ours, is richer for it. The experience is probably common to us all; only the details differ. Let us go back to ancient Greece for our origins and see what heightened awareness we can come away with.

DATELINE ANTIQUITY

Table 2.1 may seem a bit confusing at first, but all it is trying to show is when Westerners formulated their concepts about the world and the progression of how we have begun to change viewpoints about those concepts. Two themes run throughout: the Absolute on the left-hand side and the Relational on the right-hand side, which is replacing it. They are called by different names depending on the point in history you pick and the discipline doing the naming. Like a subway map, Table 2.1 is more figurative than literal. This chapter sets the scientific background that will enable us to apply it to financial economics in the next chapter.

As Table 2.1 indicates, the option and thus much of modern finance began (as Peter Bernstein informs us in his excellent book, *Capital Ideas: The Improbable Origins of Modern Wall Street*) with Thales the Milesian (624–546 B.C.). Thales is considered to be the father of Greek philosophy and a founder of Greek geometry because he was the first to prove that the base angles of an isosceles triangle are equal. His relevance to finance is as an astronomer (he made some choice predictions about the eclipse of the Sun in May 585 B.C.). Thales did not record these events, but Aristotle did some 250 years later in Book I, Chapter XI of his *Politics*.

> There is the anecdote of Thales the Milesian and his financial device, which involves a principle of universal application, but is attributed to him on account of his reputation for wisdom. He was reproached for his poverty, which was supposed to show that philosophy was of no use. According to the story, he knew by his skill in the stars while it was yet winter that there would be a great harvest of olives in the coming year; so, having a little money, he gave deposits for the use of all the olive-presses in Chios and Miletus, which he hired at a low price because no one bid against him. When the harvest-time came, and many were wanted all at once and of a sudden, he let them out at any rate which he pleased, and made a quantity of money. Thus he showed the world that philosophers can easily be rich if they like, but that their ambition is of another sort. He is supposed to have given a striking proof of his wisdom, but, as I was saying, his device for getting wealth is of universal application, and is nothing but the creation of a monopoly. It is an art often practiced by cities when they are in want of money; they make a monopoly of provisions.

Table 2.1 The History of Nonlinearity

Date	Concepts and Events	
	Absolute: Reductionism and Idealism	*Relational:* Holism and Realism
2000 A.D.		Nonlinear Pricing
	Water molecule	Funnel or system
		Evolutionary
	Physics	Biology
		Increasing returns
		Neural networks
1975		Genetic algorithms
	Capital Asset Pricing Model, Efficient Market Hypothesis	
	Static	Dynamic
	Random always	Random sometimes
	Black-Scholes option pricing model	
1972	3. Chaos	
1965		Fuzzy logic
1945	ENIAC—First computer	
	Fundamental analysis	
1930s	Neoclassical economics	
	Equilibrium	
	EINSTEIN	BOHR
1919–1926	2. Quantum mechanics	
	Pareto Distribution	
1916	Theory of Relativity	
1904	Einstein proves the existence of the atom	
1900	Bachelier—Brownian motion	
1880	1. Second Law of Thermodynamics	
	Gauss—distribution	
	Industrial Era	Information era
1792		Invisible hand
	Reductionist	Holism Interdisciplinary
	Specialization	Generalization
	Deterministic	
1648	Newton	Leibniz
	Natural philosopher	
1500	Tycho Brahe & Johannes Kepler	
	Music	
300 B.C.	Euclid founds geometry	
350	Aristotle	
400	Year observed to be 365.25 days long	

Table 2.1   *Continued*

	Concepts and Events	
	---	---
Date	Absolute: Reductionism and Idealism	Relational: Holism and Realism
460–370	Democritus	
624–546	Thales—finance begins	
800	365-day calendar	
1500	360-day calendar	

To Thales has been attributed the quote, "Know thyself," which is also applicable to many investors and heeded by few. Was it not Warren Buffett, some 2,500 years later, who said something to the effect that, "If you cannot stand the occasional 50% drawdown you ought not be in the market"? While it is unfortunate that all of the ancients do not have such a direct link to modern Wall Street, their legacy of thought is our inheritance as Westerners.

ATOMISM

Some few years before Aristotle wrote his account, a fellow Greek, Democritus, espoused *atomism*—that the world was made up of particles floating about in a large empty space and that the universe itself was a sort of mechanical system obeying a set of fixed (as opposed to mutable) laws. Aristotle, who also gave us our first understanding of the universe, which held that the Sun revolved around the Earth, rejected the first premise. No doubt Aristotle thought himself prudent in rejecting atomism because the theory was untestable. He was also quite wrong. Atomism is, of course, our basic understanding of the universe today. Aside from merely explaining the universe, atomism also offered a philosophical approach for subsequent work—that of reducing things into ever finer components.

Plato adopted atomism and called it the *demiurge*, which, as Peters mentions in *Fractal Market Analysis*, is the name of the basic philosophical urge to apply an idealistic thought or system to a messy reality. The movement receives its paternity in general from mankind but most especially from Democritus and his thoughts of fixed or absolute laws. Atomism would come to be known as reductionism and provide the basis for much of what we know. The stage is now set for a battle between looking at parts rather than the whole, looking at things idealistically rather than realistically, and looking at things in the absolute rather than the relational. The battle has raged for 2,500 years and is still going strong. The tides, however, are turning in favor of the whole, the realistic, and the relational.

THREE EXAMPLES

The common denominator of the calendar, Euclidean geometry, musical notation, and financial economics is they all superimpose an idealistic system of measurement on a messy reality. For example, Western music's notation, the octave, cannot be divided evenly between the frequencies. That is, "do-re-mi-fa-so-la-ti-do" does not divide as one would think. Music is an interesting example, and in terms of financial economics, music is germane only because it demonstrates how widely and deeply the notion of imposing idealistic theory on a messy reality pervades Western thinking.

MUSIC

Western music is based on a 12-note scale within an octave. Unfortunately, perfectly tuning the half-steps so that they are pure and without pulsations results in less than an octave. Equal tempered tuning, the most popular solution, spreads the error equally among all notes and works in most situations. The octave imposes the Westerner's love of order and symmetry upon an irregular system.

As Thomas Levenson tells us in *Measure for Measure: A Musical History of Science*:

> Unfortunately, the invention of multipart music forced instrument builders and all medieval musicians to confront one of the basic flaws in the natural history of Number sought by Pythagoras and the church alike. Accommodating the musical intervals, the fifths, fourths, thirds, and so on, created by vertical harmony—two notes sounding together—introduced a problem that was not obvious as long as those intervals occurred only melodically, with one note following another. Careful attention to the construction of a twelve-note scale revealed the impossibility of tuning the instrument so that every one of the Pythogorean consonances would be pure and in harmony with itself and the cosmos—actually building organs exposed a fundamental flaw in the musical description of the universe.
>
> Originally, the construction of an organ's pipes had seemed simple. A tenth-century text laid out the rules just as Pythagoras would have. Start with a pipe of whatever length and call it low C. Divide it into four parts, remove one and you have the pipe for the low F, a perfect fourth, related to the C by the Pythagorean ratio 4:3. Divide the C pipe into three, throw away one part, and the resulting pipe length will sound a G—the fifth above a C, representing the ratio 3:2. Then take the G pipe, divide it into three, add a part to it, and the result is the D below G—fixed by the ratio 4:3, a fourth again. The instructions go on, creating an entire scale that translates the tuning of a monochord into fixed ratios of pipe length.

The ratios work, more or less. Later organ builders came up with a slight corrective factor to make up for the eddying of air as it passes over the lips of the pipes, an effect that lowers the pitch of the pipe slightly. But when an organist tried to play two or more notes together in the polyphonic style, some of the combinations would clash viciously. The flaw was not in the construction of the instrument but in the arithmetic of sound itself.

It is a matter of multiplication. Begin with the octave, defined by the ratio of 2:1, and the major third, defined by the ratio 5:4. In the modern Western scale, three thirds fit into one octave—for example, the octave from middle C to the next C above can be divided into the thirds C to E, E to G-sharp, and A-flat to C. (On modern instruments, G-sharp and A-flat are the same note—but that's exactly where the problem lies.) Tuning organ pipes perfectly, one could find each of those thirds by Pythagoras's method: take the pipe used to create the low C, divide it into five parts, remove one, and there is the E pipe (using the correction for the lip, of course). To build a G-sharp, divide the E into five parts and remove one. To find the high C, divide G-sharp into five parts again, and once more remove one fifth of the length—thus completing the octave.

Unfortunately, while each third thus produced would be perfectly in tune with itself, the octave would set dogs barking. Based on the surgery just completed, the length of pipe, and hence the frequency of the higher C compared to the lower one, will be determined by the calculation $5/4 \times 5/4 \times 5/4$—the ratios of each third multiplied together. The sum yields a ratio of the higher pitch to the lower one of 125/64. But a note one octave above another has been understood since Pythagoras to be exactly two times higher than the original, or 128/64. In practice, those missing 3/64 translate into a hideous, dissonant tone that seems to wobble, or beat against the ear.

Our legacy is equal tempered tuning that spreads the error equally over the scale. So much for accuracy.

GEOMETRY

Geometry, although begun by Democritus, was sired by Euclid in his 13-volume work *Elements*, which was first printed in 1482 and remained a standard up until the 20th century. When Euclid articulated geometry, he made an elegant model that had three dimensions: length, width, and height. A line had one dimension, a plane had two dimensions, and a solid cube or sphere had three dimensions. In addition to the traditional three physical dimensions, we now recognize a fourth dimension of time. Spatiotemporal dimensions are the inseparable fabric of space-time. Thus, in terms of what we now know about the laws of the universe, giving an example to the reader in the physical realm is no different than giving that example in the temporal realm. For the reader's convenience we usually start in the physical realm. (*Note*: The 4D referred to earlier in graphics applications is not the same as the fourth dimension in physics, which is time. For example, if one looks at a topographical map, the mountain is in 3D and the bands of altitude, when assigned a color, are the 4th dimension, or 4D. This is technically referred to as a shaded surface plot.

Euclidean geometry works pretty well until you ask simple real-world questions like, "What are the dimensions of a Wiffle® ball, or the surface area of a cloud or a wadded-up piece of paper?" A Wiffle ball fails the 3D test for a solid because, as mathematicians say, its surface area is everywhere continuous but nowhere differentiable. In English, that means it has holes, and by definition a solid does not have holes; therefore, it is not 3D. Ditto for the surface area of the cloud or the wadded-up piece of paper. Although the definition of holes is stretched quite a bit, suffice it to say the surfaces are not smooth and contiguous. All these items reside in 3D space but their dimensions are between two and three, or a noninteger dimension. They are more than a plane or 2D but less than a solid or 3D.

Again we see the demiurge—the need to impose a neat theory of perfect dimensions on a messy reality that is characterized by noninteger dimensions. An easy example to visualize is the golden mean or ratio, which is 1.618. It is a pleasing ratio to the eye, which may explain its prevalence in Greek architecture. Strangely enough, this ratio will be found in an advanced body of math we will address later called fractional stable noises, which describes stock market movements. This unlikely link is cited on page 370 of Samorodnitsky and Taqqu's *Stable Non-Gaussian Random Process*.

Think in Pictures

Geometry is useful because it compels us to think spatially and thus graphically. And it is a fortunate compulsion, since most of us intuit better graphically or in pictures than symbolically, either verbally or in mathematical formulas. In fact, the most advanced nonlinear mathematical techniques are virtually impossible to interpret in the traditional Wall Street formats of rows and columns, but very easy with 4D graphics. In fact, whenever I attempt to solve a problem, little symbols do not dance through my mind's eye; graphical solutions do.

As a producer for the Discovery channel once asked me, what does a fuzzy logic look like? I had to admit, embarrassingly, that I did not know. The Discovery channel likes science and technology, and the producer's point was well taken. As soon as I had pictures (i.e., graphical representations) we had

something more to discuss. Nonlinear pricing is an amalgam of logic processes; however, this experience taught me that graphical output will have as much to do with the acceptance of nonlinear pricing as the performance of the algorithms themselves.

There is evidence that graphics are a more efficient way to depict complex amounts of information quickly. Most of the research comes from the U.S. Department of Defense, which seeks to keep fighter pilots intuitively well informed. Common sense states that a picture is worth a thousand words. So, why hasn't Wall Street abandoned its rows and columns of numbers approach for its traders? I think it soon will.

The idea of graphics in financial economics is not really new. William Playfair, a contemporary of Adam Smith and a mathematician at the University of Edinburgh, introduced the time series graph, or what would later become econometrics, in 1786. Now think about it. We have had 2D (price versus time) representations for over two centuries. Isn't it time to update ourselves? Andy Grove at Intel is doing everything within his power to make 3D technology mainstream as quickly as possible—not to help traders, but because he needs to capture content to justify selling ever-faster microprocessors to keep the Intel juggernaut moving forward and prices coming down. Capturing the 4D and video markets to justify the mass sales of ever more powerful chips is a battle Intel must win.

Euclid, like Democritus, had his own way with words as well. He was hired by the king, Ptolemy I, to teach him math. The king complained and asked if there was some other way to learn the math rather than having to learn all the theorems. Euclid replied, "There is no royal road to geometry," and sent the king to study. There is no royal road to nonlinear pricing either. Bravo, Euclid.

THE CALENDAR

To wit, the calendar is 365 days long but the time cycle it measures is about 365.25. The octave cannot be evenly divided between tones. Finance assumes that the movement of a time series is always random when clearly it is not, and Euclidean geometry exists in three well-defined dimensions.

The calendar is important for representing man's initial recorded thoughts of how he measured time. Time has since become a topic of physics and financial economics because it occurs in the temporal rather than the physical realm—namely, as we shall see, how perception is inextricably linked with time and, therefore, of risk measurement. Man has been at odds regarding the three ways to measure the year, presumably since time began. They are:

- Solar (365 days, 5 hours, 48 minutes, and 46 seconds), from vernal equinox to vernal equinox.

- Sidereal (365 days, 6 hours, 9 minutes, and 9.54 seconds), measured with respect to the fixed stars. The difference here arises from the precession of the equinoxes.

- Anomalistic (365 days, 6 hours, 13 minutes, and 53 seconds), from perihelion to perihelion.

None of them perfectly coincide. About 1500 B.C., the world used a 360-day year with some kludges for the remainder. About the mid-eighth century B.C. these kludges were added to make a 365-day calendar. It was not until 400 B.C., that the year was observed to be actually 365.25 days long. Julius Caesar lengthened a month in observance of his birthday, and except for varying month and quarter lengths, the Julian calendar served its users well for a long time.

However, adding an extra day every four years resulted in extending the calendar over 11 minutes beyond the seasons every year. This was not perceived as a problem for hundreds of years, but by the middle of the 16th century these added minutes had accumulated to almost 13 days. As a result, religious festivals were being observed on the "wrong" date when compared with their original season. Near the end of the 16th century Pope Gregory XIII changed the calendar to make the celebration of Easter coincide with the vernal equinox. But the rearrangements of Julius Caesar and Pope Gregory were internal and did not change the length of the year. Two and a half millennia later we are still using a 365-day calendar to measure the mean solar year. It is the imposition of an ideal system upon a less than ideal world.

THE STARS AND SIMPLE NONLINEARITY

Jump several hundred years in our chart and we move from problems in the calendar to a basic application of time—that of navigation and the problem nonlinearity exposed.

In 350 B.C., Aristotle held that Earth was the center of the universe. In 1520 A.D., Copernicus replaced that paradigm by declaring in his book *The Revolutions of the Spheres* that the Earth revolved around the Sun. In fact, as Lee Smolin tells us, "So drastic was this paradigm shift, that it gave the word revolution a new meaning—the meaning we use today in political contexts."

This heretical view earned Giordano Bruno a burning at the stake in 1600. From about this point on, the language of mathematics may be arbitrarily divided into two camps: the linear or the additive and the nonlinear or the nonadditive. Historically, linear mathematics is the type with which we are most familiar. The historical basis favoring linear interpretations of the world receives its antiquarian roots from Democritus and Euclid and its modern roots from Sir Isaac Newton and Leibniz when they formulated the calculus around 1686.

For example, if a candy bar costs one dollar, a linear or additive relationship means that three candy bars cost three dollars. So is $2 + 2 = 4$ a linear relationship. Deterministic systems like robots, where the relationships in time are fixed, are linear. Car washes and Coke® vending machines are good examples: money in, Coke out ad infinitum. It is easy to understand this simple deterministic or linear relationship, which heretofore has been the dominant paradigm for scientific interpretation of phenomena in the West.

Since nature is nonlinear, chinks in the armor of the linear paradigm began to appear immediately, most notably to astronomers when they tried to apply linear mathematics to planetary orbits. Because planetary orbits change in time and that change is disproportionate between periods, we may say that the orbits are nonlinear. Predictions that are reasonably certain in the short run decrease in accuracy over time, as the mariners who used these calculations to navigate soon discovered.

The linear view persisted probably because of practical necessity, since technology was not advanced enough to support nonlinear "proofs." Consider Tycho Brahe (1546–1601) and his student Johannes Kepler (1571–1630) when they first observed orbits. For example, if we assume that the first observation of an orbit is 1.00000 and the second is 1.00015, we may say that qualitatively the orbits are identical in that they are both elliptical or ovoid. Given the archaic state of their instruments, we might even say the orbits are quantitatively identical—until enough revolutions pass to disprove our assumptions and render our predictions inaccurate. All those numbers to the right of the decimal are called the mantissa, and they add up. Brahe's telescope was not sensitive enough to detect negligible differences and, even if it was, a quill pen and parchment are hardly adequate for heavy-duty number crunching. In fact, in a certain sense, the battle between reductionism and holism might also be characterized as the difference between the mantissa and the integral—that is, the difference many iterations to the right of the decimal point produce as opposed to the round numbers called integrals to the left of the decimal.

Determinism takes away difference in time perspective so that time flows both backward and forward. There is a certain logic to atomism and its conceptual extension, reductionism—that is, tearing things into ever-finer constituent parts until your capability of understanding or ability hits a barrier. This is fine as far as it goes, and atomism is responsible for most of the science to date, as Lee Smolin, a prominent physicist, states in his readable and informative book, *The Life of the Cosmos*. But Smolin goes on to say, "A philosophy that tells us to explain things by breaking them into parts will not help us much when we confront the question of understanding the things that have no parts at that point." Although his words are personal, they speak for many. I concur, both as a financial economics professional and as one who adopts a scientific approach. What is Smolin talking about and what does it have to do with Wall Street? This is a big topic. It is time for a pause.

By analogy, let the shifting paradigm in other disciplines, like physics and biology, as well as other industries, like Hollywood and the oil business, represent our Greek statues—things from which we could benefit if only we had a heightened awareness. Let's have a peek at what is going on in someone else's professional backyard and see ways others are using technology that might apply in financial economics. Perhaps in going over some familiar ground we will be rewarded with a new understanding and discover what has been there all along.

With a bird's-eye view that allows us to see what is going on in other disciplines, we see a struggle emerging. Simplistically, the struggle is between reductionism and holism and at what level of reality the concepts apply, for surely both exist. One easy example is a ball of string, which apparently has different properties depending on the vantage point. The ball's properties will appear to be wildly different at 100 feet and 100X, but it is the same ball of string.

It is less a struggle of what is happening than how to interpret what is happening. Reductionism is the historical precedent of the past 350 or so years and a direct consequence of Newtonian physics. Reductionism basically holds that to learn more about a thing, one *reduces* that thing to its constituent parts, and those parts to ever smaller parts. The study of atoms is now atomic physics. In financial economics, theoreticians have filled academic journals with microminutiae that few, if any, practitioners of economics, like businessmen, can understand or use. Reductionism is also illustrated in the pejorative story of the expert who, unlike a well-rounded person, knows a lot about a very little; taken to its extreme, logic implies that the expert will soon know everything about nothing.

So pervasive is reductionism that it serves as the basis for the division in academia between disciplines. Thus, the structure of the contemporary university is not prepared to cope with interdisciplinary thinking. Consider that Newton was a natural philosopher rather than a physicist, mathematician, or astronomer. Similarly, Adam Smith was a political economist. One suspects that the term exists for the commonsense reason that there is a certain interdependence between politics and economics. When was the last time you heard of a department of political economy? If this thinking seems odd, ask yourself about the many decisions that have no economic rationale but do have political consequences, such as the preservation of indefensible and much abused rent controls in New York City housing. Although the New York papers are not as attuned to a similar situation in Santa Monica, California—pejoratively dubbed the People's Republic of Santa Monica—one suspects it is not much different. As every campaigning politician is keenly aware, the obverse also holds: solutions that may be practical in economic terms, but are politically unacceptable. Consider the zero tolerance policy regarding drugs, a morally defensible position. Would it not be more practical to register everybody involved, decriminalize the activity (removing the economic incentive), and tax the usage at confiscatory levels like cigarettes? If the recent proposed settlement between the U.S. government and the tobacco companies is any guide, perhaps the drug buyers could unwittingly fund the costs of solving a lot of drug-related problems.

HOLISM

Holism, on the other hand, takes a systems approach, the *über*-view, and says that the whole is greater than the sum of its parts. Philip Anderson's-now famous example says basically that no matter how much we study about water molecules, we will never learn about the funnel—called an emergent property—that is instantly created when we pull the plug in our bathtub. We have to look at the whole thing or system, because a funnel-shaped vortex is not a property of a single water molecule but of many.

To continue the example of the academy, it is the chosen task of the Santa Fe Institute, the Prigogine Center at the University of Texas at Austin, and other interdisciplinary centers like them to cut across disciplinary lines to further articulate this cross-fertilized way of thinking. Holism as it is meant here is a catchall term for complexity, and an approach that favors generalization.

Holism versus reductionism is less a matter of right or wrong than it is of forward-thinking people versus those who have found the old ways good enough. This division also largely reflects generational differences, with younger versus older, and differences of risk tolerance, with that minority comfortable with rapid development versus the majority for whom mere existence is challenge enough. In sum, it is tomorrow versus the status quo.

Aside from financial economics, probably the most interesting disciplines to observe engaged in the battle between reductionism and holism are physics and biology. Physics has been the traditional leader in forward-thinking science primarily from the reductionist point of view for the past 500 years. And it is true that the discipline of financial economics has suffered from "physics envy," since, physicists could apply numbers more effectively to their reality than we could to ours. Equilibrium-based neoclassical economics and the Black-Scholes option pricing model are merely restated physics. Black-Scholes is actually the gas-diffusion equation, restated in one dimension because a stock can go only up or down rather than three where the gas molecule could bounce around a room. The concept of equilibrium was pinched wholesale from physics in the 1930s in an attempt to make economics more rigorous and thus scientific.

However, with the concurrent rise of holism, the computational power to model these dynamic and interactive processes, and the graphics to see the change in time, biology is now poised to take the lead. Of the sciences, only biology has the legacy of dealing with the concepts of adaptivity and evolution—concepts that more accurately describe a complex adaptive system like an economy. Unfortunately, biology also suffers from the damning comment made by Ernest Rutherford, discoverer of the nucleus of the atom: "All science is either physics or stamp collecting." By this he meant that all science proceeds from physical laws or else it is taxonomy. It is the application of Latin names and a historical account of events with no hard math to make testable theories. As we shall subsequently see, this has led to a spirited debate in biology between the natural selectionists à la Darwin and those who wish to see principles or theories at work.

Consider the following example: When a physicist solves an equation it is solved once and for all time. When your agents are electrons this is possible, since certain physical laws of the universe are either immutable or change so slowly as to appear immutable. But when those agents are people, no such assurance is possible. What could be considered an optimally good solution in financial economics one moment could be equally bad the next. The explanation begins with Anderson's concrete example that studying water molecules or their ever-finer constituent parts in greater detail will not help you at all in studying the funnel-shaped system that spontaneously emerges or self-organizes when you pull the bath plug. "Order for free" is the term mathematical biologist and visionary Stu Kauffman gave it. Obviously, the particular example of the bath is readily grasped and thus used for illustrative purposes. The operative words are "spontaneously emerge" and "self-organize." Systems both physical and temporal most assuredly self-organize and order spontaneously, but we do not know why.

On to financial economics. To what do you think Adam Smith's invisible hand refers? In 1792, why are four pin makers more productive when specialization exists—where one draws the wire, one attaches the head, and one sharpens etc., than four guys each doing every step themselves? Could the increasing productivity of pin production be an example of self-organization? It is thought to be.

Funnels, like economies, do not have parts in the systemic sense. Funnels, like the nonlinear and nonequilibrium behavior that markets exhibit, are properties of systems. Although systems are made up of constituent parts, like water molecules, all the reductionist or atomistic learning one does about water—counting the atoms, weighing them, measuring their electrical charge, and so on—are worth zilch in terms of describing their collective behavior in a system. More disturbingly, all the guys who made careers being experts in water molecules will find a new paradigm of holism being applied in their backyard. And one thing will be certain: The incumbents will stridently maintain that these new guys don't know anything about water molecules. From a reductionist's point of view, they are right. Although both schools of researchers are bound by a common term, water molecules, their views are apples and oranges. Who remembers the saying, the whole is greater than the sum of its parts? That is, the system is greater than its constituent parts.

A prime business example of the reductionist versus the holistic view oc-

curred in the mid-1970s when transistors, in the form of awkward and initially expensive calculators, replaced slide rules. Traditionalists howled and
educators lamented the decline in learning because children would no
longer learn multiplication tables. Clearly, all was not well. Similarly, one
almost feels compassion for the junior member in the family business and
the politically skilled manager whose myopia, syncophancy, or desire to be
accepted blinded them to the outside world and ultimately caused them to be
skewered by market forces. Of course, if one has ever had to sell to these
self-satisfied souls, one's compassion diminishes greatly.

In periods of rapid technological change, knowing what business you are
in is sometimes not so obvious. For example, Domino's Pizza is in the convenience business. Pizza is just the commodity. Had slide rule makers taken
the funnel view perhaps they would have realized that they were in the calculation business, and perhaps this view might have helped them make the
connection between slide rules and electronic calculators—a connection
that in hindsight seems unremarkably simple. The question is: Are you
working hard to make those seemingly weird connections between the safe
and known world and some of the stuff in this book, which may be new to
you? In five years, do you want to be reaping the rewards of your study or
still paying for your ignorance?

NEWTON, LEIBNIZ, AND THE CALCULUS

Jump another century in Table 2.1, and we now have two of the great minds,
Einstein and Bohr, dueling over a fundamental issue—the perception of
time. For three centuries the philosophical differences separating Newton
from Leibniz and then Einstein from Bohr would parallel each other with no
clear winner. It now appears that the relationalism of Leibniz and Bohr is
beginning to triumph.

Philosophically, the way we approach financial economics really goes
back to 1686 and the difference between Newton and Leibniz when they
formulated the calculus. This may seem like a long shot, but surprisingly the
connection between how these men formulated the calculus and how we approach everyday life in the money business is closer than one might think.

Basically, the difference is the absolute versus the relational. That is, Newton said one could, in effect, step outside the universe, take a measurement,
and then step back inside the universe. The implications of this superhuman
approach are dramatic. Probably the easiest way to describe this phenomenon is to compare it to the canned movie scene where the battle is raging, boy
meets girl, and intimate words are expressed. In the midst of bedlam, a tender
moment happens and the violins start to play. Our handkerchief is out ready

for either tears or triage. Strangely, the guns fall silent and ramparts are not stormed. What happened to the battle? Did the actor's union tell the bad guys to take a coffee break? No. What happened was that the filmmaker held the background as fixed, if not totally ignored, and a moment was lifted out from it. This is the dramatic equivalent of Newton's superhuman ability to step outside reality and make an observation and then step back into it. As soon as the couple profess their undying love for each other, the moment will be subsumed by mainstream events.

This is roughly the view of Newton. It is called *classical* physics and says that we can take an observation as if the background of the universe obliges us by becoming static. It is called absolute because observations have validity due to the observer. From this unique point of observation of a static universe, one can determine everything else. This is called *determinism*. Everything can be determined in three-dimensional space. All relationships everywhere for all time are fixed and linear or proportional. From a practical point of view, determinism is quite comfortable until one realizes, in this all-too-perfect state of affairs, that while it allows us to *predict*, conversely it also allows us to *retrodict*. This is not a good thing, because it conflicts with the observations that coffee always cools to room temperature, also known as the second law of thermodynamics. Radioactive decay is a good example. U_{232} never undecays. Gardens never become more orderly and grow fewer weeds. In other words, there seems to be an inherent one-way bias about the way things flow in time.

The French mathematician Pierre-Simon Laplace formalized much of Newton's structure and this philosophical approach became known as *Laplacian determinism*. Despite the fact coffee never stays the same temperature or gets hotter, determinism, even though it is a grossly oversimplified view of reality, became popular because it was simple and did an okay job—for the 17th Century. Computers did not yet exist. Determinism is a view of reality in which some points are known and others can be determined. An interesting though not obvious relationship needs to be highlighted here, and that is: Our view or understanding of reality is a *process* and progresses relative to our ability to quantitatively express it.

This institutionalized process of knowledge acquisition, known under the rubric of science is a curious process because reality and our ability to express it are never in sync. Science as the term is used here applies to all knowledge acquisition, in every discipline. Every human foible gets a chance to be exposed, because the process is neither gradual nor without trade-offs and costs. Human disposition plays a role. One can take one of two views: The retrospective view in essence says radio waves do not exist because they cannot be detected. That is, you limit your understanding relative to what is generally accepted. Most of humanity falls in this category. The other view is the prospective, which takes newer tools and sees what they can explain, even if one cannot explain everything. This book is firmly in the latter camp. Not to jump ahead, but the real reason for this book, which heightens the awareness of nonlinear techniques applicable to financial economics, is that our view of financial processes is maturing along with our ability to express reality. Think in terms of an arbitrage with matched sides; the old side is what is currently understood and accepted, and the new side is what is capable of being expressed with new tools and thus able to be more accurately characterized and, it is hoped, to be better understood.

In the Newtonian world, the calculus deals with motion. But constant motion is imperceptible. You do not feel the Earth move, and, were it not for some minor vibrations, you would not know you are traveling at Mach 0.5 in a jet on the way to London, either. What you do feel is accelerated or decelerated motion. That is the stuff of roller coasters and upset stomachs. The next issue logically raised is, accelerated relative to whom? Who is observing the motion and who is moving? Taken independently, observer and mover do not have any meaning. It is not until we ask what the relation is between them that we discover that it is relational or relative. It was not until Einstein introduced relativity that we saw how the two parties relate in time. Thus, the combination of the three dimensions of space of Newton and the fourth dimension of time of Einstein is known as *space-time* physics. Einstein gave us a better interpretation of how a fixed background and an absolute observer exist. But, however intellectually comfortable we may be with this notion, it is wrong. It may also be worth mentioning that in philosophical terms, the question of free will is moot because that also can be determined or predicted.

Leibniz, on the other hand, realized that the concept of the absolute, however appealing, was wrong, and that only relationships have meaning. This is a big shift in thinking. How can you be a husband without a wife? Or a father without a child? By definition, the terms husband and father have no meaning outside the relationship to someone else. Similarly, without the security of a fixed reference or anchor the world seems to float. However real the emotional consequences of this unanchored view, it is a scary proposition for many people to face, although we come to terms with the unfixed in limited instances such as the husband-father example or in expressing in economic terms that what someone drinks with dinner is relative since the beverage is proportional to one's wealth. A wealthy diner may have a vintage wine and a less wealthy diner the housewine. We are only just beginning to accept this viewpoint and its implications in broader terms. The definition of a cheap stock or an emerging market is a moving target. Leibniz realized this but did not have the tools to express it. Things are only defined relative to something else. Taking relational logic to its limits, things that have no relationship are by definition the same.

"The debate about whether the properties of an elementary particle are absolute or arise only from their relationships and interactions that tie it to the rest of the universe is very old," writes Smolin. "This debate dates to Leibniz and Newton and has relevance not only to theoretical physics but to financial economics. Relativity, quantum theory, and the gauge principle can all be understood to have evolved from attempts to answer this question. They all concur that properties arise from relationships."

The gauge principle can be understood in terms of an electrical charge. It is not important what the charges are but rather which are like and which are not. Posing the question today seems trivial, but in the 1920s a prominent physicist, Herman Weyl, tried a more subtle approach. In essence his question asked, "Do the conventions about charges (or differences) matter, if we are separated? When we meet can we still use our arbitrary labeling?" Weyl said, yes, we can. In this sense he followed Leibniz's *principle of sufficient reason*, which says we don't make a decision until we are compelled by a logical reason to do so. Weyl found that the way to preserve our freedom was to have the force between the charges not communicate directly but rather be mediated by a field. A field exists at every point in space and carries the charge in the sense that the charge interacts only within the immediate vicinity of the field. A charge changes a local area of the field and then is communicated to the rest of the charges via the field. Each charge feels the other only through the effect it has on the field. Change a few words and the flavor of the idea is compelling. Investors do not feel the effect of another investor directly but only via the market. Remember this concept, because you will see it later.

Since all that matters is the relationship between the charge and the field, Weyl wrote the equations that governed the behavior of the field and the charges as we prefer them. The field carries information in a way that does not restrict our conventions. As a result, we can choose differently at different times and change our minds about our choice at any time. But we can only do so if the field follows certain equations. Weyl discovered that the equations he wrote down were the same as those for the electromagnetic field! The story is not apocryphal; it is how nature really works.

The thought of charges—or anything, for that matter—being defined in terms of relationships is more than philosophy. This concept can lead to the prediction of new fields that carry forces. In this form it has become a physical principle called the gauge principle. Approaching financial economics as field theory is not covered here, but the extension is logical enough. As foundations for understanding, these concepts are not to be thrown away lightly.

What Leibniz's view means for the observer is that we have to explain the world, when we are in it, without the superhuman ability to step outside the universe and take a measurement. In terms of our movie analogy, we get to tell the girl we love her *while* dodging bullets. It is a far more real depiction but one that comes at the added cost of some complexity. Relational views like those of Leibniz and Bohr need a more sophisticated understanding of what is being attempted philosophically, and thus those views required more advanced descriptive techniques. In terms of financial-economics, our omni-science has been removed, and to articulate a more realistic model of what we experience will necessitate a shift to computational techniques—that is, com-puter-generated solutions that can handle more complex forms of information.

As it stands now, almost every bit of mathematics used in financial eco-nomics is linear. Our Newtonian paradigm holds that something is fixed while everything around it changes. To the extent we have stress testing, it is done with Monte Carlo simulations. In effect, we pull some data out of the economic system, subject it to changes as if the backdrop of the economic universe was fixed, and then reapply our results. None of the current linear techniques allows us to simultaneously make love and dodge bullets. It is that simple.

Newton, to his credit, picked the better theory over a worse philosophy. Philosophically Newton may have suspected, as did Leibniz, that ultimately the notion of an absolute observer was flawed. There is some evidence to support this in Newton's correspondence and, moreover, because of the fact that the problem that an absolute observer presents remains unresolved. Nevertheless, Newton pursued his theory because it was the most workable for his time; and, of course, it has met with some considerable success. Smolin writes, "Einstein understood this, and has been quoted by John Archibald Wheeler as praising Newton's 'courage and judgement' for going ahead to construct a workable theory against the better philosophy." From a strictly practical point of view, pursuing the absolute over the relative ob-server was the correct thing to do in 1686. The qualifying statement, of course, is that it was the most workable then. Improved understanding has changed this.

Progress, as the American physicist David Bohm was once reported to have said, is made from "dropping assumptions." The assumption of a rela-tive observer over an absolute observer, more than any other concept, is at the heart of what is now happening in physics and what is proposed in non-linear pricing. The price we pay is giving up our comfort with the old way for the probability of improving the explanations over what we already have.

To recap, the laws of motion or the calculus later laid down by Newton and Leibniz did not allow for the small changes—the nonlinearities—and without the technology to practically measure them, the linear or determin-istic viewpoint prevailed.

So pervasive has the need been to depict phenomena in predictable terms that Western thinkers rarely question this bias in our outlook. Linear or deterministic means predictable (and, in our case, randomness because time has no impact). So pervasive is this idea that some believe the goal of science is prediction, asking, if one were not able to predict experimental results, how else would they be confirmed in another scientist's laboratory? Western thought, however, has attempted to depict nature in linear terms that are too highly idealized.

About the same time Einstein proposed relativity, Werner Heisenberg, Max Planck and Niels Bohr came up with quantum physics, certainly a powerful and enigmatic explanation of the world. The two theories are in conflict, at least on terms of applicable scale, with Einstein capturing our intuitions and quite possibly our emotions because he explains things we can see, whereas quantum physics explains things we cannot see, phenomena at the atomic level. Hearing the arguments between the two approaches takes on emotional overtones because it is so hard to disregard the tactile, but nevertheless (we know intellectually) unreal. Einstein disliked the conclusions of quantum mechanics intensely. They did not agree with the world he was trying to describe. He and Bohr spent their remaining discussions arguing over whose view of the world was correct. Einstein, due to the apparent success of quantum mechanics, was stonewalled but never silenced.

It is safe to say that relativity and quantum physics are better understood today than they were in 1916 and 1919 (in final form in 1926), respectively. It is also safe to say that quantum mechanics is still not clearly understood, so radical a departure is it from our sense-indulged world. The paradoxes and explanations presented by quantumness are so inexplicable that they are distasteful and unacceptable to many—for example, Werner Heisenberg's uncertainty principle and its nonlocality. Something seems to be connected but we can't explain it.

These same philosophical arguments are taken up by Einstein and Bohr, with Einstein taking sides with Newton for a fixed or absolute position and Bohr siding with Leibniz and arguing for the relative. In financial economics it is easy to see why equilibrium became popular. It holds the background of the world fixed as we take a measurement, and then we step back inside the melee and go about our business. Unfortunately, reality is not this way.

THE THREE MUSES

Physicists borrowed from Newton and Leibniz to explain the world in linear terms. However, three major discoveries have called into question the assumption of linearity:

1. The second law of thermodynamics in the late 1800s, in which Rudolf Clausius stated that entropy increases; as a result, Sir Arthur Edding-

ton conjectured that time flows in only one direction. Coffee cooling to room temperature is a good example; once done, it cannot be undone. This is "Time's Arrow" as articulated by Ilya Prigogine, who received the 1977 Nobel Prize in chemistry. See Prigogine's *From Being to Becoming* for some insightful analysis on nonequilibrium thermodynamics, and for a more general treatment see *Order out of Chaos* (Prigogine and Isabelle Stengers).

2. The discovery of quantum mechanics in the 1926, in which Heisenberg via his uncertainty principle, stated that either the location of a molecule or its momentum could be known, but not both simultaneously, thus reducing statements about molecules in the quantum world to probabilistic assessments. For example, think of an insurer that can give you a probabilistic assessment of the frequency of occurrence of a fender bender, but not the specific time or place.

3. Chaos in the 1970s, when Mitchell Feigenbaum at Los Alamos observed quantitative universality in dynamical systems; in his own words, "A precise quantitative determination of the intrinsic geometry of the space upon which this marginal chaotic motion lives together with the full knowledge of how in the course of time this space is explored." The result is known as Feigenbaum's constant, $4.6692016\ldots$, shows that sample systems could exhibit complex behavior. This example for our purposes it suggests that predictability and unpredictability can coexist but on different scales. Think of the weather. We can predict with some certainty the coming of the seasons, but specific weather predictions a few weeks out are elusive.

THREE STATES OF THE WORLD

In terms of modeling phenomena, one may visualize three basic states of the world: predictable, unpredictable, and semipredictable. Table 2.2 graphically summarizes some nomenclature and concepts in terms of those three states. The bulk of Western thinking on economics, science and mathematics is linear and is listed in the center "random" column and the "predictable" columns at either extreme. But what about the italic columns in between? Profitability is contingent upon a broader perspective. Modeling reality accurately seems to be a very conservative move, and if the center and outside columns represent conventional thinking, then a financier will do well to remember Warren Buffett's admonition not to confuse conventionality with conservatism.

Picture a lit cigar. For the first three inches or so above the ash, the smoke

Table 2.2 Comparisons of Un-, Semi-, and Predictable Phenomena

Concept	Predictable (Exactly the Opposite)	Partially Predictable	Completely Random (Unpredictable)	Partially Predictable	Predictable (Exactly as Predicted)
Mathematics	Linear	*Nonlinear*	Linear (chaos)	*Nonlinear*	Linear
Correlation	Perfect negative		Uncorrelated		Perfect positive
Probability		*Fractional Brownian motion ($H < 0.5$)*	Brownian motion ($H = 0.5$)		*Fractional Brownian motion ($H > 0.5$)*
Distribution second moment			Normal Finite	*Stable Infinite*	
Time Series		*Antipersistent*	Independent	*Persistent*	
Equilibrium states			None	*Partial (far-from-equi-librium)*	Perfect
Finance		*New reality*	Old assumption	*New reality*	
Behavior	Your three-year-old child		Alzheimer's patient	Someone you know well	Robot
Cigar			Curlicues	*Twisted spiral*	Laminar flow
Orbits			Multiple moons (three-body problem)	*Normal orbit*	Earth's moon

rises in a smooth or laminar flow. It then gets a little twisted, and about three to five inches up it bends into curlicues. Parallels exist for behavior and cigars. Nonlinear mathematics better depicts dynamical systems or systems that change with time. Orbits, behavioral characteristics, and cigar smoke are dynamical systems. So are markets. Mathematically, nonlinearity means that results are nonadditive. A small difference today can become a bigger difference tomorrow. Results are time-dependent.

Predictable

The laminar flow approximates a linear relationship—that is, a perfect positive correlation between input and output. Simple robots like vending machines are based on this concept. The relationship between coins and the product is fixed and does not vary with time. Twice as many coins results in twice as much product. The Earth's moon, on which there is no life, is in perfect equilibrium. Perfect equilibrium does not allow for changes in time, and is true for only dead systems.

Semipredictable

It is the twisted flow, as a simple physical model and as a nonlinear relationship that lies between linearity and chaos, which best depicts the reality of everyday markets. Chaos is normally associated with a branch of mathematics known as nonlinear dynamics. However, chaos is linear according to our definition because of its complete unpredictability. Nonlinear systems are in near equilibrium that is dynamic and changes in time. Twisted flows are partially predictable; that predictability decreases with time because entropy increases.

Entropy in information theory is the amount of unpredictability in a system. Entropy is the reason microwave dishes, which communicate over long distances, have repeater stations to boost the original signal. Entropy also explains why a message passed verbally down a long line of people doesn't make it to the end of the line unaltered.

If information theory is foreign, then imagine the word represented by "B_ddh_." If you guessed "Buddha" you are correct. With two-thirds of the information, you received 100% of the message. Patterns in traded assets are no different. Yet, standard financial theory assumes that no patterns exist (i.e., movements in time are random).

In behavior, if you were to model the behavior of a family member, would you assume that member's behavior to be perfectly predictable like a robot? No. Common nonlinear sense suggests two things: First, when you say you know a person you have an intuitive (but not numerical) idea of tastes and preferences—in other words, there is limited predictability. Over time you allow this "knowing" to change, or you would give your adolescent son the same gifts he received as an infant. Markets are no different. Second, people's behaviors like physical and economic systems, exist most of the time between the extremes of predictability and randomness. A person whose behavior is truly random cannot function in society. Do you assume that, like a patient with Alzheimer's disease, you must meet your mother for the first time every time? Certainly not—unless, of course, you are a financial theorist.

Unpredictable

The curlicues are turbulence or chaos. Mathematically these flows are unpredictable. Knowing the position of any given particle tells you nothing
about where it may be in the next instant. A chaotic system is out of control
because no relationship in time exists. People with Alzheimer's disease may
be said to be chaotic because the disease robs them of their perception of the
relationship in time between events. What happens today is wholly unrelated to yesterday's or tomorrow's events.

In terms of predictability of behavior, people with Alzheimer's and robots are at opposite ends of the spectrum. No standard definition of linearity exists in this context. Therefore, we define linearity by those
conditions that are either completely random or perfectly correlated (either positively or negatively) in time. All conditions not at either extreme
are an admixture of persistence or antipersistence and randomness. They
are nonlinear. By this definition, standard financial theory assumes linearity because it assumes that asset prices follow a Brownian motion (Bm)
or complete randomness.

An unpredictable system is chaotic. The three-body problem in physics,
the Lorenz equations in meteorology, the Belousov-Zhabotinsky reaction in
chemistry, the standard feedback loop in sound and electrical engineering,
turbulence in mathematics and aerospace engineering, and the crash of 1987
in finance are all examples of chaos. In each case predictability is nil.

CHAOS

Technically the term *chaos* refers to a phenomenon in classical or Newtonian
physics where prediction is intractable because the phenomenon is highly dependent on initial conditions, which must be known with infinite precision.
Since the initial state of all of those conditions cannot be known, predictability is impossible. Chaos refers to a specific state of a nonlinear system when
it is unpredictable. Chaos is a subset of a more general class of phenomena
called nonlinear dynamics. In the early days of looking at chaos in financial
economics, it was hoped that deterministic chaos, chaos derived from the formulas of a few variables. In *Nonlinear Dynamics, Chaos and Instability*,
Brock, Hsieh, and LeBaron said, "In practice, however, there is never enough
evidence to detect high-dimensional chaos, so the best we can do is to detect
low-dimensional chaos." In the equity market they found weak evidence at
six dimensions or variables. This finding along with the fact that there was no
immediate success story led the *Economist* to publish on January 13, 1996,
an article entitled "Chaos under a Cloud." Chaos, strictly speaking, is too

narrow a term to create a realistic model of financial-economic reality. What is needed is the more general concept of nonlinearity.

James Gleick's *Chaos,* a popular account of the origins of the subject, has been responsible for much interest by the reading public. Mitchell Feigenbaum was working with a predator-prey model that was actually developed several years earlier by biologist, Sir Robert May, now the chief scientific adviser to the British government, and who is, unfortunately, no relation to the author. A predator-prey model is a representation of coexisting agents in a system, such as foxes and rabbits in an ecosystem. What Feigenbaum found was the period doubling cascade can be analyzed using tools of renormalization group theory to determine its quantitative features, which are universal for one dimensional maps with one quadiatic maxima. But it will be easier to visualize a relationship between the number of foxes alive one year and the number of rabbits alive the next. For small adjustments in the number of foxes, the number of rabbits would approach stability in a short period of time. For larger adjustments, the relationship would go into a two-year cycle before returning to stability, then a four-year cycle, and so on, then a point of period doubling when the system transitions to chaos. Small changes can lead to unpredictability.

Perhaps this fact is less remarkable in a complex system like the U.S. income tax code; it was quite simple when it was first introduced in 1918. Eighty years later, many seemingly simple changes in the rules have bred a code opaque to ready interpretation, even to the Internal Revenue Service. It is so complex that one of the perverse reasons for not simplifying it is the myriad unintended consequences that even a small change can have, especially to vested interests. A change in the tax code can have discrete—or what is mathematically called catastrophic—changes on the affected parties rather than smooth and gradual changes. A change in the code could be said to be chaotic if the change results in total unpredictability. Chaos is a subset of complexity.

CHAOS IS NOT COMPLEXITY

Complexity is the bounded degree of variety within a system and chaos is the inherent unpredictability in unstable systems. What, then, is the relationship? Chaos is not complexity. Chaos is characterized by a measurement called $1/f$ noise. Chaos is random, has no statistical memory, and therefore cannot evolve. Precisely at the point where phase transition to chaos occurs, so does complexity.

To quote Bak in *How Nature Works,* "Since all the natural phenomena, fractals, $1/f$ noises, catastrophe, and Zipf's law—occur ubiquitously, they cannot depend on some delicate selection of temperature, pressure or whatever, as represented by the parameter [relationship between foxes and rabbits]. Borrowing a metaphor from English biologist Richard Dawkins, who got it from the English theologian William Paley, nature is operated by a 'blind watchmaker' who is unable to make continuous fine adjustments." Chaos cannot explain complexity. Chaos remains unpredictable, whereas complexity describes a richer environment that can evolve or change. However, complexity is certainly included in our definition of nonlinearity, because the causality between relationships is disproportionate.

TRANSITIONS

A physical example of transitions between phase states is solid to liquid to gas. In the case of H_2O, those states are called ice, water, and steam, respectively. Usually ice melts to water and then evaporates. More difficult is when ice skips a phase and sublimates. It transits directly from solid to gas. One often sees sublimation in Colorado or New Hampshire, where the winter's snow stays on the ground through spring. Typically, the temperature is not warm enough to make the snow melt but the air is dry enough so that the snow cannot remain. The snow does not "evaporate," because it is never water—it sublimates.

As an analogy, systems go through the same sorts of transitions. The pendulum is a simple example; it can exist at a point, in periodic behavior, or in aperiodic behavior. The point is when the pendulum is still, the periodic behavior is a repetitive orbit, and the aperiodic behavior is chaos. Much work on phase transitions was done by Chris Langton at the Santa Fe Institute with a specialized branch of math called cellular automata "in silica" or in a computer. Start with a grid, and in each box is an "organism" with one rule. Let the rule run a few thousand times, and from this seemingly simple setup of automated cells comes artificial life that exhibits complex behavior. Between the states of periodicity and chaos, Langton noticed a fourth type of transitional behavior called complexity or the "edge of chaos."

SYSTEMS

The type of systems being discussed are open or unbounded and are thus dissipative systems. This is in contrast to a closed system like an electronic circuit. Economies and businesses are, by definition, open systems. Good businesses have porous or diaphanous borders, which allow significant social interaction in terms of information flow to stimulate trade. A firm is in contrast to a bureaucracy, like the IRS, where the information flow seems to be in only one direction—from you to it. Economies have varying degrees of porosity, like those in democratic versus Communist countries. *Dissipative* refers to the fact that the system requires energy to stay in a poised, semitensed, or out-of-equilibrium state. In financial economics, "energy" is loosely defined as the financial resources and collective effort required to keep a business solvent, a market liquid, and an economy productive.

In terms of life, an equilibrium state is not alive. It is dead. In an equilibrium state the system's responses are proportional, and therefore equilibrium states are linear. In death, the response is perfectly proportional or linear because there is no interaction. The Earth's moon is in equilibrium. Dormant or sleep states and normal markets correspond to slightly out-of-equilibrium states. The Earth in its stasis of life is in an out-of-equilibrium state. Radical changes in life or market activity correspond to far-from-equilibrium states. Imploding stars are in a far-from-equilibrium state. Equilibrium-based theories of economics therefore seem more applicable to the period when stock exchanges are closed rather than when they are open. Hence, the title of this book, where our objective is to price information given the economic reality of nonequilibrium and nonlinearity.

Entropy, also called the second law of thermodynamics, is the increase of disorder in a closed system. Entropy is the reason why snow melts and a cup of coffee cools. Small differences are erased and statistically become like the whole. Entropy only increases. Increasing entropy suggests that the natural state of the world as expressed by Newtonian physics is a dead equilibrium. It is not. A measure for entropy comes from information theory, which measures the quantity of information in a transmission that the system emits. This measurement is the previous "Buddha" example.

Life, of course, does not exhibit equilibrium. It exists in a out-of-equilibrium state. The atoms in my body register at 98.6 degrees Fahrenheit. In the presence of life, the temperature of the atoms in my body does not decrease to the outside temperature. In the presence of life, evolution is a reality, and complexity is a requisite part of our understanding of the universe as well as highly derivative processes such as economics. Part of the problem is that there is no general theory for nonequilibrium. John von Neumann, the father of artificial intelligence, once referred to the theory of nonequilibrium as the theory of "non elephants." The meaning is twofold. First, von Neumann uses the term elephants as a metaphor for linearity. Saying nature is nonlinear is like saying most animals are nonelephants. The statement is so broad as to be practically useless in terms of explaining other animals. It is a reflection of our state of limited development when we have to define something by what it is not, rather than by what it is. Second, the possibility of a general theory of nonequilibrium may be remote. Complexity and the edge of chaos are big steps though.

The complexity of nonequilibrium or dissipative systems best characterizes financial economics. It takes effort or some external source of energy to maintain a system in a far-from-equilibrium state. Think of your garden. It requires energy in the form of weeding and pruning to maintain it and to make it look beautiful. Left to nature, the garden would return to equilibrium or a jungle. In terms of a jungle, a beautiful garden is poised in a far-from-equilibrium state. Similarly, an untended company will face bankruptcy. Entropy says a beautiful garden will always become more disordered and never more elegant and ordered. The last word is important because we are trying to calculate within some bands of order or bounded degrees of variety called complexity.

COMPUTATION

An important facet of applied technology as it relates to finance is that our definition of what is tractable is a moving target. A problem is said to be *tractable* if the difficulty of the computation increases less slowly than the difficulty of the problem—that is, if it is computable in a reasonable period of time. In the definition of tractability, we are not concerned with how long the problem takes but rather that the time to calculate it does not rise too quickly. A problem is said to be *computable* if it is well defined but not feasible. There are many problems that are clearly defined, such as number of primes, which we are unable to compute. Common examples of uncomputable problems are the eye-catching Julia and Mandelbrot sets, commonly referred to as fractals. They are uncomputable because no amount of computation can capture their infinite precision.

It may be worth a moment to look at the converse definitions so that we may get oriented, since they can overlap. Factorization, in essence the opposite of multiplication, looks for unique combinations of prime numbers. Factorization is the branch of math upon which cryptography is built. Your credit card number on the Internet is assumed to be secure because the crypto-code cannot be broken. The code cannot be broken because it is mathematically *intractable*. That is, although an answer definitely exists, there is not enough time to compute it. Obviously, with faster microprocessors and distributed processing (using more than one processor), the definition of what is tractable and intractable is a moving target. Forty-number keys are now standard. If you download a browser from Netscape with a 125-number key, you must be a U.S. citizen and register at that time, since the U.S. government classifies this 125-number code as munitions and thus illegal for export.

INTRODUCING THE KAOS FUNCTION

Figure 2.1 shows the KAOS screen on Bloomberg, which depicts the Hurst exponent applied to Microsoft. The middle section of the graph, which ranges from 0 to 1, is but a simple crooked line. However, the nonlinear mathematics—the theory that embraces that nonlinear class of math and the paradigm shift that theory of nonlinear pricing implies—is quite substantial. Theory is catching up with reality and the relative state of ignorance is reduced. That is the good news. The bad news is there is no salve for ignorance since there is much more to know.

There is much to say about the KAOS screen and the Hurst exponent. The fractal math behind it and its impact on extant financial theory will be presented in Chapter 4 and the results from trading in Chapter 5, but at present we are concerned only with the ability to compute the Hurst exponent from a scientific point of view.

The KAOS screen runs on Bloomberg's Data General mainframes and is available to you in real-time. It is a computationally intensive screen. Although the tests have not been performed, it would not be surprising to learn

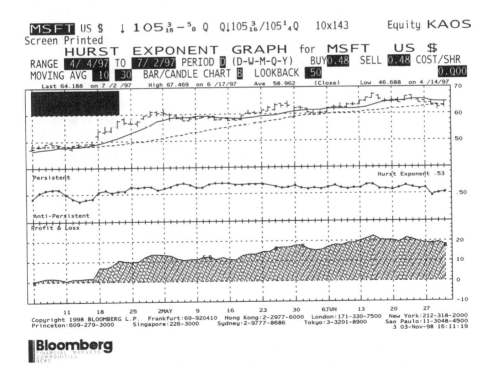

Figure 2.1   Bloomberg Screen (© 1998 Bloomberg LP. All rights reserved. Reprinted with permission.)

that the KAOS screen is one of the most computationally intensive functions on Bloomberg. When I first began using the Hurst exponent in 1994, the functional equivalent of the KAOS screen took a conservatively estimated 21 minutes to render with a single Intel 486 series microprocessor. If we apply Moore's Law loosely, that approximates $10\frac{1}{2}$ minutes on a Pentium and $5\frac{1}{4}$ minutes on a Pentium II. Used in clusters, the forthcoming 64-bit Merced chip due in 1999 may well approximate Bloomberg's speed using mainframes. If I am wrong in my estimate, because of Moore's Law I will not be wrong by much nor for very long. When Harold Edwin Hurst first devised his technique in the 1930s, he had to use a deck of cards to simulate it. Thus, the Hurst exponent has always been computable, but it is only recently that it became tractable.

What is important to remember in financial economics is that as technology progresses, whole new classes of problems that were once intractable become tractable. No longer are we just processing mundane tasks faster; we are changing qualitatively the type of information we generate because we can say something fundamentally new and different. Thanks to rapid technological development, the definition of tractability is a moving target that changes what we can demonstrate. Thus, we change information and thereby transform the business.

PROOF AND ACCEPTANCE

The first and obvious question to this change is: What constitutes proof? In science there are three basic methods: deduction, induction, and reason. *Deduction* is reasoning from theory to observation. In the presence of complexity, a condition of real-world financial economics, deduction is impossible because people are continually searching and testing new theories about what is economically viable. It is impossible to deduce why people buy and sell. *Induction* is the process of reasoning from observation to theory. *Reason* is cumulative and simply states that something is the best explanation or theory to be offered regarding the facts. Later we will see that the more appropriate term for reason is *abduction*. There are certain guidelines in constructing a proof; the most general is Occam's razor, which states that nothing should be added that is not needed. In other words, the simplest explanation is the best.

Of the three methods of proofs, in financial economics we are most prone to induction. That is, if an observation has worked more than once, it will work again. Of all the methods of proofs, induction is the most dangerous. The conclusions drawn from observations can be entirely misleading. In fact, it is wrong to think that a proof or theory can be explained this way at all. To see why, look at Bertrand Russell's chicken.

The chicken sees the farmer come in each day to feed it. This observation leads the inductivist chicken to conclude that the farmer will continue do so every day. Every feeding period leads to reinforcement of the theory. But, one day the farmer wrings its neck. The chicken's theory did not pan out. If the chicken had a better understanding, it would not draw such absurd conclusions. What should replace inductivism? Reasoning. If the reasoning is justified, then so will be the conclusions or predictions drawn from it.

Does the chicken sound like an investor in a bull market? Or a momentum fund? Or the initial public offering (IPO) market? Or the leveraged buyout (LBO) market? I think it does. Constant reinforcement every day in a rising market dulls objectivity and without the benefit of understanding leads to disaster. It will work until it does not. As I will argue in this book, far-from-equilibrium paradigms like those exhibited in biology or Boolean computer networks are far more representational of real-world financial economics than equilibrium-based economics is.

On Wall Street one can receive a non sequitur like, "You know, it is October exactly ten years after the market crashed," as I did from a broker soliciting a new account. So? Nevertheless, inductivism remains a standard because something has worked more than once. That may be the case, and in some instances inductivism may lead to a deeper understanding. But most often it does not. Inductivism, without reason, is the primary source of bad decisions in financial economics, not to mention unflattering quotes.

The 21st century will change the nature of the proof. This is a broad and sweeping statement and deserves some discussion. Prove the return on investment of a computer, or the increased productivity in a firm that the computer is supposed to enable. By our traditional measures of return on investment and productivity, we cannot prove the ROC of a computer, yet the evidence of the existence of the high-tech industry suggests that we accept it.

Traditionally, proofs were analytic. A mathematics professor wrote a multipage proof in linear math and signed "QED." In the 21st century complexity does not admit such a simple analytic proof. The new method of the proof is computational. Modeling a dynamically accurate stock market, as Arthur, Holland, LeBaron, Palmer, and Taylor did in their 1996 paper, "Asset Pricing under Endogenous Expectations in an Artificial Stock Market," at the Santa Fe Institute, is a form of computational proof. The proof is the result of thousands of iterations of a computer program. True, the results can be printed out, iteration by iteration, but that is intractable. Neither you nor I will read it, or be able to understand it in that form.

This last comment needs clarification. A closed-form solution means that a distribution of a function can be neatly represented by a formula. And in the linear world this is how it is done. Mathematicians write several pages in a respected journal, state their case with a proof, and end with the letters

QED or *quod erat demonstrandum*, Latin for "which was to be proved." It is also worth noting that the Black-Scholes option pricing model has a closed-form solution (except for American-style puts).

This traditional approach of closed-form or analytic proofs changed in 1976 when Kenneth Appel and Wolfgang Haken used computers to solve the four-color conjecture and elevate it to the status of a theorem. The question, posed in 1852, was: What is the least number of colors that a map can have that no continuous parts of the map have the same color? A proof was eventually made, but not before a lot of calculations were done accompanied by several hundred pages of printout. Similarly, when one crosses the barrier to the nonlinear world, one must solve the mathematical expression computationally because no simple formula exists. With computers this is no problem, but it is easy to see why no one would want to deal with nonlinear math without them!

The issue of what constitutes a proof is undergoing a radical change in the nonlinear world. Most investors and finance practitioners are not well versed in higher math and thus, any concept that cannot be expressed on the back of an envelope is suspect. This form of ignorance is about to become very expensive to maintain. Probability in the form of Black-Scholes was a big conceptual leap forward. Now we are seeing more realistic modeling techniques, but the proof for an evolutionary process is a highly iterative affair rather than a simple formula. The practical solution can be demonstrated in familiar terms, such as a profit and loss statement for historical incidents. As we shall soon see, David Deutsch has even more radical ideas for what will constitute a proof.

As stated earlier, the origin of the computational proof came with the four-color problem. So powerful is the concept of computational proofs that the next step has already been laid—the more exotic example from quantum computation called Shor's algorithm, as mentioned by Deutsch in *The Fabric of Reality*. The computation happens in quantum space and therefore cannot be proved by conventional—classical—methods; but it happens nonetheless!

No doubt the appeal to reason and the appeal of a proof being in a program smack of "black box" to many. Black box is a pejorative term on Wall Street, where analytical proofs are in vogue. The logic flow is trivial. If financial economics is nonlinear (and it is) and biological notions of evolution and non equilibrium are applicable metaphors (and they are), then we are justified in using nonlinear techniques such as genetic algorithms, which are very good at exploring solutions in complex environments. Nonlinear proofs are by definition computational. There is no basis for them to be accepted unless there is logic in their application to financial economics. Lastly, how can we prove *ex ante* or before the fact that a nonlinear technique, like genetic algorithms, will always work? The answer is that we cannot prove it inductively. We have to prove it by reason. By the standards of induction, if one money-losing trade occurs the theory is falsified. Yet we accept the past success of value investing inductively in terms of its results. Inductive proof will not help us because it is always looking *ex post* or after the fact. However all is not lost.

I propose the matching principle. The *matching principle* holds that the tool being applied to a problem that best characterizes the nature and results of the problem is the correct and best tool to use. That is the proof. The matching principle frees us from trying to use an outdated accounting system to measure return on investment (ROI) or productivity. For example, the proof that investment in technology roughly corresponds to an increase in productivity does exist but not within in the constructs we currently apply. Since the proof lies outside the constructs of quantifying economic performance, the linear constructs must be broadened. The same is true in mathematics. A body of math is defined, and the only way to prove something that lies outside that definition is to broaden the definition. The matching principle frees us from the bounds of classical physics in the face of a clearly quantum phenomenon such as Shor's algorithm. It also frees us from applying linear mathematics to a nonlinear system like financial economics. In Shor's algorithm, where is the proof? It is in quantum-land, not provable by our traditional notions, but it exists! Likewise, we cannot rerun a trading day and dissect the internal logic of a nonlinear process in real time to create an a priori proof. There are too many contingencies to foil our current deterministic notion of proof.

In the strict scientific sense value investing, though generally accepted, is not proved either, since one money-losing trade would invalidate the theory. Value investing is accepted not because it is proved but because it is the best explanation for that type of investing. Similarly, I argue that nonlinear techniques should be accepted because they are the best explanation of financial economics phenomena. By the matching principle, nonlinear techniques better characterize the problem and its results.

INDUCTIVE COOKIES

Much of the schizophrenic behavior of the market is due to the reality that conclusions drawn from facts are not always the correct ones. The initial public offering or IPO market is a great example. Granny first made cookies in her kitchen as a hobby and gave them away. When demand for Granny's Cookies grows too big for her modest budget, she creates an informal business. Eventually Granny's Cookies Incorporated serves the delicacies from hundreds of strip malls, and along the way the private company issues shares to the public through an IPO. If you have seen a lot of IPOs, you have probably developed a jaundiced view of stories touting the "next Microsoft." To facilitate the sale of the stock to its first owners, investment bankers price the stock at the lower end of the range of values so that it will sell the first day.

Inductive reasoning tells you that since the last three fast-food companies you bought from a certain underwriter did great, Granny's should be a smash hit. Unlike the high-tech stories, we know what a cookie is and what to do with it. Everybody loves Granny; she is a media phenomenon. On the morning of the offering, giddy in anticipation of being paper-rich, Granny gets carried away and wraps her new Porsche around a freeway entrance sign.

What conclusion can and do you draw? Are IPOs profitable? If so, which ones? It is the problem of induction in the markets in the absence of good theory that makes babblers out of very intelligent people. One observation falsifies a theory. That is why there are no theories. So sometimes it's right to buy a stock, and sometimes it's wrong.

You take a hit on Granny's and sell your position. A month later, it is Teeny Cookies, and since Teeny is also a media phenomenon, albeit a 16-year-old with blue hair, orange nails, and a new album with a voice that could devein shellfish. You buy big thinking that lightning can't strike twice. Teeny dies from electrocution from faulty wiring on stage in Beijing. It is a fiasco. The stock tanks. You have been burned twice, and you tell that banker no more fast food. Sure enough, he does not call. You see Dr. Magic's Cookies coming up on the IPO calendar. It does great. Kids love Dr. Magic's Saturday morning TV show. You tell yourself that you are not stupid, but you have done exactly everything wrong. It is embarrassing to admit it to yourself, and you are thankful that your dog does not talk back. This is schizophrenia.

CHEAPER TO STEAL

It is probably safe to say that science is a welcome thing, since, broadly speaking, it is the systematized process of knowledge acquisition. Building the logic process to explain nonlinear pricing mandates a catholic taste in many disciplines, because the terms and techniques used to explain financial economics phenomena were not developed in that field. The current literature of financial economics is not sufficiently rich to describe economic reality. This is no cause for shame, for it is true in many other fields as well. The terms come from other fields. Computer science, physics, and biology are the principle sources. For clarity we adopt original terminology and give examples from the physical, economic, or temporal realms to cement those concepts.

It should be noted that there is a general movement afoot called the interdisciplinary approach where similar phenomena, like complexity, chaos, or nonlinearity, are recognized in many disciplines. Given the tremendous cross-fertilization now happening, in a certain sense science has the flavor of a rabbinical council, where everyone is teaching everyone else. It is for the good if you can also admit that you have something to learn from the other fellow. It is our approach, and there is good reason for it: It is cheaper to borrow than to build. If a phenomenon in financial economics can be explained or a problem solved with a technique developed elsewhere, investigate it and adopt it if it proves useful. If adaptation is theft on a grand scale, I freely confess. But I admit it and I cite sources. If we are going to steal we are going to do it honestly and with attribution, because there must be honor among thieves if we are to learn from each other. While confession is in session, I also admit to some novelty in terms of interpretation, but I did not invent any of the technologies, not a one.

SCIENCE IN FINANCIAL ECONOMICS

The current mathematical framework of financial economics is predominantly linear. That is, the entire mathematical construct in financial economics is linear because the construct itself assumes that the input-output relationships are proportional or time-independent. Unfortunately, this is not so; the input-output relationships of financial economics are *not* linear. They are nonlinear, or disproportionate and time-dependent. Since markets seldom crash, those relationships are rarely chaotic. Chaos is an extreme state and only a subset of nonlinearity.

Nature is basically a nonlinear system, but linear mathematics is much easier to understand. Historically, linear math is the tool we have used to understand our world. The use of linear math is, of course, justified in some instances. However, as technology progresses, those specific instances are increasingly becoming realized for what they are—highly idealized subsets of a more general class of nonlinear phenomena. The attachment to a linear construct to depict a nonlinear phenomenon represents the human error of emotion or misplaced sentiment dislodging reason. It is illogical and reminiscent of generals who prepare to fight the last war.

Because there is a mismatch between the assumptions of the mathematics and the reality the mathematics seeks to depict, theory does not explain the facts. Explaining the facts is, after all, the goal of all science. From a superior explanation we can work with the system better to increase profits. The incongruence between theory and observable reality has contributed to the jaundiced view in which many experimental economists (read practitioners) hold theoretical economists. In financial economics there are two facts to be dealt with. First is the assumption of equilibrium. Second is the assumption of independence. In the context of financial economics the neoclassical economics of the 1930s assumes a Nash equilibrium. Equilibrium by definition is linear.

The Black-Scholes option pricing model assumes that the movement in time of time series is independent 100% of the time. The KAOS screen obviously highlights the incorrect assumption of a Brownian motion in option pricing more specifically and thus more dramatically than it does in neoclassical theory. This fact has led many to conclude that nonlinearity and the KAOS screen are only about options or derivatives. This is a limited and therefore incorrect conclusion. The phenomenon of nonlinearity challenges the entire class of linear math used to characterize financial economics relationships. Disproving the Brownian motion assumption happened to be one of the most dramatic examples; it is also now generally available to the practitioner, in the sense that it is on a major service like Bloomberg and that it can be explained simply. If the line in the center of the screen was perfectly horizontal at the 0.5 level, theory would be right and there would be no need for further work. Clearly it is not.

Like their predecessors, economists borrowed from the extant lines of linear thought. Even though the theories may not have always been accurate in the eyes of the practitioner, they fit together neatly in terms of linear mathematics. Probability theory and the partial differential equations of equilibrium physics are the roots of classical economics. For example, the frequency of a time series and probability theory are linked because the inverse of a Fourier transform is the characteristic function of a distribution.

In making classical economic theory and the portfolio theory of the 1970s, assumptions needed to be made about the future behavior of asset prices and how the returns of assets are distributed. In keeping with the linear mind-set, theoreticians assumed that the movement in time of any traded asset was random and that its returns were normally (or lognormally) distributed. While this is still the prevailing view, it is wrong and the fact that it is the prevailing view does not reflect well on the majority who maintain it.

The time series of financial markets are complex affairs that do not lend themselves to simple interpretations or formulas. Nor are they random most of the time, as Andrew Lo and Craig MacKinlay documented in 1988. Most of the time, traded asset prices persist or anti-persist. That is, they have the tendency to follow their current path or reverse themselves. "Most of the time"—what does that phrase mean? Further, what does "time" mean? What is time? Just as quantum reality does not fit within the bounds of a classical proof, nonlinearity has difficulty within the unstated assumptions of time. Most people do not have an assumption about time other than being ahead of or behind what the clock on the wall indicates. This sacred cow needs to be slaughtered.

PERCEPTION OF TIME

Time is one of the most subtle topics that man has ever attempted to explain. In fact, as we shall soon see, the nature of one's belief of time—absolute versus relational—is the proverbial nail upon which hang all the laws of the prophets of science. It is as basic as the difference between Newton and Leibniz and between Einstein and Bohr. Time is also a topic that can quickly move the focus of any discussion from the concrete, like dollars and cents, to the amorphous, including the philosophical and religious.

Like most people, my initial concepts of time came unconsciously from the experiences of everyday life, such as being late finishing homework or being faster in a race. Most experiences were finite: They had a beginning, a middle, and an end. Only in Sunday school did I learn that some things, like one's soul, are eternal. I do not remember having a problem reconciling these two concepts—time versus eternity—and therefore I now assume that as a child infinity was a word I understood. The concept of time arose later in high school physics and has stalked me ever since. Over a quarter century later as an adult, I do not believe I fully comprehend it. Perhaps I am better educated now, but certainly no wiser.

The first professional conundrum I faced with the concept of time came from a business school professor, Yakov Amihud, at New York University. Amihud told a simple story which illustrated the point that risk unfolds with time and that perception is all-important. As I recollect, it goes as follows: Imagine that you are an insurance underwriter at Lloyd's of London who has underwritten a hull. The ship sails and unfortunately sinks. You are still safe and dry but poorer for the experience.

The idea was to illustrate that risk unfolds with the passage of time, and because we are not omniscient, perception is different for different people. There are several issues at work. How frequently is the information updated? Risk does not unfold evenly. Obviously, the perception was very different for the ship's crew than it was for the underwriter. Once we all have the same perception of an event such as the ship sinking, then we are more objective. Perhaps "objective" is too strong a word, because it implies that everyone may share it; maybe we are only in agreement with each other.

The nature of time has successfully challenged much better minds than my own. Today in finance we assume that time is uniformly measured by

the clock on the wall and that all participants are equally well informed—
that is, information is symmetric, in the vernacular. We know that everyone
does not have the same information at the same time. If the purpose of study
and theory, as Keynes so aptly put it, is to defeat "the dark forces of time
and ignorance," we will also show that the idea of the clock on the wall as a
paradigm for time is also wrong.

Differences in perception quickly raise many issues. Such classics as
Charles Mackay's *Extraordinary Popular Delusions and the Madness of
Crowds*, Charles Kindleberger's *Manias, Panics, and Crashes,* Gustave Le
Bon's *The Crowd*, and perhaps even Ledwin Lefèvre's *Reminiscences of a
Stock Operator*, are the foundation of a field called behavioral finance that is
now taking root.

To the average Wall Streeter, the perception of time flows differently than
for the average Main Streeter. No doubt "a New York minute" is perceived
to happen quicker in Manhattan, New York, than in Manhattan, Kansas. If
we can apply concepts of time held by certain religions, Wall Street would
probably be Buddhist—there is only the here and now. Yesterday and tomorrow are rumored to exist; last quarter and next quarter strain the precep-
tor's ability, and beyond those is the great void.

To serve this discussion, I am fully in the relational camp. There are two
time scales: Time as I perceive it and time as I perceive what I am considering perceives it. The clock is an abstraction we can point to objectively, and
life is pleasant when my perception of time and the clock are in sync. Wall
Street works at a different tempo than does the publishing world. This is neither good nor bad—just different. How many husbands have learned to pace
their own preparations with that of their wives before going out in the
evening? For the sake of harmony in the relationship, does it really pay to
rush? We will cover time more in depth in Chapter 8.

CONCLUSION

The conclusion here is not difficult. For very good practical reasons man
chose an explanation of his world that was linear or proportionate because
that was the best he could do for that era. The linear view is pervasive in
music, geometry, and calendrics.

My colleagues on Wall Street are confronted daily with the perpetual
novelty of a system, in this case an economic one, and would rather deal
with "water" facts than "funnel" facts because the water facts are better
known, even though they may be (and invariably are) less relevant. For example, they are quite adamant in stating that the earnings are expected to be
up 4%, rather than looking at the dynamics of the stock. You can almost

hear them say, "That is not what we do." The atomistic view, is taken no matter how logical the explanation of a funnel view may be to them on a one-on-one basis.

The analogy to finance and stocks in particular is similar though not exact. Analyzing a stock in ever-increasing detail is atomistic and fine for some styles of investment. Just as technology has become an increasingly larger part of the investable universe and thus of your portfolio, and as telecommunications stitch the world together more tightly and information is communicated more quickly, dynamics will become a more important part of investing.

Newton preached a fixed velocity, a concept taken primarily from the Earth's rotation abound the Sun. In the early 20th century, the Newtonian view was shattered and replaced by Einstein's theory of relativity and quantum theory. Those theories have yet to be unified. But two facts are clear: First, the Newtonian view of the world has long been discredited as an ultimate explanation. Second, neoclassical economics, which serves as the official basis for what we learn in school and which is based on a Newtonian view, is still going strong.

Developments in science such as thermodymanics, Heisenberg's uncertainty principle, and chaos have called into question the linear view, and more fundamentally the philosophy behind that view of tearing things into ever-finer parts, called variously atomism, determinism, and reductionism.

3

Nonlinearity: A Prospective

Imagination is more important than knowledge.
—ALBERT EINSTEIN

THE VISION THING

Recalling an event at the Santa Fe Institute, in a phone call to me in 1997, Nobel laureate in physics Philip Anderson of Princeton University stated: "Theoretical economists will have virtually abandoned classical equilibrium theory in the next decade; the metaphor in the short-term future will be evolution, not equilibrium." It is safe to say few practitioners appreciate the profit potential of his statement. It will be comforting for the investor to know that a real sea change is underway, especially if one hears it from other leading minds as well.

Famed investor George Soros said in his 1995 book *Soros on Soros*: "There has been a recent development in science, variously called the science of complexity, evolutionary systems theory, or chaos theory. To understand historical processes, this approach is much more useful than the traditional approach, which is analytical. Unfortunately, our view of the world has been shaped by analytical science to a greater extent than is good for us. Economics seeks to be an analytical science. But all historical processes, including financial markets, are complex and cannot be understood on the basis of analytical science. We need a whole new approach and my theory of reflexivity is just the first step in this direction."

Nobel laureate in physics Murray Gell-Mann, of the Santa Fe Institute, echoed this view in John Brockman's *The Third Culture*: "Some dogmatic neoclassical economists had kept claiming that fluctuations around so-called fundamentals in financial markets amounted to a random walk, and they produced some evidence to support their assertion. But in the last few years, it has been shown—I believe quite convincingly—that, in fact, various markets show fluctuations that are not entirely random. They are pseudo-random and that pseudo-randomness can be exploited."

Nobel laureate in economics Paul Samuelson of MIT said regarding Benoit Mandelbrot's 1997 *Fractals and Scaling in Finance*: "On the scroll of great economists who advanced economics by quantum leaps, next to John von Neumann we read Benoît Mandelbrot." Edward Lorenz discovered (and rediscovered) the beauties of chaos and Benoît Mandelbrot created an understanding of *fractals*—both exciting developments with potential applications to engineering, biology and economics, and neither revolution possible without the availability of the modern high-speed computer."

Merton Miller of the University of Chicago, Nobel laureate in economics, said in his 1997 text, *Merton Miller on Derivatives*, "We should have learned from Benoît Mandelbrot thirty years ago, however, that large, sudden movements in stock prices, whether of individual stock or equity levels as a whole, are not really something new or anomalous. . . . Earnings and dividend flows, good or bad, tend to be *persistent* [emphasis added], like climate, and today's prices have to allow for that positive serial correlation. . . . If you like to think in terms of valuation formulas, they're highly nonlinear."

The laureates and the billionaire are not alone. In his 1994 *Complex Economic Dynamics,* Richard Day, of the University of Southern California, opined: "The general message is that complex economic dynamics must be considered as a possibility in *any model that retains essential nonlinearities.* . . . It is not a peculiar artifact but a generic phenomenon in economic processes."

Benoît Mandelbrot, of IBM and Yale, mathematician and father of the fractal, wrote in his 1997 *Fractals and Scaling in Finance*, "The study of financial fluctuations moved on since 1964, and became increasingly refined mathematically while continuing to rely on Brownian motion and its close kin. Therefore, Cootner's list of endangered statistical techniques would now include the Markowitz mean-variance portfolios, the Black-Scholes theory and Itô calculus and the like."

John Holland of the University of Michigan, father of the genetic algorithm, wrote in *Hidden Order*: "An ecosystem is a pattern in time. It is also a complex adaptive system. Complex adaptive systems abound in nonlinearities. Nonlinearities mean that our most useful tools for generalizing observations into theory—trend analysis, determinations of equilibria, sample means and so on—are blunted. . . . It is little known outside the world of mathematics that most of our mathematical tools, from simple arithmetic through differential calculus to algebraic topology, rely on the assumption of linearity."

In his *Increasing Returns*, W. Brian Arthur of Stanford University and the

Santa Fe Institute said: "Increasing returns generate not equilibrium but instability. . . . Increasing returns reign in the newer part [of the economy]— the knowledge industry. . . . The theory of using increasing returns does not destroy the standard theory, it complements it. [Hicks] felt repugnant not just because of the unsavory properties but also because in his day no mathematical apparatus existed to analyze increasing returns in markets. That situation has now changed."

In his 1996 text *The Self-Organizing Economy*, Paul Krugman of MIT remarked: "The world is full of self-organizing systems, systems that form structures not merely in response to inputs from outside but also, indeed primarily, in response to their own internal logic. Global weather is a self-organizing system; so, surely, is the global economy. . . . I have suggested that there are two principles of self-organization that seem to me to be particularly useful in explaining economic behavior. The first principle is that of *order from instability*; when a system is so constituted that a flat or disordered structure is unstable, order spontaneously emerges. The classic physical example is convection. . . . The second principle is *order from random growth*. Objects of many kinds, from earthquakes to asteroids, obey a power law size distribution."

Paul Ormerod, former head of economic assessment for the *Economist*, wrote in his 1994 book, *The Death of Economics*, "We need to abandon the economist's concept of equilibrium. A more helpful way of thinking about the economy is to imagine a living organism. The economy has the ability, when prodded or stimulated, not simply to wobble around a fixed position, but to jump to a different position altogether. In other words, the economy may not move simply up and down a curve held in a fixed position, such as the Phillips curve, but it may shift rapidly from one curve to another."

WHY HAVE WE BEEN MISLED?

By now it should dawn on the reader that some of the best minds, both academician and practitioner, are heralding a fundamental change in economic thinking. Repeat: This is no drill, this is the real thing. And it is a broad vista. To fully appreciate the terms variously used, such as evolution, increasing returns, and so on, we will have to update the scientific backdrop against which we see the world. To attempt an understanding of the above quotes without proper preparation is like pumping 200 watts of cutting-edge information though the 40-watt bulb in your brain—with predictable results.

The practical implications are far-reaching and immediately raise three important and practical questions: How can we quickly improve our understanding? What happened? Why have we been misled?

Dealing with the questions in reverse order, we find that the answers to two of those questions have been well addressed by Philip Mirowski, the Carl Koch Professor of Economics at Notre Dame in his 1996 paper, "Mandelbrot's Economics after a Quarter Century." "If Mandelbrot is right, and all the econometric models need to be smashed, then how is it possible that so many practitioners have been so grossly misled for so very long? Perhaps his most disquieting thesis is that their own flawed practices served to deceive them:

> One very common approach is to note that large price changes are usually traceable to well-determined "causes" that should be eliminated before one attempts a stochastic model of the remainder. Such preliminary censorship obviously brings any distribution closer to Gaussian. . . . The distinction between the causal and random areas is sharp in the Gaussian case and very diffuse in the stable Paretian case.

The very practice of fitting linear models, particularly those involving trended variables, acted to filter out low-frequency variance and outliers, thus effectively "prewhitening" the data. "Normal" distributions weren't normal at all: They were just artifacts of the shotgun wedding of deterministic theory with "random shocks." In other words, the reason you haven't seen nonlinear phenomena is because they get filtered out so that the filtered data fits with current linear theory. Based on a circumscribed understanding of reality, an attempt was (and is still being) made to make the facts fit the theory rather than the other way around—hardly the scientific ideal of the 21st century. In light of a superior—nonlinear—understanding of reality, the perpetuation of extant linear paradigms is one of the great ruses of modern times.

WHAT HAPPENED?

The short story is that nonlinear techniques, like the Hurst exponent, which we will explore in Chapter 4, have been either not understood, ignored, or technologically infeasible. Admitting the serial dependence, the Hurst exponent demonstrates changes many assumptions upon which extant theory of financial economics is based. The real question at this juncture, it seems, is: Do we stick with an equilibrium theory that we know, but that is wrong, or do we accept a more realistic measurement of the world and the questions that it raises?

Writing as recently as 1990 in his comprehensive *Continuous-Time Finance*, Robert Merton, who shared the 1997 Nobel Prize in economics for

his work in extending finance from a static to a dynamic or continuous state,
held for the established view:

> It was standard practice in early studies to assume that the logarithm of the
> ratio of successive prices had a Gaussian distribution with time homoge-
> nous independent increments and stationary parameters. However, the sam-
> ple characteristics of the time series were frequently inconsistent with these
> assumed population properties. One of the more important inconsistencies
> was that the empirical distributions of price changes were often too
> "peaked" to be consistent with the Gaussian distribution, i.e., the frequency
> of extreme observations was too high to be consistent with samples from a
> normal distribution.
>
> Attempts to resolve these discrepancies proceeded along two separate
> paths. The first, pioneered by Mandelbrot and Fama, maintains the indepen-
> dent increments and stationary assumptions but replaces the Gaussian as-
> sumption with a more general stable (Pareto-Levy) distribution assumption.
> Although non-Gaussian members of the stable family frequently fit the tails
> of the empirical distributions better than the Gaussian, there is little empirical
> evidence to support the adoption of the stable Paretian hypothesis over that of
> any leptokurtokic distribution. Moreover, as discussed by Cootner (1964, pp
> 333–7), the infinite variance property of the non-Gaussian stable distribution
> implies that most of our statistical tools which are based on finite-moment as-
> sumptions (e.g., least squares) are useless. It also implies that even the first-
> moment or expected value of the arithmetic price change does not exist.

Parrying, in his 1997 book *Fractals and Scaling in Finance*, Mandelbrot
successfully refutes the claim of "little empirical evidence." Further, his argument is buttressed by a growing body of evidence as indicated by the
quotes at the beginning of this chapter. What is important to realize is that in
the early 1960s Mandelbrot's work was rejected, perhaps correctly (though
painfully for Mandelbrot) in the sense that it was an outlier of the prevailing
linear view. I say correctly because one observation is typically not strong
enough to overturn a prevailing worldview.

Think of three separate levels of explaining reality, such as observation,
proof or theory, and worldview. They are, of course, intertwined but proceed
generally from the specific, in the sense of an observation, into a further
generalized body of systemized knowledge called theory, which in turn is
built on to become a worldview. This worldview is influenced by shared assumptions that are so basic as to be unstated and thus assumed as a given.

What has subsequently happened in the past 30 years is that technology
has matured and facilitated the empirical substantiation, if not proof in the
computational sense, that the world and thus financial economics is really
nonlinear. Building from the observation of the Hurst exponent, genetic algorithms, fuzzy logic, complexity theory, and so on have all speeded the

demise of our Newtonian or deterministic worldview. The reason for the claim of a paradigm shift is that observation, theory, and worldview are aligning themselves toward a nonlinear view. Mandelbrot's contribution, though very powerful, is not the sole reason for the coalescing of these various factors into a favorable aspect, yet his view is largely supported and embraced by them as the best available explanation. In this sense, he is correct and is fortunate to have lived long enough to see his view prevail. There is and will continue to be a concerted effort to extend linear-based tools to counter such a large challenge. However, in terms of order of magnitude, the prevailing forces are so large that the usefulness of linear tools and the assumption of linearity in financial economics and much of natural phenomena in general, other than for pedagogical purposes can be relegated along with Newtonian determinism to history.

The alignment of these three forces is nontrivial and is the reason that so much background must be built or restated for the practitioner. No doubt the average practitioner will see only some nonlinear results on a screen and be satisfied without contemplating their larger implications. This may always be so. With the passage of time, however, as one becomes more familiar with nonlinear techniques, one may well find oneself in an intellectual quandary of applying the odd nonlinear technique ad hoc into a linear worldview. At some point there will be the discovery of a gross mismatch of assumptions in the linear and the nonlinear approaches. The resulting confusion and frustration will hinder the progress of the adoption of nonlinearity more than the simplistic idea most practitioners currently have of applying nonlinear techniques ad hoc.

PARADIGMS

Paradigm shifts are exciting and stressful because there is no clear-cut answer to the previous question of "What happened?" Were the practitioner to question the integrity of the assumptions behind the linear/equilibrium theory and reduce the language that surrounds it to simple terms the theory might not be held in such awe or reverence. Equilibrium theory is full of "fixes" or kludges.

Were we able to hear equilibrium theory, it might remind us of the song country-and-western recording artist Johnny Cash sang in the late 1960s called "One Piece at a Time." The song recounts an assembly-line worker purloining Cadillac parts over a 10-year period. The humorous result is a jalopy that is a patchwork quilt of parts from various years! Lest one think this example not scientific, from high school physics recall Ptolemy's theory of planetary orbits. In the second century A.D. Ptolemy proposed that the orbits were elliptical rather than circular. When it was determined that the orbits were not perfectly circular, an extra variable was added, and then another. The problem here, of course, is that given enough terms we can describe anything, but we still can't explain it or fit it into a coherent body of thought like a theory.

From Miehio Kaku's *Hyperspace* we again follow David Bohm's statement, "In my opinion, progress in science is usually made by dropping assumptions!" But this is an ideal—a concept rarely encountered (and then only fleetingly) in the compromising and highly imperfect world of commerce, if it is expressed in other than economic terms. In choosing the Hurst exponent, the assumption of randomness is now dropped and we pursue the logical ramifications of that choice, wherever that may be.

Is the question "What happened?" philosophical? Yes, in that we have to admit there is a divergence between reality and our understanding of it. Is it practicable? Yes. The mathematical theory exists to rigorously express the concept. The computational horsepower exists and is cheap enough to effectuate the calculation. Is it easy to understand? Here I choose to be rhetorical and respond by asking: Is there anyone in the investment business whose comprehension of mathematics is so basic that he or she does not grasp the fact that in the gambling business the odds of the house versus the players are greater than 50–50? Wherein does the advantage lie?

Equilibrium-based financial economics cannot explain most of what nonlinear pricing has to offer. For the practitioner this may be confusing. And there is a natural curiosity to see how nonlinear pricing differs from what was (and still is) part of their schools' economics curriculum. In the simplest of terms, the Hurst exponent changes the shape of the distribution used to model returns. In Figure 3.1, the stable Paretian distribution replaces the Gaussian. The parameter used to describe the shape of the distribution is called α. When $\alpha = 2$, the distribution is Gaussian. When $1 < \alpha < 2$ the distribution is stable Paretian. It is that simple. Financial-economic time series are between 1 and 2 almost always. Rarely, if ever, are they at $\alpha = 2$ as theory would assume. The Gaussian distribution is only a very specialized case of reality, just as Euclidian geometry is. Brownian motion, Gaussian distributions, and Euclidean geometry are all highly idealized cases of reality and correspond to more realistic fractional Brownian motion, stable Paretian or fractal distributions, and fractal geometry, respectively. The former set uses whole integer dimensions and the latter set uses noninteger or fractal dimensions. The former set is the imposition of an ideal system on a messy world and the latter is the messy reality of a messy world. We will cover mathematics more in depth in Chapter 4.

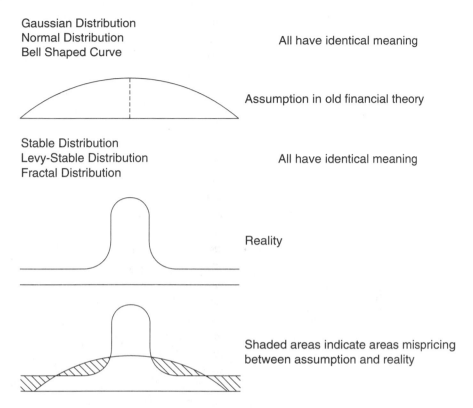

Gaussian Distribution
Normal Distribution
Bell Shaped Curve

All have identical meaning

Assumption in old financial theory

Stable Distribution
Levy-Stable Distribution
Fractal Distribution

All have identical meaning

Reality

Shaded areas indicate areas mispricing
between assumption and reality

Figure 3.1 Gaussian and Stable Distributions

WHAT GETS CHANGED?

Of course, when we admit the reality of the Hurst exponent and noninteger dimensions, we admit that *virtually every statistic produced and consumed in financial economics is obsolete*—since every moment of the distribution above the first moment of mean is infinite. Think about that. With millions of dollars of sunk costs in the form of legacy software, not to mention the additional costs of training, do you really think your financial institution or software provider is in any hurry to make you aware of this fact? In the information age the argument for nonlinearity is backed by the ultimate arbiters of reality in financial economics—mathematics and science—reduced to a simple screen on Bloomberg. The only argument to the contrary is ignorance or the inertia of habit. With your money at stake, on which side of the trade do you want to be?

Correlation or R^2 cannot be used, because it gives too much weight to the outliers. Correlation in the time domain like auto regressive integrated moving average and spectral analysis also lose their statistical rationale. Volatility, the measure of risk in finance, which is the same thing as variance, cannot be used because the second moment or variance is infinite. That is, because the tails of the distribution do not touch the horizontal axis, the moment does not exist. In risk management, diversification becomes less effective the further away the parameter α moves from 2.

The best account of why the divergence exists between the standard theory and nonlinear pricing, a sort of postmodern reality, is given by an insider, Mirowski, who makes three points:

1. Neoclassical economics attempted to partake of the ideal of deterministic explanation, but it was nowhere as successful at this endeavor as its exemplar, physics. This weakness can be directly traced to a persistent tergiversation over what, precisely, was conserved in the economic system. Without an analogous conservation principle, neoclassical economics was blocked from following physics into serious formal dynamics, including the formal structure of Hamiltonians, and instead retreated into the spurious pseudo-dynamics of *ceteris paribus* conditions. This inability to emulate the core of the ideal of deterministic explanation tarnished the entire program of imitating physics.

2. The absence of a legitimate dynamics also compromised the ideal of a scientific empiricism. What could it mean to attempt to fit neoclassical relations to time-series evidence when the fundamental determinants of neoclassical equilibrium displayed no necessary stability from one moment to the next? Indeed, most prominent first- and second-generation neoclassicals were hostile to attempts to import such techniques such as least-squares [R^2] estimation into economics; and the earliest efforts in this area were pioneered by individuals skeptical of neoclassical theory. Such disputes over the meaning of scientific activity also compromised the claims of the neoclassical theory to have attained "scientific" status.

3. There was the problem that physics continued to evolve rapidly after the mid-19th-century, whereas the neoclassical research program tended to remain mired in its original 19th century orientation. In particular, from James Clerk Maxwell onwards, physics increasingly began to incorporate stochastic ideas into physical explanations, whereas neoclassical economics did not. This progressive abandonment of the ideal of deterministic explanation has been summarized felicitously by [chemistry Nobel laureate] Ilya Prigogine:

In the nineteenth century, there was a profusion of controversy between "energeticists" and "atomists," the former claiming the second law [of thermodynamics] destroys the mechanical conception of the universe, the latter that the second law should be reconciled with dynamics at the price of some "additional assumptions" such as probabilistic arguments. What this means exactly can be seen more clearly. The "price" is not small because it involves a far-reaching modification of the structure of dynamics.

NONLINEARITY IN 20TH-CENTURY FINANCIAL ECONOMICS

The irreconcilability of nonlinearity and classical economics certainly has a history, and it is largely the story of the irreconcilability of heterodoxy and orthodoxy, or seeing the world as it is and not how we wish it to be.

Early 1900s

Vilfredo Pareto was an Italian economist who recognized that much economic information, such as household incomes, was not well described by the Gaussian curve, which could be used to describe the distribution of, for example, clothing sizes or life spans. The curve that did describe incomes had "fat or heavy" tails. The reason, as Peters relates in *Fractal Market Analysis,* is that "It is unlikely that anyone will live five times longer than average, but it is not unusual for someone to be five times wealthier than average."

It was Pareto's work that led French mathematician Paul Lévy in 1937 to generalize the density functions of distributions using the generalized version of the Central Limit Theorem. The insight was that there was not a unique solution but many. Thus, the Stable Family of Distributions, as it is known, contains three well-known distributions: the Gaussian, normal, or bell-shaped curve when $\alpha = 2$; the stable, Lévy stable, or stable Paretian or what Peters calls the fractal distribution when $1 < \alpha < 2$; and the Cauchy when $\alpha = 1$.

In 1900 Louis Bachelier wrote his PhD thesis *The Theory of Speculation* at the Sorbonne, reasoning that for every given price a financial time series had a 50–50 chance of rising or falling from that price. This idea was predicated on the observation of a Scottish botanist, Thomas Brown, from whom the term Brownian motion is derived. Brown observed a grain of pollen on a drop of water that was repeatedly "kicked." Mathematical formalism equates a Brownian motion with a random motion or noise. What was actually "kicking" the pollen was the electrons in the atoms in the water molecule. Einstein used this example in 1905 to prove the existence of the atom.

1930s

EO Wilson, a highly respected zoologist at Harvard, in his recent book *Consilience: The Unity of Knowledge*, sees below the façade of disciplinary names to their underlying and often unifying essence. Of primary interest are the lessons from biology and the inherent complexity and diversity it generates. Commenting on financial-economics in words that I cannot improve upon Wilson says:

> . . . The macroanalysis of the Classical Era was then combined with the analytic microanalysis of the Marginalist Era, most influentially by Alfred Marshall in his 1890 *Principles of Economics*. The result, in the phrase coined by Thorstein Veblen in 1900, was neoclassical economics.

In the age of complexity theory, it is prophetic to note Marshall's 1884 comment, found in *Principles of Economics* on page xiv which is also the epigraph of Chapter 8.

> The Mecca of the economist lies in economic biology. . . . But biological conceptions are more complex than those of mechanics; a volume on Foundations must therefore give a relatively large place to mechanical analogies, and frequent use is made of the term equilibrium which suggests something of a static analogy.

To continue with Wilson

> Neoclassical economics is what we have today, but there was one more overlapping period, the Era of Model Building, that brought it to fruition. Beginning in the 1930's, theorists added *linear* [emphasis added] programming, game theory, and other powerful mathematical and statistical techniques in their efforts to simulate the economic world in ever finer detail. Invigorated by the sense of their own exactitude they continued to return to the themes of *equilibria* [emphasis added] and perturbation of equilibria. They specified, as faithfully as they could, supply and demand, impulses of firms and consumers, competition, market fluctuations and failures, and the optimal uses of labor and resources.
>
> The cutting edge of economic theory today remains the equilibrium models of neoclassical theory. The emphasis is always on rigor. Analysts heartily agree with Paul Samuelson, one of the most influential economists of the twentieth century that "economics focuses on concepts that actually can be measured."
>
> Therein lies the strengths and weaknesses of present-day economic the-

ory. Because its strengths have already been abundantly celebrated by legions of textbook writers and journalists, let me dwell on the weaknesses. They can be summarized in two labels: Newtonian and hermetic. Newtonian, because economic theorists aspire to find simple, general laws that cover all possible economic arrangements. Universally it is a logical and worthy goal, except that the innate traits of human behavior ensure that only a minute set of such arrangements is probable or even possible. Just as the fundamental laws of physics cannot be used alone to build an airplane, the general construction of equilibrium theory cannot be used alone to visualize an optimal or stable economic order. The models also fall short because they are hermetic—that is, sealed off from the complexities of human behavior and the constraints imposed by the environment. As a result, economic theorists, despite the undoubted genius of may, have enjoyed few successes in predicting the economic future, and have suffered many embarrassing failures.

Among the successes are partial stabilizations of a few national economies. In the United States the Federal Reserve Board now has enough knowledge and legal power to regulate the flow of money and prevent—we trust!—the economy from spinning into catastrophic inflations and depressions. On another front, the driving force of technological innovation on growth is reasonably well understood, at least roughly in retrospect. On yet another, capital-asset pricing models have a major influence on Wall Street.

However as far back as 1939 on surveying the possibility of non-equilibrium in economics John Hicks commented that "The threatened wreckage is the greater part of economic theory." True there have been some successes with the equilibrium approach, but the greater achievements seem to be in the future after we have let go of equilibrium and the Newtonian paradigm to which we so insistently cling.

1940s

Nonlinear business cycle theory as it was generally known, existed as far back as the 1940s. It was propounded by John Hicks and Richard Goodwin in the United Kingdom, and a similar contribution was made by James Tobin in the United States. The theory suffered two setbacks. First, it was Keynesian-based and fell from favor when Keynesian explanations gave way to monetarist ones, which attempted to deal with the when and why of cycles rather than the "how" of cycles. Second, no formal mathematical framework existed in which to express it. This was to change.

1960s

Mandelbrot, an outsider to the world of economics, began publishing papers on the subject dealing with his interest in Pareto. Some papers in 1963 showed that financial time series did not follow Brownian motion or random walks but had large discontinuities. For example, a discontinuity occurs when prices close at 54 and subsequently open at 48. In theory, prices should hit every possible price between 54 and 48. Clearly it does not always happen. Eugene Fama published an oft-cited article in the 1964 *Journal of Business* entitled "The Stable Distribution of Stock Prices." Paul Samuelson and Thomas Sargent of rational expectations fame also did some related work.

This work gained some notoriety from Paul Cootner, who said: "There can be little doubt that Mandelbrot's hypotheses are the most revolutionary development in the theory of the speculative prices since Bachelier's initial work." Recall that it was Bachelier who initially reasoned that from any given price an asset has a 50–50 probability of rising or falling. Although there is no proof that Bachelier knew of Brownian motion, which is essentially the same concept, he does predate Einstein by five years in using the concept. This also represents one of the few times that economics beat physics to the punch.

A difference in approach between Mandelbrot and Samuelson also developed, and as history shows, in the short run Mandelbrot clearly lost. The difference centered around a perspective, with Mandelbrot extending the concept of Lévy stable distributed "fundamentals" and Samuelson maintaining that random price changes "proved" the market was efficient. With hindsight, it is plausible to reason, as Newton seems to have done centuries earlier, that the simple example, even though it was wrong, was preferable for practical reasons, such as the retarded state of development in collateral fields (e.g., mathematics and computational ability).

1970s

Mandelbrot had anticipated this and in his work around the turn of the decade, a shift can be seen to $1/f$ noises, fractional Brownian motion, and long-term dependence. Meanwhile, econometricians were busy with high-frequency variances like serial correlation and Markov dependence. The thought was that local linear effects could approximate local phenomena. The research did not catch on for a while with economists and caused some consternation when, as Steven LeRoy said in 1989, "it was realized around

1975 that the martingale model implied that asset prices should be less volatile that they apparently were."

In 1970, Peter Clark published his Harvard PhD thesis, which argued that fat or heavy tails in distributions of economic variates could be better modeled by subordinate stochastic processes than by stable Lévy distributions. Clark imagined that the support for the distributions of time series was not properly specified, in the sense that economic time did not flow smoothly during the trading week. In this part of the assessment he was and is quite correct, as multifractals will show in Chapter 4. Unfortunately, multifractals and the available computing power were either too new or unavailable to further explore this line of reasoning. The practice of approximating seemingly stable Lévy distributions by time-varying variances of standard Gaussian processes would become the hallmark of economics during the next decade.

Time does not flow smoothly during the trading week with any mathematical rigor. It seems intuitively plausible for three reasons: First, we assume risk unfolds with time, and we also apply an even measurement of time to the trading day. However, experience demonstrates that risk does not accrue incrementally like interest payments on a bond or erode in even increments, either. Although this concept would not be put on more secure mathematical footing for many more years, Benoit Mandelbrot, David Hsieh, Ulrich Müller, et alia did so. It follows that because volatility clusters, risk is experienced in "lumps and clumps." Krugman cites similar dynamics from the 1955 paper of Herbert Simon, the 1978 Nobel laureate in economics. With stunning accuracy, Simon describes the city size distributions with a power law. Krugman notes of Simon that "as each new 'lump' of population arrives, it either starts a new city (with probability π) or attaches itself to an existing 'clump'; the probability that each clump attracts the lump is proportional to that clump's population. Thus we have a process of random growth of clumps, with the expected growth independent of clump size." The relationship to risk management is clear: Perhaps the growth and decline of risk follows a power law function. Second, the practical effect of an unevenly flowing time can be dealt with in a nonlinear framework. Third, and however tenuous in its application to financial economics, relativity via physics holds that the fabric of space-time is curved, and gives us a rigorous reason to speculate that time can occur at different rates depending upon the observer. As appealing as the concept may be to deal with time itself as a nonlinear unit, the implications are nontrivial.

This same year saw Fama's important economic survey of the efficient markets hypothesis, where he began to break with Mandelbrot. Sargent also dropped all references to Lévy stable distributions. Others followed suit—R. Blattberg *et al.* in 1974, Christopher Sims in 1971. Clive Granger and D. Orr in 1972 went public with their disdain for Lévy stable distributions.

Also in 1972, the famous Black-Scholes option pricing model was published. It rapidly rose to prominence because almost concurrently the Chicago Board Options Exchange began trading listed options and option traders needed a methodology to value options, and here it was.

One of the major reasons Lévy stable distributions never took hold is that practitioners remained satisfied with Gaussian assumptions. At the time, the introduction of probability and computers was a material change for a clubby industry where even today technology is still not well understood nor highly esteemed. It is hoped that such pragmatic tools as the KAOS screen will help foment a change in that complacent view.

1980s

Although the 1980s were relatively quiet regarding direct financial applications, the mathematics of stable Lévy distributions continued to make progress. Mirowski's 1996 paper states that in 1986 V. Zolotarev, a major contributor, opined, "It can be said without exaggeration that the problem of constructing statistical estimators of stable laws entered into mathematical statistics due to the work of Mandelbrot." V. Akgiray and C. Lemoureaux in 1989 and Keith Knight in 1993 also contributed.

Options research also revealed something called the "volatility smile", a failing of the assumptions of the Black-Scholes option pricing model to accurately model risk of the underlying instrument on which it was used. In theory, the volatility should be constant for all strikes. Since Gaussian distribution, upon which the Black-Scholes option pricing model is based, underrepresents the possibility of large moves, traders have to compensate by heuristically "dialing-up" the volatility of far-in- and far-out-of-the-money strikes. Plotted, the kludges required to compensate for the Gaussian description of a non-Gaussian resembled a smile.

Although seemingly unrelated to finance, in 1987 James Gleick published *Chaos*, a very successful popular book on the new science of chaos with two discernible effects. First, it built publishers' confidence that a viable market existed among curious laymen for science if it was written in plain English. Second, it established a toehold in the public awareness for the subject of chaos specifically and the notion of nonlinearity generally.

Finally, Robert Shiller, the Stanley B. Resor Professor at Yale University, published *Market Volatility* in 1989. Shiller was the lone voice in academia indicating that the empirical evidence did not jibe with the Capital Asset

Pricing Model and that behavioral factors had a role to play. The reaction to his work was silence, and the silence was deafening.

1990s

The 1990s have seen a resurgence in Lévy stable distributions, from one mathematician in particular, Murad Taqqu of Boston University, who had published papers with Mandelbrot. Taqqu helped to rectify the situation by publishing *Stable Non-Gaussian Random Processes* with Gennady Samorodnitsky in 1994 and editing with Robert Adler and Richard Feldman *A Practical Guide to Heavy Tails* in 1998. Now some texts were available, and some of the applications cited in the latter work were from finance.

Tired of the typical Wall Street retort, "If nonlinearity is so great, why haven't *we* heard of it?," I rang Taqqu, a perfect stranger, and asked, "How come no one has done this sort of work before?" To his great credit the good professor listened to my plight and suggested that up until this point no one had taken a serious interest in this obscure body of math. Not having "closed-form" analytical density functions did not help—that is, formulas that can be stated a priori rather than only as a computational solution.

Practitioners also emerged to challenge orthodoxy, most notably Ed Peters, chief investment officer at PanAgora in Boston, a pension fund manager, who published the seminal *Chaos and Order in the Capital Markets* in 1992, *Fractal Market Hypothesis* in 1994, and the second edition of the first book in 1996. The fact that a *practitioner* published new work in itself represents a seismic shift. The contemporary movement probably began when Citibank pioneered the use of SWAPS several years before. Heretofore, Wall Street had taken its cue from academia because the mathematics, called partial differential equations or PDEs, used in Black-Scholes, as well as basic statistics from Markowitz's mean-variance portfolio and so forth represented a significant departure from the traditional knowledge base of most practitioners whose mathematical skills are still largely restricted to trivial financial statement analysis. Moreover, as the practical implementation of that advanced math required using and programming computers, the division was generational as well.

Physicists, mathematicians, and anyone else in a discipline where advanced math and computer skills were resident got hired and for many years enjoyed a necessary but uneasy alliance with traditionalists. Their grafting onto Wall Street culture is still not complete; in time they formed their own subculture, generally known as the "quants," for quantitative analysts. Many of these quants keep busy making new products by extending

the basic option concept by applying it to new indexes or instruments such as options on baskets or groups of stocks, interest rates, and so on, or mutating it to form caps, collars, spreads, knock-ins, knock-outs, and the like. Of course, what really keeps them beavering away is explaining to clients how to use these tools to achieve the clients' objectives. Wall Street has come up with many new products, but they are all based on the same circa 1972 assumptions. What other industry in the world can get away with using technology over 25 years old? Let that thought sink in for a moment. Who among you willingly flies a 25-year-old airplane, ingests 25-year-old medicine, watches a 25-year-old TV, or drives a 25-year-old car? To the outside observer and to many on Wall Street, it is the quants that seem the natural heirs to nonlinearity in that both approaches apply mathematics in computers. In a very limited sense this may be true, but the linear math of the quants and the newer nonlinear math work in very different ways; the assumptions and techniques are different.

It is safe to say that the approach of most mathematicians when they encounter nonlinearities is to simplify nonlinear equations to linear equations. Thus, their first move is to take away exactly what we are looking for! They do so because they seek to solve the problem analytically rather than computationally. They are trained this way. As we have said, the analytical approach is on its way to joining the dodo bird in the history books. Linear mathematicians have dealt with the notion of dynamics in the sense of a fairly constant rate of change. This concept is how one predicts the trajectory of a baseball, which enables you to catch it without an advanced degree in physics. The concept of an uneven rate of change is more indicative of what we see in real life in the markets and what the nonlinear world seeks to model. Or, to extend the baseball example, it is the speed-curve-knuckleball all at once but not always in that order for each pitch.

Mathematicians with a nonlinear background find civilian employment in such things as reservoir engineering for oil companies or in the defense/research sector modeling nuclear explosions. Now Wall Street will have to raid these places as well as learn to differentiate among types of mathematicians as they do among types of traders. Soon Wall Street will realize that linear and nonlinear mathematicians are no more fungible than commodity traders on the floor and strip traders upstairs are. They can possibly be interchanged in time, but common sense suggests that a rapid change would court disaster.

The curriculum of universities for graduate and undergraduate finance was slow to reflect the heavily mathematical reality of financial economics. It was not until 1995, almost 25 years after the introduction of Black-Scholes, that my business school alma mater, New York University, offered a degree in mathematical finance. I am proud in that I believe it was one of the first universities to do so. I was taking PhD courses in mathematics at the Courant Institute there at the time. Sadly though, I remember the internecine problems of departmental conflicts, because it was not business school professors who were teaching mathematical finance but mathematicians. Maybe it was an omen that the practical application of finance had not only outgrown, but had grown *faster*, than the skill set thought necessary to teach it.

Other changes were the decline of the Cowes style econometrics. Philip Howery demonstrated that the Wharton model could not account for the business cycle and Ronald Cooper's ARIMA style models could not outpredict any of the large-scale models. It was these models, which were so intimately connected with Keynesian economics, that were so badly affected by the oil crisis of 1973. The result of this failure was the "rational expectations" movement, which seemed to rededicate itself to ARIMA models, deterministic neoclassical economics with a representative agent, a Samuelson interpretation of martingales as characteristic of completely efficient markets.

The rejection of everything that Mandelbrot stood for was nearly complete: stable distributions, long-term dependence, the impossibility of complete arbitrage, the statistical indistinguishability of wildly divergent time series, the phenomenological (thermodynamic) approach to modeling, and the second stage of scientific indeterminism.

What makes the 1990s qualitatively different from the previous decades is the following:

1. Computing power has reached a critical mass and continues to fall in price.

2. A general awareness exists in university research that nonlinearity is a real but new field.

3. The interdisciplinary approach to problems has begun to emerge, as evidenced by organizations such as the Prigogine Center at the University of Texas and the Santa Fe Institute.

4. There is a general awareness of the availability of nonlinear techniques such as genetic algorithms and fuzzy logic to deal with new issues.

5. A general awareness exists among practitioners that linear assumptions in extant models are subject to correction.

6. Lastly, the KAOS screen on Bloomberg, which came into existence in January 1997 and refuted the assumption of Brownian motion in a financial time series, has reached the trader's desk. Nonlinearity is no longer the province of academia or arcane mathematics.

HOW DO WE QUICKLY IMPROVE OUR UNDERSTANDING?

Alas, the simple answer to how to improve understanding is the concept of disproportionality, with which you are already familiar. To do a thorough job of understanding, though, requires a step back to look at a new worldview. My interpretation of this new understanding comes primarily from Prigogine, Smolin, and Deutsch. They are quite reputable, but their views individually or collectively are not yet gospel in the scientific community. No matter, what they posit is well considered and important for our overall understanding. Three better guides one could not find. We draw almost exclusively from Prigogine's *The End of Certainty*, Smolin's *The Life of the Cosmos*, and Deutsch's *The Fabric of Reality*, all published in 1997.

To brutally summarize, Prigogine asserts that probability is a fundamental rather than a derivative aspect of nature. Deutsch uses four basic descriptors—quantum reality, knowledge, life/evolution, and computation. Smolin asserts that we cannot have a static universe and, in fact, since the universe evolves so must the laws of physics. There is some overlap, and if this text was a treatise on physics we would also explore some contradictory aspects. Briefly, Deutsch fervently maintains Hugh Everett's many worlds or "multiverse" interpretation of quantum reality. The multiverse view is logically consistent and does not violate any mathematical bounds. But, like advanced aspects of fractals, the multiverse concept would be stimulating if not mind-bending to our readership and well beyond the scope of this introductory work.

We do not need ultimately to solve the great underpinnings of the universe to sketch nonlinear pricing, but we do need to introduce these additional concepts to enrich a comparatively sterile Newtonian view. One may quickly understand that if additional aspects are needed to understand reality, then the presentation of those aspects in financial economics is not a curiosity. Rather, those same aspects are inherent in the phenomenon of financial economics itself.

In the big picture we also see occurring a melding of concepts from certain disciplines, particularly mathematics, biology, physics, computer science, and thus financial economics. As physics incorporates the dynamics of evolution, it becomes more applicable to the real world. As mathematics is applied to evolution, biology becomes more rigorous. New terms are posited, such as "biomathematics" by Ian Stewart in *Life's Other Secret: The New Mathematics of the Living World*. As financial economics academics begin to acknowledge—like John Campbell, Andrew Lo, and Craig MacKinlay do in *The Econometrics of Financial Markets*—that financial economics exhibits nonlinear behavior, then terminology and concepts from the hard sciences begin to enter financial economics. And of course, it is all tied together with computer programming.

Interdisciplinary studies such as biochemistry are not new, although at some point in time they were. What differs in the instant case is that nonlinear pricing is not a simple conceptual extension in terms of scale from biology to organic chemistry but more of a wholesale change. As a result, I believe that one of the great stumbling blocks in understanding nonlinear pricing is the fact that it is an amalgam that draws heavily from concepts which are not traditional to the background of many practitioners. Nonlinear pricing is a mélange drawn from various fields, which themselves are also undergoing rapid change. The reward for the practitioner is that as this mélange matures simple graphical representations will be found which are intuitively more appealing in the same way that any automated aspect of life is supposed to be. One will see the simple and intuitive results without knowing the relevant technologies—like the sensors, for example, that keep water levels and temperatures within certain parameters.

ERROR TYPES

Recall the simple crooked line in the middle of the graph indicating the Hurst exponent on the KAOS screen. According to linear theory, that line should be straight. It should be perfectly horizontal at the 0.5 level of a Brownian motion. Were it so, no reason would exist for this book. When we apply mathematics, and thus modeling to financial economics we have three possibilities of error: First is a simple mistake in the equations themselves. This is a Type I error and is trivial to rectify. Second are the explicit assumptions that lie behind the model. This is a Type II error. Type II errors are somewhat more difficult to rectify but not extraordinarily so. Third, and most difficult to spot, are the assumptions implicit in the worldview which suggested the model in the first place. This is a Type III error. The assumption of randomness and linearity and equilibrium in general is a Type III error.

In his 1989 paper, "How We Came Up with the Option Formula," the late Fischer Black, coauthor of the Black-Scholes option pricing model, wrote, "The notion of equilibrium in the market for risky assets had great beauty for me. . . . To put it another way, I used the capital asset pricing model to write down how the discount rate for a warrant varies with time and price." Thus, it is easy to see how the linear notion of equilibrium was perpetuated in the formation of the Black-Scholes option pricing model. This Type III error requires a substantive modification of financial economics based on new assumptions. To give an idea of how difficult a Type III change is, note Black's comments from *Institutional Investor* in January 1995 (page 12), where in the face of mounting evidence to the contrary Black defends his famous pricing model.

> The Black-Scholes option pricing model is now more than 20 years old, and critics complain that it's too simplistic and fails to consider factors that change over time. To them, that quant's quant Fischer Black, co-author of the formula, says: Phooey. The former academic and current Goldman Sachs partner told the International Association of Financial Engineers last month that "I'm completely unapologetic about using models that use constant parameters that I don't have to change the next day." The big problem with adding more factors, Black argued, is that "there are more mistakes. So if you have a choice, I favor sticking with the one-factor model." Besides that's the version a whole generation of Wall Streeters were taught in Business school.

Here caution must be exercised, because the Black-Scholes model was one of the most, if not the most, successful mathematical representations of reality in the history of the social sciences. Caution must also be exercised because there is a human element involved. Had Black lived, he would certainly have shared the 1997 Nobel Prize with Scholes and Merton. This is not possible because the award is not made posthumously. But how indelicate is it to receive one of the great honors of mankind only to have technology obsolete it within your working lifetime? Perhaps it is a sign of how rapidly technology is changing, but I do not relish chronicling the fact.

For those who are still wondering why so much disparate material, like religion, time, and the sciences, must be included in a treatise on financial economics, it is because we must rebuild nonlinearity separate by from the assumptions implicit in your worldview—the same linear worldview that has, since the birth of empirical science, received three and a half centuries of reinforcement in Western civilization. In short, we are trying to prevent Type III errors.

SCIENCE

Since financial economics happens within the universe, financial economics is, by definition, subject to physical laws. This may seem like a radical statement and in a sense it is, because in picking up a book on financial economics one expects to be met with conventions and terminology that apply exclusively to the reader's quite narrow expertise. "Quite narrow," of course, is a relative term. Expertise is probably narrow in the present age—the information age—as the structure of knowledge both broadens and deepens. The theories that organize that knowledge and help us both to explain and to understand it are spilling over traditional lines. It is for this reason that we must see the world from a wider perspective than traditionally we have done. There is a trade-off, however. For expending some effort in learning new concepts we will be able to make a more informed explanation of reality. The price we pay is that when confronted with new facts and explanations, we may be compelled to give up the comfort, often emotional or psychological, of the old ways. In this regard, this story is timeless.

Financial economics places a further burden on the acceptance but not the proof of nonlinearity for two reasons. First, for most current participants, new ways of looking at financial economics are not the difference between success and failure, since most participants are succeeding now or they would not be participants. The difference is between doing well and doing better. This places the burden of proof—in the sense of general approval by the adopter rather than empirical validity of the technology itself—on two groups: those participants who are seeking to make a marked improvement in their performance, and new participants. For example, current participants may be aware that commission or trading revenue is down and institutionally speaking it has become okay to have a new idea, while those who are in the junior phase of their careers have little vested interest in maintaining the status quo so often caused by bureaucratic inertia and are more likely to invest the time and effort to learn new technology and be less penalized for suggesting its use.

The second reason is general approval in the sense of popular market acceptance will not be expected until a dramatic success story has been recorded and has been emulated by a cadre of followers. This statement acknowledges the lemming-like behavior of most market participants. In other words, when 10% of the people know what you are doing, you are cutting-edge. When less than 1% knows, you are crazy.

The reason necessitating the change in perspective is philosophical as much as it is scientific. Much of what is "discovered" has to do with the inherent, unarticulated, and unstated assumptions we carry. In other words, it is our personal philosophy or Type III error. The development of knowledge is no more free from cycles of fashion than are more ephemeral pursuits. Financing techniques and philosophical approaches, like hemlines, have their day and their denouement. What is newly discovered reinforces or challenges the prevailing view. The discovery process itself is cyclic. In the present age, catholic tastes are favored over parochial ones. We are looking outside extant boundaries.

Not all relationships between financial economics and biology, physics, and other seemingly unrelated bodies of knowledge, are well specified or even known at present, but they are growing. The attitude in science of separate fields is now changing. Physics in Newton's day was holistically called natural philosophy. Used in this sense, natural philosophy encompasses all phenomena. We have to update our notion of what natural philosophy entails. I do not mean to abdicate the study of financial economics to the fellows in white lab coats, but the fact of the matter is that the lines, particularly academic lines, demarcating seemingly disparate bodies of knowledge are blurring. That is not to say the cross-fertilization is done easily, quickly, or even willingly. Since the 1980s, with the advent of chaos and, moreover, complexity—which are also subsequent topics in this book—the ideal of determinism or strict causality has been dealt a deathblow.

Disciplines are not completely melded but they are blurring. This is for the good, since there is no reason, save hubris, not to borrow and adapt concepts developed in another field to be used in the instant case. For example, we now have biochemistry and a host of other hyphenated disciplines, but it was not always so. Some poor devil that ended up doing biochemistry certainly did not have a degree in it because the degree had yet to be offered. Physics has absorbed astronomy, which is now astrophysics. Einstein's relativity took time out of the realm of philosophy and put it on a rigorous foundation. Physics has also taken geometry from mathematics, because gravity has determined that the three angles of a triangle do not always sum to 180 degrees! Euclid's parallel lines proof was challenged and found to be not always true. Similarly so for financial economics, which now includes—without totally absorbing—game theory, behavior, and Newtonian physics (because this is where the notions of equilibrium in neoclassical economics and diffusion in the case of the Black-Scholes option pricing model come from). Surprisingly enough, finance now also encompasses aspects of hydrology—the study of water—in the form of the Hurst exponent. Complexity, traditionally part of computer science, occurs in many fields. Where does one draw the line?

The terms "science" and "physics" are used here quite liberally as systematic approaches to determine verifiable bodies of knowledge. I do not think the financial economics practitioner will object to the terms used in this context, for two reasons. First, any practitioner is always in search of verifiable bodies of knowledge. Although investors can never achieve perfect information or omniscience, in principle they can have enough. Second, to paraphrase Einstein, by virtue of the existence of our stomachs we are compelled to live in the real world. Thus, we are all practicing economists. We have looked at financial economics as if we can step outside the universe and view it out of context as a thing apart. Clearly this is not so. It is time to change.

ILLUSTRATE A PARALLEL

I speak infrequently with Lester Seigel at the World Bank, but when I do, the conversation invariably ends with him making some thoughtful recommendation to me, which I follow. I do not know why. Once it was to take graduate probability with the eminent Ragu Varadhan and the challenging Marco Avellenada at New York University, and more recently it was to read Prigogine's new book, *The End of Certainty*. The parallel between my imagination of a nonlinear financial-economics model and what Prigogine articulated shocked me.

THE PARALLEL

In *The End of Certainty* Prigogine makes two points. One, he introduces probability as a fundamental descriptive state of the world. Two, he recognizes that asymmetry in time, which splits past from present, puts a final nail into the coffin of classical or Newtonian physics. We address these points in reverse order.

TIME

Prigogine begins with a thought from Epicurus called the *clinamen*. Epicurus was a student of Democritus, who was mentioned in Chapter 2. Clinamen is the antiquarian expression of the notion of instability. The concepts of the irreversibility of time and nonequilibrium are not new; however, their formal expression in mathematics is. Eddington called the flow of events rooted in instability "time's arrow." Unfortunately, in the deterministic Newtonian paradigm and the complete randomness of quantum physics, reversibility is completely possible. That is, the equations are the same when the signs are changed from $t +$ *to* $t -$.

Clearly this goes against observation, since elements do not undecay any more than humans become sperm and egg. The intuitive link between the low-energy nonequilibrium physics and time is an event. Low energy refers to the macroscopic world where human experience occurs, and nonequilibrium refers to the fact that systems such as financial economics and ecology change. They are not static. Although the arrow of time is not dependent upon the observer, events are our only way to characterize time.

In looking at any phenomenon, a painting for example, appearance will depend upon the distance from which it is viewed. In 19th-century American painting the parallel would be between the photo-realism of an Albert Bierstadt, John Fredrick Peto, or William Michael Harnett versus the impressionism of a Childe Hassam or John Henry Twachtman. Viewed from three to eight feet, both styles are representational but differ in their level of coarse graining with the photo-realism having a finer grain and impressionism having a coarser grain. Viewed from 100 feet, a painting is but a colored rectangle. Viewed at 75X under a conservator's microscope, paint texture can resemble a mountain range. Which view is most real? Normal viewing distance of three to eight feet is most common, but all views are equally real.

An aggregate level is a meta-level of more basic building blocks such as the notion of gross national product (GNP), which is an aggregate of all of a nation's industries, or a funnel, which is an aggregate of water molecules. In physics, *coarse graining* is the term used to express how fine a resolution one applies to reality, because distinct levels exist. Judging the level of coarse graining is an art in modeling since there is no perfect or omniscient perspective. Multiple levels are possible; however, the precision achieved at the finer levels disappears quickly when one takes a step back to view the entire painting or group of industries or water molecules.

Viewing the same thing at different levels can give contradictory results. One may choose not to invest in a company that seems an excellent prospect viewed in isolation, but whose industry is undergoing turmoil. The question of coarse graining depends on the view taken and the perceived strength of the links between levels, in this case industry and company. The meta-level or aggregate can exhibit properties that are unknown to more basic building blocks (e.g., the funnel in the bathtub versus the water molecules). In physics, time irreversibility is not a function of more basic levels such as the trajectories of atoms.

The paradox between deterministic and evolvable phenomena is resolved because these seeming contradictory viewpoints are characterized at different resolutions. For example, physically speaking, the author is 220 pounds of atoms and has enjoyed life on God's green Earth for 37 years. According to the actuary's mortality table, I have 44 or so more trips around our Sun remaining on this planet. When I am buried, my body, in terms of the Earth, will reach equilibrium. My corpse will cool down and heat up with the seasons rather than maintaining 98.6 degrees Fahrenheit. As the body decomposes the atoms will become parts of other things, presumably other carbon-based life forms. Physics proves that, "dust thou *art* and unto dust shalt thou return" (Genesis 3:19). The atoms are eternal. Although it appears that in terms of my creation, time exists, in terms of the fundamental stuff of which we are all composed, time does not. The paradox of eternal atoms and a finite life is resolved with the level of resolution and event-driven time. "Time precedes existence," says Prigogine. The application here is that time has always been, but only at a macroscopic level of an event, such as my birth, has time been marked. For example, the choice between solid, gas is probabilistically and governed stasis is a stable state like a solid or gas versus a transitory state.

The choice between phase states to stasis is probabilistically governed. In financial economics, risk is redefined as choice between phase states and is ultimately unknowable. Real-time detection of an imminent change in state can be reduced with faster feedback from real-time modeling. One has limited ability to read the future. One can only hope to achieve the future state once it is indicated faster than your competitors.

Time is an emergent concept like the funnel. The events themselves marking time are the result of self-organized complexity. Events are high-level simplicity of low-level complexity. Time is a mark of something happening. As earthlings, our standard agreement of time is the revolution of Earth around our sun, called a mean solar year. From relativity we know that no universal clock ticks away and marks the passage of time uniformly for the universe. Because a revolution is an event, the correct concept is *event-driven time.*

Were Earth to revolve around the sun in less than 365.25 days, the mean solar year would be redefined. If it happened quickly enough, time would speed up or at least our understanding of it would, since the mean solar year is all our understanding of time is based on at present. In financial economics we are aware of event-driven concepts since the technique of risk arbitrage is often categorized as an event-driven strategy. The next step to complete the concept of event-driven time is to measure time as determined by the events rather than by the clock on the wall.

In the mid-1980s when many mergers took place, often simultaneously, my personal experience was that the flow of time speeded up. Nonpractitioners of risk arbitrage may cognize the changing flow of time from some personal experience or just from thinking about the saying "a New York minute." The intuition behind "a New York minute" is that given the frenetic pace of activity in Manhattan, 60 seconds appears to elapse much quicker than in Manhattan, Kansas, where the pace is more sedate. Prigogine et alia have provided a rigorous expression for this intuition.

In my early attempts to explain this concept of event-driven time in financial economics, I resorted to an analogy in medicine. I made the parallel between a physician and a regular sell-side analyst. For a normal human or company each is appropriate, respectively. As a percentage of the total life of a public company listed on an exchange, the amount of time during which most companies are involved in a major transaction is very small; but it is very important. It is akin to pregnancy, which is only nine months out of an expected life span of 80 years or so. The amount of activity that occurs during gestation or in a major transaction is sufficient to warrant a specialized discipline. An OB-GYN in the case of medicine or a risk-arbitrage analyst in the case of finance. It is not that the family physician or regular analyst could not ultimately figure it out, but rather that a sufficiently complicated series of events happens in a relatively compressed period of time so that a specialized practice is warranted. Time speeds up.

In discussing the "reflexive" interaction between credit and economic activity, Soros says as much in *The Alchemy of Finance*. "The reflexive interaction between the act of lending and collateral values has led me to postulate a pattern in which a period of gradual, slowly accelerating credit expansion is followed by a short period of credit contraction—the classic sequence of boom and bust. The bust is *compressed in time* [emphasis added] because the attempt to liquidate loans causes a sudden implosion of collateral values."

In financial economics Soros is not alone thinking in these terms. In 1985 Gerald O'Driscoll and Mario Rizzo, from the Austrian school of economic thought, noted in *The Economics of Time and Ignorance*, "There are two important consequences of adopting our non-Newtonian concept of time. First, real time is irreversible. There can be no return to a previous period. Thus, 'movements' along a supply and demand curve do not mirror real temporal changes. Strictly speaking, as soon as we move away from a given point on such a curve there is no going back to it. Second, the passage of time involves 'creative evolution': that is, processes produce unpredictable change. A process is not a mere rearrangement of given factors, as is portrayed in deterministic models of 'changes.' If change is real, it cannot be completely deterministic: there must be scope for surprise."

Here we must make a technical point, which has been the cause of great confusion to many. Just because the element of unpredictable change is introduced does not mean ipso facto that the entire system becomes unpredictable at the moment of its introduction. That is not to say that it can never happen; but rather, unless the system goes chaotic, some element of characterization or predictability remains. If we characterize the long-term dependence or the Hurst exponent as a measure for the amount of predictability, we can then see the exact amount of predictability or the Hurst exponent varies. Similarly, as we have seen, the Hurst exponent is a scaling factor in time. The Hurst exponent becomes more jagged as events speed up. As the Hurst exponent becomes more jagged it also becomes less predictable and thus more risky. The intuition here is plain. The Hurst exponent also has a relationship to Euclidean geometry; as the Hurst exponent becomes less jagged it approximates a straight line and straight lines, by definition are very predictable. Here we see that the application of Brownian motion fails on two counts: First, it fails in its assumptions, and second, it fails to distinguish between temporal levels of resolution.

RESONANCE

The other point Prigogine makes is that change is reflected in Poincaré resonances. It is not necessary to get into the abstruse mathematics behind Poincaré resonances other than to cognize the intuition that events are a sort of frequency. When those frequencies resonate or experience a beneficial interference, the result is growth in financial economics or a symphony in music. Conversely, when there is dissonance, in terms of frequency, the symmetry is broken. Dissonance is the causal reason for instability. The upshot is that probability is a real state of the world rather than a state of mind or a dodge for interpretation without rigor.

The simple physical example of resonance is of course music. Suppose a luthier has two identically tuned guitars in his shop. We strike the A string on one guitar; the A string of the other guitar will vibrate in sympathy. It will resonate. Examples of destruction by high frequency include the old commercial for Memorex recording tapes, where a crystal glass is shattered by a soprano and we are led to wonder whether it was a live operatic singer or the reproduction of her voice. Examples of low-frequency destruction are earthquakes and jackhammers. Basically what Prigogine is saying is that if we think of causal change in the universe in terms of a glass, a soprano sings sometimes and causes change.

In financial economics, the concept of resonance is very important. Resonance is a transient phenomenon, and it is our ability to characterize it that is the intuition behind the KAOS screen. Although resonance is a word newly applied to financial economics, we know the concept. For example, stocks such as paper and forest products and airlines are called "cyclicals" because longer-term cycles can be identified. Although the cycles are not perfectly periodic, and do not correspond perfectly with credit or business cycles, the fact that some sort of recognizable cycle exists means that the concepts of frequency and resonance are not without a basis in reason. It is probably reasonable to posit that the price of Intel's shares is linked to a technology cycle that is influenced strongly by the production cycle of chips within and between generations and the discounting strategy currently being applied. The product release cycle of a new operating system from Microsoft or additional functionality from other vendors also has an identifiable role.

Again we bring the concept of resonance back to financial economics with a quote from Krugman's *Self-Organizing Economy*. "I begin with a review of the general approach to spatial dynamics used here, then turn to a specific model of a linear economy and show how the evolution of this model near an even distribution of manufacturing can be viewed in terms of growth rates of fluctuations of different *frequencies* [emphasis added]. Finally, I show why the model has a preferred wavelength, and how this wavelength depends on parameters." Krugman is looking at a spatial representation of the growth of cities. He is looking for a rhyme and reason why things tend to cluster together. Why is there a central business district, manufacturing district, Chinatown, and so forth? Another example from a simplified model is the distribution about the perimeter of a city. "Remember I started . . . with an almost but not exactly flat distribution of business around the circle. The deviation of that distribution from perfect flatness may be represented as an irregular, wobbly line. But it is generally true that, to use technical language, an irregular wobble can be thought of as the sum of many regular wobbles at different frequencies."

Arbitrage in the classic sense of being long and short 100 pounds of silver for example, is a perfect resonance. The resonance is perfect because the long and short positions are perfectly sympathetic. They rise and fall with near identical amplitude and frequency. In fact, it is the pursuit of profit by arbitrageurs that results in this near perfect resonance. Perfect resonance in classic arbitrage is a good clue for contemplating risk management, because what we are really looking for in risk management is an instrument that moves with perfect or near perfect amplitude and frequency *opposite* of the instrument or portfolio we are seeking to protect. We want to reduce risk by having a perfect or near perfect offset of the instrument being protected. That offset must occur with an explicit level of resolution expressed in the temporal realm.

Let us extend the concept of resonance. Were we to visualize a time series in financial economics as it is idealized by perfect randomness or a Brownian motion, we would see a jagged line. That is, the jaggedness would be fairly uniformly distributed. However, we also know from Mandelbrot's *Fractals and Scaling in Finance* that volatility clusters. That is, the jaggedness is unevenly applied. It lumps and clumps like curdled milk. Viewed fractally, these clusters imply that time speeds up. More importantly, the clusters are the empirical reason for financial change. That is, volatility clusters in financial economics are analogous to deviations in Poincaré resonance that Prigogine uses to demonstrate change in the universe. At lumps and clumps of clusters we should find phase transitions.

Capturing transient rather than permanent phenomena should be intuitively appealing to practitioners since they realize that there is no permanent investment truth. For example, IBM is not always a good buy for everyone. Sometimes it is and sometimes it is not. Similarly, the concept of permanency as stated by Buffett in some of his holdings is presumably restricted to those investments maintaining some status quo. Should local newspapers see significant competition from the Internet, they will no longer enjoy their near monopoly-like position as recipients of local advertising dollars. No investment is forever in the more restrictive sense of the word. What is forever or bankable is that markets will fluctuate, and if that fluctuation can be profitably characterized, an investment strategy exists.

Through the lens of resonance we can see more easily the concept of increasing returns or positive feedback. This is a period of wealth creation were the glass—to use our old analogy—is being formed. Because of the speed of electronic interaction, including the Internet, this creative/destructive process happens in much shorter timescales vis-à-vis the industrial age. The information age lives quicker than the industrial age. Because the time horizon for investing is probably measured in terms of a few years at most, the fact that resonance detects phenomena well within that range makes it more germane to the investment horizons and attention spans of investors. In other words, the dynamics of creation and destruction in the economy have been present as long as the economy has. However, when those dynamics happen outside an investable horizon, with no theory in which to interpret them or mathematics to measure them, the fact that creative/destructive processes exist is of marginal practical significance. Evolutionary processes take on new significance when the relevant timescales are minutes, weeks, or months rather than eons. It is power laws that so accurately relate frequency to events.

PROBABILITY

The reality is that the universe is out-of-equilibrium. It is in a nonequilibrium state and it is a dynamic process. Stars are born, age, and die. The fact that the timescale of the stars is much longer than human life or investment decisions is immaterial. The fact is, the universe is not static. In effect, Newton said that it is frozen. Literally the philosophical bent he left us with adopted the pose that we could step outside the thing and apply numbers to it, and then magically step back into the flow. Let's go back to our painting example for a moment. For three valid levels of reality, we have three very different descriptions. Because the dynamics of a process occur at an aggregate level, we cannot use the old physics of time-reversible trajectories; we have to use irreversible dynamics, which can be explained only in general or statistical terms because our viewpoint is far away—far away in the sense that humans do not experience reality at the quantum level any more than investors experience companies at the operational level. By the time the company files with the SEC and Wall Street analysts write their reports, from the investor's point of view that information is fairly separate from the day-to-day operational reality of the business.

With nonequilibrium dynamics the intuition is that a system, like the economy, has the option to potentially exist in more than one state. Equilibrium dynamics does not allow for this possibility. Probability in financial economics to state a constant rate of diffusion in the Black-Scholes model. The difference is that in the nonequilibrium world probability plays a fundamental role in governing the choice of states. Causal reasons at finer levels of resolution may exist, but we cannot tell what they are yet.

What is important here for financial economics is not the knowledge of physics, although that may be a positive by-product. What is important here it that we differentiate at a very early stage the assumptions we make when we attempt to solve a problem—that is, Type III assumptions, in the worldview mentioned earlier, that are taken for granted and never even questioned. It is axiomatic that the hardest thing to change in the world is an idea. It is also true that new answers are seldom found by looking at problems in old ways. Einstein said, "A good joke must not be told too many times." He was not making a literal reference to a joke but rather expressing the realization that what worked well at one point in the process of inquiry may not work well in the next. Einstein's quote captures perfectly the human sentiment that is exactly the failing in the current view of the majority in financial economics. We apply a good joke too many times, in making all problems nails because our only tool is a hammer, or looking for the keys under the streetlight when we lost them further away in the dark, or in attempting to extend the application of linear math in financial economics, when basically and precisely that is what is not called for.

Fortunately, as the pace of technology quickens, it seems that old concepts can be more readily abandoned because the old ways did not exist for a long enough period of time to become entrenched as a habit. Where the change is the most difficult is where technology meets established prejudices or commonly held beliefs, such as in financial economics. Children may be more emotionally able to change because nothing is entrenched and they have a lower inhibition to failure and change than adults do. The changes imposed by rapid advancements in technology will compel us to become more neotenic or juvenile in these respects.

We will devote some attention to resonance. It seems unusual for financial economics; however, since it does occur within the universe, which is subject to physical laws, it is enlightening to explore where the two bodies are congruent, where they differ, and where they intersect. Chapter 5 dealing with the KAOS screen discusses the specifics of how the screen in effect acts like a tuner and strength of signal indicator to characterize this transient resonance. Chapter 11 provides the basis for the intuition of how a time series such as those in financial economics can be thought of as a frequency.

DERIVATIVE SCIENCES

Starting with physics at the most fundamental level of the known universe, the vertical chain in Table 3.1 is basically how we have seen the world and reasoned.

Table 3.1 The Old View of Sciences in the World

Derivative	Economics, politics, etc.
↑	Human behavior
↑	Biology
↑	Organic chemistry
↑	Chemistry
Fundamental	Physics

From particles we build atoms, and from atoms we build molecules and then compounds. Somewhere along the way from atoms to compounds, physics becomes chemistry. A special branch of chemistry called organic chemistry has a preponderance of carbon-based molecules used for living things. Life is introduced and chemistry becomes biology. Higher up the food chain, more complex forms of life merit their own disciplines such as human behavior. A subset of that behavior is called financial economics, but if financial economics is the study of individual choice to optimally allocate scarce resources, then in a sense all aspects of behavior may be said to be economic.

The extant chain is unsatisfactory because the things we observe are more complex than can be explained by basic sciences. The leading sentence of the Science subsection earlier in this chapter, "Since financial economics happens within the universe, financial economics is, by definition, subject to physical laws," is quite true. However, in terms of a chain of causality, particle physics has little bearing on any trading decision. The only time physics is of value in financial economics is metaphorically speaking when the concept of gravity is invoked with the saying "what goes up must come down"—or so it is hoped if one is currently losing money.

NEW REALITY

In an attempt to make a more informed picture of reality Deutsch in essence proposed the accompanying chart (Table 3.2). Many of the concepts dealt with in nonlinear pricing have no meaning when viewed traditionally in terms of Newtonian physics and need a richer structure to support them. One of the real mismatches we now have is between the explanatory power of theory and the complexity of reality. It is a principal reason for the frustration or disinterest altogether with theory. After all, how can one be expected to cognize financial economics in terms of evolution, as Anderson *et al.* insightfully suggest, much less in terms of nonlinearity or complexity, unless one has some framework or some underpinning linking these highly derivative concepts?

To get that underpinning we have to restate the basics. We no longer have to try to express the rich and complex fabric to which the world admits in highly idealized (and discredited) Newtonian terms. This restatement is the intellectual equivalent of removing constricting clothes and blinders from the eyes all at once.

Table 3.2 The New View of Sciences in the World

Quantum Theory	Life/Evolution	Knowledge	Computation

THE FOUR MAIN STRANDS

The essence of Deutsch's approach in Table 3.2 is to take the irreducible concepts of quantum theory, life/evolution, knowledge, and computation and move them to the status of fundamental descriptive building blocks. In so doing, we are compelled to accept more fully the logical conclusions each strand presents, individually and in concert. While each strand is accepted in a limited sense individually, their acceptance in full mandates a large conclusion—that of leaving the familiar Newtonian world behind. The argument for change is characterized by any fundamental situation where logic must prevail over emotion. This Type III change is not a trivial thing to attempt, nor witness. But it is for the better.

LIFE/EVOLUTION

In the jump from chemistry to organic chemistry, which studies carbon-based life forms like you and me, no particular magic can be found that constitutes "life"; ergo life must be a fundamental strand. In other words, the thinking in 1998 is that if we cannot measure "life" then it must be inherent. We can measure life's effects but not the phenomenon itself. Also, life seems to be inextricably woven into any meaningful explanation of reality.

Deutcsh also mentions research by two respected cosmologists, John Barrow and Frank Tipler, who posited that it is the future course of human life that will determine the life of the universe. They considered what the effect of life would be after our sun turns into a red star and concluded that life will make a major qualitative change to the galaxy and later to the entire universe. Therefore, there is no explanation of the universe without life or more specifically, the objective knowledge embodied by life. The simple example to cognize is that the oxygen in Earth's atmosphere is a product of the photosynthesis of plants. Thus, temperature regulation of Earth is codependent on Earth-based life forms. This is the controversial Gaia hypothesis. Moving up to a cosmosian scale, life in general will affect the life of the universe.

Deutsch's definition of adaptation is also useful. "The degree to which a replicator is adapted to a niche is the degree to which it causes its own replication in that niche." More generally, an entity is adapted to its niche to the extent that it embodies knowledge that causes the niche to keep that knowledge in existence. If we change a few words, we see that a firm's profitability is the degree to which it is adapted to its market niche, and the degree to which it is profitable allows it to replicate (grow or spawn competitors). The play on words is more than semantics and is in keeping with the view that the behavior of a firm, which is part of an ecosystem in time, can be explained with biological terms.

The progenitors of evolution are Darwin, late of "survival of the fittest" fame, and more recently Richard Dawkins, who extended this concept in *The Selfish Gene* and *The Blind Watchmaker*. In essence, it is not the species but rather the gene variant which must survive the test of fitness. Darwin had the right idea but he had looked on too large a scale—the species rather than the gene. As previously stated, genes are the biological embodiment of knowledge.

Although I am sure Soros did not anticipate that his Theory of Reflexivity would find a conceptual ally in cosmology, it is there. Soros maintained in Reflexivity that the perceptions of market participants could materially affect the *fundamentals* of an investment. The reasons he gives are that markets are biased and markets anticipate. The examples he gave in the *Alchemy of Finance* of the stock market are the conglomerates in the 1960s and 1970s. Reflexivity is also exemplified in the credit market with prices affecting the value of collateral in real estate investment trusts (REITs) in the 1970s. Without the concepts of probability and nonequilibrium at the fundamental level, such recursive behavior is difficult if not impossible to express. Soros admitted as much at the time of his first writing in 1985. Regrettably, Soros's book received a muted reception. A few money managers I informally polled were bewildered. I suspect the real reason was because the intermediate concepts in physics, mathematics, and biology linking Soros's intuition and his nontechnical articulation of that intuition, had yet to be expressed in a more rigorous and accessible form. It is hoped that some of those terms will be sketched in the present work. In dealing with reflexive interactions, it is interesting to note that even the terms describing the interaction between entities, such as coevolution and symbiotic and parasitic behavior, come from biology.

If a biological parallel can be made between a market and its participants and between the two genders, then looking for clues for rational choices governing the interactions between the two sides will take us into the economics of sex. Richard A. Posner, the erudite chief judge for the Seventh U.S. Circuit Court of Appeals in Chicago, has written *Economic Analysis of Law* and *Sex and Reason*. Both seek to optimize. The former optimizes equity in law and the latter rational allocation of scarce reproductive resources. Steven Pinker's *How the Mind Works* echoes costs inherent in sex.

These texts, while seemingly out of place in a financial economics treatise, are more relevant now than ever. To the extent an economy is thought to be and is evolutionary, the reasons why we trade genes for procreation and how we trade them yield clues to how we trade for other resources.

The simple explanation of how males and females trade genes, according to the *Economist*, is that the process is coevolutionary. Males peddling cheap sperm perpetually innovate new ways of seducing females with expensive eggs. To stay competitive, females have to invent new ways to become blasé. If either gender is allowed to evolve strategies and is then unleashed upon a control group, that gender will be disproportionately successful. This is the same reason underdeveloped economies are often less in favor of free trade with developed economies. In aggregate, both sides benefit; however, the developed economy, like the more evolved gender, will benefit disproportionately.

According to biologists, the reason why we must endure the high cost of sexual reproduction is that gene mutation is, in the long run, a superior strategy to thwarting biological enemies. Were the nemesis to evolve, and if humans only replicated or cloned themselves (resulting in an exact genetic copy as opposed to reproduction, which results in a mix of both parents), over time the nemesis would have the advantage.

The concept of coevolution is powerful and serves as the basis for the theoretical foundation of nonlinear pricing for a few of reasons. First, it is relational. From Herman Weyl we see that we need to state something in terms of something else since the fixed backdrop of the Newtonian no longer exists. Second, coevolution allows complexity and self-organized criticality to be manifest. Third, coevolution is an apt metaphor to generate and interpret nonequilibrium.

Thomas Ray, a pioneer in artificial life, gives some insight in his paper "An Evolutionary Approach to Synthetic Biology: Zen and the Art of Creating Life." Within the context of coevolution we can generate complex software by articulating relationships at the local level between participants and at the global level between participants and the environment. In our case, it is investors and the market which should remind you of charges and the field from the previous chapter.

Although the details are beyond the scope of this work, Ray mentions two concepts that can easily be seen at the conceptual level. First, we recognize that synthetic biology inhabits a non-Euclidean space. The connection to nonlinear pricing is simple. In terms of the matching principle, we are using a tool in the form of a computer to generate solutions that are like those generated by the real world. That is, the spatial topology of random access memory (RAM) in a computer is fractal. Thus, the space in the virtual reality generator in which we are creating solutions is fractal, as is the reality of financial economics. Ray says, "What is the distance between two locations in memory? In fact, the distance cannot be measured in linear units. The most appropriate unit is the time that it takes to move information between two points. . . . A space in which all pairs of points are equidistant is clearly not a Euclidean space."

Second, coevolution, like sex and the predator-prey model mentioned earlier, can approximate equilibrium, out-of-equilibrium, and far-from-equilibrium conditions. This is called the Red Queen effect, from *Alice in Wonderland*, where "in the face of a changing environment, organisms must evolve as fast as they can in order to simply maintain their current state of adaptation. 'In order to get anywhere you must run twice as fast as that.' " Simply put, when the rabbits and foxes are truly competitive, their state resembles an equilibrium. In the case of investors and the market, this corresponds to the time when the risk-free rate of return is earned. Change can come endogenously from the participants or exogenously from the market. This is the reason we need a model and a paradigm that can handle multiple levels of resolution. Ray further states, "The Gaussian principle of competitive exclusion states that no two species that occupy the same niche can co-exist." Curiously, this may provide an important clue as to why, in terms of nonlinear pricing, perfect equilibrium is never possible.

Back to sex. Considering that we cannot meet all prospective mates within our reproductive time frame, how do we make the decision with whom to breed given the fact of finite time and the bewildering array of possibilities? In terms of how to make love, Posner's, Pinker's, and Ray's works are not romantic in the least, but in terms of why or how much they are eminently practical. But then, so is biology, as Dawkins said in *The Selfish Gene*. John Maynard Smith asks a similar question in *Did Darwin Get It Right?: Essays on Games, Sex and Evolution*. Biological processes are not irrational.

I strongly suspect knowledge has a locus. This sentence is an unintended double entendre. First, knowledge is embodied physically, whether biologically in a life form or mathematically in a virtual reality. Second, locus has meanings in both genetics and mathematics. In mathematics it is a series of points and/or lines that satisfies one or more given conditions. In genetics locus is the position on a chromosome occupied by a particular gene.

There exists a subtle but real attraction for certain repeatable patterns of behavior. This attraction could also be characterized as a fundamental reason that is distinguishable from random. The chaos fans will see the relationship between a locus and strange attractor in phase space. The biologists will identify with a better than random interaction. The practitioners in financial economics will see the same phenomenon as a bias in the markets. Some rational process, whether of allocation or otherwise, seems to be a theme that runs right to the core. We may not call it rational or even financial economics; maybe we call it self-organized complexity. But there is something, however nebulous its current state of articulation. To conclude that there is no knowable process is so scary as to be unacceptable.

KNOWLEDGE

Knowledge, or more accurately the theory of its acquisition, is the second strand. The framer of our process is philosopher Karl Popper—also a great influence on Soros—who maintains that it is the process of conjecture, test, refutation or acceptance, and new proposal that leads to real knowledge.

Popper's method of knowledge acquisition marks a change from the inductivist or prediction-oriented methods indicated by Bertrand Russell's chicken in Chapter 2. Deutsch says, "In regard to science as a *problem-solving* process, inductivism regards the catalogue of our past observations as a sort of skeletal theory, supposing that science is all about filling in the gaps in that theory by interpolation and extrapolation." We begin with a problem—something that needs to be explained. We posit a thesis and attempt to persuade via reasoning and empirical evidence that our explanation is the best one available. This is the objective of all scientific reasoning. The refutation is based on experimental testing. Whatever the conclusion, a new level of understanding is reached and the process begins again.

Theory based on observations alone is called inductivism. Without an overriding explanation, the observations are prone to much misinterpretation. Inductivism rests upon the mistaken idea of science as seeking predictions based on observations, rather than as seeking explanations in response to problems.

Reasoning must be paramount. Computer models, while they can tell us much, are limited by available data. A computer model of Russell's chicken would not be a great advantage, for example, and runs the risk of being inductivist since there is no understanding what the model is trying to tell us, in the greater sense of the term. In financial economics this is often a real problem since the number of data points available to work with is typically much smaller than in many other disciplines. What software can do is to extend human capabilities where speed and voluminous data are concerned. Software does an exceptional job at pattern detection. However, once the pattern is articulated, it still must be placed within some organized body of thought we call a theory to have real explanatory power. Patterns in financial economics data produced by nonlinear pricing, by themselves have descriptive power but not explanatory power. For example, the Hurst exponent describes a nonlinear time series but does not explain why it is nonlinear. In sum, the numbers tell us a lot, but they cannot tell us everything.

COMPUTATION

The argument for computation as a fundamental strand is based on the Turing principle, which holds that a computer—a virtual reality generator—can be built to express any physically realizable environment. A virtual reality generator is akin to a flight simulator for training pilots. It is also the reason why the nonlinear models that seek to emulate market dynamics or any other phenomena are important for our understanding of nature. To the extent we can build a virtual reality of the market we can develop better explanations and thus better predictions.

The proof of such a virtual reality rests on a *diagonal argument* first used by Georg Cantor to prove that there are infinite quantities greater than the infinite number of natural numbers. A diagonal argument is one where a list of entries is imagined and then that list is used to construct a related entity that cannot be on the list. Diagonal arguments are at the heart of modern computation as put forth by A. M. Turing. They were also used by Gödel for his incompleteness theorem. Simply put, a body of math cannot be used to prove a statement which exceeds the definition of that body; hence it is incomplete. The homology to finance is clear. Nonlinearity cannot be demonstrated with linear math because linearity is only a highly idealized subset of a more general nonlinear reality. Return on investment is a linear concept. The high-tech business is characterized by nonlinear concepts like increasing returns. If you are still confused, then attempt to calculate the ROI of a computer. It is a mismatch of linear constructs applied to nonlinear phenomena.

Deutsch goes on to illustrate via the Turing principle, alternate worlds must exist and that the laws of physics mandate their own comprehensibility. Again, we do not need to draw such a large conclusion but include this as a matter of completeness.

The practical aspect of virtual reality in financial economics is much more modest. Computation is important because if we succeed in creating a virtual reality of the stock market—the beginning steps of which have already been taken at the Santa Fe Institute—then we have helped change the nature of the proof from a formula to a computational proof. That is, the proof exists in the sense that a virtual reality, like the actual one it so accurately emulates, has indicated it is so.

Think of a pilot. We assume that if a pilot has spent enough time in a 747

simulator and that the simulator is very lifelike, then we can satisfy ourselves that a computational proof of the pilot's flying ability exists. But we
can never write a formula a priori proving the fellow can fly. Even after 400
hours of real flying time in the left seat, there is no guarantee that the pilot
will not crash on the next flight. Perfecting this virtual reality to change the
qualitative nature of the question being asked is the reason, at least in the
scientific sense, that faster microprocessors are necessary—as we shall see
later in this chapter.

In this context, it is also useful to keep in mind computer games, like
Riven and Quake,™ which hit the market in 1997; these are good examples
of the commercial drivers of state-of-the-art 3D and multimedia. Although
built with teenagers, primarily boys, in mind, they are not trivial. The requi-
sites of reflexes, spatial logic, reasoning and a nonlinear style of play make
these games our best common training ground for the virtual reality simula-
tors to come in industry and defense. An example of a nonlinear style of
play is reaching a location, such as a well, for the objective of water and
noticing an ax leaning against a nearby tree. The ax is not relevant to the immediate scenario but has relevance in a later scenario, and will have to be
remembered and retrieved.

Over Christmas break 1997, I witnessed Avery Rose Smith, age *three*,
initiate and perform solo using the above-mentioned skill set on a game
called Putt-Putt. Her sister, Dylan, age seven and a half, understands, in an
intuitive sense, the biological basis of nonlinear pricing, because she plays
Tamagotchi™. This $11.99 Japanese game on a key ring is a virtual reality
that requires several inputs over time to maintain the Tamagotchi's "life,"
including warmth for incubation, medicine for illness, food for hunger, pun-
ishment for misbehavior, and cleaning when the Tamogotchi defecates!
Failure to do any of these in some generalized and unstated period of time
results in the Tamagotchi's illness and ultimately death. The biological dynamics are much more lifelike than any static doll ever could be. Not surprisingly, it is Kim, their mother—with three children and one husband, my
best friend Garrett—who has the best idea of the dynamics of Tamagotchi.
In biology the only finality is death. One does not play and score and win or
lose. There is no scoring. Tamagotchi is a *process*. Kim tends to Tamagotchi
for a few moments intermittently throughout the day between feedings,
bathings, cryings, and so on of her small children ad infinitum. Perhaps females, in their role as mothers, have an important lesson to teach in terms of
dealing with processes without a sense of finality.

Although these children and teenagers in general are not conscious of the
fact yet, they are preparing themselves for many activities in the 21st century, including trading and risk management in financial economics. The
broadly distributed skills of hunting and mechanization in their own epochs

were the sort of American know-how that made money and won wars. Perhaps computer gaming is the information age's answer to the skills of the agricultural and industrial ages. If the Turing principle is appropriately a law of physics, then resorting to analytic proofs will not be necessary. The computational proof or proof "in silica" (referring to the silicon of microprocessors) will be sufficient. The Turing principle is the physical embodiment of knowledge.

WHAT ARE THE LINKS?

Evolution and Knowledge

Popper by his theory of knowledge says that knowledge can grow only by conjecture and refutation—in other words, evolutionary epistemology. There are differences, to be sure. Biological mutation is random whereas human problem solving, in terms of creating new conjectures, is complex and directed. There is also no biological equivalent to argument. Biology is slower because it must exhaust more options.

But stronger than the differences are the similarities. Evolutionary success depends on the survival of objective knowledge. In biology, evolutionary success is called adaptation. Is useful information encoded in the niche? Inferences are not drawn from observations alone, but observations can help detect weaknesses in inferences. Discerning the needs of a crying infant does not seem any easier than discerning the wiles of an unruly market. Perhaps the Popperian process of conjecture and refutation to reach a solution happens so intuitively and quickly that it is subjective if not instinctive.

Quantum Physics and Computation

The Turing principle does not explicitly state the link between physics and computation, so we have to look below the surface. Physical variables can store, interact, and transmit information. That such a process is stable depends on quantum theory. Highly adapted replicators depend on virtual reality generation and universality. This process can be understood in terms of the Turing principle.

More esoteric aspects of quantum computation are mentioned, including the fact that quantum computers with very limited functionality have already been built at IBM Research in Yorktown Heights, New York, by Charles Bennett in 1989. Immediate commercialization is not a prospect, but the fact that the thing exists at all means that it merits some attention. Also, the presence of Shor's algorithm, invented in 1994 by Peter Shor at Bell Laboratories, and Grover's algorithm merits this same attention. Quantum factorization in cryptography is the direct threat mentioned earlier to current methods, specifically the RSA method now heavily used on the Internet.

We spoke earlier about the changing nature of the proof. We have moved from a simple analytical proof spelled out with a few linear formulas to a computational proof depending upon computer simulation. Quantum computation will further change the nature of the proof. Because the quantum computation takes place at the quantum level, in those parallel worlds maintained by Deutsch, where is the proof? We are not able to express it in the visible universe. Bigger conceptual changes are in store, although it is impossible to say when.

It is also important to realize that if we are in the information business and there is a real and identifiable link between quantum theory and the processing of information, we should make ourselves aware of it.

There is a further twist. The *New York Times* reported on July 22, 1997, that Dr. Nicolas Gisin of the University of Geneva had performed the twin-photon experiment. That is, he confirmed a statistical relationship between photons created from seemingly nothing at all—at a distance of over seven miles. The great mystery is how they communicated, which we now believe to be a physical impossibility. The question is, why is a numerical correlation between two particles different from information? The answer is not clear but may have some bearing on the encryption problem mentioned previously and the concept of a nonlocal analysis.

Evolution and Quantum Theory

The fact that the future behavior of the universe and life are codependent in an evolutionary sense establishes this link. Life has an effect at the largest and smallest scales of the universe. "The largest-scale regular structure across universes exists where knowledge-bearing matter, such as brains or DNA gene segments, has evolved." says Deutsch.

CONCLUSION

Deutsch goes on to state his case for the acceptance of nonsequential time. That is, if a multiverse exists as he concludes from quantum interference, by definition, time cannot flow. Here I choose to leave the argument, not because it is not well argued; it is. I leave because of my own limitations. I do not yet understand the direct applicability of a multiverse to financial economics well enough to present it.

This has been a long chapter. We have covered much ground that will be new to many in financial economics. Yet there is no way to appreciate Anderson's quote at the beginning of this chapter without increasing the reader's background. The quote again is, "Theoretical economists will have virtually abandoned classical equilibrium theory in the next decade; the metaphor in the short-term future will be evolution, not equilibrium." Given that the description of financial economics is not well served by equilibrium and that nonequilibrium is a far more powerful concept embraced by mathematics, physics, and biology, perhaps the practitioner will conclude, rightfully, that a real sea change is underway and practical opportunities exist for those who seek them.

Not only is it important to introduce new concepts such as probability, nonequilibrium, evolution, and knowledge, which some leading minds are incorporating at the root-level description of reality, but we must attempt to see how the interrelationships between those concepts are being thought about. With a richer descriptive palate, we may begin to interpret more clearly how the very complex phenomena of financial economics may be more accurately cognized.

4

Fractal Analysis

There was a crooked man, and he went a crooked mile,
He found a crooked sixpence against a crooked stile;
He bought a crooked cat, which caught a crooked mouse,
And they all lived together in a little crooked house.

—NURSERY RHYME

If you think it is just a *bit* eccentric to use a children's nursery rhyme as an epigraph in a book dealing with such a serious topic as money, then you are in for a real show. "Crooked" is of course an oblique reference to the Hurst exponent. The calculated effect of injecting yet another anxiety-producing source of uncertainty—in this case our shattered notions about finance— makes the subject all the more surreal.

Maybe you think I'm crazy like Yossarian in Joseph Heller's *Catch-22*. Believe me, if I was crazy, I would not be worrying about what makes stocks go up and down. On the other hand, since no one knows what makes stocks go up and down, if I was not crazy, what would be different? As Gilbert and Sullivan said, "Things are seldom what they seem,/Skim milk masquerades as cream./Lowbrows pass for upper-crust;/We accept it, 'cause we must."

Let me be clear. Do you know to what "Ring around the Rosie" refers? Ring around the rosie, pocket full of posies, ashes to ashes, we all fall down. Ring around the rosie refers to the ring of red blisters surrounding the flea's bite during the Black Death of medieval Europe or the bubonic plague of 17th-century London. Posies were thought to protect you from the plague, sort of like wearing garlic to protect against vampires. Ashes to ashes refers to when they stacked the corpses, stiff from rigor mortis, like logs on a funeral pyre and burned them. And we all fall down dead from the plague. The fact is your children recite this and you have no idea to what it refers.

The parallel to finance is transparent; things are seldom what they seem. People, grown-up people, recite all sorts of statistics in finance and you (and they) have no real idea of how well those statements refer to the reality they are supposed to describe. Trillions of dollars are at stake and everyone is a bit hazy on what is really being said. Because of a crooked line called the Hurst exponent, we all fall down. It is enough to make you crazy.

FRACTALS

There is no way to add rigor to nonlinear pricing without addressing the mathematics. While nonlinear pricing has a fractal structure, this chapter could easily be a book. In fact, it has taken Mandelbrot, who sired fractals, four books and he is still publishing. Thus, we strongly reiterate that accuracy has been sacrificed for accessibility and direct interested readers to Mandelbrot [1997a,b,c, 1972], Feder [1988], Schroeder [1994], Peters [1994, 1996], McCulloch [1996, 1997], Samorodnitski and Taqqu [1994], Adler, Feldman, and Taqqu (eds.) [1998], Baille [1996], Rachev [1996], Rachev and Mittnik [1997], Olsen *et al.*, Fama [1963], and Granger and Teräsvirta [1993]. And we note that this chapter, "Fractal Analysis," could easily be called "Mandelbrot Analysis" since Mandelbrot, the man, is as interesting and complex as the fractals themselves.

Fractals are not new in concept but are new in application to financial economics. Although fractals have been applied in many disciplines, financial economics seems to be their natural home. Their newness in application in financial economics holds much promise for future researchers and the opportunity for financial-economics to become the leader among the disciplines in fractal analysis. The concepts discussed here were born and developed in fields other than financial economics. Thus, the introductory examples given do not necessarily come from financial economics. Where possible, we will try to make a direct connection. Where it is not possible, conventionally trained practitioners and academics will have to use their mind's eye to visualize how a concept from another discipline may be applied to the instant case.

CONCEPT

The presence of the Hurst exponent, hereinafter referred to as **H**, presents a concept that is philosophical on one level and practical on the other.

As Jens Feder says in *Fractals*, Mandelbrot can offer no more rigorous definition than, "A fractal is a shape made of parts similar to the whole in some way." Although this definition may seem a bit abstract to the practitioner, it is generally agreed that this field is still rapidly evolving and thus will become more rigorously defined with the passage of time. It is also important to note that the intuition that led Mandelbrot down this path is graphical. That is, he saw pictures in his head. The mathematical expression of graphics is geometry. Expressing solutions in the form of graphics is also a central theme of this book. Personally, I find formulas as awkward as large numbers expressed in Roman numerals. The key to understanding anything is to get past the terminology and symbolism to the underlying concept those things are trying to express. Do not get stuck in unfamiliar territory. Keep moving.

Nonlinear pricing uses a fractal structure. A fractal has two defining properties: *self-similarity* and a fractal or *noninteger* dimension. A graphic example of self-similarity is scaling, such as a fern leaf, where a small leaf is qualitatively similar to a larger leaf. Invariant scaling means that an object is qualitatively similar at a large scale, at a small scale, and in between. Fern leaves, conifers such as Christmas trees, snowflakes, bronchi in mammalian lungs, river deltas, the surface area of clouds, and a wadded-up piece of paper are all simple physical examples of fractal scaling. For those who have been seduced by the colorful and entertaining chaos pictures, namely Julia and Mandelbrot sets, they are also fractal because viewed at resolutions of power 10X, 50X, or 72X, they are qualitatively similar.

A more restrictive and complex attribute of fractals is self-affinity. *Self-affinity* is proportional scaling in two dimensions. Self-affinity is what happens when you pull diagonally on your browser to increase the viewing area. Java allows the web page to be viewed to scale proportionately in terms of length and width. As Mandelbrot in his 1997 *Fractals and Scaling in Finance* says:

> Many geometric shapes are approximately isotropic. For example, no single direction plays a special role when coastlines are viewed as curves on a plane. In first-approximation fractal models of a coastline, small pieces are obtained from large pieces by a similarity, that is, an isotropic reduction (homothety) followed by a rotation and a translation. This property defines the fractal notion of self-similarity. Self-similar constructions make free use of angles, and distances can be taken along arbitrary directions in the plane.
>
> But this book deals mostly with geometric shapes of a different kind, namely, financial charts that show the abscissa as the axis of time and the ordinate as the axis of price. The scale of each coordinate can be changed without regard to the other. This freedom does not prevent a distance from being defined along the coordinate axis. But for all other directions, the Pythagorean definition,

Distance = $[(\text{time increment})^2 + (\text{price increment})^2]^{0.5}$

makes no sense whatsoever. It follows immediately that circles are not defined. Rectangles must have sides parallel to the axis. Squares are not defined, since—even when their sides are meant to be parallel to the axis—there is no sense saying that time increments = price increments.

There is a linear operation that applies different reduction ratios along the time and price axis. It generalizes similarity, and Leonhard Euler called it an *affinity*, because its matrix is diagonal. It follows that for graphs of functions in time, like price records, the relevant comparison of price charts over different time spans involves the scaling notion of self-affinity.

This distinction is important since we must be able to view time series on their own characteristic time scale, or what Olsen & Associates calls "intrinsic" time, rather than on clock time, which is how we do it now. That is, time, according to the time series, may elapse quicker or slower than what the clock on the wall is indicating. We direct the reader specifically to "Fractals and Intrinsic Time—A Challenge to Econometricians" by U. A. Müller *et al.* of Olsen & Associates. This concept is belabored because it is so important.

The notion of a characteristic time scale other than that indicated by the clock is known heuristically but not rigorously, nor have its implications in financial economics been fully realized. For example, we understand that "children grow like a weed" compared to their parents and the growth rates of start-up companies experience "dog years"—a reference to the fact that a year in a human's life equates roughly to seven in a dog's. Conversely, we also know that old people are slower than their children and bureaucracies experience "turtle years"—a reference to the fact that giant sea turtles have a very slow heartbeat relative to humans and have a life expectancy of about 200 years. In sum, the idea of fractal scaling is the rigorous but intuitive and logical extension that certain observations are relative to the observer.

The difference is that we are not discussing the concept of relativistic time in terms of a cosmological context but rather in risk management and moneymaking. In the context of financial economics, relativistic time is certain to be a difficult pill to swallow because it is an alien concept. However, it is for this reason that the science background is necessary—to prove that the concept has a place in the pantheon of great thoughts, and that physics is the boundary of what is permissible in financial economics. Lastly, and because of the novelty of the idea, it is also important to state that it does not matter whether one believes such a thing or not. In the scientific sense, what matters is whether a thing is true or not. In the information age what is true or not can be an excellent indicator of whether a thing can help make money or not.

Woe be to the firm that sees profit without the requisite level of understanding of how that profit is achieved. The structure of this argument helps to explain why Wall Street has had such growing pains (read: incurred such losses) with respect to derivatives. Like many a human endeavor, such as sea and air travel, derivatives are not inherently cruel, but they are terribly unforgiving. The basic reason is that derivatives take some time to understand—time which no one in pursuit of profit has. Derivatives also take some background in terms of mathematics to understand a body of knowledge, which is alien to traditional Wall Street. Only the profit half of the equation was grasped. Understanding, the other half, is painfully catching up.

A fractal dimension is a noninteger dimension. A graphic example is the surface area of a cloud. Although the cloud resides in 3D space, it fails the Euclidean definition of a plane (2D) and a sphere (3D) because its surface is nowhere differentiable. A financial-economics time series is almost always between a line (one dimensional or 1D) and a plane (2D). A random time series known mathematically as Brownian motion where $H = 0.5$ has noninteger dimension of 1.5D. A persistent time series where $H > 0.5$ is closer to a line, and conversely, an antipersistent time series where $H < 0.5$ is closer to a plane. Both persistent and antipersistent time series are examples of fractional Brownian motion (fBm).

It is the invariant scaling characteristic of fractals that makes them so powerful. In *The End of Certainty* Prigogine said, "As we shall see our formulation requires an extended function space. This new field of mathematics, which uses generalized functions or fractals, as Benoît Mandelbrot called them, is now playing a critical role in the understanding of the laws of nature." As we see from the above paragraph, Euclidean geometry does not possess a fine enough resolution to describe many aspects of reality with the mathematical rigor with which fractals can describe a wadded-up piece of paper. Historically, when faced with this challenge mathematicians moved to Reimann geometry, the geometry of curved surfaces like the windscreen of your car. There are others such as Hilbert space to describe phenomena in quantum land. Sadly, none of these spaces described by various geometries solve our problem completely.

This is the reason Prigogine needed an "extended function space." Our simplistic wadded-up piece of paper is the exact analogy to the more sophisticated phenomena Prigogine *et al.* are now describing with mathematical—that is, fractal—rigor. The questions addressed by Prigogine such as the physics of populations, and the irreversibility of time are the very questions financial economics needed to have answered to make the math more representative of reality and to cast financial economics off from its Newtonian moorings. Strangely, it is a chemist and a mathematician, contemplating reality on an intellectual plane inaccessible to most of us, who have helped to solve some practical problems for Wall Street.

Infinite scaling and fractional numbers are very important in financial economics because time series are discontinuous and volatility clusters. As we have said earlier, when volatility clusters, time speeds up; however, the geometric expression of that clustering or speeding-up of time has to become more jagged within the same space of finite points. That is, we have to express more information within the same constraints. The simple picture is real estate. If we make an analogy between the density of people and information, and the finite points in which the information is bounded and a city block, then the only alternative is to build a high-rise. The density has to go somewhere, so it goes up. A time series does not go up; it becomes more jagged. To use a technical term, it becomes a *multifractal*. Multifractals are, as the term implies, fractals of fractals. In terms of financial economics, mutlifractals are not needed everywhere, nor are they needed all the time. But when volatility clusters or prices jump, a mechanism is now available to express those phenomena accurately.

DOMAINS AND SPACES

The word "space" has a few different uses in this book. Cyberspace is the abstraction within the computer and the network. Meatspace, as the digerati say, is where we shake hands. It is physical reality. Solution-space, as it is used in problem solving, is the abstract space where a solution is thought to lie. In mathematics, we need one dimension of solution space for every variable in the problem. For example, $x = 7$ has one variable, and the solution can be geometrically represented in one dimension or a point on a line; $x + y = 4$ has two variables, and the solution of whole positive real integers is a series of coordinates on a plane (0,4), (1,3), (2,2), (3,1), and (4,0). We cannot visualize above three dimensions. Above 3D, the terminology of physics and computer science diverge. In physics, 4D is time and in computer science it is the application of color to a area like a mountain called a shaded surface plot.

The problem with financial economics in meatspace is that so many dimensions are involved, potentially infinite, that we cannot take them all into account. This is the reason for the dispute about the existence of chaos in the strictest sense. High-dimensional chaos, as it is called, is impossible to detect. Fortunately, the high dimensionality of financial economics need not be the death knell for modeling, since we are able to make some sense of real-world problems now. That is, via approximation we can reduce the number of variables to a manageable number. For example, it is reasonable to posit that two important factors which affect the stock market are interest rates and earnings expectations. That obviously does not say that these are the only factors or that they affect the market equally or with uniform degrees of consistency.

Domains refer to how something is viewed. There are four primary ways: space, time, frequency, and phase. The space domain refers to the relationship between variables regardless of when they happened. An example is the yen–mark relationship or the interest rate–stock market relationship. The time domain refers to the relationship between variables regardless of where they happened. An example may be the origin of trades on the New York Stock Exchange. Once upon a time, trades had to originate on the floor. Now trades can originate wherever there is access to a telephone. Time still has a meaning but space does not. The frequency domain refers to the representation of patterns in time. For example, the tendency of a stock to close at or near the strike price of an option is a regular occurrence. The changing nature of commodity contracts as they approach expiry where the use of margin is restricted is another. Phase-space is the representation of patterns in space. We will give the example of two men on a beach shortly. Phase-space is useful for visually detecting patterns that may otherwise not be evident. What is important to our thesis is stated by Bak and Chen that, "We and our colleagues suggest that fractals can be used as snapshots of self-organized processes. Fractal structures and flicker [$1/f$] noise are the spatial and temporal fingerprints, respectively, of self-organized criticality." Recall that **H** scales geometrically and temporally. We have two very different ways of seeing the same thing.

PHASE TRANSITIONS

In Chapter 1, we mentioned the need for 3D and 4D visualization as a major point. What we did not mention was what we needed to look at in 3D or 4D. Of course, one simple example of plotting is time versus price versus any other variable one may wish. This is definitely an improvement over what currently exists but is not the punch we are looking for.

Jack Cohen and Ian Stewart's in *The Collapse of Chaos* wrote one of the best accounts of phase transitions I have ever read. With some modifications, I have paraphrased the excerpt on a wholesale basis here.

Imagine you are on a beach in Southampton, New York, and there are two ice cream sellers murmuring, "Ice, glacé, gelato" as they hawk the gourmet goods. On a beach a mile long, one would think that they would be at the one-quarter and three-quarters mile markers so no customer would have to walk more than a quarter of a mile to get ice cream. Instead, each eyes the other's customers and therefore moves a little more to the center to capture that business. Pretty soon both ice cream sellers are together at the half-mile marker competing for additional business. This example also explains why political parties, most notably in the United States, become more centrist.

It would be fairly easy to draw a map of these two fellows as they move about. What we are more interested in is to create a map of all the possible places they might be. We call this a map of *phase-space*. Each position these fellows can occupy is called a state in phase-space. A continuum of your dog's emotions may be thought of as a simplistic 2D version of a phase-space map. Those emotions range from violent to amorous but exist most of the time in the tail-wagging mode.

What is found in many maps of phase-space is that phenomena being measured typically exist in some discrete orbit or geometrical shape, just as most of the time you exist at home, at the office, or in transit between them. Viewed in phase-space, of all the possible places one could be all of the time, most of the time your peregrinations take on a fairly stable geometric shape.

One of the most famous maps of phase-space for weather looks like the number 8 turned on its side and creased in the middle. Lorenz discovered this in 1961. These orbits are called *strange attractors*. They are so named because the orbits were considered strange and the attractors reflected the fact that most phenomena exist within some bounded degree of variety called complexity.

Strange attractors will become the new method of viewing risk measurement because they are rich enough to capture the real dynamics of an investment. An investment that does not exceed its bounded variety for some period of time will be considered a safer or less risky investment than one that does. It is a tool with scientific origins that better depicts reality than the discredited linear statistic called volatility.

If the reader has perused any of the literature in the area of nonlinearity, no doubt he or she has seen the word *fractal* and wondered what the logical connection was between fractals and nonlinear concepts, such as chaos. The logical connection is that the strange attractor has a fractal dimension. All this says is that the geometry of the orbit is between a plane and a solid. The bounded variety has a noninteger dimension between two and three.

A more sophisticated answer is that as we begin to look at phenomena in 4D, we now have a more realistic geometry with which to articulate phenomena. Or, to use an analogous situation, we can see a picture in higher definition with a better lens. We can see the phenomenon in greater resolution or detail—better than mere rows and columns where one would never see orbits intuitively as geometric pictures. Fractal geometry is more intuitive and more detailed since more dimensions and thus more information are included.

BEFORE THERE WAS HURST'S EXPONENT, THERE WAS HURST'S EXPLETIVE.

HURST DEFINED

Named after the British dam builder and hydrologist H. E. Hurst
(1900–1978), who looked for patterns in the Nile River delta in 1930s, **H** is
a nonparametric statistic. That is, **H** does not make any assumptions about
what it is calculating. This flexibility is its ultimate strength but also a weakness if lots of computational horsepower is not readily available. Obviously
that is no longer the case. The reason that linear mathematics is not appropriate in financial economics is that the assumption of linearity inherent in
the calculation is incorrect.

Hurst's problem was simple. If he built the dam too high he would waste
resources; if he built it too low, the dam would not achieve its purpose.
Hurst began to wonder about the possibility of a relationship between annual rainfall and the level of the reservoir. Not only was Hurst concerned
with the relationship between rainfall and reservoir but between extremes of
high and low water as well. Fortunately, the Nile is an ancient area and had
records on papyrus going back almost a millennium. He transformed the
data into a number of segments and then examined the logarithmic range

and scale of each segment versus the number of segments. So-called rescaled range (R/S) analysis showed that the rate of rainfall was highly persistent. That is, it had the tendency to keep doing what it had been doing. In other words, it was partially predictable. Several other time series in nature were also found to be highly persistent because they did not scale evenly.

Uneven scaling is in direct contradiction to Einstein's 1900 scaling called Brownian motion which stated that the distance (R) a particle travels scales proportionately with the square root of time (t). Thus, with (m) as a constant:

$$R = m \, (t)^{0.5}$$

This concept would become the basis for power law scaling and the basis for the Black-Scholes option pricing model. In the 1960s Mandelbrot would change the exponent of 0.5 to reflect the reality of some time series found in nature, beginning with cotton prices in 1963. So:

$$(R/S)_n = (n \times \pi / 2 \,)^{0.5}$$

Mandelbrot named this the Hurst exponent (**H**) in honor of its founder. There are several ways to calculate **H**. The most traditional is R/S analysis, which is a nonparametric statistic produced from the following steps:

1. Transform a time series of length **N** into a new series of **N – 1** by taking the logarithm of each element divided by the previous element. For a series

   $$(a_1, a_2, a_3, \ldots a_n)$$

   create

   $$[\log (a_2 / a_1), \log (a_3 / a_2), \ldots \log (a_N / a_{N-1})]$$

   Call each new segment **b**. Call the length **n**, such that **n = N – 1**. The new series is:

   $$(b_1, b_2, b_3, \ldots b_n)$$

2. Divide this second series into contiguous segments **S**, each with length **c**, such that **S × c = n**.

   $$S^j = |\, S^1 = (b_1, b_2, b_3, \ldots b_c) \,|$$
   $$|\, S^2 = (b_1, b_2, b_3, \ldots b_{2 \times c}) \,| \; j = (1,2,3, \ldots n / c)$$

   where   S is the subseries
    s is an element in the subseries
    s^j_i = the ith element of jth subseries

3. Find the mean of each subseries **S**.

$$\text{avg } (S^j) = 1 / c \sum_{i=1}^{c} S^j_i$$

Create yet another series based on the divergence of each subseries from its mean, or

$$d^j_i = s^j_i - \text{avg } (S^j) \text{ with } c \text{ elements in each } \mathbf{d}.$$

4. Form a derived series of the accumulated divergences

$$x^j_i = \sum_{k=1}^{i} \text{ then } X^j = [d^j_1, (d^j_1 + d^j_2), (d^j_1 + d^j_2 + d^j_3 \ldots)]$$

5. Find the range of each subseries **d**.

$$R^j = {}_{max}X^j - {}_{min}X^j \text{ for each}$$

6. Calculate the standard deviation for each subseries.

$$\sigma = [1 / c - 1 \sum_{i=1}^{c} [(s^j_i - \text{avg } (S^j)]^2]^{0.5}$$

7. Divide each range of accumulated divergences by their standard deviation, find the R/S value for that subseries, then take the sum of all these R/S values and divide by **c**, the number of different subseries.

8. Plot the logarithm of R/S against the logarithm of the length of the subseries into which the original series has been divided for each run of steps 1 through 7.

Bloomberg returns this calculation to you over digital lines in roughly 1.75 seconds for any time series for which it has data. It is for this reason that I earlier said that the KAOS function depicting the Hurst exponent was very possibly Bloomberg's most computationally intensive screen. Although the concept of serial dependence is quite simple, the calculation as indicated above is a bit involved.

Further is the V statistic, which can detect the boundaries of an aperiodic cycle. An aperiodic cycle has no absolute frequency. We divide the R/S by the square root of the segment to obtain:

$$V = (R/S) / n^{0.5}$$

DENOMINATORS

The common denominator of the calendar, musical notation, the geometry of Euclid, and Brownian motion in financial economics is that they all superimpose an idealistic system of measurement on a messy reality. To wit, the calendar is 365 days long but the time cycle it measures is 365.25. The octave cannot be evenly divided between tones. Financial economics assumes that the movement of a time series is random when clearly it is not. It is no more appropriate to use a Brownian motion in financial economics than it is to use a plane to represent the topography of the Tetons. Euclidean geometry exists only in three well-defined dimensions.

There is also another point worth mentioning. In general, the various disciplines such as mathematics and science do not progress at an even rate. Mathematics does not work like a stonemason who methodically builds layer upon layer to create a wall. A more realistic physical picture would be that of a stonemason starting the frame of a drawbridge on one side of the castle, while someone on the other side has already built a wall to the second level. There is also specialization. One specializes in carving and another in creating stairwells. The skills are specialized enough that a worker in one discipline has little or no knowledge of what the other is doing, and the group meets only infrequently to renew a discussion on the blueprint in progress.

Further, because of the creative process, it is not uncommon to receive glimpses of how to build the second story before the understanding of the theory for the foundation is complete. Because of the individualized nature of progressing knowledge, the blueprint is only the vaguest of concepts. In fact, a blueprint usually emerges in the form of a survey article long after the castle of Babel becomes an identifiable structure. Fractals are sort of this way. Perhaps fractals are analogous to string theory in physics, which has been called a bit of 21st-century science that was accidentally discovered in the 20th-century. This may seem like an odd comment but it is important because fractals are only a part of a broader mathematical expression of non-linearity in the world.

Nevertheless, a working definition of fractals exists. In a practical sense, fractals are a *property*, just like mass, charge, and spin are physical properties. The difference is that fractals are not a fundamental physical property. This comment is prompted by a videotape I once saw where the narrator pointed to a financial economics time series and said, "Here is a fractal." That statement is incorrect: rather, all time series in financial economics *exhibit fracticality*. A straight line is not typically fractal, but then, neither is it representative of a time series in financial economics. Similarly, no physicist would listen to you for very long if you pointed to an object and said, "Here is a mass." Table 4.1 may help to clarify the relationship between the physical and temporal dimensions.

A physical example of fractals and a good parlor trick is the following question: "Is the length of England's coastline finite or infinite?" Be careful. One is tempted to say finite, because England could be bounded by a big but finite square. The real answer is that England's coastline is infinite, because

Table 4.1 Physical versus Temporal Dimensions

Physical Dimension	Temporal Dimension
Wadded-up piece of paper	Minute
Fern	Day
Snowflake	Week
Mammalian lung	Month

it depends on the length of your ruler. A yardstick will capture more nuances and thus more length than a mile-stick, an inch-stick will capture more than a yardstick, and so on ad infinitum.

Obviously the coastline is fractal because it scales. A two hundred meter segment is just as jagged as a two-millimeter segment. It also has a noninteger dimension, because the degree to which the coastline is jagged means that it is more than a line and less than a plane. And the jaggedness grows finer with the sensitivity of the ruler.

In the previous physical examples we illustrated objects with dimensions between 2D and 3D and a coastline between 1D and 2D. We now show another example between 1D and 2D, but we transfer from the physical to the temporal dimension.

We address time series. A time series is jagged like a coastline and its fractal dimension can be measured. The basic relationship between a Euclidean dimension and **H** is:

$$D = 2 - \mathbf{H}$$

where $D = 2 - \mathbf{H}$
$\mathbf{H}$ = Hurst exponent

There is also a relationship between **H** and $1/f$ fractional noises. It is:

$$b = 2 * \mathbf{H} + 1$$

where b = spectral exponent
$\mathbf{H}$ = Hurst exponent

The relationships between fractal dimensions, the Hurst exponent, and fractional noises are given in Table 4.2.

A little cogitating here will help. A perfectly persistent time series is a straight line or 1D. A perfectly antipersistent time series, which is always reversing itself, is a plane or 2D, and a Brownian motion or random time

Table 4.2 Fractal Dimensions, Hurst Exponents, and Fractional Noises

Times Series	Fractal Dimension	Hurst Exponent	Fractional Noise
Persistent	ID—line	1.0	Yes
Random	1.5D—Brownian motion	0.5	No
Antipersistent	2D—plane	0.0	Yes

series has a dimension of 1.5D—perfectly equidistant between a plane and a line.

Now thinking geometrically, which is easier to predict, a straight line or a plane? If you guessed a straight line you are probably correct, and the mathematics of non-Gaussian distributions will bear you out. A highly persistent time series is and should be less risky. It should be priced as such. For a persistent time series, an option or a swap which is priced assuming randomness results in the seller undercharging for risk for far-out- or far-in-the-money strikes because there is a fat tail and thus a higher incidence of a large-magnitude movement than the normal distribution implies. Conversely, the buyer is overcharged where the curve of the normal distribution exceeds the empirical distribution's curve. This strike is typically + or − 10% to 15% of the current market price.

Detecting mispricing for antipersistent time series is more difficult to prove since that body of math has not been invented yet. Fortunately, time series given sufficient duration in financial economics are persistent almost always.

One of the interesting thoughts with direct risk management ramifications is continuously and maximally antipersistent time series. The everyday example is "double or nothing" since a maximally antipersistent time series always reverts in the extreme. If the risk is always double or nothing, then won't that be appropriately discounted? Since if it is always that way, it is not that risky. True, it may be more volatile, but is it more risky? This seemingly obscure example suggests that maximal risk is found at $H = 0.5$ since there is no characterization possible other than random, and brings into question the idea of volatility or the concept of a time series bouncing up and down vis-à-vis itself as a proxy, for total risk. It is a poor proxy, but if it is to be continually used then the change in volatility may be a more relevant partial measure, since it is the unexpected change that is considered risky. Assuming independence, the expected return over time of double or nothing must be unity. With dependence, however, we see that volatility does cluster and that more sophisticated nonlinear techniques must be used.

SELF-SIMILARITY

Time series exhibit statistical self-similarity (i.e., viewed without labels, minute-by-minute, hourly, daily, weekly, etc., time series look like each other). An important aspect of this fact is that time series in financial economics tend to have no characteristic scale. And if they have no characteristic scale, then as Mandelbrot said, "A process that has no scale has the scale of the observer." The upshot is that it is meaningless to speak of an investment in terms of nonlinear pricing without also stating a corresponding investment horizon. This is why we mentioned earlier that the assumption of a Brownian motion fails in discerning any investment horizon or degree of temporal resolution. Scaling is a powerful tool, but as Peters notes in *Fractal Market Analysis*, small variations can and do occur depending on the size of data included in the sample. The issue is analogous to volatility in the sense that it makes a difference whether the sample is taken weekly and multiplied by 52 to annualize it, or monthly and multiplied by 12, or if the entire period is used.

The concept of differentiated perception is intuitive in financial economics or there would be no reason to ever sell or buy. Unfortunately, stating an investment horizon in other than the vaguest of terms has not been a strong point for many investors. Reasons may often have more to do with tax consequences or portfolio decisions than the investments themselves. The issue of timing is also mitigated since most financial institutions structure part of their employees' compensation based on amount of assets gathered. The age-old problem of sell-side analysts issuing stock recommendations in gradations of desirability to buy rather than to sell is also noted.

Thus, the imposition of a highly idealized Euclidean geometry upon a messy reality on the verge of the 21st century seems a bit anemic. From the point of view of human nature, though, it is all too understandable to attempt to express the unknown with familiar tools. As practitioners, our task is not to perfect a coherent theory but to profitably exploit inefficiencies when and where they exist.

NOISES AND POWER LAWS

Power laws are ubiquitous in financial economics and in nature. A power law describes a phenomenon by expressing it as a number raised to some power—what one usually sees is a straight line on a chart of, say, the frequency and magnitude of an earthquake. An earthquake that is 10 times more powerful is 10 times less likely to happen. This is the Gütenberg-Richter Law. There is Zipf's law for the frequency of words in English and other assorted examples. Krugman in *The Self-Organizing Economy* cites Herbert Simon, who suggested that the size of U.S. cities approximates a power law. In *How Nature Works*, physicist Per Bak showed that the avalanches in his sandpile were power law distributed.

More technically, the *power spectra* is the squared magnitude of the Fourier transform, which are expressed as homogenous power laws in the form $f^{-\beta}$ as a function of frequency f and where ß ranges from 0 to 4. It is called a law because the power expression is almost always true over all scales. A spectral exponent of zero is white noise (named after white light) and has a constant power spectrum. Integrated over time, white noise becomes brown noise (after Brownian motion) where $\beta = 2$.

Pink noise, also called $1/f$ noise, is widely found in nature and has an exponent of $\beta = 1$. Manfred Schroeder posits one reason for pink noise's ubiquity is "their genesis through parallel relaxation processes." The example Schroeder gives in *Fractals, Chaos and Power Laws* is one of an electron in an excited state trapped in a semiconductor "where it remains for an exponentially distributed time interval with relaxation time interval τ." More important for our purposes is the concept of multiple relaxation processes. Think of the four phases of a heartbeat or any other biological process that expands and contracts. Mandelbrot also wrote about this in *The Fractal Geometry of Nature*. After a large run-up the market, often it will be down the next day. Reporters write something to the effect that "the market paused to catch its breath." Mathematically this is an aperiodic cycle. $1/f$ noises are not considered to be a common part of the financial economics literature, but they are prevalent in nature, especially in acoustics. The link from acoustics to financial economics is simple; they are both seen generically as time series processes.

Markets are characterized by black noise processes where $\beta = 3$, because events such as disasters come in clusters like volatility does. Schroeder cites a very interesting quote from A. Barclay's 1509 translation of *The Ship of Fools* that "Wyse men sayeth . . . that one myshap fortuneth never alone." The contemporary version is, of course, when it rains, it pours. It is because of this clustering that Mandelbrot coined the terms the Noah and the Joseph effects, named after the biblical accounts of the Flood and the seven fat and seven lean cows, respectively. The Noah effect refers to wide-ranging phenomena like floods and market crashes or the infinite variance syndrome. The Joseph effect is, of course, serial dependence and a black noise process, which describe the tendency to cluster, as is the case with volatility or personal wealth.

In fact, nearly 100 years ago the Italian economist Vilfredo Pareto (1848–1923), working in Switzerland, found that the number of people whose personal incomes exceeded a large value follows a simple power law.

Pareto created a distribution to describe this phenomenon, variously called the Pareto, Pareto-Lévy, stable, and most recently, the fractal distribution. Later, Herbert A. Simon, the 1978 Nobel laureate in economics, in 1995 would write *On a Class of Skew Distribution Functions*, which noted the prevalence of power laws in economics. Other examples of power laws in economics and the fallacies of trading schemes based on them are discussed by Mandelbrot [1963a, b]. Power laws are also interesting for a more important reason: They are thought to be strongly indicative of nonequilibrium systems and thus self-organization, as mentioned repeatedly in Kauffman's *In Search of Complexity*. In other words, power laws are a necessary though not sufficient condition for complexity.

Table 4.3 illustrates the corresponding distributions, noise and power laws, and names of motions. Mathematically the terms noise and motion are interchangeable; however, their usage has evolved differently. It is entirely correct though stilted to refer to Brownian motion as Brownian noise. The terms come from various fields but are interrelated. The best explanation comes from Schroeder's witty and insightful *Chaos, Fractals and Power Laws*.

THE MATH

The most mathematically rigorous explanations of Table 4.4 come from *A Practical Guide to Heavy Tails* edited by Adler, Feldman, and Taqqu, and Samorodnitski and Taqqu's *Stable Non-Gaussian Random Process*. In looking at the matrix of independence and dependence and possibilities of distributions we find the relationships shown in Table 4.4.

Table 4.3 Distributions, Noises, Power Laws, and Names of Motion

Distribution	Noise and Power Law	Name of Motion
	White f^{-0} Independent of frequency Pink f^{-1}	
Normal Mean—finite Variance—finite	Brown f^{-2} Dependent on frequency	Brownian motion
Stable Mean—finite Variance—infinite	Black f^{-3}	Fractional Brownian motion
Cauchy Mean—infinite Variance—infinite		

Table 4.4   Distributions and Assumptions in Time

Assumption in Time	Distribution	
	Gaussian	*Fat Tails (Stable)*
Independence	I CAPM, EMH, Black-Scholes	II α-Levy
Dependence	III fBrownian motion	IV fStable motion

Quadrant I

This is the traditional state of affairs, where iid (independent and identically distributed) variables are assumed, the math fits neatly together, and life is good. The body of research is several hundred years old, so many of the properties are well known. There is a relationship between frequency and distribution. And, in fact, the limit of a Brownian motion is a Gaussian distribution. From fast Fourier transforms, the easiest way to visualize this is the pendulum of a grandfather clock. The tick-tock-tick is both a frequency and a distribution. The relationship between the two is that the inverse of the Fourier transform is the characteristic function of a distribution. While the moment-generating function may only sometimes exist, the characteristic function always exists.

Once we acknowledge **H** is < or > 0.5, the notion of Brownian motion and the mathematical equivalent of a linear Garden of Eden is dead. However, by itself **H** is not a strong enough statistic to prove a priori whether we should be in Quadrant II, III, or IV. It is, however, clearly strong enough to knock us out of Quadrant I and, it is hoped, out of historical complacency. It is for this reason that earlier I made the claim that randomness is dead. At this point the judgment about distributions comes into play. It does not seem to be very difficult.

Again one may wonder why we have persisted so long in Quadrant I when clearly we should be looking somewhere else. Perhaps collectively, we are like the drunk who loses his keys.

The policeman asks, "Where did you lose them?"

The drunk replies, "Over there."

"Then, why are you looking under the streetlamp?"

"Because," the drunk replies, "that is where the light is."

Maybe all the research behind linearity and iid is analogous to the light, even though the solution to our problem lies outside its illuminating beam of knowledge. Perhaps it is only our turn in the history of science to expand the beam of knowledge.

The number of distributions is infinite. Change a point of the data and the distribution changes too. Of all possible distributions, only a few have names and of those few that have names, only a few have had their properties extensively documented. Oversimplification of this sort—assuming Gaussian returns when clearly they are not, or Brownian motion when clearly it is not—has its place in three separate instances: (1) when the technology to measure other than assumed mathematical properties does not exist, (2) when the technology exists but is not cost-effective, or (3) for teaching introductory-level students. The practical question is not what is the real distribution, but rather what distribution best approximates the reality being modeled?

Quadrant II

Peters [1994, 1996] gave a good treatment of the relationship between Lévy-stable or α-stable distributions and a financial economics time series, which links the shape of the distribution and the time series. The concept of linking distribution shape to time series is analogous to the relationship between a Brownian motion and Gaussian distribution and is *very* important. The relationship is:

$$\mathbf{H} = 1 / \alpha$$

where $\mathbf{H}$ = Hurst exponent
α = shape of an α-stable distribution

Obviously, when $\mathbf{H} = 0.5$, $\alpha = 2$ and a Brownian motion and a normal distribution are mathematically linked. However, when $\mathbf{H} > 0.5$, $\alpha < 2$ then fat tails emerge. Most time series in financial economics over a sufficiently long duration approach $\mathbf{H} = 0.6$.

Independence with coin tossing is a concept that you learned in junior high statistics—maybe in the classroom, maybe behind the schoolhouse. Coin tossings are independent, because the first tossing has no effect on the second tossing. One may consider the stock market independent *if* the day the after the market crashes your client is *indifferent* to buying or selling. In all probability this will not be the case.

Not surprisingly, in terms of available material Quadrant II follows Quadrant I. The suspect reason is the preservation of the assumption of independence.

Quadrant III

Quadrants III and IV are less well developed. Since we know that distributions in financial economics are not Gaussian there does not seem to be much applicability for the intersection of fractional Brownian motion and Gaussian distributions.

Quadrant IV

Fractional stable motion is the least developed area. Heavy or fat tails and dependence are the most correct paradigm for three reasons: One, because as we have already seen via H, dependence or serial correlation exists. Yesterday affects today. Two, because as we have seen from Fama [1964], Mandelbrot [1965, 1997], Peters [1994, 1996], Lo and Mackinlay [1988], and from all the evidence of volatility "smiles" and clustering that fat or heavy tails exist. Three, and the least provable reason is, because this is what my instincts lead me to conclude after all my research and a decade's worth of experience as a practitioner.

Collateral research was also done by Peter Clark at the University of California at Davis, whose PhD thesis we mentioned earlier. In a phone conversation on October 19, 1997, with Clark, he mentioned that clearly dependence and fat tails were established. This places him squarely in Quadrant IV but with a slightly different methodology. He maintains that variance is finite but varies with time. It sort of expands and contracts accordion-style. This is not an unreasonable assumption, as the tails do not go to zero as the number of days increase.

Clark says the variance is not infinite but finite and that if we make variance a variable we can achieve the same effect. In addition, he claims that as the number of days get shorter, whereas the zero variance is incorrect, varying variance seems to create fat tails during short time periods. Clark is clearly a very forward-thinking researcher and maintains the notion of fat tails and serial correlation or dependence. The only problem, of course, is that none of the methods that create fat tails can also deal with persistence or $H > 0.5$.

CAPITAL USAGE

As a practical matter, Schroeder illustrates two questions with which nonlinear math may help us—risk management and capital usage. How does one maximize the expected rate of increase on one's capital knowing that the

chances of winning, p, are better than even ($p > 0.5$)? How much of one's
capital should one risk for each spin of the wheel? The answer comes from
information theory, in fact, one of its earliest applications to gambling. In a
landmark paper John Kelly, Jr., proved that in order to maximize the rate of
increase of one's capital, one should bet the fraction $2p - 1$ of the current
capital. And of course, for $p \leq 0.5$ one should abstain completely and find
another pastime. The expected exponential growth of one's capital is then
given by the factor $2^{C(p)}$, where $C(p)$ is Shannon's channel capacity of a binary symmetric with error probability p.

$$C(p) = 1 + p \log_2 p + (1 - p) \log_2 (1 - p)$$

Thus, for $p = 0.55$, for example, one should risk $2p - 1$ or 10% of one's capital for every spin and expect a rate of enrichment of $2^{C(0.55)} = 0.005$ or 0.5%
with each spin (read: trade).

Most people, including financial economics professionals, use the word
"probability" colloquially rather than in its precise mathematical sense. As
Holland said, most of our tools for measuring probability assume independence and is therefore almost always the wrong concept in the precise
sense of the term. What most people really mean when they say probability
in financial economics is degree of membership function, which we will
address in Chapter 6 dealing with fuzzy logic. Probability and **H** are identical only at **H** = 0.5. However, since most of the small movements are
bunched about the center of the distribution, it may be a useful rule of
thumb to work with more confidence in **H** = 0.55 for probability than **H** =
0.7. The higher **H** gets, the more likely it is to occur than as predicted by
the normal distribution.

RISK MEASUREMENT

I am about to take JP Morgan to task. However, to their credit I note two
things. First, they are not alone—not by any means. The name of any commercial or investment bank, public or private pension fund, money management firm, consultancy, accounting or law firm, foreign or domestic
would have sufficed. The only difference is RiskMetrics™ has made Morgan a prominent example. Second, the issuance of a risk-measurement
standard was a generally positive development in financial economics in
that creating a standard is smart in the information age since standards are a
winner-take-most market. Unfortunately, though, Morgan's standard is
wrong. The standard is, of course, by definition generally accepted. But
then so was the horse and buggy until the automobile came to dominate the

roads. Being generally accepted though is distinct from being mathematically accurate. Morgan's calculations are no doubt precise, but the question is, how well do those calculations refer to reality? This is what determines whether they are accurate. We saw the same concept from Einstein in Chapter 1: "So far as the laws of mathematics refer to reality, they are not certain. And so far as they are certain, they do not refer to reality." Specifically, we see a certain linear construct that does not accurately refer to a nonlinear reality.

The further the distribution is from $\alpha = 2$, the less diversification works. Diversification as it is currently measured by Morgan's RiskMetrics™ and almost everyone else's methodology for that matter assumes that $\alpha = 2$. This would be a correct assumption if the returns followed a Gaussian distribution and $H = 0.5$ or a Brownian motion. Clearly this is not so. However, on page 15, section 2.0, entitled "Statistical Assumptions," of the *Technical Document* of October 1994, Morgan states, "We assume that prices of financial instruments follow a stable random walk and their changes can therefore be approximated by a normal distribution." Clearly they are still squarely in Quadrant I. However, section 2.1 is entitled "Are changes normally distributed?" How curious! After they tell us what they do in section 2.0 according to one method, they ask in section 2.1 if assumptions used in section 2.0 are so. How can this be?

Section 2.1 begins, "How reasonable is the hypothesis of normality? The debate on the exact distribution in securities prices is certainly not closed. . . . Over the last few years, a number of studies have questioned the representation of financial markets as a random walk. Tests of normality have been performed on various sets of financial instruments from equities to bonds. Most of them conclude that:

- Return distributions have **fat tails** (there are more occurrences far away from the mean than predicted by a standard normal distribution called kurtosis).

- The **peak around the mean** is higher than predicted by a normal distribution (it is a condition called leptokurtosis)

- Asset returns are often **negatively skewed** (there are more observations in the left-hand tail than in the right-hand tail)."

There you have it, quoted directly from Morgan's document. Now, either returns are normally distributed or they are not, and a time series in financial economics may be most accurately portrayed by a Brownian motion or it cannot. Equity time series tend towards $H = 0.6$, which results in an α of 1.67, obviously less than 2.0 or normal. There is a difference between what is currently accepted and what is correct. The conclusion is clear. Risk is *un-*

derstated when the Gaussian distribution is assumed because in fact the tails are fatter that they are assumed to be. The practical effect is diminished for smaller movements than for larger ones. The same is true for hedging. But this is precisely where we want risk management to work most.

The applicability of normal distribution to something that is not normally distributed is incomprehensible to the hard scientist, since the overwhelming amount of evidence and explanations support a different conclusion. But perhaps the hard science view ignores the peculiar sociology of financial economics.

We have said earlier that belief does play a role in financial economics because it is self-referential. To be "correct" one has to guess what everyone else will be guessing. Sometimes this self-referential analysis can, as Soros has noted in his theory of reflexivity, change the underlying fundamentals. However, no amount of belief can make a market conform to an arbitrary mathematical notion like a normal distribution or a Brownian motion. The market is what it is. Unlike opining on the desirability of a certain stock as an investment, the mathematical characterization of the returns of a financial market has a unique solution for a given point in time. One answer is correct. The market returns are either normally distributed or they are not. The choices are mutually exclusive.

The research refuting the randomness of time series in financial economics is all throughout this book but begins with Mandelbrot and Fama in the early 1960s. If more financial economics professionals were aware of the argument, one would like to believe that their response would not be so muted. Of course, the realpolitik argument may be invoked. No one cares if a bank believes the moon is made of green cheese, only what is the angle from which to profit? The answer, of course, is that mismeasurement creates a spread between assumption and reality. Given the self-referential process in financial economics, in a certain perverse sense it is good that false beliefs are perpetuated, since it allows others with better information to profit from them. Some dupe has to be the other side of the trade.

To the extent that establishment firms take the attitude, with respect to keeping their old linear beliefs that "What is good for General Motors is good for America," others will profit. There is also a large-firm dynamic at work. However obvious it may seem to the interested observer, it will be no more trivial for a major player in financial economics to change and institute nonlinear pricing than it will be for GM to someday build a high-quality small car. Bureaucratic inertia in the form of myopic decisions from thousands of touchy timeservers will ensure that. The evidence is pretty damning. Were this trend not true, then the previous decade would not have seen millions of Japanese imports flood American roads.

LEGAL DIMENSIONS

There are also legal dimensions. When the facts changed, Keynes changed his mind. If most financial institutions change, they will have to admit in effect that they were wrong. And if they were wrong, there is a potential for liability. Unfortunately though, the research predates the issuance of RiskMetrics™ by about 30 years. There is a wonderfully circular argument I once heard a restructuring specialist ask management in a public meeting about the sale of the corporate aircraft. It went, "Why did you sell the airplane if we needed it?" And, "If we didn't need it, why did you buy it in the first place?" It was a catch-22. A similar argument will keep large firms from changing their risk management beliefs. First, there is a lot of money sunk into legacy software. Second, if a client incurs losses because assumptions are changed and the client does not understand them, what is the legal argument? Ours is an increasingly litigious society. Ten years ago, the defendant probably would have prevailed, but today?

The defense will argue that the Gaussian distribution is the accepted standard. But enough respected dissenters have emerged to cause any jury to question the accepted ways. At the end of the day, everyone one will be arguing math, with the prosecution showing a picture of the normal distribution superimposed on a stable distribution. Now here is a big bank pushing a linear standard that clearly is not so and the jury knows that this was known over 30 years ago. What is the jury supposed to think?

Other than caveat emptor, perhaps a general warning should be issued: *Technology is challenging our beliefs.* Truth in advertising may demand this but your marketing department won't like it. As nonlinear pricing becomes better known it will emerge as a competing standard for the same reason that imported Japanese cars exist.

As we have mentioned, $\mathbf{H}$ is a paradox because it is a scaling factor in both a temporal *and* a physical dimension. Thus, the greater $\mathbf{H}$ is, the faster it scales in time and the closer it is geometrically to a line. Conversely, the lower $\mathbf{H}$ is, the slower it diffuses and the more it geometrically resembles a plane.

REGULATORY ISSUES

There are wider issues at stake, however. Capital adequacy for commercial banks was agreed to in the 1988 Basel Accord, which "called for banks to retain capital equal to 8% or more of the 'risk-weighted' assets (i.e., loans)" as the *Economist* in "The Real Risk in Banking" of February 28, 1998, tells us. The article goes on to say, "Most regulators agree that change is needed. What form should it take? A good alternative is coming from banks themselves. Many already measure risk using their own formula, far more refined than the Basel rules. Banks such as JP Morgan and Credit Suisse have built and published sophisticated computer models which show the maximum likely loss on portfolios of many different loans." There is a difference of course between credit risk, which is much harder to model, and portfolio risk. The real and overriding question though is: To what extent do the models resemble reality?

Another article, entitled "Model Behavior," in the same issue of the *Economist*, ends with "The models are clever, all right. But how much relation they bear to reality may not be clear until after the next recession." Not to confuse credit with portfolio models, but the issue of mathematical relevance to reality stands tall. If the relevance does not exist, then the mathematical constructs are gratuitous.

TIMING

Thus, with multifracticality we can see different perspectives in time. Stocks scale at different rates. No longer is the view of growth or rate of change in time constant as it is with randomness or Brownian motion. In fact, if the financial markets were accurately represented by Brownian motion as just discussed with information theory, there would be no advantage. Now we see why our assumption about time is so important. We used to believe in physics that in the universe one grand Newtonian clock beats at the same rate for all observers, and in financial economics that all participants are rational and possess perfect information. This restrictive assumption has been relaxed somewhat in the "weak form" efficient model but not for time. To make demonstrable progress in risk management it must be. The assumption of a uniform time for all instruments must be allowed to float like an exchange rate. Time must be allowed to be thought of and measured according to the dictates of what is being measured rather than from the abstraction of a clock hanging on the wall, or clock time.

Clearly, a uniform viewpoint of the world and a uniform diffusion rate are not consistent with reality. As a result, no linear formula(s) can yield a priori results. With multiple viewpoints in time, the most efficient way to sort through all the variables is to evolve one's way through them for the simple reason that the aggregate effect of all those multiple viewpoints, what we call the market, is a moving target in time. That a linear ideal is assumed is no surprise; but reality is not a simple beast.

THE INFORMATION ERA

It is no more possible to separate nonlinear pricing as a thing detached off by itself from the cyberspace in which it occurs than it is to discuss grape growing without talking about the farm. They are inextricably linked—application and technology that makes the application possible. It is for this reason that this chapter is a mélange of environment and phenomena. We may approach the late Marshall McLuhan's view that "the medium is the message," if we work hard enough to understand the message—nonlinearity—and the medium—cyberspace. To do this we have to look at several fields simultaneously: good old stocks and bonds, the portfolio theory of the 1970s, some advanced mathematics, and, of course, the rise of the digital era, that makes nonlinear pricing an instant reality.

On 22 October 1998 Lou Gerstner, chairman and CEO of IBM on CNBC, declared "the era of the PC is over." In 1992, roughly speaking, we entered the networking (i.e., Internet and intranet) phase, which really blossomed in 1995. In the latter part of the networking phase, multimedia—3D and sound, in the form of mass entertainment—will become necessary as semiconductor makers seek to ensure that the market can financially justify the need for ever faster chips. In a broad sense the network era in financial economics is not yet over. E-commerce is still just getting going with such firms as www.amazon.com for books and www.cdnow.com for compact disks (CDs) leading the way in general retail. Stock trading on-line is beginning to grow. Proxies can be voted on www.proxyvote.com. Instanet, the private Reuters-based service for passive stock trading is growing and fixed-income services are being investigated. OptiMark comes on line in late 1998. Wit Capital offers initial public offerings on-line. On-line financial economics is maturing, as the promulgation of rules on January 13, 1998, by the Securities and Exchange Commission clearly indicates. There is also another application brewing that will be ripe for nonlinear pricing, the regulation of markets themselves. I refer specifically to the over-the-counter or dealer market, better known as NASDAQ (National Association of Securities Dealers Automated Quotations system, which has recently merged with the American Stock Exchange. The heart of the problem lies in the transparency of markets and the perceived fairness that must be self-evident to individual investors. In an auction market like the New York Stock Exchange, a privileged participant is the specialist. Specialists are privileged with knowing buy and sell orders that are not transparent to the market. However, their role is identified and their monopoly regulated. With dealers listing quotes on a screen, the process is less clear-cut because they can act as both agent and principal. The SEC has never been completely comfortable with this fact. Using nonlinear pricing in a quasi-regulatory role is unusual in that it is neither profit producing nor risk management *per se*, but the technologies are certainly flexible enough. The result is a cleaner market, the preservation of transparency, and the goodwill of the individual investor, which is the political Holy Grail of the SEC.

One of the more humorous asides of the NASD-ASE merger was a general lamentation from floor brokers that (cheaper) electronic trading put them at a disadvantage, which of course it does. They justified their higher commissions by insisting that the value they added was almost impossible to quantify. No doubt the political clout to preserve their jobs will exist for some time, but I remember musing to myself, "Sweetheart, you are a floor broker and this is Wall Street. Justify your place at the trough in terms of dollars and cents, or get ready to join the dodo birds." As an example, look at London International Financial Futures Exchange, London's bricks-and-mortar futures exchange, which boasted a 70% market share in German government bond futures. The Germans responded with an all-electronic version called Deutsch Termin Bourse which is cheaper, better, and faster. Now the guys at the Chicago Mercantile Exchange and Chicago Board Options Exchange (CBOE) see the handwriting on the wall. Equity in the form of member-owned exchanges is in the crosshairs of progress. The new world order does not include them.

Now that we have done away with brokers, ask yourself: With systems like Deutsche Bank's Autobahn that allow you to make a market at different levels and split spreads, why support a sales force? Clients only want execution, anyway. In a nonequilibrium world that is probabilistically governed, how much value can a sales force in the form of sports-knowledgeable guys with a wicked sense of humor and girls who are attractive and agreeable add? Conversely, a client will pay for superior analytics in the form of nonlinear simulation because the client knows that partial predictability exists.

Technology is driven by consumer acceptance, which is being driven by a younger, more computer-literate clientele. Moreover, in financial economics, reductions of cost will continue to mandate further automation. It now costs a bank roughly a penny to process a paper check and only one one-hundredth of a cent to process it electronicly. WebTV, low-cost (now $700) "thin clients," and the second-generation Internet that is currently being studied under an initiative of a consortium of universities, will speed the acceptance of the networking phase. Probably the single biggest barrier to the Internet is the telephone companies. Regulation has resulted in a culture driven more by politics than by market forces and has left them unable to respond quickly, if at all, with new products and services as the labored birth of Integrated Services Digital Network attests. This is in stark contrast to the

Ayn Randian, American-capitalist, super-dynamism of Silicon Valley. The real question is: Can Silicon Valley and the information age afford to continue to let the telephone companies be backward?

At some point, the novelty of networking, will also become passé, probably by 2001 when either asynchronous digital subscriber lines (ADSL) and/or cable modems are established and home appliances become smart. Even now, the Next Generation Internet Initiative is growing at www.ccic.gov. Wireless communications will be established and computer-to-computer traffic will have surpassed voice traffic in about 2003. By then, in Intel time, the latest version of their flagship processor, the 450 MHz Pentium II at the time of this writing, will have taken over networking, modem, video, and graphics acceleration. State-of-the-art processing for the "Wintel" standard will have moved from 32-bit to 64-bit, with the 1 GHz chip code named Merced. Although 64-bit processing is already available in the UNIX world, Intel is the standard used here because it better represents the mass market. In terms of development and adaptation, the networking period is shorter than the PC period. A fact of technological progress is the general trend to shorter rather than longer product cycles. What then?

ADAPTIVE PROCESSES OR INTELLIGENT NETWORKS

We will enter the era of the adaptive process. That's what. Legions of intelligently networked computers will monitor a general class of processes called adaptive processes, of which nonlinear pricing is but a financial-economic application. An adaptive process is any process that changes with time and which needs to be simulated in as close to real-time as practicable and whose results must be graphically displayed. Financial economics is not the only commercial application; airlines and health care management are also data-intensive, but financial economics is a whale of an application and one that is ready for harpooning. Risk management simulations could be run, giving the firm an up-to-the-minute view. Plausibility scenarios could be run. Although these simulations are run now, they are built on linear assumptions and thus subject to much improvement.

Assuming that we have not impinged on physical boundaries like the "point one" barrier, where a single electron is impeded from navigating a substrate, chip speeds will continue to double. Legions of networks will begin to monitor in real-time processes where time is a dependent variable. No longer will we assume that a time series is always random. We now are able to measure it.

BOTS

Bots are a prime example of an adaptive process. As Andrew Leonard tells us in *Bots: The Origin of New Species*, bots are software robots that pervade the Internet. The mention of bots in a financial-economic treatise is important for a couple of reasons. First, as a cutting-edge piece of technology, bots occupy a high-level status in the creations of man because they have been endowed with autonomy, however limited. Autonomy is the ability to do certain tasks with a minimum of initial direction. The best search engine on the Net is Digital's AltaVista. The bot behind it is Scooter. Bots take on aspects of their creators and so there are good guys and bad buys. Scooter is the model Netizen, but an underworld exists. The behavior ranges from annoying but not harmful to outright thievery and destruction. If the object of war is to destroy your enemy's ability to wage it, then along with computer viruses, one would be surprised if the Department of Defense has not given some consideration to potential destruction wrought by warrior bots. After all, mechanical robots are already used for clearing minefields.

Second, as financial economics moves on-line, bots will move into financial economics. Bots exist in limited senses such as Bloomberg's equity search function (ESRC). ESRC can be set up to run automatically every night. However, ESRC cannot modify its own search; if the evolution of bots is any indication, ESRC soon will. The application is obvious. A money manager requests a response to some set of conditions to be continuously returned to him or her; since the objective is always the same—profit over some investment horizon—we must let the set of conditions that give rise to that profit change with the market. The trade-off in cost is that the money management firm will need traders and analysts with better skills but the firm will need fewer of them.

The rudiments of the adaptive processes phase already exist—thousands of interconnected computers and largely autonomous bots. The degree of autonomy will grow. Soon bots will be able to modify their own search in progress. This is an important concept in nonlinear pricing. Dynamic hedging, index arbitrage, or any aspect that is time-dependent already requires a response time quicker than what any human is capable of. The adaptive agents of nonlinear pricing are fuzzy logic and genetic algorithms, which experience data and adapt their way through to the preferred region of solution-space. Since the preferred region in solution-space is continuously changing with the market, the adaptive process must be continuous as well.

The essence of the adaptive processes phase is a mission control–style setup where some live process is continuously monitored and "adaptations" or nonlinear solutions are continuously given. This definition obviously goes far beyond financial economics. In financial economics monitoring is already extant in the sense that the trading floor exists. What has not been matched with those live data-feeds is a continuous real-time nonlinear solution.

If you do not consider yourself one of the digerati, Nicholas Negroponte's *Being Digital* and Esther Dysan's *Release 2.0* are probably the best general primers for life in the digital age. Kevin Kelly's *Out of Control: The Rise of Neo-Biological Civilization* is also a good read. As Lee Smolin suggests in *The Life of the Cosmos*, biology is the metaphor that may lead us to new breakthroughs. Kelly suggests this with computing in the 21st century. *Out of Control* weaves a rich tapestry of vignettes, which range from gladiator robots to modeling the nonlinear behavior of the animal world. It will be the rise of neobiological thinking coupled with the immense power of massively paralleled processors in supercomputers that will propel the qualitative change to adaptive processes to new heights. Will we have to wait long? No. It is already being done.

If the adaptive processes phase sounds too abstract, ethereal, and surreal, remember the next time you call DHL to locate your package the "voice" you hear belongs to a bot.

WHEN THE CHIPS ARE UP

Microchip producers, primarily Intel, regularly make multibillion-dollar bets by building manufacturing plants called fabs, with the philosophy that the movie *Field of Dreams* made famous, "Build it and they will come"— not exactly the budgeting rationale of most of corporate America (which suggests that we identify a market and fill an already existing need) but one that is feasible in the high-tech business because of the "hockey stick" graphs of increasing performance.

Looking at Table 4.5, one may recollect that doubling games are very uninteresting for the first 25% of their existence. But after that, look out! One may recall the apocryphal story of the emperor who granted a favored subject one wish. The subject asked for a grain of gold to be placed on the first square of a chessboard and doubled every square thereafter. A penny on the first square is $92,000,000 billion on the last. The emperor quickly figured out that he had been duped!

What most people do not perceive in viewing the table is that somewhere along the hockey stick there is a *qualitative* change as well. That is, we do not continue merely doing the old process or inquiry twice as fast; we make a qualitative change in the nature of the question asked and begin doing a new and different kind of process or inquiry. Every 18 months or so, according to Moore's Law, a successive generation of chips radically skews—in

Table 4.5   History of Intel's x86 Processor

Intel Chip	Date	Initial Cost	Transistors	Initial MIPS
4004	11/71	$ 200	2,300	0.06
8008	4/72	300	3,500	0.06
8080	4/74	300	6,000	0.6
8088	6/79	360	29,000	0.3
PC PHASE BEGINS				
i286	2/82	360	134,000	0.9
i386	10/85	299	275,000	5.0
i486	4/89	950	1,200,000	20.0
NETWORKING PHASE BEGINS				
Pentium	3/93	878	3,100,000	100.0
Pentium Pro	3/95	974	5,500,000	300.0
Pentium II	5/97	750	7,500,000	400.0
786* (Merced)	1998	1,000	8,500,000	500.0
ADAPTIVE PROCESSES PHASE BEGINS				
886*	2000	1,000	15,000,000	1,000.0
1286*	2011	N/A	1,000,000,000	100,000.0

*Industry estimates.

fact, doubles—the price/performance ratio of processing MIPS or millions of instructions per second.

ADSL, previously mentioned, promises to make a qualitative change in the throughput of the Internet by increasing the bandwidth roughly 30-fold by Christmas 1998. Think of bandwidth as the diameter of a pipe as if were we discussing plumbing. Going from 52,000 kbs on regular analog copper phone lines to about 1.5 million kbs will change in a fundamental way what the Internet is and how it is thought about. In terms of volume of bits, data will surpass voice by about 2001. In terms of communications protocols, fax and data are not time-dependent. In contrast, voice and video are. Building networks to support this are currently Level 3 Communications, IXC Communications, Williams Companies, and Qwest Communications. Level 3 plans to have its fiber-optic cable network completed in 2001. The idea of a stockbroker showing a 3D graph of nonlinear pricing to a client in the private chat room of the corporate intranet is about to take a big step forward.

Continuing this line of thinking, one does not go far before bumping into George Gilder, who in *Forbes ASAP* said, "Actually, the law of the microcosm makes distributed computers (smart terminals) more efficient regardless of the cost of linking them together. The law of the telecom makes broadband networks more efficient regardless of how numerous and smart are the terminals. Working together, however, these two laws of wires and switches impel ever more widely distributed information systems, with processing and memory in the optimal locations." Regardless of the nuances of fiber optics, regulatory considerations, phone company bureaucracy, and possibly even his timing within a two-year constraint, Gilder is basically correct in his claim of cost reduction per millions of instructions per second or MIPS and increased capacity as measured by throughput in megabytes per second. As an adaptive process nonlinear pricing is hungry for ever more and cheaper microprocessor cycle speed and bandwidth. Fortunately, the trend favors this stance.

One of the great counterintuitive arguments of technology is, "Who needs faster processors?" History has proved the questioner wrong because increased capability leads to new applications like nonlinear pricing. It is worth noting that this question demonstrates the retrospective rather than the prospective view as well as a distinct lack of imagination. Technology is more prospective and that prospective vantage point in time is all-important. The answer has two levels. First, to the average consumer: You don't need a faster processor to type a letter. You need a faster processor to stay current with industrial and academic standards. An example of staying current is getting ready for the enhancement of multimedia for mass entertainment in the form of 3D, with Silicon Graphics' OpenGL, Microsoft's Direct X, and Intel's MMX 2. Sound is more important, with voice commands and since radio is now broadcast and records are now sold on the Internet (not the physical recording—the right to download the electrons!). Second, the scientist, the daydreamer, and anyone who wonders "what if?": One needs a faster processor to change the qualitative nature of the question being asked. The qualitative difference, which is really the important issue, is the type of question we get to ask with enhanced computational ability.

In Chapter 1, three examples of this qualitative change were given: The movie *Toy Story*, Levi Strauss using modern techniques of measurement, and Landmark Graphics' 3D seismic imaging in the oil business. None of these applications are merely a 100% improvement in faster routine applications, like processing lists of inventory or customers. They are really new ways of manipulating information. Less sexy and less graphic but better examples of nonlinear techniques already at work are: neural networks, a technique modeled on the connection of synapses in the brain, from HCN Software (over-the-counter stock symbol: HCNS) in San Diego, which are used to detect anomalous behavior in credit card applicants and thus reduce fraud. Both John Deere (NYSE: JD) and i2 Corporation (OTC: IWTO) of Irving, Texas, use genetic algorithms, a nonlinear evolution technique, for improving assembly lines and delivery schedules to factories, respectively. Olsen Associates of Zürich specializes in a non-linear, high-frequency analysis of currencies to give currency traders a partially predictive edge.

Strangely enough, the practical implementation of this qualitative change owes a huge debt to the fact that the U.S. and several other nations have banned nuclear testing. If we, as Americans, want to maintain defense capabilities, and we do, then the only alternative is to *simulate* explosions. These simulations require ever more and faster computational ability and all but ensure the future of American supercomputing. The result is the Advanced Strategic Computing Initiative funded by the Department of Energy and begun in 1996.

For example, Janus, the 9,072 Pentium Pro processor behemoth built by Intel and now the world's fastest supercomputer, was recently installed at Sandia National Laboratories. It is noteworthy only because it broke the "teraFLOPS" barrier—that is, trillions of floating operations per second. A floating operation is the kind that keeps track of the decimal and all the bits and pieces to the right of it. This is the mantissa mentioned earlier which adds up after lots of iterations. To translate, simulating nuclear explosions and nonlinear pricing are the same kinds of calculations—FLOPS. Chips are only getting faster, we have a government mandate to keep building the supercomputers, and we have a real need in financial economics to improve risk-reward performance. From the *New York Times* of September 3, 1997: "The increase in power has almost no precedent," according to Dr. William J. Camp, director of computational science, computer science, and mathematics at Sandia. "In one fell swoop, we've raised computing power by an order of a magnitude." Less than six months later, on February 13, 1998, the *New York Times* reported that the DOE signed a $85 million contract with IBM to build a 10 teraFLOPS machine. "To put this into context," Secretary of Energy Federico F. Pena said, "we will be able to do in less than a day all of the calculations that were performed at the weapons laboratories in the first 50 years of the nuclear weapons program."

The U.S. federal high-performance program has upped the goal to a trillion calculations per second by the end of the century. By the year 2020, petacrunchers capable of reaching a thousand trillion calculations per second may be possible, although new technologies and programming methods will be needed to reach that level.

We are now, in 1998, at that point of the hockey stick where an unseen but real inflection point indicating a qualitative change has been reached for financial economics. With the late model P6 family, the Pentium IIs and the P7 Merced, the x86 family of chips are now powerful enough. Graphics software and accelerator cards are robust enough to display the results intuitively. The Internet is progressing nicely so we can move all these files around, security issues are being addressed, and bandwidth is increasing. Supercomputers have a promising future ahead of them. Nonlinear techniques have established a beachhead in industry, however modest, and most importantly, our understanding of the world is more sophisticated. We are there.

To use a metaphor, whereas biologists have long experimented in vitro we now can do so "in silica"—referring to the silicon of microprocessors; 2D simulations are commonplace, 3D places an additional burden, and having a simulation unfold in 4D takes very powerful machines—which now fortunately exist. Soon Los Alamos will get their Silicon Graphics/Cray supercomputer and Lawrence Livermore will get theirs from IBM. The Argonne National Laboratory has taken a different route, since its focus is energy rather than defense, and has specialized in MPP—or massive parallel processing—with IBM's SP-2. MPP is also quite advantageous for nonlinear pricing since the problem can be chopped up into bits—processed in parallel—and reassembled. Competing evolutions are run simultaneously and then compared for fitness at their conclusion.

There is another salient point to be drawn from Argonne. Part of our reasoning is based on computational proof, which took a major stride forward at the Argonne National Laboratory in November 1996, when a computer program written by Dr. William McCune proved the theorem behind the Robbins conjecture. It is not important to know what the conjecture was, but rather that it was certifiably hard and had stumped mathematicians for 60 years. A machine proved the theorem. This is a far cry from the simple four-color theorem mentioned earlier and a giant step away from the traditional method of what we call "proof."

Technologically speaking, one should be a bit of a daydreamer because what is a daydream today has a very reasonable possibility of becoming a commercial reality within the time frame of myopic investors. No longer will the proof of the analysis be written on paper—it is too complex. The proof is a process in a computer.

LOOSELY COUPLED SETS

This is an advanced topic and a great idea that has its origins with Richard Morley, who, as BooBoo said of Yogi, is "smaaarter than your average bear." Dick is a bear of a man who hibernates in the woods of New Hampshire in his office called "The Barn." Outside of his annual Santa Fe conferences on chaos in manufacturing, he is not well known in the popular sense, but he is to those who are cogniscent of nonlinear thinking.

During a recent pilgrimage to The Barn, Dick blew me away (a great compliment) with the concept of loosely coupled sets. Like all great ideas, loosely coupled sets are remarkably simple. The idea is modeled on the neuron in the human brain. Neurons are notoriously lousy sensors. If a neuron was bathroom scale it would only indicate light, medium, or heavy. If a neuron was a ruler, it would only indicate short, medium, or long. What is powerful about loosely coupled sets is that there are more states of mind than there are neurons in your brain roughly 10^{20}.

Whatever real-world problem one contemplates, it scales quickly in level of difficulty. But loosely coupled sets scale even more quickly. Remember our definition of intractability, that the level of difficulty scales quicker than the ability to compute its solution. Conversely, if the ability to compute a solution to a problem scales quicker than the problem's difficulty, then broad classes of problems which were once thought to be intractable are now tractable. It is another example of our view of the world changing with our ability to measure it. No metric within the loosely coupled set is robust by itself. Only when they work dynamically in concert does their emergent property of robust description become evident.

Conceptually, loosely coupled sets segue nicely into thousands of dumb sensors—or "jelly beans" as they are known in the industry—which are making automation a reality. Practically, loosely coupled sets take many, many imprecise measurements. The intersections of those many measurements result in a fairly precise solution. For example, we could take the measurements of stride, height, weight, hair color, and so on. from a crowd and identify you with great precision. The idea is that the solution to the myriad vague inputs is almost always precise. It is strange but true.

CONCLUSION

The mathematics in this chapter may be complex to the financial economics professional; however, the conclusion is not. The assumptions of Brownian motion and normally distributed returns are not correct. When these assumptions fall, nearly every tool in financial economics falls with them, because nearly every current tool is based on them. In Mandelbrot's own words, the discrepancies between the assumption of Brownian motion and the facts are as follows:

- *Apparent nonstationarity of the underlying rules.* The top diagram in Figure 4.1 is an actual record of prices. Different prices look dissimilar to such an extent that one is tempted not to credit them to a generating

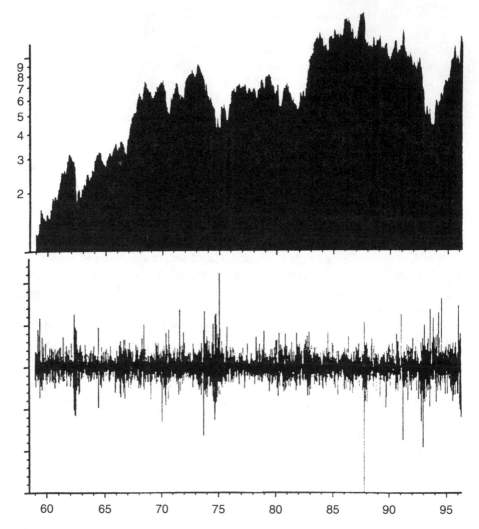

Figure 4.1 Apparent Non-Stationarity (Reprinted with permission from *Fractals and Scaling in Finance* by Benoit Mandelbrot. © 1997 Springer-Verlag New York, Inc.)

process that remains constant in time. While a record of Brownian motion changes look like a kind of grass, a record of actual price changes (bottom diagram) looks like an irregular alternation of quiet periods and bursts of volatility that stand out from the grass.

- *Repeated instances of continuous change.* On records of price changes, discontinuities appear as sharp peaks rising from the grass.

- *Clear-cut concentration.* A significant proportion of overall change occurs within clear-cut periods of high price variability. That is, the peaks rising from the grass are not isolated, but bunched together.

- *Conspicuously cyclic (but not periodic) behavior.* For example, the real price series shown in Figure 4.1 shows conspicuous cycles. It will be seen that the preceding discrepancies can be traced to two characteristics of a more theoretical nature.

- *The long-tailed ("leptokurtic") character of the distribution of price changes.* An especially sharp numerical test of the instability of the sample variance is provided by the analysis of cotton data in Figure 4.2 over 50 subsamples of 30 days; the sample variance ranged a hundredfold.

- *The existence of long-term dependence.*

Clearly from this list we have concentrated primarily on the last point, called the Hurst exponent, or long-term dependence.

Fractal analysis is a mixture of what and how. The what is fractals or the rigorous mathematical characterization of time series. In extending function

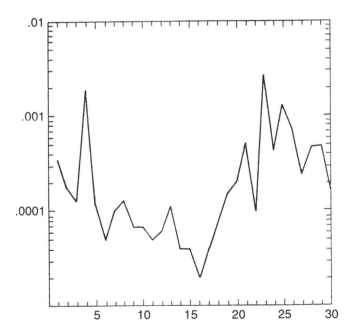

Figure 4.2   Long Tailed (Reprinted with permission from *Fractals and Scaling in Finance* by Benoit Mandelbrot. © 1997 Springer-Verlag New York, Inc.)

space, fractals play an important role in explaining physical reality and thus provide additional force for the nonlinear paradigm to be adopted in financial economics. The how is the computational environment necessary to execute that advanced mathematical analysis.

The mathematical technique and the ability to process it are codependent, or coevolutionary, to use a term from biology. Both are necessary in terms of making fractal analysis a practical reality for the financial economics practitioner.

5
Results of the Hurst Exponent

Nothing in the world can take the place of persistence. Talent will not; nothing is more common than unsuccessful men with talent. Genius will not; unrewarded genius is almost a proverb. Education will not; the world is full of educated derelicts. Persistence and determination are omnipotent.

—Calvin Coolidge

DOES HURST WORK?

Yes, Hurst works because fractals are a property of a financial time series. The Hurst exponent can be used on any time series 100% of the time. However, the most desirable profit and loss (P&L) pattern of steadily increasingly profitability that can be seen in the Intel example occurs only intermittently. The reason is that the Hurst exponent detects transient phenomena. It may not be possible to profitably trade Intel on a 23-day lookback 100% of the time. It is like asking, whether risk-arbitrage analysis works. Well, you can apply it 100% of the time, but the period of time that it will really make a difference is only when a stock is in a deal. In the total trading life of the stock, the percentage of time the stock is in a deal is very small—but, financially speaking, very important.

If one thinks in terms of arbitrage, then the Hurst exponent is a statistical meta-arbitrage. It is the practitioner's ability to rapidly characterize the Hurst exponent of a time series versus the assumption of randomness for a time series by the market.

To cement the concept of Hurst, look at Table 5.1. One intuitive way to think about the term nonlinear is in terms of human behavior. Think of someone with Alzheimer's disease, which literally severs the perception of time between events. From the patient's perspective, every time she sees her husband, she is meeting him for the first time. This phenomenon

Table 5.1   The Three States of Behavior and Finance

	Randomness	*Partial Predictability*	*Perfect Predictability*
Behavior	Alzheimer's	Know well	Robot/Coke machine
Finance	Portfolio theory of the 1970s Black-Scholes option pricing model	Nonlinear pricing	Does not exist

is in mathematical terms, random. That is, no memory exists, literally or statistically.

At the opposite end of the spectrum from perfect randomness is perfect predictability. A robot, like a soda machine or a car wash, is a simple physical example of perfect predictability. But, in reality, for example, a wife does not have to meet her husband for the first time every time. Because you know your spouse well, you know whether he or she will prefer the beach or the mountains for a vacation, or a football game to the opera. Mathematically speaking, partial predictability exists. And the degree to which that partial predictability exists is dynamic, not static. It changes a little bit over time.

If a phenomenon is completely random or perfectly predictable 100% of the time, then it may be said that time has no effect, and thus the relationship may be characterized as linear. The relationship is linear because it is always random or always perfectly predictable. If that phenomenon is *always* at either extreme, then time has no effect. If, however, that phenomenon falls in between the two extremes of randomness and perfect predictability, then time produces an effect. The effect is varying and disproportionate and therefore may be characterized as nonlinear. Moreover, the phenomenon does not stay at a particular point of partial predictability; it fluctuates.

What we are really dealing with is nonlinearity, which suggests at least partial predictability. The mathematically rigorous title of the KAOS screen should probably be HRST for Hurst or NONL for nonlinear. But KAOS won for marketing reasons.

The Hurst exponent on the KAOS screen is proof positive that the assumption of randomness is overly restrictive. The Hurst exponent measures the statistical long-term dependence in a time series. In English, this means that yesterday affects today and that today affects tomorrow. And you can now measure—or quantify—the changes in time between the prices of traded assets. You have an objective rather than a subjective—or heuristic—

EXAMPLE   151

measure, which is all you have now. Technology has improved. It also means that randomness is dead.

Without the preparation to change your frame of reference—or paradigm—there is probably very little in your conventional background to prepare you for nonlinear pricing. For example, logically, you cannot use both the Hurst exponent and a least squares regression on Bloomberg, because each screen offers mutually exclusive views of reality. Once you (and your competition) see this competing standard, several issues are raised and you have to start thinking about why you do things a certain way. There are really only two choices: Embrace the new way and accept the fact that technology is changing our beliefs or live with the old way and continue to look over your shoulder.

Think for a moment: The math underlying financial theory is 25 years old. Given a choice between a commercial aircraft five years old and one 25 years old, which would you prefer to ride in and why? To continue, with the exception of the grandfather clock, art, and antiques, do you use *one* piece of technology in your home that is 25 years old? Car, kitchen appliances, stereo, telephone, TV, VCR, air conditioning, prescription or over-the-counter drugs, computer—anything? Well, then why do you accept 25-year-old financial technology? The real answer is that you do not know.

EXAMPLE

Ideally, our objective is to characterize, using the optimal combination of four variables listed at the top of the KAOS screen and one assumption, a smooth and steadily increasing P&L statement indicated at the bottom of the graph.

CAUTION: Most people assume that since they are *seeing* three 2D graphs, such as time series, a graph of the Hurst exponent, and a P&L, that a *visual* relationship should immediately jump out at them, and if it does not, their brain clicks off and they cease thinking, like Uncle Momo from Brooklyn who saw this and asked, "So where do I buy and where do I sell?" In fact, the relationship *can* be visualized, but only in multiple 4D—in essence a film clip—something that neither Bloomberg nor this book is capable of displaying at this time. The Hurst is calculated from the time series, and the P&L is merely the summary of a search of multiple entry and exit combinations using the Hurst exponent. The relationship between the Hurst exponent and the P&L is *logical,* not visual.

Figures 5.1 and 5.2 show the DM, a prime example.

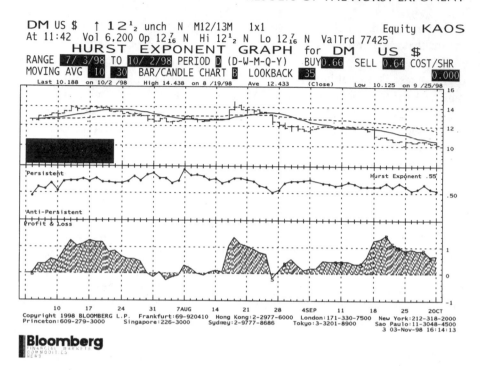

Figure 5.1   Bloomberg's KAOS screen illustrating the Hurst Exponent for DM
(© 1998 Bloomberg LP. All rights reserved.)

ASSUMPTION

The one assumption is: *The further we wish to look ahead, the further we must look back in history.* No simple rule exists in finance or the hard sciences to articulate the exact relationship between length of history and length of forecast (e.g., for every period going forward use 10 periods of history) needed in a model. The only guide is intuitive, conjectural, or experiential. I grasped the intuition of this concept when I read Churchill's account of his antecedent, John, Duke of Marlborough. Churchill said, in effect, that the more a man knows his own history, the further he can see. Perhaps knowing the contretemps to which Marlborough was repeatedly subject as keeper of the Grand Alliance, which Churchill documented in the early to mid-1930s, fortified Churchill for his leadership role in World War Two.

In this sense, judgment is required, and it is the quality of this judgment that still makes economic analysis more art than science. Obviously, one should not blindly throw a tool at a problem unless one has

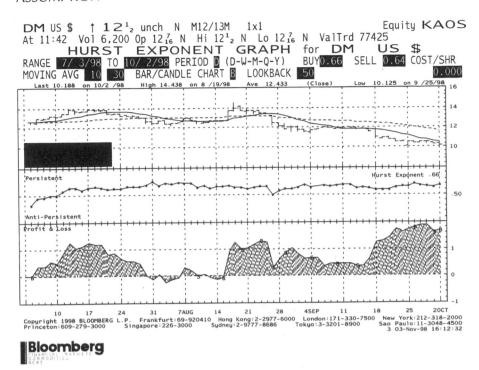

Figure 5.2 Another Bloomberg KAOS screen illustrating the Hurst Exponent for DM (© 1998 Bloomberg LP. All rights reserved.)

knowledge of both the tool and the problem and understands what one is looking for.

Common sense suggests that we will look back further into a candidate's history if he or she is being interviewed as a partner of the firm rather than as a entry-level staff member. Why? Because we can reasonably assume that: (1) the candidate's future with the firm is viewed on a longer-term basis, and (2) he or she will have a larger impact on the firm's fortunes. Thus, more due diligence or history is warranted.

Further, there is no science which states that for a near-term horizon, like day trading, that a 15-day lookback is right and a 33-day lookback is wrong. The relationship between future and past is posited in general, not specific, terms. If you ask why, the real answer is that you have just bumped into a phenomenon that science cannot yet explain. Pity. You will have to rely on common sense and experimentation. I do not view this as a failing, since I have never heard of any value investor being able to reduce to a simple rule the number of profitable quarters he or she needed to examine before justifying an investment. The real answer is gray, not black and white.

THE FOUR VARIABLES

The information listed at the top of the KAOS screen includes:

1. Transaction costs
2. Lookback period
3. Lookback denominator
4. History

Transaction Costs

Transaction costs on the KAOS can be set on the default page in Bloomberg so the P&L being viewed is after transaction cost but pretax. The P&L also states the return in points rather than in percent. For our example, the return is 100 points in about four months. The return calculation is not made since costs of capital and the ability to use margin vary among users. However, these variables notwithstanding, the return is substantial.

Lookback Period

Locate by trial and error one stock among any of the approximately 71,000 on Bloomberg, (or any of the other myriad financial instruments) that exhibits a smoothly upward sloping P&L statement. To do this you will need to manually screen lookback figures ranging from 12 to 250 days. The P&L is dynamic since each lookback period yields a unique P&L, and thus there may be none, one or more profitable P&Ls. These lookback periods may be conceptualized as profitable cycle lengths or "sweet spots." Golfers and tennis players instinctively understand that if they find the sweet spot on the club or racquet, the ball will have very good performance with very little energy. Where no sweet spot exists for a range of lookback periods, one may conclude that the application of the Hurst exponent cannot profitably characterize the behavior of a stock during this six-month period. It suggests that in the shorter lookback periods, steadily increasing profitability as a function of the Hurst exponent is a transient or intermittent phenomenon. It happens often enough but I do not know why. The Hurst exponent also tends to smooth out at about 50 days or so, and I suspect that this is a major clue in determining a level of temporal resolution. That is, a special place on the *timescape*, which is a temporal version of a landscape.

Once the lookback number has been determined, it must be monitored frequently to see when the stock changes cyclic lengths. It will. There is an instinctive desire to associate this cyclic length or phase transition with other phenomena, like news and financial reports. The instinct may be as basic as the need to understand a new way of interpreting information in terms we are already familiar with or as grand as using conventional interpretations in an effort to determine a basic property of the stock as a member of a complex adaptive system. We will visit complex adaptive systems later but the gist of the idea in analyzing or interpreting complex phenomena is to determine where the levers or points of inflection are located and when. To those conventionally trained, obviously interest rates may be thought of as a lever in a complex adaptive system like the economy. On its surface, this seems to be a good line of inquiry. However, I do not think my ideas in that area are ready for public scrutiny. It is also noted that, generally speaking, the further the lookback period, the smoother the Hurst exponent becomes. Even so, the Hurst exponent rarely, if ever, defaults perfectly to 0.5 as theory holds.

BACK TESTING

In the course of discussing nonlinear pricing, one receives many garden-variety, "How many angels can dance on the head of a pin?" questions. Two of my favorites are, "How much back testing have you done?" and "How much data do you need?" The trick in testosterone-laden boardroom conversation, where the object is score quick points by stumping the other fellow rather than real inquiry, is to answer questioners with the same swiftness and lack of forethought with which they asked. For the reader, though, the answer will be deeper.

In response to the former question, a simple reminder that the Microsoft example, Figure 5.1, like any KAOS screen, is by definition an *historical* example. For Microsoft, during the previous six months, trading was profitable. The quantity or duration of back testing can be adjusted with the variable No. 3, the lookback denominator and variable No. 4, the length of the lookback denominator's history.

I intuit that the question of how much back testing usually refers to the quality rather than the quantity. Judgment is needed here. How much is the Intel of today like the Intel of four years ago? I suspect that, as a high-tech concern, Intel is less comparable to its historical self than a consumer non-durables company like Gillette or Procter & Gamble is to its historical self. Other than to determine consistent profitability, a three-year back test for technology will probably not yield as much insight into Intel's future as it will for Procter & Gamble's. About the only way to answer the quality issue is to establish the veracity of the Hurst exponent and direct the questioner to see Peters [1996], Mandelbrot [1997], Samorodnidsky and Taqqu [1994], Taqqu [1998], Feder [1988], Korsan [1993], and almost anything from Olsen & Associates and the Santa Fe Institute.

Lookback Denominator

Five different lookback denominators are offered: day, week, month, quarter, and year. Intuitively, for those investors with a nearer-term investment horizon, a nearer-term time period will be used. Different denominations allow one to scale one's perspective in time—that is, to zoom in or out depending on one's purview. Intimately linked with the lookback denomination is the amount of history points and the length of time they cover.

History

The length of the history is bounded on the KAOS screen by the parameters indicated in Table 5.2. As a practical matter, though, most historical data in Bloomberg typically dates from the early 1980's.

If that is not sufficient, then just asking "How much back testing do you require to validate the concept?" is advisable. Invariably, they do not know, so there is no uniform response. They do not know because they have never reconciled the mismatch between analytic techniques, which tend to be used at discrete intervals in a static universe, and computational techniques, which are dynamic and can be used continuously. If the questions get spurious, then it is a good sign that the inquirer is more predisposed to a duel than to achieving a real understanding.

Many do not think their questions through very clearly which leads me to suspect that they are mere curiosity seekers. When I am asked how much

Table 5.2   Lookback Denominators

Denomination	Number of Points	Length of Time
D	180	Six months
W	260	5 years
M	240	20 years
Q	120	30 years
Y	60	60 years

data is needed I feel like replying that I don't know. If you are a dyed-in-the-wool value investor, how many annual reports do *you* need? Support and criticize from all points of view. The answer, by and large, is that those doing the asking have never thought it through in those simple terms. Somehow this does not excuse one from having a precise answer at the ready. Perhaps the precision of the computer has lulled these inquisitors into assuming that there is a precise number for everything. And if there is a precise number, there must be a precise reason for it. Don't waste too much time with these people.

P&L

In additional to indicating profits, the real value of the P&L is threefold: (1) it indicates if a given lookback is profitable for a specific period of time, (2) it shows the nature (e.g., smooth or bumpy) of the profitability, and (3) it serves as backtesting for the chosen lookback period.

It is important to note that the P&L graph displayed in Figure 5.1 is for completed trades, and thus, it is a *closed* P&L. While your position is open much can happen. I do not pay too much attention to investors who desire a steady 1% increase in assets per month, or who are greatly upset with drawdowns. These investors are either psychologically unsuited for investing in the stock market or are naive and after a Holy Grail. Even Buffett said those not prepared for a 50% drawdown should not invest. No doubt more managers promise what investors want to hear than they can deliver. I suspect it is theoretically possible to approximate the Holy Grail, with some token percentage increase each month, but I have not taken the question further.

PERSISTENCE, RANDOMNESS, AND ANTIPERSISTENCE

The center band of Figure 5.1 graphically indicates the three possible states that any time series, financial or otherwise, may occupy. They are: persistent, random, and antipersistent. These three states are intuitively analogous to the three possible states in which H_2O may exist: as a solid (ice), as a liquid (water), or as a gas (steam).

This would not be a very interesting statement were it not for the fact it contravenes a current and very important assumption about finance: that financial time series are random 100% of the time. Mathematically, a random time series is called a Brownian motion (Bm). Were that assumption true, that crooked line would be perfectly horizontal at the 0.5 level. Clearly it is not.

Changing this seemingly innocuous little assumption also changes many other assumptions that were built on and around it. Specifically, it alters option pricing and eveything built on it, such as SWAP pricing and hedging assumptions. It also changes the assumptions which underlie risk management.

FREQUENCY OF SAMPLING DATA

The simple rule of thumb is that more data is better. But this statement needs qualification. The Hurst exponent statistically detects long-term memory, which is the bias in a time series known mathematically for our purposes as fractional Brownian motion (fBm). Thus, more data over a longer time period is better—my heuristic benchmark for equities is at least three years.

Think of this intuitively: let us say you have entered a transaction with another person. The consequences are binary: You can either: (1) lose half your wealth or (2) have the time of your life. To assess the situation, would you rather have one 10-hour interview or 10 one-hour interviews? Most of us would opt for the latter, since the implicit assumption is that shorter exposure over a longer period of time will result in a more accurate characterization since we will see the person under more and varied circumstances. An example is the theory of courtship as viewed by a nonlinear mathematician: The transaction is marriage and the payoff is predicated on Spanish-based community property laws, like those of Texas, which state that all property accruing to the marriage is owned 50–50.

DAY TRADING

Getting intraday data is not so useful since more points on a given day do not tell you more about longer-term cycle lengths. Currency and futures traders have shorter-term horizons because their respective markets seem to be set up that way. I do not have proof of this, but I have never met any buy-and-hold managers in these fields, either. The Hurst exponent is a low-frequency, and thus longer-term, indicator. High-frequency analysis, data collection, and forecasting, is done by Olsen & Associates in Zurich.

TURNING A POSITION

No rule is stated for how effective the Hurst exponent will be for different investment horizons. The profitable periods for any given lookback period are, as one might expect, intermittent. Again, the Hurst exponent describes

TEACHING AN OLD DOG NEW TRICKS

but it does not explain why this is so. Intermittency seems very acceptable since as any money manager will attest there are times to be long, short, or out of any given stock. Transitioning from long to short to flat is called a phase shift.

How do you tell when a market is changing from one period to another? It is not easy, but is best done with a high-speed computer analysis. Without the 4D graphics, probably the easiest way to explain how to detect a phase shift to exit a position is to look for the P&L leveling off.

COMPARISONS WITH TECHNICAL ANALYSIS

I have not familiarized myself with much of the technical literature. However, for the sake of making nonlinear pricing more relevant to the community of technical traders, I offer some cursory comparisons for two such techniques—momentum and Elliot wave.

Nonlinear pricing is anticipatory and conceptually analogous to momentum in that, like any other historical technique, some relationship exists between yesterday and today. There are, however, three important distinctions to be made:

1. Momentum is linear and **H** is nonlinear.

2. **H** filters purely random movements from a time series.

3. Momentum says nothing about reversal or antipersistence.

We have already seen the first distinction by highlighting the differences between linear or proportionate relationships and nonlinear or disproportionate relationships. Second, it is possible for a time series to go up-up-up or down-down-down for a purely random reason. The Hurst exponent measures the changes in time and measures the degree to which a time series is random. Momentum cannot do this. Third and most importantly is that momentum is a great technique until it does not work. Stocks or any financial instrument, may go up (or down) for a long period of time, but they do not do so forever. At some inconvenient point, they reverse direction. Momentum is analogous to the Hurst exponent when a time series is persistent for long periods of time. However, since momentum is a linear statistic, it says nothing about the possibility of a time series reversing itself.

Elliot wave is linear, but it does have a slightly more sophisticated concept in that it scales like a fractal. However, unlike a fractal, the scaling is proportionate and linear. A simple physical example of proportionate scaling can be seen in the cross section of a seashell. A fractal is a noninteger dimension.

THE RADIO

A simple way to think about the detection of intermittent profitable patterns in a financial time series is to think about a good quality hi-fi receiver or tuner. Receiving a radio station's broadcast on a stereo receiver clearly means that the stereo's tuner resonates or is in tune with the broadcast frequency. On better models, there is also a "strength of signal" indicator. In nonlinear pricing, it is the financial time series that "broadcasts" a signal. The question is, how do we profitably tune in to it?

The radio analogy is accurate. The strength of signal is analogous to the increasing profitability of a financial time series. Using the appropriate lookback period as indicated by the upper part of the KAOS screen, we can determine if a profitable resonance exists by looking at the P&L. Sometimes no lookback period is profitable, but often there are many. If, for example, an increasingly profitable P&L exists, one may infer that investment horizons of varying lengths are identifiable. This evidence supports Peters's *Fractal Market Hypothesis*, which holds that a healthy, liquid market exhibits investment horizons of varying lengths. Conversely, unhealthy markets, especially those prone to a crash, have a uniform investment horizon, which is very short-term if not immediate.

One naturally asks, why do financial time series exhibit profitable cycles sometimes at possibly different lengths, and at other times not at all? I suspect there is an explanation but, as yet, I do not know it. Questions such as this are, at worst, part of the very humbling frustration in working in a new field and, at best, a spur to future researchers. State of the art of nonlinear pricing describes but it does not explain. And, in fact, to keep my sanity at times, I privately posit that even the goal of explanation may not be a reasonable one. Maybe we must be content with the idea that we are doing a good job if we just improve our description of financial markets by using nonlinear techniques on what is clearly a nonlinear phenomenon.

To continue our radio analogy, it is also common for radio signals to drift—that is, for the signal to sway slightly in and out of the receiver's reception frequency due to interference from atmospheric conditions, buildings, or changes in signal strength. Remember, the radio station's broadcasting frequency is fixed and it is the tuner that must be changed when things affect the signal between the broadcaster and the receiver. To keep the signal strength strong (i.e., profitable) one must slightly adjust the tuner. Whereas the radio station broadcasts at a fixed frequency, the financial time series changes. It drifts, sometimes quickly and sometimes slowly. The retuning as the signal drifts is the process of detecting transitions in the lookback in the time series and partly the job of the genetic algorithm.

Manually assessing all the possible combinations of lookbacks and history lengths is a large task and an impractical one for real-time trading. The search or optimization for increasing profitability is properly done on a mainframe or supercomputer. Moreover, in mathematical terms, this is not an ordinary search that has occupied the fields of operations research and the like for many years. It is a nonlinear search. And that necessitates a nonlinear improver called a genetic algorithm, which we will discuss in Chapter 6.

As we now see, the Hurst exponent is just one technique of nonlinear pricing. There are several others, but the Hurst exponent is important for three reasons: One, it is a simple concept. Two, it is on a private system widely used by the financial community. And, three, it contravenes a tenet of financial theory of the 1970s.

Detecting resonance in a time series is loosely analogous to curve fitting. Curve fitting to an extent is not bad. It is over–curve fitting, in which models explain history with 20–20 hindsight, that is bad. Over–curve fitting is analogous to generals preparing to fight the last war. Like any investment technique, judgment is required. In this instance, it is to determine the degree to which curve fitting is allowed. Allow too much and one will go forward looking through a rearview mirror; allow too little and one might as well be just guessing.

If the Hurst exponent acts as a strength of signal indicator (where profit equals signal strength) and a genetic algorithm acts as a tuner (to continually identify upward sloping P&Ls), then we have created a sort of stock market radio that tunes in to the profitable frequencies of a signal. Does it sound crazy? Perhaps, but the simplistic illustration of a radio helps to make the point much easier to people unaccustomed to thinking in terms of nonlinear math.

EXAMPLES WITH OTHER INSTRUMENTS

We have chosen the deutsch mark at random and looked at larger lookback intervals of 35 and 50 days. Peters made insights as to the actual markets. We do not go that far. We say only that for the periods reviewed the Hurst exponent did a profitable job of looking at the mark. Any other instrument for which Bloomberg has data, such as international equities, fixed income, currencies, and commodities may be so characterized.

HYPER-TIME

Scaling refers to time. The concept of scaling is a bit more subtle. I call scaling hyper-time, and it is somewhat analogous to fast-forward on your VCR where events unfold in real-time (the time on your watch) but quicker than real-time would normally allow us to see. We have seen some examples in man's history where the concept of time is quite important, such as Pope Gregory changing the calendar or the mariners having trouble with their log books of the stars. Hyper-time is our first brush with exploiting the ability to profit from the differential between perceptions by different investors—one of the major advantages of nonlinear pricing.

If viewing a film clip in fast-forward takes 8 minutes and the normal play (i.e., real-time) takes 15 minutes, our real-time advantage is 7 minutes—a veritable lifetime to some market participants. The difference between reality and our VCR example is that in a VCR, the film clip has but one outcome, while in real-life there are many. If we could somehow run several computer simulations very quickly, (1) we could derive some sort of time advantage, and (2) more importantly, we could get a better idea of the possibilities to evolve so we can make a judgment as to which possibility will be the most probable. Thus, we have a quantitative advantage in time and a qualitative advantage in probable outcome. One of the goals of nonlinear pricing is to evolve plausible or investable scenarios in hyper-time. Hyper-time can be summed up as getting a reasonable idea of what will probably happen just a little before everyone else does.

Being able to rapidly evolve scenarios in hyper-time may seem a bit novel. It is not. Intuitively it reminds me of when market participants wait for more information before making a decision—by implicitly playing out future scenarios in their head.

There is a conceptual connection between Hugh Evertt's "Many Worlds Interpretation" of quantum reality and evolving the most plausible scenario in hyper-time. In sum, life at the quantum level is quite unlike the reality we experience directly as humans. It is dictated by Heisenberg's uncertainty principle, which says that one cannot know the place and momentum of an electron simultaneously, thus reducing life on that plane to probabilistic assessments. The reason is that to measure something, first we must see it, and refraction of light off the electron, in this case a mere photon, is large enough to alter the atom's trajectory.

The contra-view is called the Copenhagen Interpretation. Schrödinger gave the famous example with his cat in a box. The cat is neither alive nor dead until we open the box! Evertt, then a graduate student at Princeton, in 1957 offered a rival interpretation in which parallel universes exist. That is, there is a dead cat *and* a live cat and we invoke reality by choosing one path and by not choosing all the alternatives. Although quantum reality has the flavor of good science fiction, Evertt's view is fully consistent with known theory and mathematics. It is easy to see why Niels Bohr, the Danish physicist and Nobel laureate who sired quantum physics, said, "Anyone who is not shocked by the quantum theory does not understand it."

The connection to waves or the sweet spot I mentioned earlier also has a basis in science. It is this: According to de Broglie's wave equation, macroscopic objects, like people and things on our plane, have individual quantum wave characteristics. Well, if a phenomenon in the social sciences is a thing, and I think it is, then it, too, has a characteristic wavelength. As Max Born proposed in the 1920s, quantum waves are not like waves in the water; they are waves of *probability* amplitude which interfere to give probabilities. Thus, using nonlinear pricing in the form of rapid prototyping to ascertain ahead of the market what will probably happen is unusual, but at least the concept has a foundation in science.

What we find when we evolve these scenarios in hyper-time is typically the transient characteristic cycle length of the time series. The simple concept of characteristic cycle length is resonance. An example is the luthier's shop in which many fine guitars are displayed, all perfectly tuned. A visitor plucks the A string of one and all the guitars resonate and sound A. In physics, falling into place with other characteristic cyclic lengths is called phase lock. Other examples are: falling into step with many strangers on a crowded New York City sidewalk, clockmaker's shops where all the pendulums are in sync, and probably bull markets. I say probably, because I believe the herd instinct is an example of phase lock and investors being in sync, but I have a more difficult time proving it than the above examples. In Appendix 1 *Survey of Nonlinear FE*, W. Brian Arthur of Stanford University and the Santa Fe Institute takes the base concept of resonance or phase lock and extends it into "increasing returns" as demonstrated by the Betamax–VHS™ war and how increasing returns leads into disequilibrium.

In reality there are a multiplicity of waves with changing frequency, amplitude, and phase shift. Stock markets exhibit them all at once, that is why linear math, like fast Fourier transforms, or FFTs, do not work. FFTs assume periodicity, a sort of regularity and a form of linear thinking.

Obviously, if your assumptions and thus your model, are too crude to articulate a rich environment, you may conclude that either aspects of reality do not exist or that the model is not as robust as it could be. As a nonparameterized statistic, the Hurst exponent allows for a richer expression of reality. The use of advanced descriptors, such as the Hurst exponen,t is consistent with good science, since one may reasonably posit that if theory does not fits the facts, then good science mandates that we modify the theory. Modifying extant financial theory is both a reality and a practicality, because in 1998 we are at a point in technological development where cost-effective technology has tilted the trade-off in balance between accuracy and simplicity back to accuracy.

MY OWN BEST CRITIC

The killer assumption surrounding all historically based investment strategies strikes when the future fails to conform to our expectations of it. Firstly, all investment strategies are historically based and then projected forward for some period of time, and it is hoped with some flexibility in their parameters. For example, value investing presupposes that the market will realize in due course that our value is the correct one, since a low price/earnings (P/E) multiple, high cash flow, and unique franchise value have been rewarded before. Risk arbitrage is predicated on the assumption that most deals are consummated. Small-cap investing assumes that smaller companies will grow faster than the blue chips, which has usually been the case. Nonlinear pricing is no different in this respect. It assumes that the mathematical characteristics of a financial time series will vary somewhat but not so drastically that it renders the technique unprofitable in the long run. Fortunately this is true, since markets crash less often than they trend or drift.

The reason certain technologies, especially neural nets, may be weak is as follows: Neural nets and other adaptive agents are typically trained over some set of historical data and then are turned loose on data that they have never seen and are expected to predict the future. They do so for a little while and then fail. I think the primary reason they fail is that the data over which they were trained was not sufficiently representative of all possible future states that might arise.

The practical solution may include: (1) updating the starting point of the data each day, just as a human does, (2) shortening the time horizon to be predicted (i.e., using neural nets to peer around the corner rather than as a crystal ball), (3) using trading discipline to look for consistency of profitability, and (4) keeping your expectations in check.

No investing technique, value investing included, is going to predict the next crash. Partial predictability is what we are doing here. If a crash comes, my shorts will do great and the longs will suffer—just like everyone else's. If there is a difference, it is that nonlinear techniques are conceptually superior because they are being used to characterize a clearly nonlinear phenomenon, like the financial markets.

Longer-term prediction is not so unreasonable in many fields. Consider the distribution of the heights of individuals versus wealth. Finding an individual 10 times as rich as another is much more reasonable than finding one 10 times as tall as another. In fact, it was this very phenomenon that led Italian economist Vilfredo Pareto to create a distribution, variously called the Pareto, Levy-Pareto, stable, or fractal distribution, to describe the realities in the field of economics, which renders conventional tools much impaired. As a practical example, HCN Software of San Diego uses neural nets to detect credit card fraud. My hunch is that neural nets are okay for this application because the variability of the data is less than the fluctuation of market prices, which make a neural net appear "brittle."

Predicting the next crash is an impossibly high hurdle for nonlinear technology in its current state of development. It is a hurdle that even the superior humans have trouble clearing. Enthusiastic proponents of anything new often overpromise to induce change. The new thing visibly fails in some respect and the positers of this impossibly high standard then dismiss the whole affair and say, "I told you so." This is true often enough. But then, so is the realization that any current method has its shortcomings and that progress is contingent upon something new—or we go back to living in our caves.

DETERMINING LOOKBACK

Obviously, the ability of the default lookback period of 25 to consistently pick periods of steadily increasing closed P&L is not robust. The values in the lookback calculation range from 12 to 250. The screen in its current state is accurate, but what is really needed for true day-to-day operations is batch processing and an automated search procedure to continuously monitor the Hurst exponent. What is needed is a real-time nonlinear search procedure to determine fairly quickly which value of the Hurst exponent best conforms to whatever criteria we deem important for the portfolio. In Chapter 8 we select components of the S&P Index.

The intuition behind what you are seeing is as follows. Given a highly sensitive indicator of tendency such as the Hurst exponent and the fact that only certain characterizations out of hundreds of lookback periods—each of which generates unique buy/sell signals—can we detect in near real-time useful signals?

The reasons why are simple. As nonlinear technologies are used in concert, the manipulation of the concepts can become involved. It is a bit like taking a PC and making three modifications at once. When there is a glitch, and there always is, you don't know where to begin your diagnosis. So, look for the desired results first. The most important result in this test is the steadily increasing P&L. The things we did not ask it to do are important, but they are the results of a process. It is more important, to establish the process first.

There is also another major reason for emphasizing a steadily increasing P&L. Since ultimately the closed P&L is the single most important factor in this type of money management, it will also be the most important for gaining the confidence of users who do not have the background to assess nonlinear pricing.

Beating the market is a concept of local analysis. The question then becomes, over what period of time? Whereas the process of a steadily increasing P&L is a nonlocal analysis that operates over an arbitrarily long period of time, profit maximization is also a local rather than a general solution. In terms of logic it is a poor a business model as earthquake and stock market crash prediction. It takes perfection to call the first crash and perfection and some very long period of time to call the second. At this point even if people believed you, would they pay you a retainer for a long time to keep them from losing money? Probably not. The expected loss would be discounted because it is a loss prevention rather than an income gain, and the difference of what the expected loss is and what you are charging to prevent that loss would be discounted again to the present. There is no business in this business.

Amos Tversky's experiments in behavior sort of bear this out. Faced with a certain loss (the fixed cost of the earthquake prediction service) people will take their chances (with the quake or crash). Conversely, they will pick a more certain profit (a steadily increasing closed P&L) over the riskier possibility of a potentially greater one (making the most money). Of course, the analogy is not perfect since Tversky assumed that expected outcomes were identical. The subtlety for the existence of investors paying for risk management services is that those services are nonlocal. That is, they occur every day, as opposed to analysis, which is local to a single point in time.

Keeping what you have can often be as smart as or smarter than getting more. The concept is roughly expressed in the saying, "Don't work harder, work smarter." Or, when dealing with tax considerations, "It is not what you make, but what you keep." Tversky's research suggests that, given equal outcomes, a sure bet in the face of a gain is preferable and taking one's chances in the face of a sure loss is preferable. Yet, strangely, Wall Street focuses primarily on profit making rather than profit protecting.

This further suggests that profit-making analysis will command a premium in price over loss-prevention analysis in the market. But should it? Ironically, it is only the profit-making strategies that are frequently discussed. The opportunity for nonlinear pricing will probably be in risk management since the profit-making strategies are cherished, whereas no one really cares how the money is kept, just so long as it is. Yet the underlying technology in nonlinear pricing is identical in profit making and profit keeping. Weirdly, one may think that profit-making services would be the logical application since they command a premium in the marketplace. The reason is sociological. People don't want to be told how to do their job or what their business is.

PRICE AND QUALITY

In short, the price = quality error is identical to looking at the wine list and picking the wine by price. Past the distinction of red versus white versus other is where most people's analysis breaks down. It is moronic and we know it and we do it anyway. What an interesting experiment it would be to list the wines alphabetically with no reference to price! When the patron asks the waiter, for there is no sommelier at this restaurant, "What do you recommend?" the waiter would reply, "Sir, since I am not you, I cannot have your tastes." The patron does not know what he wants or at least he cannot articulate it. He is in a cold sweat and his ignorance over this facet of life puts him at risk of being made to feel inadequate—the great fear of men—in front of his lady.

While no restaurant would accept such a study in the name of sociology, the circumstances are not too dissimilar to the investment manager and the investor. The reference to no price obliquely refers to Buffett's thought that he would not care if the stock market was closed for a while. Would a patron really object to sampling a taste of three separate wines? If is complimentary, of course not. In keeping with the standards of the restaurant, the wine class is called high-quality but not rare so the patron knows he won't get stiffed on price. The waiter does not put the patron on the spot by asking any questions to which the patron may not have an answer. The patron appreciates the brief ceremony and service gets to choose his preference. It is hoped the restaurant develops a relationship with its client.

Why not use the same unobtrusive techniques to discern generally what the client wants in terms of risk, duration, and expected payoff preferences? After all, clients (and firms) are no more able to articulate risk-reward profiles than they are a good wine tasting note. In objectively characterizing the risk-return profile of an investment, after stating the historical returns, the level of objectivity of the presentation declines very rapidly. Since most investors will never achieve an adequate level of sophistication, it will be up to the institutions to assess it for them in an unobtrusive way, just like doctors assess vital signs.

As we begin to look at economic variables and their interrelation, we quickly find that theory is a consideration in forming how those variables are modeled. The real difference between the value you place on the portfolio today and the value ultimately realized is price. Why price? Because it is simple and it is the ultimate arbiter—but each price is associated with a certain point in time. Unfortunately, price is a highly derivative concept. Price has a lot of information condensed into it. Look at the differences in Table 5.3.

Price is easy and the economic climate is uncertain. Behavioral specialists have said that when the outlook is uncertain and people are in a relative state of ignorance, they tend to look around and follow somebody else's course of action, because it is easier and cheaper to pinch another's opinion than to build their own. To become a bull market there must be some fundamental rationale for improved and sustained performance. Prices go up, people are rewarded, and the process begets a self-fulfilling prophecy. Prices rise above intrinsic values and people buy because the price is going up. The dynamics have more to do with the supply of money and the supply of stock. The result is a bubble. Were processes held in higher regard than prices, one would like to believe that bubbles would have a harder time materializing.

At some point anxiety over the possibility of the loss of the unrealized profit coupled with some break in the fundamental picture in terms of disappointing earnings or rise in interest rates due to inflation or a political event may come about which causes a shift to a sale. Coupled with a uniform viewpoint about bleak future prospects, the investable horizon or expecta-

Table 5.3 Process versus Price

Process	*Price*
Assume that valuation is right	Assume that price is right
Assume that market is wrong	Assume that market may be right
Fundamental (multivariable) analysis	Technical (univariate—i.e., price) analysis
Nonlocal (multiperiod) result	Local (uniperiod) result

tions collapses. In an effort to protect unrealized gains, investors rush to sell, which causes a superquick self-reinforcing process as other investors seek to protect their losses. This is a crash.

Of the two indicia, price is far easier to interpret than valuation or process. This leads to the bifurcation in modeling of price prediction, which is thought to be more technical analysis, and valuation versus price, which is associated with fundamental analysis. Because of the difference associated with the perspective in price, and thus, of time, price prediction in essence says we don't care what the price is, as long as we know what the price will be. This is different than saying the price is wrong. They are agnostics, not atheists.

Valuation people have to begin with the assumption that the price in the market is wrong and that their valuation process will ultimately indicate a price range judged by the market to be correct. They are betting that the market is, in Buffett's words, "a voting machine in the short run and a weighing machine in the long run."

The distinction between price and valuation is important because clients cannot judge valuation on their monthly statement—only price. This leads to another question, why not publish valuations on the monthly statement? As financial economics moves on-line and adaptive valuations become real-time, I think they will have to. In essence, institutions will be forced to make a market on their own beliefs. They will have to state a target price for their investment and a time horizon over which they expect that valuation to yield the expected price. Remember, in fractal analysis since we can split clock time from intrinsic time, valuations are not open-ended; they have an expected duration. This also lays the groundwork for risk management. Once the expected duration and result are stated, it follows that anticipated drawdown or risk will be part of the analysis.

In sum, investors will judge investments not only on price, although that will always be a final arbiter, but also on the analysis's expected return, duration, and risk. If the expected return, duration, and risk are right, the anticipated price should generally follow.

INTELLECTUAL CAPITAL

The point over valuation is belabored because when we model intellectual capital, we have to choose the best process for how the answer is derived. Intellectual capital cannot be proved inductively since there is no metric for potential smarts that will result in a kinetic and timely profit. The current method of induction is: The intrinsic value of software is hard to measure.

Smart people make software. High-tech companies can have desirable investment characteristics, such as a high P/E multiple, large market capitalization and so forth. Ergo, intellectual capital must exist. Maybe intellectual capital is the wrong conclusion and a better conclusion is that investors are old-fashioned monopolists. Investors bid up software companies because they realize that a few successful high-tech companies can have most of the market since high-tech can be a winner-take-most market.

Intellectual capital cannot be proved deductively because markets are too complex and too weakly causal. What passes for deduction is as follows; for example, if the sustained market valuation of a company is $100 per share and the book value is only $10, the $90 differential exists and it must be accounted for somehow. Maybe the market has wishful thinking and gives too much credit for software people. Maybe that $90 differential, called intellectual capital, is actually a composite of intellectual capital, good management, timing to market, and plain good luck.

Intellectual capital is best inferred or abducted because a sustained valuation exists and we recognize that extant metrics cannot measure intellectual capital and that the people are highly trained and educated. At present, the concept of intellectual capital is not rigorously expressible; when it is and thus becomes falsifiable, a whole new set of tools will the join list of inputs for nonlinear pricing.

STATEMENT OF RISK

Ironically, no mutual fund has published guidelines on risk. The first reason is because no one can measure it. That is, volatility is measured now but this simple metric cannot fully characterize the myriad concepts that are lumped under the rubric of "risk." The second and more important reason is because of liability, which is why prospectuses are lengthy tomes of legalese. Unusually, it seems that if standards for risk, duration, and expected profit could be agreed upon, then investors would be matched more accurately with their preferences than by using such nebulous terms as the income strategy fund or the sector-rotation growth fund. The only well-defined word is "fund."

The result would be safer for investors because they would get a better idea of what they want and for money managers since they would more accurately match clients to preference profiles. The logic is simple and follows an oft-used strategy of consulting. Ask clients what they want, and give them what they want. It should be harder to get fired since consultants can always argue that they gave the clients what they wanted.

It is also axiomatic that knowing your clientele is a successful business strategy. If your organization is skilled at some particular aspect of investing, does it not make more sense to service the clients that match your profile rather than just ranking them on the size of their accounts? Assets under management is an issue, but dealing with the wrong sort of clientele and their money will shorten your life.

MODERN FINANCE TAKES A STEP FORWARD

In looking at price versus process in an analysis, recollect the physical nature of physical processes, at least as described by Prigogine in *The End of Certainty*. Those processes are irreversible. Remember the cup of coffee whose temperature seeks the level of its environment? And the relational view of Leibniz and Bohr? And that instability or nonequilibrium, as measured by resonance, gives rise to the marking of the passage of time? It means that your valuation techniques are off and that means $$$. In 1994 in *Investment under Uncertainty*, Avinash Dixit and Robert Pindyck did a good job of integrating the concept of irreversibility into orthodox financial economics and came up with some surprising results. Among other things, they found that the net present value calculation can give erroneous results because it ignores the concept of "irreversibility and the option of delaying an investment." For the same reasons, they also found that the "orthodox view of production and supply going back to Marshall" is contradicted. Now, the concepts of irreversibility and the ability to wait are examples of the more advanced treatments of time, which we argue for in this book.

What Dixit and Pindyck did not do was include the serial dependence admitted by the Hurst exponent or its larger conclusion of nonequilibrium, although they do approach the latter. As evidence of the interdisciplinary approach, they also give some examples in sections such as "Marriage and Suicide" and "Legal Reform and Constitutions."

To me the conclusion is clear. Their work is a rigorous explanation and an intermediate step from equilibrium to evolution in financial economics as earlier indicated by Anderson. Perhaps the larger conclusion to be made is that like, Thales the Milesian, the philosopher who first used the option, contemplating the larger issues is neither a waste of time nor of money.

CONCLUSION

We have seen three interesting facts from the KAOS screen: (1) A simple metric called Hurst, which is available on Bloomberg, supports our claim to nonlinearity and refutes a major tenet of randomness, which is widely held as a standard in finance. (2) On an intermittent basis the profitable may be exploited. (3) Visualization in full detail requires multiple 4D, or a sequence of shots, a more sophisticated interface than is currently seen on Wall Street. In the next chapter we will see how our reasoning has led us to thinking in linear terms in a nonlinear world.

Economics is a complex adaptive system which has nonlinearity as a property. Nonlinear means that the input-output relationship is disproportionate. The Hurst exponent characterizes a nonlinear time series in three states: persistent, random, and anti-persistent, The portfolio theory of the 1970s assumes that a time-series is random 100% of the time. The Hurst exponent demonstrates that a profitable arbitrage may intermittently exist.

6

Nonlinear Technology

Vagueness is no more to be done away with in the word of logic than friction is with mechanics.

—CHARLES SANDERS PIERCE,
founder of abduction

Three nonlinear technologies are introduced in this chapter: genetic algorithms, fuzzy logic, and abductive logic. Although the names may be unusual, the concepts are very straightforward. Genetic algorithms are "improvers." Fuzzy logic approximates, and abductive logic is reasoning by inference. All are widely used concepts in financial economics. Continuously seeking the greatest return per unit of risk is an example of improvement. Coalescing and generalizing about disparate bits of information to reach a buy or sell decision is approximation. Since we can never know all the facts, hypothesizing a plausible solution is logic by inference.

Using nonlinear technologies to characterize nonlinear phenomena such as those found in markets is in keeping with the matching principle. The matching principle says in essence, we should use screwdrivers for screws and hammers for nails. In other words, the type of tool must match the type of phenomenon being characterized. Nonlinear tools for a nonlinear reality. Using nonlinear tools to characterize patterns of traded assets in financial economics is nonlinear pricing. What is being characterized is the pattern of the traded asset, but the inputs used to characterized that pattern transcend the definitions of fundamental versus technical analysis. That is, if we used only price to characterize the price pattern, then our application falls closer to the technical view. If, however, we use more traditional measures such as a history of earnings, sales, and other such fundamentals, with percentage of market share, estimated industry growth rates, and a qualitative assessment of management, is our analysis not more fundamentally oriented? Our traditional distinctions between technical and fundamental analyses are breaking down and losing their effectiveness. The analysis is still nonlinear pricing, since it uses nonlinear technologies to pick out patterns in the asset.

IMPROVE WITH GENETIC ALGORITHMS

Genetic algorithms are one of our fancy tape measures. Genetic algorithms are best suited to improve. They are often called optimizers, but John Holland, their inventor, corrected me on this term and indicated that some users of genetic algorithms have forced the role of optimization on them. No matter, genetic algorithms can improve, maximize, or minimize, even in the presence of other constraints. Genetic algorithms are superior to previous methods because they do not make any assumptions about the data or environment being modeled. How they optimize is quite a novel approach. Parent-equations actually "breed" child-solutions with components or genes that are desirable in terms of the criteria being optimized. Agribusiness does the same thing with plants when for example they develop strains of vines for wine grapes, which have been optimized or bred to be resistant against certain pests like phylloxera. Horse breeders and society matrons will also instantly recognize this approach. Although genetic algorithms were developed in the computer science field by Holland in 1975, the mathematics or algorithms mimic nature's biological process, where genes are transferred by reproduction from parents to child. His central insight was that the binary representation of 0's and 1's in computer code was strung along like genes in a chromosome.

Hence the name genetic algorithms. Mathematics and computer science are merely keeping pace with biology. After all, sheep were first cloned in 1997 and cows followed in 1998. A proposal for human cloning for infertile couples was also made in 1998 by a Chicago-based physicist.

THE BIRDS AND THE BEES

What happens during sex? I did not know until I read a book, several in fact, on genetic algorithms. It is probably safe to say that few minds are smitten with the combinatorial representation of genetic crossover and mutation represented in computer code. Nevertheless, a greatly simplified view of sex from a more clinical perspective will enhance one's appreciation for the intuition behind genetic algorithms. No doubt that appreciation will also enhance the overall experience as well.

What really happens during sexual reproduction is male and female chromosomes, the stuff of hair color and gender or, more formally, the biological version of encoded information, are shuffled between parents. These big molecules bump into each other while swimming about and chromosomes that are geometrically similar exchange bits of genetic information. That is, similar in the sense that the chromosomes' surfaces are reciprocal in the shape like the male—female union of any electrical or plumbing connector. This is the recombination operation, which is often referred to as crossover. There are many types of crossover and this is the first of three major operators in a genetic algorithm. Biologists call it crossover because chromosomes literally crossover during the exchange.

The incidence of crossover depends on fitness of the individual chromosomes. Fitness is the degree to which an individual can compete in its environment and is determined by the positive values of bit strings. Luck or random process also has a small role to play. A gene refers to a specific attribute that is encoded in the genotype's chromosome string. Alleles are particular values that the gene can take. In eyes this would be green, blue, and so on. The position on the chromosome is the locus. Genotype refers to the individual bit strings. Phenotype refers to the desired result such as blue eyes. In the language of nonlinear pricing, using computational techniques we try to achieve a phenotypic objective like minimum risk per unit of return. We do this by ensuring that genotypic representation of the program conforms closely with reality.

Mutation is the second operator and is a random change of one gene in an encoded bit of information. In biology, mutation can be a destructive process and fortunately has a lesser presence than the other operators. In financial economics mutation is important because it prevents *over-fitting*. Over-fitting is the loss of generality in forming a solution. In essence, the over-fitted model describes hindsight with 20–20 vision by over-fitting past data and, in so doing, loses the flexibility to look ahead and predict new situations. Over-fitting is particularly prevalent in models using linear and older nonlinear technology.

Selection is the third operator, and it chooses which of the alleles will be crossed over—that is, which traits will be passed on to the next generation. Depending on the type of selection, randomness can have a role to play. In sum, genetic algorithms and adaptive processes in general are the techniques that are able to efficiently sort through the huge cosmos of solution-space.

BIO-COMPUTING

Genetic algorithms and similar evolutionary strategies are the everyday expression of biology-based computing or what I have dubbed bio-computing. Bio-computing, like quantum computing, is important for several reasons. First, bio-computing is a high-performance nonlinear technique that has been back tested in nature for millennia and performed well. Second, bio-computing illustrates a theme of this book, which is that very strong links

exist between fields—in this illustration biology and information processing. Third, the concept of bio-computing is rather deeper than arranging
computer code to simulate evolution.

The third point addressed here is the actual use of DNA molecules to
process information. Our subject is Leonard Adleman of the University of
Southern California, who started out at the Federal Reserve in San Francisco
transferring funds. He got bored, borrowed a computer to solve a recent
problem he had seen, and got hooked on mathematics. He studied primality.
This is the search for prime numbers used in factorization that we discussed
earlier. It was his colleagues at MIT, Ronald Rivest and Avi Shamir, who
were working on encryption. Later the trio would become RSA, Security
Inc., makers of the most widely used encryption software on the Internet.

Adleman later took an interest in biology and made the connection that
DNA is a Turing machine. In other words, DNA is a computer. DNA can be
encoded with information just like a conventional program instructs electrons on various paths. The result is chemical reaction rather than a printout.
The "AND" command is done by separating sequences and "OR" is done by
combining them. The improvement in performance over conventional standards is astronomical.

It is also interesting to note that researchers at Stanford University have
attached skin cells to the back of a microprocessor.

It will probably be the emerging science of molecular biology or nan-
otechnology—the science of building stuff at the atomic level—and the
concept of the Turing machine that will unite the capabilities of quantum
and DNA-based computing several years hence. No matter, the conceptual
links have been made. The conclusion is inescapable. As the computing
power and algorithmic efficiency improves by orders of magnitude, problems thought to be intractable will become tractable and our view of what is
doable will change as well. If one needs further confirmation of the trend of
the biological invasion of computing, ask yourself, why is harmful computer code called a virus and why are defects called bugs?

To continue the theme, evolution is very important. An increasing amount
of software will have to be grown or evolved. The reason is simple: cost. The
creation of applications is one of the most inefficient processes in high-tech.
A programmer can crash a program with one ill-placed semicolon. How
many lines of codes can a programmer really do in a day? Fifty or 60 lines is
a good rule of thumb. As applications become more user-friendly, they also
become much more complex. Applications today are millions of lines long.
No single human can know it all. Even if individuals know the functions of
sections of the software, they can find only the bugs that occur at the meta-
level of interoperability by slow and expensive trial and error. This is why the
ancient software that runs the air traffic control system and even the space

shuttle has not been replaced. Better stuff exists but the testing is too expensive. We cannot have airplanes full of people *almost* landing. Since no one can ever make a list of things one has not thought of, more mundane applications are released in beta and the market does the testing. Anyone who has ever reported a bug is a software developer.

HARDWARE

The concept of evolution even applies to hardware. Genetic algorithms are being applied to chip design unbounded by normal human design constraints. Research is now being done at the University of Sussex to allow the configuration of the chip's circuits to evolve. The possibility is now open for the continuous real-time dynamic evolution of circuitry to match the application. Another good example is the use of living cells and natural polymers in materials science to create man-made plastics. Christopher Over of Cornell University said, "Most polymers formation is random, yet enzymes and the natural polymers beat the system—they're nonrandom."

It is not important to know what an enzyme or polymer is. What is important is that the concept of bio-computing is successfully being applied to the physical realm just as we in financial economics apply it to relationships in the temporal realm. It is also important to note that the themes of nonrandomness and self-organization run quite deep. They are by no means limited to financial economics. Lastly, the fact that a bio-computing approach can "beat the system" implies a very powerful paradigm for quickly finding temporal relationships in financial economics. The theme of nonrandomness or partial predictability or bias in directed evolution is analogous to the persistence exhibited by time series in financial economics. Financial economics time series are not random and neither is nature. Bio-computing is a statistical or probabilistic approach, but it is not necessarily random.

OUR EXAMPLE

The optimized criteria are called the *objective function*. For our very basic application in the KAOS screen the objective function is: maximize steadily increasing profitability, and minimize drawdown or P&L fluctuations.

The two variables we are using here, lookback and profitability, are not linearly related. That is, profitability does not increase with lookback. The real answer is that sometimes it does and sometimes it does not. The brute force or linear way to solve this problem is to throw the largest amount of hardware possible to calculate every possibility. This method would probably solve our constraint of getting results in a timely manner, but it would blow the budget for the management information systems department. There are cheaper and smarter ways to optimize than using brute force, and they are genetic algorithms.

INDUSTRIAL APPLICATIONS

John Deere & Co. not only uses nonlinear techniques such as neural networks to manage part of its pension fund, but it uses genetic algorithms to optimize its production lines. Portfolio managers and production line engineers both face immensely complicated nonlinear tasks. Genetic algorithms can help solve both. It is more than coincidence that a firm involved in agribusiness makes use of software that simulates biological processes. Perhaps the corporate knowledge of biology and genetics within John Deere & Company made them receptive to the idea of using software that mimics biological processes. The Smithsonian has even given Deere an award for it! The farmers are one up on Wall Street.

There is another important conceptual link to be made here. Kelly's *Out of Control: The Rise of the Neo-Biological Civilization* is recommended reading and does a fine job of detailing how the paradigm of biology is an excellent model for so many organisms—like an economy. In financial economics terms, *Out of Control* refers to the collective effort of many individual parties, such as Adam Smith's invisible hand, but the central control of none. "Neo-biological" simply means that nature has given us a model to interpret, many complex things like financial economics. And in fact, the concept of evolution is a central tenet of nonlinear pricing. It is the same message espoused by Anderson, Holland, and other leaders of complexity.

FINANCIAL APPLICATION

Genetic algorithms are fascinating, and the best laymen's introduction has been provided by John Holland himself in *Hidden Order: How Adaptation Builds Complexity* and *Emergence: From Chaos to Order*. Dave Davis's *The Handbook of Genetic Algorithms*, Melanie Mitchell's *An Introduction to Genetic Algorithms*, and Richard Bauer's *Genetic Algorithms and Investment Strategies* also do a good job. If we want to extract information and view it with respect to making a profit, that goal is appropriately enough called an "objective function." We can search through a lot of variables in a hurry. Given a handful of variables, can genetic algorithms evolve solutions? That is, can we find the needle in a haystack? It is not a promising search on its surface, but the odds are quite good.

The needle represents the size of the solution and the haystack solution-space. And genetic algorithms are a fast and fairly efficient search mechanism. With thousands of iterations and ever-faster central processing unit (cpu) cycles, we literally grow the solution, just like a greenhouse grows plants. It is in keeping with Kelly's *Out of Control* and John Train's *Dance of the Money Bees*, and is an example of the paradigm shift to biology from physics as a hard science model for financial economics. It also is nonlinear and shows what Anderson was saying: that evolution will replace equilibrium.

We can breed horses that have desirable characteristics for racing and corn that is resistant to certain viruses. And we can also do it in financial-economics. In fact, in financial economics we will find some of the most useful applications of breeding for superiority because it can be quickly and quietly done in a computer and without any of the negative aspects the subject of breeding usually encounters.

What has made genetics so tough and even boring is that corn has a characteristic cycle of one year and research can run a million years. At present one can't compress that into one month. If one could, feeding the world might become easier. But you can't, and that is why geneticists use drosophila, the fruit fly, to experiment. In one year you can go though a lot of fruit fly generations.

In cyberspace our generational length is primarily determined by the speed of the microprocessor. Speed is also gained by chopping up the problem to use multiple processors or parallel processing and, to a certain extent, algorithmic efficiency. As these techniques move further into the mainstream of financial economics, practitioners will demand answers more quickly and they will demand faster processors. Actually, nonlinear pricing will become one of those applications that are enabled by faster processors, which is why the relationship between nonlinear pricing and microchip speed is symbiotic.

The general effect has been to compress our characteristic length and see the world in a new way. By doing this we have used technology creatively to extract information that was not previously possible and have altered the nature of the information business.

There are a host of issues that need to be optimized in portfolio and risk management, the most basic of which is consistently determining and obtaining the maximum unit of return per unit of risk incurred. Previous applications should stir a lot of imaginative uses of genetic algorithms in financial economics.

WHERE IS MY SLIDE RULE?

Previously, we have briefly outlined what genetic algorithms are and we have shown in a very limited example that genetic algorithms are a practical technique in financial economics. Genetic algorithms are a powerful enough tool that is worth the effort to rethink our entire view of financial economics. This is a bold statement and one that should give pause to the sobriety of the speaker and all supporting evidence. I will reiterate Anderson's prediction, "Evolution will replace equilibrium as the paradigm for economics within the next decade." And I also offer just about everyone else whose name appears in this book.

Rethinking financial economics from an equilibrium model to an evolution model is a real nonlinear shift but a timely one. As products are embedded with microcontrollers, they become "smart." This smart environment will facilitate the capturing of relationships of which we either were previously unaware or only suspected. But these relationships have to be interpreted, and they will be highly nonlinear. Some relationships will deal with the degree to which your bread is toasted and others will have a more direct impact on the bottom line.

One of the easy examples of this sort of dramatic change is the demise of the slide rule in the face of the calculator in the mid-1970s. In hindsight, this example is amusing. Just like equating the phenomenon of Alzheimer's disease in behavior to Brownian motion in financial economics to express the lack of memory, human and statistical, respectively. I am quite fond of these stories because once the phenomenon of no memory, for example, is articulated in terms that are readily understood, a grin emerges. The grin emerges as if to say, "Of course, meeting my mother for the first time every time is a preposterous idea!" Unfortunately, once the issue is translated back into financial economics, the grin of innocent self-conscious humor transmogrifies to self-conscious nervousness, which seems to say, "What does he know that I do not?"

CATCH-22

Now that you are aware of the magnitude of change that nonlinear pricing presents, one of the great challenges is to determine when to do something about it. Like starting a business, buying a house, getting married, or starting a family, there is no ideal time to change how you think. Once you are old enough to understand the issues and to have something to lose, you might also be too old to change. As Yossarian would say, "It is a catch-22."

Nonlinear shifts, the biological-like growth that most technological advances present, builds sub rosa, where they are not of much interest. By the time they are obvious, it is usually too late to do much about them. Survival suggests a more proactive stance, where you seek out ideas and circumstances that are percolating, and you know about them long before they are obvious.

Listen: Do you really think the white-socked, pen-protector-pocketed engineer who made slide rules or the investor in the slide-rule-making company was thinking any differently about their career and family when the microprocessor emerged? Probably not. After all, the microprocessor was initially written about in engineers' hobby magazines not the mainstream business press. When Intel's first chips appeared in watches, they were dismissed by Warren Buffett—not a good omen for the technologically illiterate investment community. Like any investment idea, it did not come with a warning flag attached. No investment idea ever does.

If techniques like genetic algorithms are ever to assume a prominent place in financial economics, we will have to see our way clear to rethinking our biases in financial economics. This is an intimidating task and technological development pushes that deadline closer. I am thankful that Professor Holland was kind enough to take the time to listen to my application's thesis and offer some assurance that the problem had been reasonably conceived and matched to the genetic algorithms' capabilities; that is, the type of answer the genetic algorithms were capable of delivering and the type of question being asked of it seemed to be reasonably matched.

One of the hardest tasks in nonlinear pricing is not throwing technology at problems, but to have a secure enough understanding of the capabilities and limitations of the technology and the diagnosis of the problem being addressed that they match. The analysis goes deeper in terms of conceptualizing the morphology or the form and structure and the physiology or the functions of vital organisms. Few comprehend your financial challenges as well as you do. But to make the leap to employ new techniques, you need some security in their viability and your own understanding. More than by a how-to recipe, the application of nonlinear techniques is better served by a guide on "how to conceptualize" about specific examples in financial economics. We will not be able to cover them all here. Unless you have an understanding at the conceptual level, nonlinear techniques will prove elusive.

BLENDING OF MAN AND MACHINE

Creative use of technology to articulate financial relationships as *Toy Story* did in Hollywood presents an issue for the traditional ways in which Wall Street views and pays money managers. We always want to know the breakdown in performance between man and machine. Assessing this breakdown will become increasingly more difficult. Look at the doctor with his CAT scan and the pilot with his navigation instruments.

Financial economics has a strange sociology. We accept the blending of man and machine in other disciplines, but much less in our own. As Michael de la Maza notes: First, there is no box blacker than the human brain. Computer code, by contrast, is well defined. Second, an adaptive process can by definition adapt in a systematic fashion. Humans, in contrast, tend to be less flexible. Money managers tend to be good at one style but rarely more than one, and, as the behavioral arguments to be presented shortly attest, they are prone to misperception. It is fine to be risk-averse, but in accepting the outcome of an investment decision, what are the boundaries?

APPROXIMATE WITH FUZZY LOGIC

"Markets are among the most nonlinear, noisy, asynchronous, ill-measured, time-varying, and multi-dimensional systems known to man. The user must often break down the problem into smaller systems of fewer dimensions. Even then the user may find little help in the quasi-linear math of models of econometrics or portfolio analysis. Fuzzy systems offer a practical way to transfer the vague judgments and wisdom of the user to a quantitative and nonlinear approximation model. The math of the fuzzy system is not fuzzy but the user need not know the math to use or tune the fuzzy system. The user can program the system in words or sentences." So wrote Professor Bart Kosko, director of the Signal and Image Processing Institute in the electrical engineering department at the University of Southern California, in Cox's *Fuzzy Logic for Business and Industry*. It is a big statement and we will explore it.

BACKGROUND

Let's start with the big picture stuff. It is difficult for the Western mind, so enamoured of Cartesian exactitude, to accept the concept of an inherent fuzziness in nature. We impose a duality. Either a thing is, or it is not. And with this clean and binary approach we leave out the big hole between "is" and "is not" called "sort of." However, if we can at least point to a concept in physics, we will sound more rigorous. That concept is the well-known uncertainty principle, which holds that we can know the position or the momentum of an electron but not both simultaneously as articulated by Heisenberg in 1927. The dual nature of light as both a particle and a wave, and the multivalued states of quantum computation might be other examples. In biology, the parallel might be the indeterminate state between genders that, contrary to common sense, can be difficult to determine. It is as if a phenomenon was to exist between the clearly delineated phase states of ice and water, like slush. The thing is neither fish nor fowl. In terms of procreation, the phase-state of being "a little bit pregnant" may be very brief. However, in terms of financial economics that transitional or indeterminate phase-state may have a much longer duration.

These uncrisp transitions between phase-states are important and thus indicate a real role for the concept of fuzziness. Remember the pendulum example? When the pendulum is at rest, its swing can be described by a point. This is period one. When the pendulum's swing can be described by a continuous figure like a figure eight it is periodic. This is period two. When the pendulum's swing goes nuts, it is chaotic. This is period three. But between periods two and three is period four. It is the transition to chaos that indicates the subtle realm of complexity or the edge of chaos and it is fuzzy.

We will see in Chapter 9 that one of the best reductive or simplistic views of a complex adaptive system is the proposed layering of hierarchies where different things happen on different levels, just as decisions are made on the divisional, corporate, industry, and national levels. It is the concept of fuzziness that will allow for the transiting from one layer to another. But let us stick to the physical example for now. If a space full of particles is inherently fuzzy, then by Heisenberg's uncertainty principle, a corollary follows that a vacuum must also be fuzzy, too. In a vacuum the energy is usually zero. Heisenberg's uncertainty principle is sort of a loophole in physical law, because it allows for the energy to vary a bit and thus for particles to appear and disappear. When the energy is above zero the virtual particles may appear and not contradict the law of conservation of energy.

So much for heavy-duty physics. In the workaday world physical laws may be a bit too basic to help us with our tasks, but certainly the principle of fuzziness is very useful. Nothing of any real use can be stated ex ante about financial economics without approximation.

APPROXIMATING WITH FUZZY LOGIC

The KAOS screen is simplistic in that it uses only the instrument's price as a variable. Obviously profitably navigating something as complex as the financial markets requires us to look at instruments vis-à-vis each other. For example, a low interest rate implies that equities should do well. Thus, there should be a direct relationship between fixed-income instruments and equities. Determining what the absolute level of a stock should be involves looking at its fundamentals, earnings, sales, and so on, various economic reports, and credit ratings for corporate fixed income. There are also commodities like oil, gold, and real estate. In other words, in the real world, we tend to look at the entire picture and make an internal judgment as to how much that will affect our outlook on a particular investment.

To look at variables vis-à-vis each other is an approximation and the non-linear approximator is fuzzy logic. In short, fuzzy logic does away with R^2 or what we all know as regression. Why? Because R^2 assumes that many variables such as stock returns being regressed are normally distributed. We have shown that they are not.

INDUSTRIAL APPLICATIONS

A luxury sedan taking a corner at high speed is tasked with delivering a smooth ride. How does the suspension adjust so quickly, with the variables of forward motion, roll, pitch, and yaw? The answer is micro-controllers, which are small microprocessors that have embedded firmware—software that is particular to that chip, just like the multiplication tables in your handheld calculator. These variables are never quite the same twice but they can be approximated vis-à-vis each other to yield a single result—the degree of steadiness in the suspension.

A great benefit to finance is that the weightings between and among variables is auditable. That means we can actually peer inside the fuzzy logic program and determine the degree to which bond yields affected stock prices. We thus avoid the "black box" accusation.

KNOWLEDGE ACQUISITION

We have not covered the more technical aspects of genetic algorithms and fuzzy logic because they can be readily referenced. Once one sees why they are valuable, the specialists will take over. What is more important here is to realize why we need such things and how they can be used to improve performance. Let us use the analogy of a bridge builder. As an executive, it is our job to see the forces that give rise to the need for a bridge and to select a site. It is for the architect and engineers—the technicians—to design a viable structure. But it is not their job to determine the need or select a site.

As we have said, genetic algorithms are an improver and fuzzy logic is an approximator. There is no process in financial economics that does not use both improvement, with a goal toward optimization, and approximation. They are powerful concepts. Probably the thought that first strikes most financial economics practitioners is that these nonlinear technologies deal with computers and math and, therefore, are technical. The logic behind such a conclusion is not particularly robust but it is common enough. The error of this conclusion is illustrated by Gwangyong Gim and Thomas Whalen at Georgia State in a paper dealing with "Dimensions of Knowledge."

Referring to Table 6.1, typically what Wall Street calls analysis is the "Declarative" column—it is knowing what. The quantitative aspect of knowing what is called technical analysis, and the qualitative aspect is called fundamental analysis. Technical analysis is associated with price movements and the near term, whereas fundamental is associated with causal factors and the longer term. These definitions are not precise though, nor is the pairing sacrosanct. Fundamental analysis certainly uses numbers and computers and technical analysis certainly requires some qualitative assessment of the outside world, although this assessment is implicit to the model maker and user but not explicit in the model.

Nonlinear pricing is less concerned with knowing what, since the dynamism of the markets ensures that this is always changing and becoming obsolete. We are very concerned with knowing how. If we can always know how, then we are always in business. The difference between knowing what and knowing how is the difference between having a fish (knowing what) and knowing how to fish. If one knows how to fish, it does not matter that one does not have a fish at present, because one knows how to catch another.

The original chart included neural nets in the quantitative/procedural quadrant. Genetic algorithms have been substituted. First, in my experience,

Table 6.1   Types of Knowledge and Its Representation

Type of Knowledge	Representation	
	Declarative (Know What)	*Procedural (Know How)*
Quantitative (nonsymbolic)	Regression models	Genetic algorithms
	Fuzzy logic	
Qualitative (symbolic)	Written summary	Genetic algorithms

neural nets are too brittle for financial economics. This is probably because the parameters of raw financial economics data vary too widely. Neural nets however have found some success in characterizing consumer behavior to detect credit card fraud. Technology may solve the brittleness problem eventually. Second, and more importantly, the weightings between the levels of neurons in the neural net are not transparent, as they are in fuzzy logic or as they can be in genetic algorithms. Transparency is an important issue because the human who is being advised may need to see those weightings. Without transparency, we have a true black box. Having said that, neural nets are nevertheless related conceptually as C. W. McColloch and W. Pitts first determined in 1943, since the neuron and their demonstration of these nets, when combined with infinitely large memory, are Turing machines.

Since nonlinear pricing is concerned with knowing how rather than only knowing what, the traditional distinctions between technical and fundamental analysis are severely compromised. The precise point of fuzzy logic is to make rigorous the relationships identified in natural language by the practitioner. The fact that qualitative descriptors admitted by natural language can be introduced into a model without much if any, programming experience, all but destroys the traditional distinction between fundamental and technical analysis. Even in the brain of the analyst and the investor, the facts of "good management" and "dominance in its market" have only an approximate effect on the price of the asset. That is, we know these aspects are good, but the question is *how* good are they? This is the thrust of fuzzy logic. We now have a geometric technique to convert qualitative assessments into a rigorous format. Conversely, we also have a technique that can render some qualitative description of a quantitative event. Rarely is there a price movement that does not go wanting in search of a reason. True, the reason that fuzzy logic yields will be in terms of factors identified in the model, but, given a sufficiently robust model, this is a huge improvement over the guesswork that now exists.

In contrast to fuzzy logic, which approximates the effects of factors given, genetic algorithms can be used to determine what those factors might be. In a highly nonlinear world it is safe to assume that relevant factors affecting price are changing. What is important today may not be so sometime hence. One of the very exciting areas of research explores how these two technologies can be used recursively. Fuzzy logic can be used to approximate inputs, and genetic algorithms can be used to optimize how those inputs are processed.

Both quantitative and qualitative inputs are valid, but the real improvement comes from their further integration and the shift from a declarative to a procedural basis for knowledge acquisition. As we shall subsequently discuss, the distinction between knowing what and knowing how has further consequences. The aspect is time. Knowing what implies a point in time. Knowing how is a process and thus implies multiple points in time. Knowing what applies only to now, since whatever we know now is time-sensitive and will be changed as the market and other circumstances change. To address the need for more accurate nomenclature, we propose adoption of the terms from physics: local and nonlocal analysis.

LOCAL VERSUS NONLOCAL ANALYSIS

The traditional distinctions between fundamental versus technical analysis are no longer valid. A better characterization of analysis is local versus nonlocal. Local refers to a price for a single point in time and nonlocal refers to a process or multiple points in time. Obviously, day traders are more interested in local analysis since their decision is a point decision. Conversely, pension fund managers are more interested in process and thus nonlocal analysis since their decision is decidedly longer-term. It is ironic to note that often those most amenable to the use of nonlinear technology as a decision support tool are the investors with shorter horizons. As Chapter 5 showed, this time horizon can be extended, not in years but certainly within the time frame of several weeks to months.

The more logical reason for determining the effective use of nonlinear pricing is the answer to the following question: What is the time horizon at which the analysis or the ability to characterize patterns breaks down? Think of nonlinear pricing as a radar screen in time. Obviously one uses radar to the extent of its visibility. This seems to be a bigger mental hurdle for so-called longer-term investors than for shorter-term investors. In fact, most investors are opportunists but are loathe to admit it since the justification for their investment decision is based on an amalgam of factors that are not reducible to any coherent reason or theory that would be acceptable to a committee. That is not to say an opportunistic decision is wrong. It just says extant theory is not robust enough to capture many of the real-life aspects necessary for investment success. Alternatively, most investors cannot express their heuristic bias in more rigorous terms. It is hoped that nonlinear pricing will both extend extant theory to include more lifelike descriptions and that investors will avail themselves of nonlinear pricing to extend their ability to characterize investment decisions.

LINKS TO FINANCIAL ECONOMICS

There are two very important conceptual and practical links to be made between these nonlinear technologies and financial economics. They were solidified for me in a phone conversation with Ed Peters. The first link is fuzzy logic and behavioral finance. The second link is complexity theory in general, especially as expressed by genetic algorithms, and "the 'Austrian school' [of economics] founded in the 1870s by Carl Menger," writes Michael Prowse in the *Financial Times*, February 28, 1994. Ludwig von Mises fleshed out the concept in his *Human Action*. It is surprising that researchers in these four fields have not made better use of these connections, if they have made use of them at all. Their subsequent integration on a more formal basis will contribute much to our understanding of the markets and nonlinear pricing.

Since we have covered the technologies in some depth, we will devote a few paragraphs to the financial economics side. Behavioral finance is a recent and growing field that seeks to characterize investors' behavior. The two classic examples are given by Amos Tversky. First, when faced with a choice between a certain but favorable outcome of $70 in hand and a 70% chance of winning $100, most people chose the former even though the expected values are identical. However, when the outcome is unfavorable and the choice is between a sure loss of $80 and the 80% probability of losing $100, most people chose the latter. Again, the expected values of the outcomes are identical. This suggests a skewed or asymmetric preference between gains and losses. Everybody loves a sure bet, despite the fact that if it was sure, it would be not be a bet. The second example illustrated the inability of people to mentally segregate accounts. This experiment involved either initially paying $40 for a theater ticket or paying $20, arriving at the theater, and discovering that one had lost the ticket. Would one then buy a second ticket? Most people said no, since they would be poorer, even though the expected values are identical.

A practical example would be the typical *Fortune* 500 company that suspends its dividend and whose senior management must face wailing pensioners at the annual meeting for "stealing their dividend." Even after the chairman explains to a widow that one can manufacture her own dividend by selling some stock and receive a preferential tax treatment by doing so, since dividends are taxed twice—once at the corporate and then at the personal level—the widow laments that she "never touches principle." A possible converse of this is the "wealth effect." That is, when portfolio values rise, we are more likely to spend, even though we do not lock in that value with a trade and are thus subject to the portfolio's possible subsequent decline in value. Other examples of mentally segregating accounts occur in life insurance, where one can buy term life and invest the difference, or portfolio managers who will "invest only their profits."

Intelligence is another factor. Unlike Garrison Keillor's mythical Lake Wobegon, where all the children are "above average," individuals' assessment of their own abilities as typically above average is no myth. Perhaps it is this stance, which allows us to analyze and thus develop an overconfidence, that gives rise to our problem. The logical conclusion, which is too painful to contemplate and too politically incendiary to mention, is that there are about 140 million Americans making the upper half of the class possible. The practical manifestation of this open secret is that, unlike Europe or Japan, America maintains the myth that everyone should go to college. We have universities and colleges of all ranks. A few are world-class, but some are trade schools or high schools by any other name. Since this is bound to be a sensitive point, let me be clear. It is good, if not noble, to strive for self-improvement. The Commonwealth of Virginia, in conjunction with industry, has done a great job of getting community college systems to train people for a job that is waiting for them when they graduate. This is the system working at its best. What is misleading is to build up the idea of college as *the* ticket to everyone's dreams. It is for many, but not for everyone, and that is the perception to which I refer. I don't know that Britain's Oxbridge tradition, France's Grand Écoles, Japan's Todai–Tokyo University, or Germany's system of segregating technical and university students at the high school level is superior. But they do not suffer from the misperception that those institutions are for everyone. This passage has as its roots the economic assessment of education provoked in "Education Policy Analysis" and "Education at a Glance 1997" published by the Organization for Economic Cooperation and Development (OECD) in Paris. It is fair to say that mirrors can be a painful instrument of introspection.

Lastly, as Tversky illustrated, is the shifting issue of investor's perception. One such example comes from Bruce Clarke, president of PanAgora Asset Management in Boston in a speech entitled, "Why Smart People Make Dumb Choices." He suggested that often investors let price be their guide to quality. Bernard Wysocki reported this in the *Wall Street Journal* and summarized other factors as well, such as, "Social proof. In uncertain situations, watch what others do. Representativeness. In judging the future, figure it will be similar to something you know. House-money effect. If you have a winning year as a money manager, you make more aggressive bets the next year. Commitment. Once you have placed your bet, you become more confident that you have a winning hand."

A few months earlier, *Fortune* had reported on some of the research done on positive feedback loops that can lead to disequilibrium by Ivo Welch and Sushil Birkhchandani at UCLA and David Hirschleifer at the University of Michigan. The essence of the theory of informational cascades "is that people often imitate others' actions when making choices with limited information about what's best." In other words, it is expensive to gather information and hard to make a decision by yourself. The easier route is to find out what someone else is doing and copy it.

All this behavioral evidence suggests the answer to the question, why are markets nonlinear? The answer is because we are nonlinear and collectively we are the markets. It begs the question, why is our behavior nonlinear? Because we can be fooled by frames. Because we would rather see ourselves in a more flattering light. Because we are not indifferent to gain and loss and the commensurate risk that must be incurred. It is axiomatic that investors exhibit a schizophrenic tendency when they want to be both bond and stock investors simultaneously. They want the security of the predictability of returns of a bond and the higher aggregate returns of the equity market. Make lots of money but don't make any losses is the investor's war cry.

Fuzzy logic does an excellent job of expressing these biases in more rigorous terms. Human decisions and biases, like these and most others, are not formulated in a binary style like a light switch; they are in shades of gray. They are qualitative. They are approximations. True, the decisions may be expressed in a binary manner such as buy or sell, but they are not formulated that way. Of what use is a more formal expression of human decisions and biases in the form of a model if we cannot include our biases in loss aversion and inability to mentally segregate accounts?

The other link involves complexity and the Austrian school of economics. The best current source is Gerald O'Driscoll and Mario Rizzo's *The Economics of Time and Ignorance*. There was a sort of schism in financial economics in the 1930s when much of the profession decided that the wholesale application of equilibrium physics to economics would make the latter "more scientific." The Austrian school decided that the mathematical framework was too unrealistic to accurately portray the rich environment of political economy and continued on with a qualitative rather than a quantitative description of financial economics. At the current juncture, it is time for both schools to talk again since the framework to discuss that richer fabric is extant, as this book attests. Neoclassical economics does not have to abandon math per se, but it will have to include a tremendous amount of nonlinear math to update its description of the world in terms of current technology. The best guiding light in this vein is Day and Chen's *Nonlinear Dynamics and Evolutionary Economics*. In so doing, neoclassical economics will necessarily metamorphose to some other descriptor. The Austrian school should include math in the form of complexity theory and nonlinearity in general in an effort to make it more computationally tractable, and thus extend its influence.

ABDUCTIVE LOGIC

Abduction means reasoning by inference. We arrive at the necessity for inference from several routes—first as a matter of logic, second as a result of defuzzification, and lastly as a need to replace randomness and equilibrium as assumptions for the future for financial economics modeling. We discussed logic previously. Deduction is reasoning from the whole to the part, which Socrates gave us as A = B, and A = C, then A = C. Deduction is truth preserving that does not work in complex adaptive systems like financial economics because the causal relationships are too weak. Induction is reasoning from the part to the whole, where we look at only the facts to make predictions without a higher-order synthesis of the facts called a reason or theory, the perils of which have been illustrated with Bertrand Russell's chicken. Abductive logic is inferencing from facts to their best explanations, and successful abduction results in truth creation.

Although financial economics professionals do not know themselves as practitioners of abductive logic, in fact we are. We routinely posit the best explanation possible based on the facts at hand. The creation of these facts is based on techniques of measurement and extant theory. However, the economy of ideas is changing and those yardsticks are not keeping pace.

We saw a prevalent example with the nonadjustment of the consumer price index (CPI) in 1997 for political reasons. On a micro basis, how well has the notion of book value expressed the true value of a software firm? Not very well at all. Even when discrete measurement can be applied, value is still a question since the economic value a barrel of oil is much more concrete than a gigabyte of 0's and 1's. Can we conclude that the efficacy of our traditional financial-economic yardsticks is being degraded in the face of an information economy? I think so. Inferencing—computational solutions—will have to become more robust. Abduction prevents the error of looking *only* at the data. What if the data is incomplete? What if part of the data is wrong? What if an element of the data is contradictory to the best prevailing explanation of all the facts? Well, that is what science is. A reason that will explain *all* the facts is usually impossible. What we usually have is a theory like the capital asset pricing model (CAPM) or Black-Scholes option pricing model that does the best job of explaining most of the facts. To conclude that nonlinear pricing includes *only* the numerical inputs of historical data would be a huge misconception. With fuzzy logic we are able to accept input in the form of multivalued logic, better known as qualitative assessments or natural speech from humans.

Second is defuzzification. This odd-sounding word means nothing more than attempting to draw precision from generality. It can be done to an extent and relies on inference. Fuzzy logic is particularly good at abduction and with it we are able to make the best possible statement in the face of imperfect information.

Third, when we assume that time series are random and that equilibrium will be obeyed, this is an a priori assumption about the future, but the assumptions do not take into account any facts. In contrast, a persistent time series and stably distributed returns are an abduction since they take into account some but not all facts. Every time series has a unique distribution; even a stable distribution is an approximation, but it is one that better fits reality than almost any other alternative. Abduction is not an old field but it is one that will play an increasingly important role in financial economics.

INFERENTIAL REASONING

If research is stealing from many and plagiarism is stealing from one, then this section is pinched wholesale from *Abductive Inference* edited by John and Susan Josephson. The reason is simple. Although Charles Sanders Pierce (1839–1914) is credited with siring the concept of abduction, not much is written on the subject, and what is written is still largely in the province of computer science and to a lesser extent medicine and defense. To my knowledge the word "abduct" does not appear in the financial economics literature. "Pierce contended that there occurs in science and in everyday life a distinctive pattern of reasoning wherein explanatory hypothesis are formed and accepted. He called this kind of reasoning 'abduction.' "

Abduction means reasoning by inference. Abduction is a simple concept and one that is sure to spread into financial economics as we move further into the information age. The application of abduction is very straightforward. We need to determine the best possible explanation for all the metrics, primary or otherwise, and qualitative information that we have in order to discern the best possible investment *ex ante*. In fact, like the concepts of nonlinearity, fuzziness, and adaptation in financial economics, we already abduct although we do it without calling it such formally. What does an investor do when he or she takes into account lots of facts and constructs a mental hypothesis as to how that investment should play out? When we put that mental hypothesis that is usually described in words into software, it is called abduction. As relationships in financial economics become complex and performed by computers, intuitive processes must become more formalized.

To further acquaint you with abduction, we give some examples in different fields. Diagnosis in medicine is largely inferential since we seek to fit the best possible theory to the known facts. Given what we know, what is largely true? Is the diagnosis always true? No. Misdiagnosis unfortunately exists. Testimony in law is another example. A simple example follows.

Much of the research for air-based target acquisition and friend or foe determination was funded by the U.S. Air Force in the 1980s. Consider the problem of an F-16 fighter pilot flying combat air patrol at 300 knots. He receives a call on tac-air of possible foes in a valley at a clearing. There is the valley and the clearing. As he makes his approach to the grid coordinate and acquires the target, he receives conflicting information. Yes, there are huts. Yes, there are women and children. Looks like friendlies. All of a sudden his wingman spots several people bearing what appear to be logs on their shoulders facing the planes. But wait—these people are rice farmers and live in huts; logs are suddenly no longer the best explanation. Maybe a better explanation for "logs" is Russian-made shoulder-mounted surface-to-air missiles (SAMs). The abductive pilot assist flashes green and the pilot's thumb instantly depresses the "expend all ordinance" button. Napalm turns the village into an inferno. His wingman confirms "a good kill." Later, ground troops confirm the body count and a weapons cache. The elapsed time from target acquisition to friend or foe determination is less than 20 seconds.

This example is graphic, but it is also real. Americans did not beat the British by dressing up in brightly colored uniforms and marching in a straight line in the European tradition of the 1700s. They did it wearing deerskin clothing and hiding behind rocks. The prior example would have been far more benign if the enemy were another pilot and the hostile intent mere "radar-lock"—what air-to-air missiles use to lock on to other aircraft. Hostile intent instantly overrides the composition of the villagers. It is true that what appeared to be logs *could have been* logs. It was certainly not proved *ex ante*. But with near instant response time of SAMs in a known hostile environment in a state of war, logs = SAMs is the best possible explanation. The prudent course of action is to shoot first and ask questions later.

The parallel to financial economics is clear. We also face incomplete and conflicting information, and we never know everything we would like to know to make an investment decision. Rapid response time is an issue since financial economics information is heavily time-dependent and action is mandated. If one never makes an investment, then the client does not need you to invest in cash. Not making a decision is making a decision. We go with the best possible explanation at the time. Also, abduction is emergent and thus may result in a more certainty than the premises upon which it is built like Morley's loosely coupled sets.

THE ECONOMICS OF SECRECY

Given the self-referential nature of financial economics and its goal of profitable processes, there are two main schools of thought on secrecy: those who are secretive and those who are not. Among those who are and believe it is for the better is Doyne Farmer of Prediction Inc. in Santa Fe. The reasons espoused for secrecy are myriad: Why give anything away? Knowing what does not work can be as valuable as knowing what does. If everybody has the secret formula, your profits will be arbitraged away. Those who know don't tell and those who tell don't know. There is some merit to these arguments. On balance, though, as evidenced by this book, my belief is more strongly allied with Richard Olsen of Olsen & Associates in Zurich. Again the reasons are myriad: As long as markets are heterogeneous, exploitable patterns will occur. Patterns will change as they have always done. Recognizing these patterns is what money managers do. And since information is not acted upon uniformly, heterogeneity is maintained. If Black-Scholes is an example of the secret formula, did promulgating it destroy or build a $119 billion derivatives industry? The point to be made here is that people are heterogeneous and thus their use of information differs. There are probably 20 sell-side analysts who make part of their living by having an opinion on IBM. Pick one. Every buyer uses the information in a different way. Why will the users of nonlinear pricing be any different? They probably will not. Soon there will be 20 nonlinear pricing models of IBM.

Lastly, the issue of secrecy is ultimately an issue of competitive stance. Since all financial institutions want to pay as little as possible for nonlinear modeling expertise, or anything else for that matter, it may be financially advisable to sell to a lot of institutions at a lower price like Dr. Olsen does than to become secretive and thus captive like Dr. Farmer is to a Swiss bank. Since owners and managers of financial institutions are rarely the entrepreneurs of high-tech applications, the issue of how to allocate success to technology is difficult. Traditional financial economics theory does not admit an answer any more than it does for calculating the return on investment of a computer. Sellers of information processes want to capture increasing returns, and buyers, unable to judge the true value added, are willing to pay for only a service. Commodity vendors like Bloomberg have taken this approach. Ultimately they must keep adding services, such as TV, radio, sports scores, and the KAOS screen, so they are perceived as a utility. Why? When was the last time you thought about whether to purchase electricity or water?

Again, one error commonly made is to assume that the issue of secrecy is binary—either totally disclosed or totally withheld. Common sense suggests that neither extreme is probable since there is no economic incentive for the former and the force of competitors inhibits the latter. There is an incentive to disclose about what you do, but not necessarily how you do it in detail. The issue is better stated by the *Economist* in their 1993 "Survey of the Frontiers of Finance": "It is betting in other words that the financial-computer industry will soon be like the computer business, not the drugs business: patents will be irrelevant and technology will be everything." This is also my belief.

Of course, this has not stopped Citibank and Merrill Lynch from taking out patents, probably as a precautionary measure. Merrill Lynch took out U.S. Patent No. 4,674,044 for an "Automated Securities Trading System" and Citibank received U.S. Patent No. 4,731,640 for an "Automated Investment System." As S. C. Glazier notes in *AI in Finance*, the courts are becoming friendlier to the idea of protection of intellectual property. Software developers are not even required to submit source-code, which is the nitty-gritty of any application. Oddly enough, it was Merrill Lynch that pioneered this thrust when it received U.S. Patent No. 4,346,442 for its Cash Management Account in 1982 and successfully defended it against PaineWebber in *PaineWebber v. Merrill Lynch*, 564 F Supp. 1358 [D. Del 1983].

HUMANS

The issue of secrecy leads into more human issues. Technology is typically not accepted unless it is understood to a degree by at least some critical mass of people. This phase is important because the people who purchase it are typically the least likely to understand it. There is nothing particularly cutting-edge about the typical senior manager in a big company. Senior big-company and cutting-edge types parted ways long ago in their careers. Because technology purchases of this sort tend to be expensive and thus higher-level decisions, senior managers need reassurance that they are doing the right thing. In other words, it is the sentiment captured 15 years ago by the saying "No one ever got fired for buying IBM." To stay current, we should probably substitute Microsoft for IBM.

Typically a senior manager will play Mr. Big Picture and say, "Come see us," and will then hand you over to his minions. For example, Mr. Big Picture will introduce you to Mr. Riso, "who does all this sort of stuff for the bank," and promptly excuse himself. Mr. Riso instantly surmises that

(1) this was not his idea, (2) he has never heard of the word "nonlinear," (3) it will cost money, and (4) it can't possibly fit into the bank's current strategic initiative, which is rolling out Windows 95.

Sociology plays a big role. In the military it is always more risky to be in a unit that is not your specialty such as infantry officer in a tank unit or a communicator in an aviation outfit. The reason is simple: You are a second-class citizen. The commanding officer will choose his own over the outsider. In the same vein, in-house boffins may see nonlinearity as a threat rather than a savior, reasoning that they will get blamed for this since it sounds like math and computers, "which we are supposed to know about, and we are a cost center not a profit center. These people are telling us how to do our jobs." Making the issues public will also make them harder to resist. Eventually senior management will call Mr. Riso and the boffins in on the carpet for a business chat.

CONCLUSION

Genetic algorithms, fuzzy logic, and abductive logic form the foundation of the practical implementation of nonlinear pricing. We have seen the reason why formulas cannot be used is because the Newtonian world and inductivism are dead. Nonlinear pricing will replace the formulas, and computational solutions using technologies will be how it is done.

The technologies in this chapter are not really that new, but they are new in terms of application to financial economics. However, their implementation poses some conceptual hurdles, which will require an increased role of the machine in investment decisions and analysis as well as the way we think about gaining and using knowledge. The last issue deals with our rate of absorption and acceptance. The threat of potential theft exists but the real value is being able to be creative with the technology and match it to a problem. This hurdle is not trivial since the unlikely mix of mind-sets between traditional financial economics practitioners and hard scientists has to profitably harmonize.

7

Biology and the S&P

The Mecca of the economist lies in economic biology. . . . But biological
conceptions are more complex than those of mechanics; a volume on Foundations
must therefore give a relatively large place to mechanical analogies, and frequent
use is made of the term equilibrium which suggests something of a static analogy.

—ALFRED MARSHALL,
Principles of Economics (1884)

WAVE OPERATORS

Do you remember that contrived bit of legerdemain called the matching principle? The matching principle holds that we use the tool that best characterizes
the problem and its solution with the intent that in a metaphorical sense we are
using hammers on nails and screwdrivers for screws. We use the matching
principle on genetic algorithms to introduce wave operators so that genetic algorithms move further out from the Darwin/Dawkins/Smith view that natural
selection is sufficient to explain evolution. Specifically, we add another level of
meta-operators above the genotypic level called *wave operators*. Wave operators are—like an ocean wave—nonstationary and aperiodic and their operand
is the population dynamics of the phenomena being described. They are sort of
a tuner that looks for the intermittent period which may be characterized by
self-organized criticality, but which always runs differently than clock time and
which is characterized by a power law distribution. Thus, using our model with
two levels we can look at interactions at the company level and the market
level. We move the concept of adaptive resonance to the Stu Kauffman/Steven
Rose/Richard Lewontin view in which some degree of contingency is allowed
to happen—just as in real-world financial economics. However, we do not
move so far as Brian Goodwin, who holds that contingency is all.

There is a basis in the thinking of evolutionary economics to suggest that
wave operators are prudent. The reasoning is as follows: Philosophically

genotypic Darwinism is too deterministic, as Rose discussed in *Lifelines: Biology Beyond Determinism*. From other sources cited earlier we know that pure determinism is too reductive an approach to analyze such derivative applications as biology and financial economics. With the reductive approach, in Feynman's words, you "will get 'down the drain,' into a blind alley from which nobody has yet escaped because 'Nobody knows how it can be like that.' " In fact, many biologists, physicists, and financial-economists, especially those mentioned in this book, are in a larger sense of their work moving away from reductionist solutions. Biologically there is reason to believe that contingency in the form of self-organized criticality plays a role in determining our current state of development. Finally, and most importantly, in evolutionary economics, which is by definition highly nonlinear, we also recognize that like biologists, we "cannot replay the tape" and if we did the results would certainly be different. The word "tape" here has a double entendre. In biology, tape refers specifically to Stephen Jay Gould's use of the term as a fossil record for which archaeologists dig. In financial economics, tape refers to the executed trades on a stock exchange and serves as a metaphor for the greater financial economics record.

In our transit from equilibrium to evolution, wave operators allow us to capture events called self-organized criticality and more importantly remove us from the burden having to assume that all participants maximize rationally all the time. As genetic algorithms are currently set up, they are Darwinian and can detect only maximum rationalization, primarily in the form of optimization. However, as financial economics practitioners, we know that life is suboptimal since omniscience and perfect rationality are but ideological constructs for the linear world of equilibrium. We also recognize that events in financial economics are loosely causal. Sometimes the two levels will be mutually reinforcing and thus resonate and sometimes they will not and the results will be destruction or, in terms of frequency, dissonance.

How then to rationally introduce irrationality? Well, we could just perennially select the penultimate choice. But this seems arbitrary and inelegant. More to my way of thinking and more importantly within the context of nonlinearity, we could extend the concept of operators to a local *and* a nonlocal level. That is, true to our relativistic world we look at the company in light of the market and the animal in light of the species. For in truth they are not separated in reality but only in the model, which is an extension of our mind. Or, to recap our movie scene, looking at the company in light of the market is *homologous* to making love while the bullets are flying. The word homology is like analogy but stronger. Analogy connotes a surface relationship, while homology denotes a similar type of origin, and thus a much deeper relationship. The shared relationship between biology and financial economics in this instance is of course the simultaneous interaction of population and individual operands.

Locality is an important issue. Recollect our ball of string viewed at 100 feet or 100X. Here the illustration of the ball of string fails in more sophisticated examples because in biology and financial economics we have multiple localities. We need to see both population and individual dynamics to be satisfied with our description. Often the dynamics work in synchronicity at two different levels; sometimes they do not. Sometimes the individual fails (e.g., dies or goes out of business) without affecting the population. Sometimes the population fails in the case of dinosaurs or the market crashes and individuals are thus seemingly inadvertently affected. Conversely, sometimes a rising tide (e.g., market) lifts all boats (e.g., companies).

We see the same phenomena in the struggles for the perpetuation of life and for economic survival. Typically we have seen life at the species level, but Dawkins said no, look at the level of the gene; otherwise we cannot explain altruism. For example, an animal illogically sacrifices itself for the good of the collective's gene pool. Can we posit an analogy, even homology, between a gene in biology and an individual in financial economics and a species in biology and a firm in financial economics, respectively? Genes and individual humans are singular members of a species or firm group, respectively. If so, then we can speculate about the following.

INTELLECTUAL CAPITAL

In the information age, the intellectual capital movement is the ultradeterministic and Darwinian thrust to reduce financial economics to the level of people which are analogous to genes. Intellectual capital introduces many metrics that are not traditional to generally accepted accounting principles (GAAP) and Federal Accounting Standards Board. The measurements for intellectual capital may be better indicia of the direction in which the firm is evolving than as a potential or kinetic measure of the collective economic value of what is in people's heads. This is not necessarily a failure any more than Columbus failed to discover India, only to find America. True, in the strictest sense it was a failure in the sense that India was not discovered, but what a consolation prize! God and science move in strange ways. In sum, it is reasonable to posit that if we can better discern the direction in which a firm evolves, we may better discern its value. True, this is not how most intellectual capital people have thought of their discovery. Nevertheless, seeing the direction in which a firm is evolving and the rate at which it is doing so does lead to a better informed assessment of value, which is, after all, what we all want to know.

EXPECTATIONS ABOUT PREDICTIONS

One of the logical consequences of introducing some degree of contingency in our modeling assumptions to reflect the real world is that we must also realize the limitations contingency imposes upon us in prediction. In the linear world predictions are easy, though not necessarily very accurate, since we can assume that a time series will be random forever or that markets are always in equilibrium. It is an easy extension of theory because time as a constant plays no role.

The realistic expectations of prediction in the relational age are less what "will be" in the sense of an oracle rather than how it "probably could be." With multiple simulations we will have a better idea of how it could be and thus more probably how it will be than mere reliance on the assumptions of randomness and equilibrium.

After all, a simulator cannot predict that the pilot will not crash in real flight; what it can do is to replicate reality as well as possible and enough times so that we will know more probably what to do.

BIOLOGY

Biology may seem like a luxurious diversion for the harried financial economics professional, but let us consider two important factors. One, in the new and nonlinear world the assumptions of Newtonian determinism are dead. Two, given the claim of biology as a new paradigm for financial economics it seems necessary, even prudent, to be an interloper in the world of some of the planet's most prestigious biologists. Our goal is not to become biologists but rather to see how they solve problems. Consider for a moment that genetic algorithms have their conceptual and practical roots in computer science, mathematics, and biology. Now genetic algorithms also have applications in financial economics. Concurrently the linear assumptions in financial economics are falling. The logical conclusion is that if genetic algorithms are to progress, and more specifically if simulated biologically-based techniques are to progress in financial economics, then we must have some appreciation for what the tool is trying to do and its origins. In contrast, anyone who slaps a bunch of numbers into a nonlinear program and expects to have an intelligible answer is likely to find the effort wasted. In sum, biology is important because it is man's best metaphor for complexity.

Unfortunately and realistically, biologists are as fractured a discipline as financial economics is. The principle division is the Darwin/Smith/Dawkins interpretation of evolution, which holds that the historical record of natural selection is explanation enough. In a philosophical sense, this view compares with our deterministic paradigm. It is objective, rational, and incomplete and therefore wanting. Genetic algorithms are firmly Darwinian. And while this view does need updating, the fact that the math exists to do this at all is a big step for us. In time, it may be hoped that the viewpoints of Gould/Rose/Kauffman/Lewontin will provide the insight for future researchers to midwife the lineal descendants of Holland's genetic algorithms, whatever that post-Darwinian reality may be called. At the opposite end of the spectrum is Goodwin, who holds that contingency is all. Life is a series of unpredictable accidents. Somewhere in between are Gould, Rose, and Kauffman who say something to the effect that both extremes have some merit but self-organizing complexity may have descriptive power as well. Power law distributions are a necessary but not sufficient condition for self-organized criticality. Pursuing self-organized criticality is of course not complete, but this is where the next big ideas and gains will come from. It is no mistake that the extremes of biology with respect to selection resemble the differences between determinism and randomness, much like the old ideas of financial economics.

HISTORICAL VERSUS EXPERIMENTAL SCIENCES

It has been said that there is no biology without history. Of course, there is no financial economics without history, either. Paleontologists are the historians of biology; less grandiloquently in financial economics our short-term historians are called stock analysts and for a longer retrospective, just historians. Part of the problem inherent in the approach of either discipline is that they begin with a historical record and seek to explain from that. Physics, on the other hand, does not begin with a recollection from the days of Archimedes but rather with an experiment. This is a crucial difference, one that has relegated everything that cannot be fully described by equations to the role of "soft" rather than "hard" science.

This distinction is the basis for Rutherford's acerbic comment that "All science is either physics or stamp collecting," by which he meant that science is either doing experiments or labeling things taxonomy. The wholesale effect of nonlinear modeling in financial economics will be to elevate the field to a more experimental rather than merely descriptive nature. In sum, the power to model is the beginning of the power to experiment.

We can see the nascent stages of this power to model in the works of Ray and Langton in artificial life and Kauffman and Bak in self-organized criticality. These developments are by no means complete but they are compelling. For example, power laws are a necessary but not sufficient condition of self-organized criticality; however, power laws are widely found in nature,

including in financial economics. We also know that equilibrium-based economics cannot explain markets 100% of the time. Thus, self-organized criticality is a very strong clue that indicates where we should be looking for our tool. It is true that the nascent stage of any development produces more heat than light. Is this not to be expected? In adopting a philosophical pose, I invoke the arbitrageur's dictum. The only time an arbitrageur's knowledge is QED or, as the lawyers say, "perfected" is the day the deal closes—far too late to make a profit. Therefore, we must be actively part of the process in information gathering and assessment to make that profit whether it is measured in dollars and cents or scientific fame itself. The biological-like growth rate of technological developments themselves supports this stance.

COMPONENTS OF THE S&P INDEX

To look for those "waves" or periods of resonance in large-scale money management applications we ran a simple preliminary experiment. Could we find resonance in components of the S&P? The answer is, yes, we did. One can make money with this stuff. The tabulating and graph are reproduced in Table 7.1 and Figure 7.1.

The experiment assumes that we are a $1 billion plus hedge fund. We are very risk-averse and thus decided to run only "balanced money." That is, we were almost always plus or minus a few percentage points of being 50% long and 50% short at all times. We chose components of the S&P Index to obviate individual stock risk and maximize liquidity and marginability. We also thought the ability to go short was a better test of nonlinear pricing than the more restrictive long-only rule that pension and mutual funds must follow. The inability to go short also perversely makes these types of funds a one-way ride. Lastly, since we are a large money application we restricted trading frequency to about once every four to six weeks. This was a soft constraint that was violated occasionally but not materially so.

These assumptions seem to get around some of the initial obstacles in relating technology directly to money. The problem is scale. Since most technology is linear, its predictive power is very robust but not very applicable. Therefore, if the focus is on accuracy, proponents of linear technology are compelled to focus on nearer-term horizons, smaller margins, and small money applications. If the focus is on methodology, they can go further out, but the results won't have much bearing on reality. Unfortunately, all these constraints often preclude technology's adoption even in large applications.

Did the experiment outperform the market? This is almost always the first question asked and one we considered the least important at the preliminary stage of development. The reason is as follows: If there is no indication of resonance, then continuing along the same line of reasoning is pointless and very expensive. The first thing to test is whether resonance can be detected. If it can be detected, then the next step might be to beat the market. Conversely, if we cannot find resonance, a new approach should be tried. In this case 80% of the components beat their respective measures. The return for all indexes in the S&P for the period October 5, 1996, to May 5, 1997, was 18.04%. The aggregate return for part of those indexes was 14.726%. So, in the beta stage of development we lagged the total S&P by a few percentage points. That is bad. However, it is significant that these results were achieved (1) with balanced money and (2) without leverage is compelling enough to merit further work. In its completed stage, this balanced money application of nonlinear pricing did consistently beat the market. Those results, however, are not disclosed for competitive reasons.

Notice we did not ask to:

• Beat the market.

• Make the most money.

• Minimize daily or weekly fluctuations in the open P&L.

Table 7.1 Average Profitability of S&P Components

Average Profitability	14.726%

		SPAUTO	SPALUM	SPBEVA	SPBEVS	SPMEDA	SPCONM	SPFODW	SPFOOD	SPGOLD	SPELEC
Begin Index	a	266.97	435.48	465.23	2608.89	8473.15	461.28	575.40	1015.44	292.15	75.93
End Index	b	278.09	488.73	579.43	3739.01	7724.38	571.13	610.57	1355.75	206.99	73.77
WINTLB	d	14.07	204.77	57.06	984.98	1288.35	7.22	80.71	110.85	83.41	–13.66
Return in points WINTLB % Return	d/a	5.27%	47.02%	12.26%	37.75%	15.21%	1.57%	14.03%	10.92%	28.55%	–17.99%

	SPENTE	SPCARE	SPDRUG	SPHMO	SPMED	SPHWAR	SPMONY	SPOILI	SPRAIL	SPRETA
a	2328.90	573.88	2195.88	276.92	333.46	862.54	262.65	544.01	536.98	376.43
b	2806.46	871.27	3289.92	322.88	410.85	919.94	381.82	716.35	624.63	405.96
d	359.22	219.53	84.24	–6.15	35.14	–59.03	67.33	95.15	62.61	154.47
d/a	15.42%	38.25%	3.84%	–2.22%	10.54%	–6.84%	25.63%	17.49%	11.66%	41.04%

	SPRETF	SPREST	SPSHOE	SPPRNT	SPSTEL	SPTELP	SPTOBC	SPTELC	SPPOLU	SPAIR
a	810.51	502.42	1107.37	121.27	74.16	407.01	1530.38	394.70	305.78	332.16
b	849.49	545.57	1405.05	117.83	71.69	433.40	2137.52	381.36	303.99	377.07
d	47.59	91.38	20.47	–16.26	–5.73	18.89	1725.85	34.70	173.58	122.94
d/a	5.87%	18.19%	1.85%	–13.41%	–7.73%	4.64%	112.77%	8.79%	56.77%	37.01%

	SPHOSP	SPINSU	SPMETL	SPNGAS	SPRBNK
a	130.90	311.11	341.04	566.13	256.09
b	143.79	409.49	326.58	693.66	375.97
d	–10.01	7.58	72.57	–3.18	30.63
d/a	–7.65%	2.42%	21.28%	–0.56%	11.96%

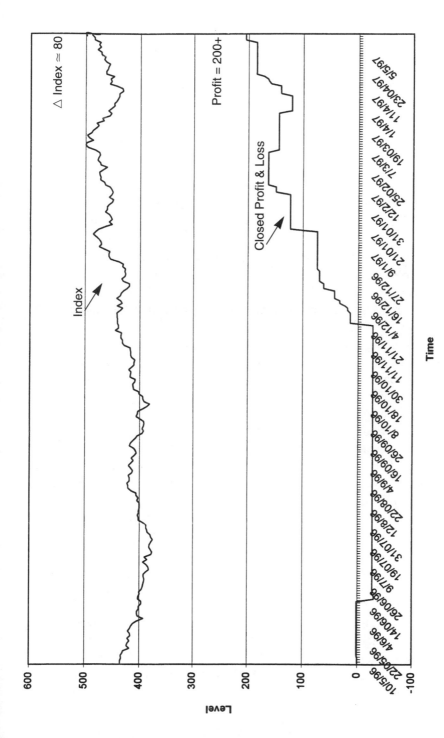

Figure 7.1 SPALUM-Aluminum.

We did ask for the following trading constraints:

Hard

- A steadily increasing closed P&L.
- A 15% or less drawdown.
- The ability to go both long and short.

Soft

- A soft damper on trading frequency.

We express resonance in the form of a steadily increasing closed P&L. The reason is simple. A business is a repetitive sequence of events for profit. If we can identify resonance profitably we have a business. Beating the market, making the most money, or minimizing fluctuations is not a business. Consistency in terms of profitably finding resonance is. Mathematically speaking, balanced money is not zero risk, but it is an acceptable approximation and a concept that is readily grasped by most people. The additional constraints limit drawdown to 15%. That is, no component may lose more than 15% of its value. Many people are concerned (overly, in our opinion) about minimizing open position fluctuations. Although the technology is capable of performing this task, we viewed it as unnecessary since a balanced money approach would go a long way toward dampening those interday fluctuations. We imposed no further constraints.

The algorithms trained on data from January 1995 to October 1996. We looked at a period of eight months from October 1996 to May 1997, which was generally a rising market and an out-of sample period. This means on October 5, 1996, we opened for business and the algorithms saw that day and every day thereafter happen when we did. They had to provide answers on a forward-looking basis.

The calculations of the investments in the subcomponents were equal-dollar-weighted. That is, an equal amount of money was invested in each component. Standard institutional commissions of seven cents per share were charged, so the return of 14.726% is after commissions but before the fees that a manager would charge. The return is also pretax. The funds were not leveraged.

There are three steps that were taken when this product moved from an experimental stage to a beta. They are:

One, the simulation uses only 30 of the total available number of the S&P components. We ran only 30 of the S&P components, but there are 90 in total. We chose these 30 in particular because they are unreconstituted. In 1991 Standard & Poor's reconstituted the majority of the index components so that the internal weightings of those components would better reflect actual business practices. For production all 90 components would be run and some adjustments made for the reconstituted data. We did explore a few of those reconstituted components and expect the results we present here to be representative of what we would find of the 60 or so remaining components.

Two, all 30 components were run under a uniform set of variables. We adopted a quick and dirty approach that prevented the algorithm from specializing—we kept it as a generalist. Note that this specialization has nothing to do with over-fitting or adapting of the algorithms themselves; it has to do with inputs that are particular to that time series. Just as all analysts are the same in their generalized capacity as analysts, their inputs may vary widely. In terms of resources, the woman who analyzes domestic consumer nondurables may have little in common with the fellow who analyzes Latin American debt. For production we would do more work in tailoring the inputs for each time series. For example, the price of pulp has a potentially important impact on the paper and paper products component.

Three, our hardware was good but not great. We were using a multiprocessor workstation. We could generate answers in terms of hours, which given an investment horizon of weeks is quick enough. For production we would have better gear, more programmers, and the systems people to baby-sit it.

BACK TO THE KAOS SCREEN

Obviously, the ability of the default lookback period of 25 to consistently pick periods of steadily increasing closed P&L is not robust. The values in the lookback calculation range from 12 to 250. The screen in its current state is accurate but what is really needed for true day-to-day operations is batch processing and an automated search procedure to continuously monitor the Hurst exponent—that is, a nonlinear search procedure to determine fairly quickly which value of the Hurst exponent conforms best to whatever criteria we deem important for the portfolio. In this case, we selected components from the S&P Index such as airlines or banks. If we trade a component we do not have risk associated with an individual stock. This model is not complete. It is not necessary to show that it is done, only that it can be done.

The intuition behind what you are seeing is as follows. Given a highly sensitive indicator of tendency, the Hurst exponent, and the fact that only certain characterizations out of hundreds of lookback periods—each of which generates many unique buy/sell signals—can we then detect in near real-time the transient sweet spots of profitability?

CONCLUSION

There are different levels of resolution in financial economics and not every technique may be equally applicable to every level. Currently genetic algorithms are a huge step forward for science and financial economics in particular. Their influence has not even begun to be felt. The results demonstrated here are but a simplistic computational proof of what is possible. More advanced problems await us. However, genetic algorithms are Darwinian and lean toward the deterministic view. In the future, if biology is any indicator, we will have to go beyond genetic algorithms as a Darwinian/deterministic operator to a post-Darwinian operator, which I have called the wave operator. It is a class of operator that works on the system or population level rather than the component level.

8

Father Time

If you knew Time as well as I do, you would not talk about wasting *it*. It's *him*.
—THE HATTER TO ALICE,
in *Alice's Adventures in Wonderland*

Sometimes an analogy can be a useful tool to make a point. One of my favorite analogies uses sports. At a dinner party once, I was asked, "What is the difference between a mutual fund and hedge fund?" Before I had formulated a response, one of those pretty girls who adorns the galleries of art dealers chimed in, "Oh, that is easy. Mutual funds are for people who wear Polo and hedge funds are for people that *play* polo." She may not have known the difference but she certainly understood it. We are going to use some examples from children's books to change how we think about time, and, like sports, you do not have to know it to understand it.

The definitive reference for this chapter is *Alice's Adventures in Wonderland*. You may know it but you probably don't understand it and are thus a bit lost like poor sweet little Alice. The Cheshire-Cat asked Alice, "Where are you going [with your linear analysis]?" Alice said, "I don't know." To which the Cheshire-Cat responded, "Well, if you don't know where you are going, then any road will get you there."

Using a pincers movement of logic I want to compel the reader to "think outside the box." In most cases this trite phrase, "the box" is used only as a metaphorical container. In our case, the box also has a literal representation—it is the 4D world we inhabit. And the challenge will be to cognize concepts without the constraints of our spatial senses, just as we cognize radio waves. We need to use concepts like tesseracts from other dimensions to help us.

The first pincer is this: Financiers will not summarily dismiss the discussion of time, because they are vaguely aware that it has legitimate roots in physics, even if they do not know exactly what it is. This is the stick. The carrot is the use of children's books, our common ground between generations and disciplines, which are also appealing if for no other reason than that you have probably read them, and forgotten them. At the end of this chapter you will derive an unexpected benefit from reacquainting yourself with this body of knowledge. Moreover, lest you appear foolish in the eyes of your own children, no reader can complain that there were too many formulas. In fact there are none. Your special reward awaits you.

Machismo has a role to play too. In the pincers movement, logic is closely allied with emotion. The fear of losing money or missing a profit because of the difference in perspective competes with the greed of increasing gain. The goal now is to outline the concepts we saw applied in the last chapter in the workaday world.

TESSERACT

In 1962, Madeleine L'Engle wrote *A Wrinkle in Time*; like many of the best children's books, its real message is too subtle for a literal interpretation. Perhaps it is more accurate to say that it is meant for children of *all* ages. *Gulliver's Travels*, written by Jonathan Swift in 1725, is another example that comes to mind, but this is a polemic or political satire. Closer to our point is Lewis Carroll's *Alice's Adventures in Wonderland*, written in 1864, and *Through the Looking Glass*, which followed five years later. Lewis Carroll was the pen name of Charles Dodgson, a deacon cum mathematician at Oxford. Wonderland is a place where the effects of quantum weirdness, such as the Cheshire-Cat dematerializing slowly and leaving only his grin, could be presented in an unintimidating way to the most open-minded group of people on the planet. It is highly probable that when you first read *Alice in Wonderland* you did not immediately make the connection between the tunnel to Wonderland and quantum cosmology. Your patience is about to be rewarded. Things are getting, as Alice cried, "curiouser and curiouser."

A Wrinkle in Time, which won the prestigious Newbery Award for children's literature, also has some odd effects. I first read the book when I was 12 and thought it might be a good physics primer for financiers since there are no formulas. The wrinkle in time is illustrated by an ant walking along a taut piece of string of about six inches or so in length. When the two ends of the string are brought together, the distance between endpoints is obviously shortened and a loop or wrinkle is created. More realistically, the surface of space-time is conceived as a bedsheet, rather than a piece of string.

The trick in conception is to think beyond the normal three dimensions. Remember that the first dimension is a line. Squared it becomes the second dimension or a plane. Square the plane and we get a third dimension or a cube. We cannot visualize the squared third dimension, but it is time. To continue, the story says:

> "That's right," Charles said. "Good girl. Okay, then, for the fifth dimension you'd square the fourth, wouldn't you?"
> "I guess so."
> "Well, the fifth dimension's a tesseract. You add that to the other four dimensions and you can travel through space without having to go the long way around."

In other words, to put it into Euclidian terms, or old-fashioned plane geometry, a straight line is not the shortest distance between two points. The story continues, "As she [the witch] spoke the great white body began to waver, the wings dissolved into mist. Mrs. Who [another witch] seemed to evaporate until there was nothing but the glasses, and then the glasses, too, disappeared. It reminded Meg of the Cheshire-Cat." The Cheshire-Cat could evaporate like a rolled-up blind on a window, presumably by accessing a higher dimension.

HURRY UP

For the impatient financier, unaccustomed to things as abstract as children's books in a treatise on finance, and who may consider their inclusion a digression, I ask your continued forbearance. The logic is as follows: Financial economics is a *process*, which happens *in time*. In financial economics, either time is treated basically as a static process in the sense that is viewed through discrete snapshots or frames, which is what quarterly and annual reports are, or it is viewed as a random process—a concept of which we hope to have disabused you with the Hurst exponent.

Viewing a company in static frames seems as awkward and as unnatural as viewing a movie frame by frame. But before motion pictures, your grandparents did exactly that through viewfinders. To add humor to history there is an apocryphal story of a Hollywood impresario who, on being told that sound could be integrated into motion pictures, dismissed the idea because if people wanted to hear sound, they could go to Broadway shows. In essence motion and sound add dimensionality.

Although this example is simple, the extremes of static or random are clearly not a very sophisticated treatment of the subject of time in financial economics. And if you have ever experienced anything meaningful in *any* financial market, you know neither assumption gibes with reality. The common denominator of these two approaches is that they are both linear or constant. That is, they either are always static or always random. Time either does not affect it or if it does affect it, it does so at a uniform rate. What if time is not linear, like the ant on the wrinkled string? Moreover, markets are open only five days a week, but information flows seven, meaning that two days exist where information may flow and not immediately be reflected in the prices. Perspectives in time are worth considering because neither static nor random concepts mesh smoothly with reality.

As we note from physics, time is not a trivial notion. And in the same breath, I also note most financiers do not note physics. I do not mean that financiers are ignorant of time, but our professional methodology for treating the subject of time—so that it is either static or random—is trivial in the sense that it is overly simplistic in terms of experiencing the world as a practitioner does.

For example, relativity is an interesting concept but it does not seem useful on the human scale until we consider the effects telecommunications and networks have had. Peter Schwartz, chairman of the Global Business Network, a research group that advises corporations, said in the July 1997 *Wired* that the result of waves of technological innovation will be a "networked society" where technology has *compressed time and space*. If we return for a moment to our sunken ship and to the Lloyd's underwriter, we can see that had a real-time communications link existed, it would have compressed time and space—but mostly time, in the sense that the minds of the crew and the underwriter would be in touch. And as a result, *their perception gaps about the future would be narrowed*. This is a very important concept. The underwriter knows in real-time and with stark realism that the crew is on their way to Davy Jones's locker. To continue the parallel, it is the speed of air travel— planes and rockets—that has helped to compress space. To explain the difference in perspectives we have to either invent new terminology or borrow extant examples. In this chapter the examples happen to come from physics and biology because they have treated the topic most extensively. It is this perception gap that is at the heart of the difference in financial economics between buyers and sellers or owners and managers, whether it is executive compensation or asset allocation or investment analysis. No real progress is going to be made in any of these issues until progress is made in how our discipline treats time. The good news is that the "networked society" and the "smart" products of the 21st century will serve as data collection points, which in turn can serve as a basis to narrow that perception gap.

Thus, I have to treat a topic that is considered sort of a sacred cow in the sense that it is so basic an assumption that we normally do not even consider it for discussion. But consider it we must, for one simple reason—risk unfolds with time. The unfolding of risk may be commensurate with time or it may not. Since many investors perceive that reward increases with risk, we will assume that they are commensurately related. The old linear way of expressing this concept is that they are perfectly positively correlated. To use this concept as it is defined we have to assume that they are normally distributed; in reality this is not so.

It is often assumed that risk unfolds commensurately with time. This does not mean that $1/24$ of the daily risk measurement evaporates every hour all the time, but it can. It means that when a risk event happens, time changes speed. Remember that we can now show that our simplistic measurement of risk lumps and clumps. That is, it goes multifractal at those speeded-up periods. The concept is borrowed from relativity. The time value of money still holds. If there is no risk then time is slow and the return demanded by investors approaches the risk-free rate of interest. By definition, risk has to unfold commensurately with time, because they are both events and the only marking of time we have is events.

As risk is encountered and approaches the singularities or warped periods of space-time, time speeds up. This statement for all practical purposes is what happens when volatility lumps and clumps and is the reason why we need a measurement at a finer resolution of space-time, called fractals, to measure it. The lumping of volatility has several sources, in particular Müller, *et al.'s* 1993 paper "Fractals and Intrinsic Time—A Challenge to Econometricians."

It also means that if risk is great enough, a singularity is reached and the return required becomes infinite, such as an act of God or a plane crash. Risk and the time value of money both increase. We express this concept today as low volatility and low risk-return ratio and high volatility and high return. The concept of space-time is more robust because the asset is considered in context; volatility, in contrast, deals with only the asset in isolation.

In applying models and expecting a priori solutions, we conceive of risk as a function of time (e.g., the stock averaged 20% volatility today, or your rent-a-car insurance premium is $8 for the minimum coverage today). Moreover, risk can vary, but time is always assumed to flow at an even rate. This assumption is so basic that it is never even stated.

CHILDREN'S MATH AND SCIENCE

It is basically physics that gives us the idea of an unevenly flowing time and biology that via evolution gives us a clue on how to treat unevenly flowing time. And so they seem like a useful place to start. The tesseract, as you may have gathered, is not merely the product of a fecund imagination of an author; it is the product of something far more sinister—a mathematician. A tesseract is a hypercube, an attempt at the spatial representation of the invisible fourth dimension, time. The best visual attempt we have is Salvador Dalí's painting *Christus Hypercubus*, which hangs in New York's Metropolitan Museum of Art. It depicts Christ as being crucified on a tesseract, an unraveled hypercube. A tesseract and Alice's Looking Glass, which is the gateway to Wonderland, are mathematically related concepts. The Looking Glass, as Kaku tells us in *Hyperspace*, deals with cuts in the fabric of space-time expressed in Riemann geometry. Dodgson wrote these books as a way of explaining a hypothetical trip from Britain through a tunnel in space to Wonderland. The 20th-century name for this tunnel or twisted fabric of space-time is a black hole or a wormhole.

Riemann geometry is merely the geometry of curved surfaces like the windscreen on your car. Although Mrs. Whatsit, one of the witches in *A Wrinkle in Time*, used her skirt to illustrate the planar fabric of space-time, a wadded-up piece of paper is a more realistic static model. A more realistic dynamic model is a piece of paper that keeps getting recrumpled. It is a complex surface.

The little bit of taut string with an ant on it (see Figure 8.1) is useful only because we measure time in uniform, discrete chunks called hours or days. We thus conclude wrongly that this is how events "flow."—that is to say, linearly. This is not so. Like our three previous examples, of music, calendrics, and geometry, all of which impose a rigid measurement on a less than rigid system—so does time. We measure it evenly, but what if the stuff we are

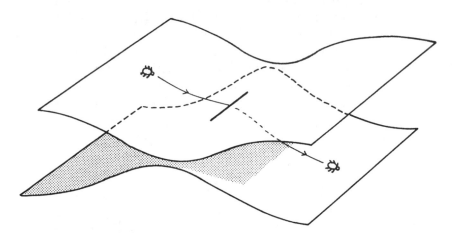

Figure 8.1 The Ant and Riemann Geometry (From *Hyperspace: A Scientific Odyssey Through Parallel Universes, Time Warps, and the Tenth Dimensions* by Michio Kaku. © by Oxford University Press, Inc. Used by permission of Oxford University Press, Inc.)

measuring happens unevenly? What if it comes together like the ends of the string or, more realistically, like a drunken accordion or Slinky? That is, the paper does not stay crumpled in one particular way. It is always recrumpling.

This idea sounds heretical, and you might well demand a refund for this book except that the concept has a basis in physics and is part of our universe. It also might explain why people can be rational investors and still make very different investment decisions. Everyone's perspective is different. And it is changing. And those views are changing at different rates. Investors may be considered rational in that they are internally self-consistent with what they know. However, their actions might be illogical from a different informational point of view. But how can we seemingly have these different views all at once? That is, how can it be that, as Justice Felix Frankfurter said, "Reasonable men may differ." If they are rational, viewing the same set of facts, how can they arrive at different conclusions, other than

THE PAINFUL DIFFERENCE BETWEEN TWO DIMENSIONAL AND THREE DIMENSIONAL ANALYSIS.

the explanation of having different points of view? If time flowed as uniformly or smoothly as per our current assumptions and measurements then the fabric of space-time would be planar. In fact it is not as evidenced by relativity and in financial economics by the lumping of volatility. With a uniform Newtonian clock, investors' viewpoints might still differ, but the fact that time is happening at different rates makes a uniform viewpoint more unlikely, if not impossible.

Einstein, via relativity, in essence said: one, that space and time are part of the same stuff called space-time, and two, that the surface of space-time is curved. The fabric of space-time is warped and everyone's vantage point is different. However, the claim of rational choice is consistent within individuals but not within markets. And not when viewed globally.

DIMENSIONS

Flatland: A Romance of Many Dimensions written in 1889 by Edwin Abbott Abbott, another man of the church and mathematician, and headmaster of the London City School, is instructive. Whereas *Through the Looking Glass* deals with higher dimensions, 3D and above, *Flatland* deals with lower dimensions, 2D and below. Although sold as science fiction, *Flatland* is both satire and mathematical mind stretcher. *Flatland* is a thinly veiled but scathing parody of the English class system in Victorian society. It is a world of only 2D, where higher social status is denoted by more sides. Thus, high priests are circles, the nobility are hexagons, men are squares, soldiers are triangles, and women are lines. The irony is that the upper classes are polygons with equal sides, but their views do not embrace equality. *Flatland* is the story of a man or a square that discovers a 3D world and is ridiculed for it.

When someone is imprisoned, the cell is merely a closed figure. If someone from the 3D world were to come to *Flatland* and remove the prisoner, from the viewpoint of the other prisoners he would simple vanish. He was lifted into the third dimension, in the same way the Cheshire-Cat vanishes into a higher dimension.

In *Flatland* we are compelled to deal with the unreality of the world in 2D, as an analogy for passing beyond our 3D existence into higher dimensions. Though this may seem like quite an academic exercise, it is not. The laws of physics often simplify in higher dimensions. An example is the general who can better direct the melee if he leaves the battlefield (2D) and moves to the hilltop (3D). What is often incomprehensible viewed in one way may make sense viewed in another. The KAOS screen would make more sense to the viewer in 3D because the logical and visual relationships would be congruent. The logical fact of the Hurst exponent would be matched with its visual application over multiple periods explaining the logic of the P&L. To continue, financial-economics relationships will make even more sense viewed in 4D—a continuous series of 3D frames—so that time will be taken into account.

When you see a price quote on your screen, this is a 1D representation. When you see a graph of trading prices versus time, this is a 2D representation. Now the representations in the financial world we are trying to capture are far more complex than a 2D representation we currently use and even the 4D representation we are capable of spatially, so why limit ourselves? We are underutilizing our assets or human potential. This is the greatest argument for updating Wall Street's interfaces to 4D. The objection to 4D used to be cost; however, cost is becoming less of an issue as 3D will be standard in 1999 with MMX technology from Intel and ActiveX from Microsoft. More technically, just as the surface area of a cloud has as fractal dimension between 2 and 3, even though it resides in 3D, so does a 2D representation of financial economics that resides in $N =$ dimensional space.

It is also worth mentioning that in mathematical modeling, the solution to the problem is contained in space and the dimension of that space is determined by the number of variables in the problem. Thus, $x + y = 7$ has two variables and the solution is represented in 2D solution-space, like the simple price versus time graph commonly seen for stocks; $x + y + z = 23$ has three variables and the solution-space is 3D; and so forth. Solution-space has as many variables as the problem requires. Since the number of variables is arbitrary, mathematical statements are generalized with the term $N =$ dimensional, where N is the arbitrary number of variables. When we encounter real-world problems that are $N =$ dimensional hard, we need some very powerful techniques to search that very large solution-space; hence the use of many technologies in nonlinear pricing.

Parenthetically, about 10 years ago, when the late Carl Sagan was working on his novel *Contact*, a story of extraterrestrial intelligence, he asked some physicist friends, Kip Thorne and Michael Morris at the California Institute of Technology and Ulvi Yurtsever at the University of Michigan, to see if time travel was possible given the then current state of physics. In 1987 they solved this problem and published their results in the *Physical Review Letters*, one of the most respected journals for science. Both the gentlemen and the results would be easier to dismiss if they were not scientists and did not follow the rules of science, but they are and they did. *Contact* became a movie in 1997 and it is another example of science fiction moving closer to science fact. Jules Verne with his submarines and spaceships would be proud.

HEAPS OF TIME

Julian Barbour in his tour de force *Absolute or Relative Motion: A Study from a Machian Point View of the Discovery and the Structure of Dynamical Theories: The Discovery of Dynamics* offers many insightful thoughts about the relationship between space and time. As the title of this weighty tome implies, it is a big subject. What it lacks in brevity is compensated for in thoroughness. Barbour's view is even a more radical departure from those we have encountered. He maintains time is a "heap" and those possible moments are culled like pictures from a party with no particular order.

Like Deutsch, Barbour's view of time is heavily influenced by quantum physics. We include this observation for completeness and note that the notion of heaps may be more in keeping with the quantum-influenced view of the world, but it is less intuitive to the human experience. The best possible explanation is one of resolution. Viewed at the quantum level, heaps may be the reality versus an interpretation of flow at the human level. Remember we mentioned earlier that atoms are eternal and that time exists with my birth. Said another way, time is marked when all those atoms are lumped together as a zygote in the womb but not when atoms exist individually. If time is marked by the occurrence of events, then what may be said qualitatively about time? That is, will the nature of biological events give rise to a different sort of time than nonlife events?

COMPRESSION

It was Einstein who introduced the notion that time meanders and burbles like a brook. It flows unevenly. This compression or warping of the fabric of space-time is the human-level parallel of relativity. Compression can be a desirable thing in financial economics because it may bring perceptions of the user and the provider of capital closer together, as our Lloyd's example illustrates, and thus reduce transaction costs or friction. The compression is also uneven in the sense that perfect information is never attainable. The perceptions of providers and users of capital can never be unique, because they are not the same entity. This is another way of saying that they cannot share the same place in space-time. Perhaps Gauss's principle of exclusion is related. The physical explanation is that they are different DNA structures, which have been modified by their own experiences. This is not as complex as it sounds. Humans have unique DNA codes, which can be modified. Smokers can help to produce cancer by smoking. Cancer is the abnormal growth of cells caused by a defective gene. If as a result of imminent death your view of the world and priorities change and different things become important, there is a good chance your investment outlook will likewise change. That two cannot occupy the same position at the same time is known by anyone who has been in a fender bender. In fact, it would be insanity to assume that they possibly could be or in financial economics to assume that they could have the same perspective on the same information—symmetric information is the technical term. But what about the temporal world?

If you jump to the conclusion that temporal perspectives may vary as evidenced by the problem of determining the length of the year, you are on the right track. Whereas geophysicists using 3D seismic analysis mentioned in Chapter 1 have some aspects of their business rooted in the physical world, the financier's world is rooted solely in the temporal domain. No one has ever seen "a finance" anymore than they have felt the Earth rotate. The processes that financiers must characterize in time and to which they must ascribe finite values, however imperfectly, are their cross to bear.

Many financiers love to summarily dismiss things they do not understand for the simple reason that they do not understand them, as if their lack of understanding will protect them. In the short run, they may survive, but not in the long run. To make progress and build upon their predecessors' foundation, financiers of the 21st century will have to know more than did their counterparts in the 20th.

FINANCIAL ECONOMICS

In 1998, we are making initial steps to lay off insured risk on the capital markets. If you were managing a portfolio of those insurance contracts, would you rather hear about events in real-time or read about them in tomorrow's paper? The answer is now because by tomorrow, when everyone else gets the news, the value of the insurance contracts will tank as the liabilities become known. We do not have to turn to such an exotic example. As Bloomberg knows, most of Wall Street votes with their wallets to have information now rather than later.

The imposition of the assumption of randomness is our first step in making time continuous. This is how the basic concept of a static analysis was extended and it was the seminal work of Merton, who applied the work of famed mathematicians Norbert Wiener and Kyoshi Itô. Itô's lemma is part of stochastic calculus—the calculus of random variables. And mirabile dictu, financial economics took a big step forward! Equilibrium and thus randomness could be used as proxies for the future. Thus, models could be built and assumptions made. Merton developed and codified many, if not most, of these concepts in his *Continuous-Time Finance*. Although the famous Black-Scholes model does not bear his name, his contributions are integral and should probably be reflected on its masthead.

The basic question we have to ponder is this: What happens if time, like the previous three examples of music, the calendar, and geometry, is a perfect system imposed on a less than perfect world? What if time, to use the musical terminology, is an even-tempered measurement of a phenomenon that does not occur evenly or smoothly? We measure time in uniform discrete chunks, called hours, days, and so on, but does it really occur that way? What if it does not progress smoothly and linearly? The lumping of volatility as characterized by fractals suggests that it does not. What if the relationship itself between the observer and the observed changes with time?

There are physical concepts to support the fact that time is not even or smooth as evidenced by relativity, where gravity warps the fabric of space-time like a rock in the middle of the bed warps the planar fabric of the bedsheet. This is a very important concept. In the physical world the relationship between the observer and the observed changes with time, as when our car comes to a bumpy halt as a train next to us accelerates. We can also see in biology that infants and children, who are said to grow like weeds or kudzu, have a rapid growth rate—as perceived by their parents. Is it that way for the child? If your reference group is everyone else in kindergarten or in the retirement home, then growth or the rate of change may seem normal. Normal in this example is a constant rate of change relative to the observer. Parents, like investors, necessarily have a different time horizon, but it is not static. It is changing, too. A year to a parent is proportionately less of their total life and patience is a probably a by-product of that.

In financial economics, emerging markets and small companies, like children, develop very quickly. But the rate of growth is not constant. It is not constant for larger companies, either, but the example is more dramatic for small-capitalization companies, known as small caps. The notion that the perceptions between observer and observed themselves are changing does not give us a quick solution, but the intuition that it is so brings us much closer to the relational rather than the absolute notion that separated Leibniz and Newton 300 years ago. If those changes are relative and thus in a sense evolutionary, then this is also in keeping with the evolutionary and nonlinear techniques we will have to model those changes.

One might immediately be tempted to leap to the conclusion that those changes between the observer and the observed are themselves random. This is partially true in that randomness exists and is a necessary part. But the changes themselves and the relationships between those changes are not *totally* random. If we accept the fact that everything is random, then a fortiori any sort of planning or analysis is by definition pointless. It is also intellectually unsatisfying because it explains nothing, which is a scarier proposition for mankind than trying to explain something because not attempting to explain anything emasculates our sense of self-worth. Fortunately though, partial predictability exists and there is enough partial predictability to warrant analysis or modeling. As a species, we feel better with the hope as we begin the day anew that we have attempted to extend our mastery over what Keynes called the "dark forces of time and ignorance."

Aside from time series analysis, one possible clue for contemplating partial predictability comes from biology. Your children are a genetic mix of you and your mate. They are not an exact copy of you. That would be a clone or perfect predictability. Nor did you produce progeny with no relationship to you as parents. That would be a truly random selection of the gene pool. You did produce a child who has a mix of genes, and that mix was influenced by randomness. You can see this in your neighborhood, if not your own home. Some children are a spitting image and some children offer no discernable clue, excepting DNA analysis, that they are their parents' issue. Moreover, the child does not grow randomly although growth is uneven. Also, we see one of the odd things about the universe is that chaos and order can coexist, as Peters explained in *Chaos and Order in the Capital Markets*.

Risk has usually been viewed as a function of time. We will now posit that time as a function of risk may be a better way, because with the compression of space-time (instant communication) money will be made or lost when those blips of high-risk, fast time occur. Time is now a variable rather than a constant and this is a departure from traditional practice. Yet. probably the best example is that most stock returns are gained in a fairly short period of time—fairly short relative to the total time invested. Insurance is sold in tranches. Why not sell mutual funds that way'? Moreover, why use tools that are fixed to measure something whose rate of change is clearly variable?

RISK AND THE HURST EXPONENT

One of the more disturbing aspects of the Hurst exponent (H) concerns risk and the perception of time. There is a simple mathematical link between H and the physical dimensions. Where $H = 1$, or is perfectly persistent, H corresponds to a line or 1D. When $H = 0.5$ or is random or a Brownian motion, it is equal to 1.5D, a fractal or noninteger dimension halfway between a line and a plane. And where $H = 0$, or is perfectly antipersistent, the corresponding physical dimension is a plane or 2D.

The concept behind risk and its measurement of volatility is this: The more something bounces up and down vis-à-vis itself the riskier it is. Physically, being in a boat with more roll—the side-to-side motion—is riskier

than being in one with less roll. If we take the notion that risk is characterized by volatility (not the math, just the notion) then, conversely, should not
a less up-and-down motion be less risky? Is not a line, 1D, then the least
amount of risk because it experiences the least amount of up-and-down?

The reasoning is subtle because it hinges on perception. If a stock is in a
steady state of the Hurst exponent 100% of the time, then it is not risky in a
sense because that state will be perfectly discounted and reflected in the
price of the stock. This is the same sort of behavior people exhibit when
they prefer to deal with someone who is a grouch 100% of the time rather
than deal with someone who is pleasant one day and markedly not the
next—which is captured by the masochistic saying "Better the devil you
know". Unfortunately, stocks do bounce around between persistence and
antipersistence and this can be crazy-making.

To continue, if a stock exhibited perfect persistence or a straight line, it
would imply that the price history is steady. In practice, the steady state of
the Hurst exponent is approached by event-driven examples such as bankruptcy or merger arbitrage, where values are locked by easily identifiable
circumstances. In theory, assuming a zero-valued stock could stay listed, it
would be perfectly persistent and thus very predictable and not risky. It
would also be a dead company. Now, the Hurst exponent is also a scaling
factor in time. If time does not scale for a dead company, what can we conclude? Would it be accurate to say that there is no risk? No. There is risk. It
is just that risk exists which is not captured by the constant perspective of
the time series itself. It is also worth stating that Brownian motion cannot
scale. Assuming randomness is like always seeing the world through a
50mm lens with no opportunity to improve on seeing the stars or the microscopic or to join Jacques Cousteau's colleagues underwater. Randomness is
a very singular view and the mistakes perpetuated by using it will persist until there is a change.

Contemplating a stock with a steady Hurst exponent is like asking, does
time slow down for a dead man? For the observer it does not slow down,
but for the dead man it probably does because the deceased is in equilibrium without an event. Thus, we have a split of perceptions. As an arbitrageur, I can attest that stocks in a steady state have risk that cannot be
fully characterized by volatility alone. The event we speak of in "event-
driven" strategies is often a judge's decision or a corporate action such as a
tender offer.

If the steady state at a non-zero value could be produced by a company
with an even stream of earnings, then it would begin to exhibit bondlike
behavior, because the only question left for the investor (assuming a *de
minimis* risk of insolvency) is the interest rate at which to discount the

earnings stream. Companies traded on the "pink sheets" are also approaching the steady state, but they run into a different problem, that of infrequent trading.

UPSHOT

Given that volatility lumps and clumps or exhibits what we call multifractal time like a bedsheet, how can one reasonably expect any risk-management program to calculate meaningful results when the assumptions are wrong? Time moves like an ant on a string that is stretched out and the ends brought back together. Maybe an elastic or rubber band is superior in concept to a piece of string. This is why equilibrium-based economics will never portray the real essence of economics.

OPTIONS

I was once asked, "If everyone gets your formula, won't the profit just be arbitraged away?" I did not bother telling this fellow that there are no formulas in nonlinear pricing, that we use computational rather than analytical solutions. I merely replied, "Did publishing the Black-Scholes option pricing formula build or destroy the $119-billion derivatives industry?" All derivatives, including embedded options in convertible bonds and SWAPs, which are complex combinations of puts and calls, are but variations on a theme. The reasons that the industry did not go away are many. And several things are true, such as the claim that real liquidity has moved "upstairs" from the trading floor to the dealing rooms of large financial companies. Cost is a major reason, since it is easier to buy a custom-made put on a basket of stocks than to buy the puts individually. Demand for derivative products has increased as knowledge, often painfully acquired as in the case of Bankers Trust and Metallgesellschaft, for example, has spread.

The real reason the derivatives have not gone away is the difference of perspective in time. Of the five inputs to the basic Black-Scholes model—stock price, interest rate, duration, volatility, and strike price—three are very unambiguous—stock price, duration, and strike price. The calculation for the interest rate curve, which corresponds for the duration of the option, is involved but attainable. The real problem is the perception of volatility, which is ambiguous. The basic difference is between historical volatility, which is calculated from past prices and is used as an input for the formula, and using implied volatility, which uses current market prices to impute an option price. Historical volatility is retrospective and implied volatility is prospective. Thus, the same option model can yield very different answers.

The right answer is elusive. Exigency may demand a historical calculation, but common sense says that current market conditions should be more relevant. The problem, as many mathematicians have discovered, is that modeling a nonlinear phenomenon like volatility with linear math becomes intractable. Time series do not behave as a random walk or a Brownian motion, and the normal or Gaussian distribution does not reflect the real returns of stocks as evidenced by the "volatility smile," which is documented extensively in the academic literature.

Theoretically, according to Black-Scholes, volatility should be uniform for all strike prices. Plotted it would be a horizontal line. Instead, traders, who are aware that the model does not accurately reflect the real risks at strike prices far removed from the current prices of the stock, called far-in-the-money or far-out-of-the-money strikes, compensate heuristically by "dialing-up" the volatility. The higher volatility is reflected in higher prices either far-in-the-money or far-out-of-the-money of the strike range. Plotted, this curve resembles a smile.

Philosophically, the more one lets the reality of the phenomenon dictate the model, the further one moves from what is accepted in terms of extant financial theory. I maintain, as any good scientist does, that the theory must fit the facts. And in the case of finance, our goal is to more accurately articulate the relationship between risk and reward in time as they are, and not how we wish them to be. A new concept has to replace the old. Merely extending the old way is comforting in the sense that certain assumptions are shared, but in doing so we also perpetuate the problems of the old way, which does not work as well as it could. And the implications are enormous because so much money is at stake. It means that millions of dollars in legacy software code has to be scrapped and rewritten. It also means that all the risk-management tools, which share many common assumptions, also err. All the hedges are wrong. Try explaining that to your client after you have just booked a $300 million SWAP, because if you don't someone else will.

For the financial economics professional the mathematical reason for the error in measurement to which the previous statement refers is as follows: Although we can calculate a finite variance from a sample, there is no relationship from that sample variance to the population variance—a critical link in the reasoning. More simply put, we can calculate a finite variance of IBM from some portion of its recent history, but there is no relationship that links the current sample of IBM's history with its population or overall past and future. The reason is because the returns of IBM are not normally distributed. They have a heavy-tailed distribution, as Mandelbrot and Fama pointed out over 30 years ago.

TIME AND DATA

In financial modeling there is a conundrum. Prices exist only during market hours. But the world time line continues and information continues to flow even though the markets are closed. Therein lies the conundrum. One is intermittent and the other is continuous.

Do we take the quick and dirty approach and pretend that weekends and holidays do not exist and assign them a value of zero? A similar conundrum exists when, strangely enough, the Japanese equity market closes for lunch. We usually do take the quick and dirty approach. This conundrum will become more important as instruments trade on different markets, as evidenced by the popularity of non-U.S. companies seeking access to U.S. capital markets. More importantly, as fuzzy logic continues to include greater amounts of qualitative information into numerical models, we realize that this type of information is not restricted by market hours. The time line of the world and thus of information still continues but diverges with the closing of every relevant market and converges with that market's opening. Maybe it is easier to say that the time line of the market emerges and collapses into the world when the market opens and closes, respectively.

OTHER WAY AROUND

Rather than looking at risk as a function of time, for many investors looking at time as a function of risk may be more practicable. In an increasingly risk-averse era, we want limits to expected risk. The closest concept is that of risk tranches in insurance, where exposure limits are clearly defined. With better real-time information and processing, which compresses space-time by narrowing the gap between the users and providers of capital, risk measurements can be made.

Gas mileage is a simple concept. Say we get an average of 25 miles per gallon. We get fewer miles per gallon accelerating than we do cruising on the highway, but the unit of the gallon stays constant. Flip the concept around—how many gallons per mile do we get? We can consume a fixed amount of gas quicker accelerating than we do cruising. But here mileage is the constant. And it is true that slowing our acceleration will give us better gas mileage. Substitute risk per unit of return for miles per gallon.

Suppose the greater the risk, the greater the return for some given period of time. Now, instead of getting a 14% return per annum on an investment, where for simplicity, risk is defined by the old notion of volatility, what about fixing the risk and letting time and the return vary? The risk-averse investor will be able to say, I will buy (expose my capital to) 100 risk units in your fund. If the reward via return within the risk parameters is met, the investment is continued. If the risk parameters are exceeded, the investor will either demand a higher premium in the case of a bond or a greater return in the case of an equity, or exit the investment. But now we have a way to define our risk exposure. Funds can now be sold in tranches.

The use of capital for certain classes of investors is defined less by time than by exposure to risk. Pension funds are a case in point. Their investors are less concerned than, say, hedge fund investors about making money in absolute returns than they are about preserving capital and making money in a relative return or beating the averages and having definite levels of risk exposure.

Compensation programs' attempt to narrow the perception gap is important as evidenced by efforts to compel employees to adopt a shareholders' point of view, or, as I would say, to narrow the perception gap between employees and suppliers of capital.

Since most money is made in an investment only at those times, there's no sense tying up capital and sitting around waiting for the returns to just happen. Is this short-termism? Perhaps. But with better measurements we can make better decisions. Opportunistic is how I prefer to think of it. It does mean that there is a closer perception between user and supplier of capital, though.

Take advantage of risk-reward that meets your parameters. To do that you will have to have an investment horizon in mind. Most investors already have an implicit horizon in mind, in that pension funds have a different horizon than day traders.

What changes is the investors' perception of time since mechanisms exist that narrow the perception gap and allow them to monitor and model it in real-time. No longer is the relevant yardstick 90 days or beating the averages. The relevant yardstick is amount of risk borne, regardless of the return or the time it takes to accrue it. We will be measuring the greatest return per unit of risk. Time will be a variable. And it will vary. The investments that give the greatest return per unit of risk will be the most stable. Curiously, this circuitous reasoning brings us back to a recent paper by the famed finance professor and Nobel Laureat Franco Modigliani and his granddaughter, Leah, now at JP Morgan, which also argues for efficiency. It was rejected, illogically in my opinion, by many finance professionals because real returns are thought to be preferable to risk-adjusted returns. That is, funds with a high absolute return are preferable to those which achieve the highest reward per unit of risk because the latter funds have a lower absolute return. When the former group of funds is adjusted for risk, their desirability is severely mitigated. Perhaps a good bear market will help these investors and professionals to rethink the absurdity of their position.

Assuming that risk unfolds proportionately with time, then reasoning backwards, since returns do not unfold at a steady 1% per month as most investors would prefer, risk does not either. And since risk does not unfold smoothly for the investment neither does time even though we continue to use fixed measurements for time.

Conceptually time is not taut like Mrs. Whatsit's skirt or smooth like the bedsheet. We are not applying relativity or Riemann geometry or tesseracts or any other exotic form of math to finance other than as a pedagogical aid to change your concept of how things *may* happen. Once this is done, you will see why linear approaches to financial economics are never going to be right other than in the most general of terms and why the goal of an a priori solution will remain unsolved other than in the most general of terms—so general that the solutions will count as only opinions.

Once we throw out Newton's idea that time is taut and that there is one big universal clock ticking away and everybody and everything beats to it, we arrive at a more relative notion of time. Here everybody and everything beats to their own clock and sometimes they are in sync, but mostly they are not. When all the participants of the market, like nodes on a network, are voluntarily participating, we have a very accurate and highly nonlinear view of the world and the economy and of markets in general.

Once we admit the complexity of the task, we must also look at the tools that help us to characterize it. Because of the market's dynamism, a priori solutions and linear techniques used to obtain them are often, as John Holland noted, "severely blunted" despite our insistence on using them. Because of all the possible states in a market that can occur, stating rules from the top down or the bottom up, other than in the most general of terms, seems futile. It is better to flip the concept around and interrogate the market and let the market tell you by what rules it is playing. We saw this in the risk arbitrage example, where sometimes it was smart to overpay and sometimes it was not.

The number of rules and the conditions under which they are applied become unwieldy very quickly. There is too much information to order in too short a period of time to be practicable. Fortunately, nature has provided us with the evolutionary paradigm, which is also highly nonlinear. Nature has found a more efficient way of ordering and processing complex bits of information and it is as complex as real life comes. The mathematical expression of this technique, as we have already discussed, is called genetic algorithms. A multiplicity of varying perspectives of market participants and other economic variables require a high-dimensional solution-space.

... AND THEY LIVED HAPPILY EVER AFTER

In sum, higher dimensions are not only a reality but a necessity for financiers. Kaku goes on to say, "In fact, Riemann's theory of higher dimensions, as interpreted by Lewis Carroll, has become a permanent part of children's literature and folklore, giving birth to other children's classics over the decades, such as Dorothy's Land of Oz and Peter Pan's Never Never Land." This sounds like a good start for your continued reading.

At the beginning of this chapter, I promised an additional benefit to you. Here it is. In an age when time with your children is at a premium, they will thank you for reading these books to them and spending time with them even though you may also have practical motives in mind. All the golf courses, bars, and offices in the world cannot muster the innate wonderment available to the little one in your lap and thus to you.

9

Nonlinear Pricing—
Advanced Concepts

Be regular and orderly in your life so that you may be violent and original in your work.

—GUSTAVE FLAUBERT

This chapter reconciles Soros's Theory of Reflexivity within the context of nonlinear pricing. Soros's intuition is correct but it took Ilya Prigogine, a Nobel laureate and probably the world's premier scientist in nonequilibrium physics, to build a scientifically credible case. By his own admission Soros brings a complex mind to bear on the complex subject of financial economics. Certainly the same is true of Prigogine in science. To the average practitioner in either discipline who finds the thinking of these men remote, this chapter will present a challenge because it exists at a rarified level of understanding.

This chapter is in three parts: Part I is the science background to put the Theory of Reflexivity in context. Part II is the Theory of Reflexivity interpreted, and Part III posits nonlinear pricing in general terms. If you want to see "how it really is," look at Kevin Kallaugher's famous cartoon (Figure 9.1). At its most visceral level, financial economics is not about math, science, or anything else written on paper. It is about buying what everyone else buys before they buy it and selling what everyone else sells before they sell it. The emotions of fear and greed, not the dispassionate attributes of intellect or judgment, seem paramount. If you are right and make money no one will care why. If you are wrong and lose money, no explanation will suffice.

But if we are ever to see "how it really is," we must first begin by trying to explain "how it might be." Given the evidence we have gathered, what

Kevin Kallaugher, KAL. The Baltimore Sun, Cartoonists and Writers' Syndicate—
used with permission.

special insight and imagination can we apply to make nonlinear pricing a better articulated and more coherent hypothesis? First we will reintroduce the matching principle.

Matching principle—The type of information being characterized must be matched with the technique best able to characterize it.

This principle does not seem to need to be stated. If phenomena are nonlinear then we can dismiss certain linear tools because they violate the matching principle and are no longer the best ways of characterizing information, even though they may be industry practice and therefore generally accepted. To paraphrase Warren Buffett, if 40,000 people have a bad idea, guess what? It is still a bad idea. But whatever the prevailing sentiments in theory, fashion, fads, trends, or customs, the world of financial economics is not immune. Invoking the matching principle to rid ourselves of linear math is tantamount to landing an expeditionary force on a beach and burning the ship. Any temptation to leave the new nonlinear world is quickly quashed.

We know for example that a recording is a better representation of a symphony than is a score sheet. In layman's terms, if one only has a hammer, then every problem looks like a nail. The differentiation here is to distinguish nails from screws or bolts. If a paper representation is inferior for a temporal phenomenon like a symphony, why is it the medium of choice for financial economics? What about 4D?

Although we have seen a history of nonlinearity in Chapter 2 and some formalization in financial economics in Chapter 3, it is the thoughts of practitioners, typically money managers, that I most value. They are the reports from the trenches. Their history is succinct and they are all from men of my father's generation. It begins in 1972 with *Dance of the Money Bees* by John Train, who first used a biological metaphor to express a phenomenon in financial economics—the degree of "excited-ness" that a fund manager can exhibit over a stock, that will in turn cause other bees or managers to follow. Swarm theory is now a discipline of computer science. Then to Jerry Goodman, alias Adam Smith, who in *Paper Money* in 1981 stated that Newtonian determinism was "dead." Inflation and the oil crisis were his cues that the way we "saw the world" was wrong. The post-Newtonian view is now becoming widely accepted.

In 1987 Soros wrote *The Alchemy of Finance*. It was the first serious attempt by an accomplished member of the workaday world to wrestle with the nontrivial subject of nonequilibrium-based economics. Soros's approach, as befitting his background and generation, comes from the philosophy of Popper, who also espoused the concept of "open society." Soros's intuition of nonequilibrium in financial economics is accurate; however, his terminology is self-admittedly impressionistic. The nonequilibrium view, too, is becoming widely accepted.

Had Soros been my contemporary rather than my senior, he almost certainly would have taken advantage of the maturation of the collateral concepts in science, mathematics, and computing to express Reflexivity. His reward for having the courage to explain what he saw in terms available to him was silence from the Street and indifference from the academic community. Fortunately history will treat him more kindly than they did.

In 1992 Ed Peters, the first of my contemporaries to write, published *Chaos and Order in the Capital Markets*. As befits our generation and background, the intuition of our father's generation finds itself expressed in terms of a more scientific bent. *Nonlinear Pricing* is the next salvo.

PART I—BACKGROUND

Philosophy

In searching for this nonequilibrium expression, I may be as welcome as Soros was, and yet he persisted and I know why. His financial success may have made him impervious to criticism and praise, but that is not what made him persist. The root reason is found in the philosophical aspects of non-equilibrium. You see, one of the moral casualties in the world of Newtonian determinism is free will. The reason is that free will can be determined, so there is no free will. Once we leave determinism, we began an indeterminate future, our free will and the realization that to change things you have to actively be part of the process. That is, we cannot stand apart as the isolated observer admitted by Newtonian determinism. To use our old movie example, we are inextricably part of the show and are thus compelled to make love while the bullets fly.

Unfortunately, since we are human and not divine, we are fallible. Even though we must act with what is right, what is right may not be ideal from an omniscient point of view. Therein lies a burden. In terms of reaction from the outside world, this can be painful and humiliating; however, in terms of being true to one's self there is no alternative. The reconciliation of possible adverse effects cannot be tallied only on a balance sheet. This is why we persist.

Thus, it is at the meta-level of realization that the concepts of philosophy, which finds its expression as Soros's Open Society Foundation, and financial-economic theory, which finds its expression as the mathematics of nonequilibrium, are in sync. Perhaps a more accurate term for this meta-level of realization is the political economy of free will. Certainly Adam Smith would have approved. I suspect the evident discrepancy between the literal and philosophical levels occurs because people have not been introspective enough because they have not been challenged enough. Soros's views were tempered by the hot fires of extreme conditions as a child trying to survive World War II and mine are from military service. These are extraordinary events in terms of normal suburban existence—an existence which, by definition, is not challenging in the extreme. Maybe a real challenge helps one in sorting the wheat from the chaff about what is really important in life. I can not offer any science to support this claim, but I strongly believe that it is true and privately speculate that this is why corporate America hankers after a transformational weekend at places like Outward Bound.

The reasons for the apparent charity from Soros's foundation are also clear. There are certain philosophies that have a transcendental aspect to them. On a personal scale, with the decision to have and care for a family comes the mandated change in view that one may no longer think only in terms of one's self. On a societal level, with the realization of knowing about the benefits of an Open Society comes the collateral responsibility to ensure that it is widely available. Another simile might be the paradoxical thing called love. One of the best ways to get love is to give it. Giving is having. That is, one cannot give what one does not have. So the only way to ensure that you always have it and will receive it is to keep giving it away. Because we are dealing with social phenomena, to use one of Soros's favorite examples, there is a reflexive aspect much like the concept used in the French language where the subject is also the object.

Happily for a man like Soros, who sees political economy as a philosopher, help is on the way. In *The End of Certainty: Time, Chaos and the New Laws of Nature* Prigogine notes, "Mankind is at a turning point, the beginning of a new rationality in which science is no longer identified with certitude and probability with ignorance." We agree completely with Yvor Leclerc when he writes, "In the present century we are suffering from the separation of science and philosophy which followed the triumph of Newtonian physics in the eighteenth century." Jacob Bronowski beautifully expressed the same thought in this way: "The understanding of human nature and of the human condition within nature is one of the central themes of science."

Popper also saw the heart of the argument of this book when he said, "I regard Laplacian determinism—confirmed as it may seem to be by the *prima facie* deterministic theories of physics, and by their marvelous success—as the most solid and serious obstacle to our understanding and justifying the nature of human freedom, creativity, and responsibility." For him, "The reality of time and change is the crux of realism."

The attempt to reconcile determinism and indeterminism dates from Epicurus who thought he had found a compromise with the *clinamen*. As told by Lucretius, "While the first bodies are being carried downward by their own weight in straight lines through the void, at times quite uncertain and at uncertain places, *they deviate slightly from their course*, just enough as having changed direction." Stephen W. Hawking would later invoke the anthropic principle, but neither man could explain how these things could come from a deterministic understanding.

In contrast, Einstein and Spinoza in an attempt to keep the unity of nature reduced man to mere automata. Until the expression of temporal asymmetry and indeterminism finds itself in the laws of dynamics, there is no solution to this dilemma. Clausius was the first in 1865 who gave us the term *entropy*, which in Greek translates as evolution. Eddington then conjectured that entropy must follow the "arrow of time." The solution has recently begun to emerge. It is expressed in probabilities rather than certitudes.

Probabilistically expressed indeterminism may constitute Soros's third category of truth; true, false, and the indeterminate or reflexive. It is strongly analogous to the degree of membership function found in fuzzy logic. Again conceptually, indeterminism has its roots in antiquity. One of Aristotle's famous "Laws of Thought," a forerunner to what became known in mathematics as "The Law of the Excluded Middle" as put forth by Parmenides around 400 B.C., holds that a proposition is either true or false. Heraclitus refuted this, saying that a thing could be true and not true simultaneously. To admit a probabilistic assertion also admits the ability to be wrong, or, in Soros's words, "to recognize one's inherent fallibility."

Politics

From Chapter 2 recall that the evolutionary epistemology of Popper as put forth by Deutsch as one of the four strands of reality holds that real knowledge can only be falsified but never verified. Human existence evolves in the fog of understanding from explanation to explanation, with progress marked by explanations which fell by falsification to superior explanations. Were we to admit a universal truth no longer subject to question, we would halt inquiry and thus progress. Whereas Deustch treated this process of hypothesis, testing, falsification, and hypothesis in the scientific realm, Popper and Soros saw the process as fundamental to the human condition. In this sense they are in agreement with Deustch. Because the process is fundamental and therefore irreducible, it must be necessary.

The only political context that admits such open questioning, testing, and so on with no rigidly held ideology is a democracy. Though not without imperfections, the United States of America's implementation of this ideal is the exemplar. Those places where dogmatism still holds sway, as evidenced by totalitarian regimes, are the antithesis of an Open Society. Seen in this light, Soros's foundation work in Eastern Europe is a simple natural extension of what makes him get out of bed in the morning.

Economics

The conceptual jump to economics is easy. A society is a group of people, as is a market. What this group does and how it behaves has different names depending on whether the context is politics or economics. At a macro level there may be no discernable difference since they are two sides of the same coin of political economy. After all, the principles that govern how I treat me govern how I treat my wealth, which is a product and thus extension of me. They are the same. The schism or unrest comes when rules from one group are imposed on another. As seen from this vantage point, the extant body of financial economic literature makes little sense. Reconciling the two in a rigorous way is what we will attempt. And the outcome is bound to be as alien a creature as if we were to treat politics in more scientific terms.

We begin with the concept of equilibrium as a conventional notion brought in wholesale from physics over 50 years ago and based on the discredited idea of Newtonian determinism. Equilibrium is a static measure that has suffered a fatal blow from a changing weltanschauung known as the post-Newtonian or relational view. This relational view is grounded in the best methods of knowledge acquisition that mankind has at present, and is confirmed by various disciplines. The relational view supports concepts such as nonequilibrium, evolution, nonlinearity, and almost every other term in this book. Curiously, when Prigogine begins his discussion in *The End of Certainty*, he does so with a quote from Popper's *The Open Universe: An Argument for Indeterminism:* "Common sense inclines, on one hand, to assert that every event is caused by some preceding events, so that every event can be explained or predicted. . . . On the other hand, . . . common sense attributed to mature and sane human persons . . . the ability to choose freely between alternate probabilities of acting. This 'dilemma of determinism,' as William James called it, is closely related to the meaning of time."

This change has been caused by advances in technology which have allowed us to measure or quantify the world with greater precision and generality. Beginning with Copernicus, who introduced math to describe planetary movement, this is the simple description of the history of Western civilization. The only difference now of course is that the change to a nonequilibrium view is happening about the second millennium after Christ and it is happening to the fundamental concepts we use to articulate the emotional subject of financial economics.

Expanded Physics

This section expands two limiting assumptions of current financial economics: equilibrium and randomness of a time series and explores Table 9.1. Both of these concepts are defunct legacies of Einstein's deterministic space-time physics applied to financial economics. We immediately see two things: First, that both equilibrium and randomness were serviceable approximations that have been applied from an old and discredited paradigm of physics and second, that financial economics is a higher-level

Table 9.1   Comparative States

EQUILIBRIUM	NEAR EQUILIBRIUM	FAR FROM EQUILIBRIUM
Neoclassical	Nonlinear Pricing	
economic theory	Theory of Reflexivity	
TIME AND VANTAGE		
Reversible	Irreversible	
∞- ← t → +∞	t → +∞	
Retrodict and predict	Partially predict	
All vantages are equal	Some vantages are better	
ROLE OF PRICES		
Passive		Active
Price taker		Price maker
DESCRIPTIVE PROCESS		
Absolute	Relational	
	Dialectics	
SOLUTUION TECHNIQUES		
Analytic	Computational	
Formula	Simulation	
RISK		
Risk increases	>	>
SCIENCE PARADIGM		
Physics	Biology	
APPLICABLE TIME		
Almost always	Nonlinear pricing	Theory of Reflexivity
does not apply	almost always applies	applies sometimes
CAUSALITY		
Causal	Weakly causal	
Determinate	Indeterminate	

phenomenon than physics in that it is more derivative. In other words, there is a *mismatch* in the levels of theory and phenomenon, which results in a lack of explanatory power for equilibrium-based theory. It is unreasonable to assume that a more fundamental theory will adequately explain the richer environment of more complex phenomena. Clearly, as we saw on the KAOS screen, a financial time series is not random 100% of the time, and clearly markets do occasionally crash.

Since financial economics has borrowed from Newtonian physics before, and since we have expanded physics beyond Newtonian determinism, it makes sense to return to see what physics and other fields have done in the subsequent decades to determine if any new developments or interpretations may add to our understanding of financial economics. It sounds limiting to keep referring to physics as the sole provider of answers and in a sense it is.

However, the physicists' tradition for unfettered inquiry seems more robust than our own. How else can I explain a deterministic view that ceased to be credible in physics over 70 years ago but is still alive and well in financial economics? The physicists' traditional limitation is the fact that their agents are electrons. In financial economics our agents are anticipating and self-referencing people. This fact alone argues for a more biologically-oriented approach.

However, what may not be obvious is that physics has grown in this century to incorporate or subsume other fields. Physics—as a metaphor for knowledge—has structurally changed to become both broader and deeper. Astronomy is now astrophysics. The study of the universe is now cosmology. Frank Tipler's Omega Point—the physics of global general relativity—incorporates eschatology! Closer to financial economics are the fields of geometry and more importantly time. As we saw in Chapter 4, the Hurst exponent is clearly related to fractal geometry because a time series exists between the Euclidean definition of a line and a plane. The Hurst exponent is also a scaling factor in time. Geometry was once thought to be a field of mathematics. However, relativity changed that. With the successful challenge to Euclid's parallel theorem, we see in fact that the three angles of a triangle add up to 180 degrees only in highly idealized circumstances. When Einstein introduced relativity and found that the fabric of space-time is curved, a triangle does not necessarily have to sum to 180 degrees because gravity is now a factor. Thus, geometry may be reclassified as part of physics. It was also relativity that put the notion of time on a rigorous foundation. Prior to that the subject of time was solely the province of philosophy. Moreover, physics has grown to incorporate the quantum world. With the compelling proposal by Deutsch that life/evolution, computing, and knowledge are part of the description of the physical world, it seems that physics has grown again. Since the Hurst exponent is a scaling factor in both time and geometry and because both time and geometry and much else are now part of physics, we can now trace a direct link via the Hurst exponent from its application in financial economics through physics.

Life/evolution, computing, and knowledge are all germane to financial economics. Financial economics is growing increasingly dependent on computing. Financial economics is created by life, as certainly without it there would be no need for a market of exchange. Because of the perpetual novelty of evolution, we must use computational rather than analytic solution techniques. Prigogine has extended physics to include population dynamics. Smolin has also explored the idea of a biologically based interpretation of physics since the cosmos evolves. Bak looked at dynamics in terms of self-organized criticality. Biologists have also made advances as Kauffman has done with complexity theory and as Rose has by looking past the deterministic ultra-Darwinists in biology. Computer scientists such as Holland have borne biologically inspired mathematical modeling. Respected economists such as Romer and Day have also made inroads incorporating dynamics, nonlinearity, and mathematics. Clearly the discipline in which the explanation is applied is easy to recognize, but the mélange of activity leading to that reasoning can be quite eclectic and presently exceeds the purviews of run-of-the-mill MBAs or CFOs. At this level of abstraction, there is not much that is intuitive in physics or financial economics. Like the semiconductor worker, you need to have the background. The approach of sort of figuring it out, whether it is making the leap from mechanics to electronics or linear to nonlinear financial economics, is dead.

There is also no denying that financial economics occurs in the physical world and thus is subject to its laws. As we have seen with the well-known Moore's Law, physical laws are *the* limiting case of what mathematics and thus financial economics may or may not do. The fact that we are usually ignorant of that ever-moving boundary of the limiting case is no reason to pretend that it does not exist. It is a bit like a 10-year-old boy denying the existence of sex because he has yet to encounter it. Nor will it do to be satisfied that the boundary is too far away to be material to our present thinking. As technology progresses those bounds are more frequently touched. The historical case is thermodynamics in the form of a steam engine, which gave rise to an economic boom in the 19th century. Electrodynamics in the case of electricity is a more contemporary example. The transistor, computer, and the Internet continue this tradition by pushing electrons through physical mediums as fast as possible. More pertinently to financial economics is the fact that technology is rapidly moving the boundary of what was once intractable to what is tractable.

It seems very reasonable that knowing those boundaries will make for more informed economic decisions. Knowing that something is physically possible is often a very important first step in determining if it is do-able and finally if it is feasible or cost-effective to do so. Finally, knowing what is possible is not the same as knowing how to get there and that is the reason a *process* for the method of knowledge acquisition is vital. To date, our best is Popper's method of proposal, testing, refuting/accepting, and new proposal, which is also a part of Deutsch's thesis. An explanation may not be verified, but it should stand until it is falsified. Randomness and equilibrium are now falsified.

In reality we are in a world of multiple fluctuations. Those fluctuations are manifestations of fundamental properties arising from the microscopic level of unstable dynamical systems. The irreversibility of time starts at the most fundamental level and is magnified though atoms, molecules, life, humans, and finally human activity. The eminent biologist Stephen Jay Gould said as much when he penned the following:

> To understand the events and generalitics of life's pathway, we must go beyond principles of evolutionary theory to a paleontological examination of the contingent patter of life's history on our planet—the single actualized version among millions of possible alternatives that happened not to occur. Such a view of life's history is highly contrary to conventional deterministic models of Western science and to the deepest social traditions and psychological hopes of Western cultures for a history culminating in humans as life's highest expression and intended planetary reward.

It is here that we see the explanations of biology and physics begin to merge. In financial economics we are at the nascent stage of considering the multiple alternatives caused by the instability inherent in the universe. Dixit and Pindyck in *Investment under Uncertainty* suggest we take waiting into account—that is, the cost of doing nothing—and strongly note the fact of irreversibility. Ron Dembo and Andrew Freeman in *Seeing Tomorrow: Rewriting the Rules of Risk* raise the point of regret, an attempt to price a contingent and irreversible event.

Again, happily for Soros, the convergence of biology and physics to describe the nonequilibrium world of financial economics dovetails nicely with philosophy as well. Popper says, "My own point of view is that indeterminism is compatible with realism, and that the acceptance of this fact allows us to adopt a coherent objective epistemology of the whole of quantum theory, and an objective interpretation of probability." In truth one cannot meaningfully state anything in financial economics without referring to time, resonance, and resolution.

Resonance and Time

"Time precedes existence" is Prigogine's quote. That is, "Time has no beginning and probably no end." Time is marked by events that result from inherent instabilities in the medium of the universe and thus is an emergent phenomenon. Just as evolution in biology cannot be studied at the level of the individual, the flow of time is a global property. This was the cause of Ludwig Boltzman's failure when he attempted to emulate Darwin's approach over a century ago.

These instabilities are characterized by resonance, and viewed from different levels of resolution they seem to have unique properties. That is, at the atomic level of resolution, time does not seem to exist in the sense that it cannot be measured by an event. However, once those atoms reach some critical mass, which can be associated with an event, such as a zygote in the womb, time can be marked. This simple fact recognizes the irreversability of time. Simply, the symmetry of time—the ability to predict and retrodict—is broken and no longer dependent on an observer. And it is this fact more than any other which contributed to the demise of determinism. The observer is no longer necessary. In other words, when the tree falls in the forest and there is no one to hear it, it still makes a noise.

Characterizing inherent instabilities is a concept called nonequilibrium that allows for conditions to achieve different states. The multiplicity of resonances occurring at different levels of resolution are characterized by a complex or fractal solution space. One of the best methods we have of dealing with the change in states and the complexity to which they give rise is called biology, particularly the concept of evolution. Occasionally a simple high-level state is reached called self-organizing criticality. Thus, self-organized criticality is a product of irreversibility. But the price of realizing this is the destruction of the equivalence between individual levels of statistical description. This, in turn, is why linear mathematics and formulas and the analytic approach will not work. Having said that, reversible time and thus equilibrium do exist, but in the main are merely highly idealized notions and thus subsets of a more prevalent irreversible time and nonequilibrium.

In financial economics our resolution is primarily determined by the temporal realm and the level of aggregation. That is, an organized exchange is a level of aggregation of prices and it can be viewed over varying investment horizons. Time is marked by the event leading from the level of resolution. This is the insight behind a relational time and specifically supported by Müller et al.'s "Fractals and Intrinsic Time—A Challenge to Econometricians." The frequency of prices is, strictly speaking, a price analysis. Resonance is the mutually beneficial interference of frequencies and takes on an added richness when other variables are added to describe the environment of the time series. This is the traditional realm of fundamental analysis and value analysis.

Resonance is very important and dates back to when Poincaré proved that dynamical systems were nonintegrable because dynamical motions are not isomorphic with respect to free noninteracting particles. The reason is the existence of resonances between the degrees of freedom. In other words, a frequency corresponds to each mode of motion. Instead of particles we use financial variables. Prigogine continues, "The simplest example of this is the harmonic oscillator, in which a particle and a central point are given. . . . When we force a spring to deviate from its equilibrium position, it vibrates with a characteristic frequency. Now let us subject this spring to an external force that can be varied. When the two frequencies, that of the spring and that of the external force, have a simple numerical ratio (that is, when one of the frequencies is either equal to the other, or two, three, four ... times larger), the amplitude of the motion of the spring increases dramatically. The same phenomenon occurs when we play a musical instrument. We hear the harmonics. Resonance 'couples' sound." In essence, this is the concept behind nonlinear pricing from the theoretical point of view. Later in this chapter we will explore resonance by substituting a time series and market for the spring and external force, respectively.

In a system characterized by two frequencies when their sum is zero or the ratio of their frequencies is a rational number we have resonance. However, as Poincaré showed, there are "dangerous" points where the sum of the frequencies was not zero but their reciprocal. That is where resonances diverge. This simple fact was long overlooked and when it was comprehended by KAM theory, which dealt with the influence of resonance on trajectories. It lead to a new formalization of dynamics. "According to Kolmogorov Arnold & Moser (KAM) theory, we observe two types of trajectories: 'nice' deterministic trajectories and 'random' trajectories associated with resonance which wander erratically through phase space. So some points in phase space take on complex values like chaos," writes Prigogine. Resonances are a nonlocal event that cannot be described by a single point in phase-space or an instant.

In looking at a spectrum of frequencies like a time series, or information about an investment, we do not want to see all frequencies but only what is useful for our purposes. This is in essence the observation the late physicist Richard Feynman made about the eye and all frequencies of the electromagnetic spectrum. The eye is a filter. It is also what Warren Buffett intimated when he said that you do not have to swing at every pitch or invest in every opportunity.

Erwin Schrödinger in *What Is Life?* makes a parallel between the open dissipative systems of physics and biology and the concept of negative entropy or "negentropy." An open system like your garden or business will "dissipate" if it is not maintained. In scientific terms this maintenance is called negentropy. Entropy is the amount of disorder in a system and follows time's arrow, so it only increases. In information theory we gave the example of a measurement of entropy as "Buddha." Thus, to keep the garden neat and the business profitable as open dissipative systems, negentropy must be applied. See Table 9.2.

Prigogine makes a link between the interaction of matter to achieve a flow of correlations and suggests that the same may be true of people in terms of a flow of communication. If so, then new qualitative descriptors

Table 9.2 Nonequilibrium Systems

Condition	Physics	Financial Economics
Equilibrium	Entropy at a maximum Negentropy at a minimum	
Near-equilibrium	Decrease in energy	High willingness to trade Liquidity
Far-from-equilibrium	Increase in energy Entropy at a minimum Negentropy at a maximum	Low willingness to trade Lack of liquidity

may be in store for future researches to describe the interaction of people and the market. An increase in energy increases randomness. Energy is also associated with a frequency. Here is an interesting speculation. Can we make a conceptual link between negentropy and liquidity? Both are required to keep a system maintained—one physical, the other financial. Without liquidity, markets crash. If so, then the state of far-from-equilibrium in physical and financial systems paradoxically suggests an inverse relationship. More liquidity means less energy, or randomness and a near-equilibrium condition. Correspondingly, more energy means less liquidity and a greater susceptibility to far-from-equilibrium conditions. In financial economics this negentropy or energy might be thought of as the kinetic state of the desire for improvement. The active pursuit of this improvement is what the investor does every day at the office. Perhaps the apparent contradiction between an increase in energy and investors' lack of willingness to trade is that energy manifests itself in stress, which paralyzes them. Collectively they are known as the market.

Thus it is entropy or the increasing amount of disorder in a system and negentropy in the form of the active pursuit of improvement which form the countervailing forces that are the bounded degrees of a variety in a system called complexity. Schrödinger attributed negentropy in biological systems to conscious sorting demons—humans in financial-economics to circumvent the second law of thermodynamics. Although negentropy is ill-defined in financial economics with respect to a direct measurement, it is indirectly measurable at the global level through the cumulative effects of resonance. Because of Poincaré resonances, irreversible dynamical processes lead to long-term memory effects—just as those detected by the Hurst exponent. Dynamics as such can be seen as a history of correlations that begins to "see" in nonequilibrium, as Prigogine says. The conclusion is that equilibrium is "blind" and gives us a false image.

Reasons Why Financial Economics Is in Disequilibrium

Let us quickly review some reasons why financial economics is not in equilibrium and therefore nonlinear. Reasoning from our physical universe we note that the universe is not in equilibrium. It is dynamic, not static. Using the *anthropic* principle and thus reasoning from our existence, we and all living things are not in equilibrium. Physically, we are in equilibrium when we are dead. Our expectations are in equilibrium when they are sated. Extending the example, life also implies by its very existence an organization, though perhaps not optimal, that is certainly better than random. Life may be considered a unique form of energy with a purpose. Philosophers may say consciousness, existence, and bliss are the goals of all living things. More fundamentally in biological terms it is surviving and procreating. Thus, the energy is directed. It is energy with the purpose of living. Lastly, extant equilibrium-based and thus linear theory has not met with complete success in explaining economic reality. Until that goal is met, the need for an improved understanding is mandated.

Any efficient system like a cosmos or a company exists in a semi-tensed or out-of-equilibrium state. Some organization exists and is compelled to exist to achieve some purpose. For example, demonstrating the dynamics of traffic jams Bak on the last page of *How Nature Works* called this the critical state. It is the most efficient state that can be achieved dynamically by a system. A simple physical demonstration of dynamic tension is the muscles that hold your arm in the shoulder. You may have seen someone suffer the effect of a stroke when the arm slumps and has to be held in place with a brace. The dynamic tension is gone.

The critical state recognizes that higher throughput could be achieved but only at the expense of greater instability. Bak calls this a critical economy as opposed to an equilibrium economy. Evidently healthy economies sometimes experience large shocks, which we should accept. Karl Marx, he goes on to point out, thought that capitalistic economies lurched from crisis to crisis and that fluctuations in prices, unemployment, and so on could be smoothed out with a centralized economy. This real-time experiment in planned economies failed in the case of the Soviet Union. Only the most left-leaning people might consider the verdict still out in communism. Bak concludes that the fluctuations that we sweat through are actually a normal sign of a healthy economy and not something we should try to avoid. In that case, investors should either accept wider swings in their returns or pay a higher premium for smoother ones!

In a business, different functions are required and held in place with incentives such as pay and rewards. Things have to get done for life to exist. Were everyone left to one's own devices, without the discipline of any over-all companywide objective in mind, chaos would reign. There would be no organization. If purpose-directed energy is allowed to cease, then the system will wind down. Entropy or the amount of disorganization will increase. Paint would begin to peel off your house, burst pipes would not be replaced, invoices would not be sent, and services would not be rendered. Energy without direction is a return to the wild.

Markets exist in this same semi-tensed state since they exist for a pur-pose. What supplies this energy? Energy required by the market is supplied by humans, Schrödinger's "conscious sorting demons," who gather and as-similate knowledge (K) to bid their expectations for the purpose of im-provement or profit. They bid to live.

Necessary and Sufficient Conditions for Emergence in FE

Three conditions are necessary and sufficient for emergence or autocatalytic behavior in financial economics. They are:

- *Volume.* We must have volume because it marks both the passage of time and mandates the generation of prices. Volume is also the best in-dicator of liquidity or willingness to trade, even though it is *ex post.*

- A *divergence of perceptions.* As a result of volume, we find a mandated divergence of opinion. If this were not true, we would not have buyers and sellers.

- *Unmet expectations.* After some experience with the divergence of per-ceptions we will see unmet expectations. That is, one side of the trade will be disappointed with the failure or lack of subsequent success of their trade. As a consequence, we have the emergence of market insta-bility and dynamics.

Resolution

In making an analogy to financial economics, the difference in vantage is not physical but temporal and thus informational in the sense that an advan-tage in time is an advantage in information. Knowing something sooner can be a definite advantage. Soros in his Theory of Reflexivity—and even in most serious analysis—attempts to abduct or to gain this advantage. Obvi-ously the quality of abduction is very important since it is time-dependent, and because of imperfect information, the impact of the analysis can only be local. No single analysis can be uniformly accepted and acted upon by all participants in a market. It cannot be grasped by all people or agreed upon. The reasons are myriad—lack of intellectual acuity, risk profile, and so on. On a larger scale the barriers may be political intransigence or lack of will in the case of austerity measures.

Those participants who favor the historical record exclusively are—because it is supposedly less controversial and therefore conservative—inductivists. Induction works beautifully in a deterministic world since from a few known points everything else can be determined. Unfortunately, when the assumption of determinism falls, the blind faith in inductivism becomes misplaced. The upshot is that it is actually safer to be abducting and proactively assuming some intelligent amount of risk than it is to be avoiding all risk. With a relational view, inductivism is tantamount to driving forward while looking through the rearview mirror.

Arguing from pure logic, applying induction to the markets should result in failure more often than abducting does. This may account for why Soros's performance based on hypothesizing is more successful than trust departments. Changing in the face of ever-changing circumstances may actually be less risky on average. Imperfect **K** or knowledge means that perfect predictability is impossible, but partial predictability is possible. For how long and how certain or robust is the partial prediction? These are difficult questions. First, the length of an aperiodic cycle is in perpetual flux. Obviously the longer the investment horizon, the less susceptible it is to short-term fluctuations. This is intuitive. The real answer is that cycles have to be continuously monitored. Hurst is the indicator of choice. It is almost impossible to answer the question of how strong or robust without multiple sequential simulations to actually demonstrate it visually.

Often there is a real opportunity for miscommunication because practitioners' practical experience and intuitive knowledge far outstrip their ability for rigorous expression of that knowledge. Senses finely honed in the marketplace are crudely articulated with a formalism that typically ceased being deveoped in high school with the concept of percentages of probability. Formally speaking, they forget that high school probability assumes independence—an assumption directly disproved by the serial correlation evidenced by Hurst. Moreover, as any etymologist knows, language is a living thing and meanings are ultimately determined by usage. Informally speaking, the usage of probability in the vernacular is a catchall phrase that bears little resemblance to its mathematical definition.

Ed Peters gave an insightful example during a lecture illustrating the concept of membership functions versus probability. Membership functions are the province of fuzzy logic and deal with the concept of overlapping sets. His example dealt with fetid water. Given a choice of drinking from a pool that was, probabilistically speaking, 90% fetid or one that had a 90% membership function of fetid water and pure water, from which would you drink? Neither alternative looks good. Option one says nine times out of 10 you are dead. Option two says that 10 times out of 10 you are dead because the water is nine parts crud and one part pure.

Terms

We have defined the following terms previously but we have not integrated them on a conceptual level.

- Complexity or the bounded degree of variety within a system and the self-organized criticality that it occasionally exhibits are high-level properties of financial economics. For example, after about 50 days, equity time series approach a steady state of about $H = 0.6$, a sort of self-organization in the timescape—the temporal version of a landscape.

- Resolution refers to the level at which we look at things. Self-organized criticality is a top-down approach and Darwinism is a bottom-up approach. Neither is sufficiently robust to explain everything individually. We care about what their intersection can provide us about the thing we wish to explain.

- Resonance is the mutual beneficial interference of frequencies. Power laws are indicative of frequency of occurence. Resonance is how we will determine the relationship of phenomena vis-à-vis each other. Resonance is how intellectual capital might be reconciled with physical capital, open versus closed systems, and increasing returns reconciled with decreasing returns.

- A relational approach, which can be a descriptor such as coevolution, looks at things in terms of each other. It is not one frequency or time series we wish to look at in isolation; it is one or more of them in a relational context. And in context means relative to the market or relative to other time series.

- Multifracticality measures the degree to which time speeds up; this of course, has a direct effect on the frequency and resonance. Another way of thinking about frequency is phase. Lastly, it is not an identical frequency or phase we care about. According to Webster's, the definition of resonance for physics is, "the effect produced when the natural vibration frequency of a body is greatly amplified by reinforcing vibrations at the same or nearby frequencies from another body." We must modify this definition for financial economics by striking the word "body" and substituting the word "process." It is the reinforcement or amplification of this resonance that gradually moves a market from near-equilibrium to far-from-equilibrium. An example is the self-reinforcing process that leads to a bull market. Although favorable market conditions may initiate the process, it is the raised expectations of **K** and the positive feedback in the form of rising prices that exacerbates the trend.

- Computational solutions are the only method that can capture this process. The best solutions include nonlinear technologies such as the generalizations of fuzzy logic and the highly iterative improvements of genetic algorithms. We cannot state a formula for a fast-changing resonance, but we can characterize that change with some generalization and a highly iterative technique as was demonstrated in Chapter 7, "Biology and the S&P." Finding these improvements is the systematic extraction of **K**. Almost every time we traded we had an informational advantage over the market. This advantage translated into a profit.

Near- to Far-from-Equilibrium

What causes transient behavior and thus the change in states? As we have seen, the cause for instability is inherent in the universe. We have detected instability in various ways in financial economics. Soros noted that freely floating exchange rates are inherently unstable. Romer, Krugman, and Arthur noted that increasing returns, which characterize the information economy, lead to instability. Siegel noted that at some point in time a diffusion process becomes biased and leads to dissonance and thus nonequilibrium.

Soros distinguishes near-equilibrium as a state when conditions are easy to change and far-from-equilibrium as a state when conditions are hard to change. This can be interpreted as follows. In near-term conditions, the flow of resonances is less persistent. As a result, they have not autocatalyzed or self-organized into phase lock. Imagine lots of people walking down a New York City sidewalk. Often, at just the right speed and density of people, they will fall into step. This is phase lock. The process of this self-organization is autocatalytic. No external force acted upon it. It just emerged. Another illustrative example is Kallaugher's cartoon at the beginning of this chapter. The beginning part of the sell phase is near-equilibrium. At the end of the sell phase we are far-from-equilibrium. The interaction of people and their effects as measured by the time series and other variables has pushed or aggregated the resonances above a threshold.

The more technical reason is bifurcation occurs at the points where resonances have a non-zero, noninteger denominator. The research to determine which frequencies (e.g., time series) to use to model has not been done in financial economics. My intuition leads me to suspect that it is a logical extension of the S&P analysis in Chapter 7. Here we found that resonances exist and can be profitably characterized. The next step is to determine the properties of their divergence. This work will go a long way in ascertaining what rules apply when.

Velocity and Persistence

The speed and density of people on the sidewalk are analogous to velocity and persistence. If velocity is slow enough then, as Soros contends, markets have a chance to adjust and thus prevent what would normally be a disastrous scenario. Persistence is a function of density. That is, the denser the field, the more persistent the interaction. What makes their conceptualization challenging is that they need to be taken simultaneously.

Persistence allows the flow of resonances to become stronger as a result of this attraction. To form a shift in state, ultimately they will have to become strong enough to overcome interfering forces. I think the best way to visualize the buildup stage of the flow of resonances is to use the concept of aggregation as it applies to cellular automata which forms "patches" as it begins to organize state-space. The inflection point where rapid growth is achieved resembles a biological growth. Red algae in the sea, like a network, have the same growth characteristics. The Internet is over 20 years old. For many reasons it perked up in 1992 and by 1995 it was a widespread phenomenon. This inflection point where a marked change in the rate of growth occurs is Kelly's "tipping point" or Holland's "lever" between a near- and a far-from-equilibrium state. This strength is not unlike a magnetic strength of attract-repulse. Attraction gives a feedback mechanism; the result of the process is often reflected in a run-up in prices. In the initial stages of feedback it is quite weak.

Going back to Weyl's field theory in Chapter 3, I suspect the answer to Soros' question about the distinction between near-equilibrium and far-from-equilibrium has its roots in the strength between and among certain metrics.

Change

The change from a near- to a far-from-equilibrium condition has been stated technically as a bifurcation point. It has also been noticed by Soros as a qualitative change as it has by Holland as a lever and Kelly as a tipping point. These are the points where the speed and velocity of persistence push resonance to a new state. Visualizing this state is what I proposed in using the cellular automata maps. There are two important points to be made here. One, attempting to ascribe causality to this tipping point may be in vain. The reason is that we are seeing a phenomenon like the economy at a high level of resolution; thus we will have to accept a great amount of indeterminacy. For example, a lowering of interest rates may not be a strong enough causal reason to change states. The quality of change will vary. Second, quantifying the flows of resonances, or what Holland calls the tagging problem, is nontrivial. This is why I believe some metrics used to describe resonance are standard GAAP/FASB concepts and some will have to be nonstandard, the so-called secondary and tertiary metrics.

For example, as demonstrated by quantum superpositioning, information is a physical quantity. As a result, it is the laws of physics that govern what is computable. Thus information stands in light of fuller possible characterization in terms of the fundamental forces of nature. If we can admit this then we can admit that descriptions from the physical world may provide invaluable clues. For example, the strength of persistent interaction that gives rise to resonance admits no descriptor to give a quality of that strength, in much the same way that volume adds a dimension to price. Such a descriptor would be very useful in determining a move to general opinion such as the market's current affair with Internet stocks. Could developing a more refined view of resonance and the tipping points or levers using weak or strong force interaction give an insight into the measure of strength?

Static and Dynamic Disequilibrium

Soros also speaks of static and dynamic out-of-equilibrium conditions. The difference can be illustrated with the example of a house. The equilibrium condition for a house is ruins since this is what time and weather will reduce it to. Repairing it by adding paint, fixing the plumbing, and so on, or what we refer to in a systemic sense as adding negentropy, results in a static far-from-equilibrium condition. That is, it will stay that way for a while. In financial economics this state corresponds to market conditions that do not correspond to a reality, such as the latter stages of a bull or bear market. In contrast, a pencil poised on its point will fall over very quickly. This is a dynamic disequilibrium or so-called punctuated equilibrium and corresponds to markets that change more quickly. Determining what causes markets to shift suddenly between states is why tipping points or levers are so important. In turn, determining tipping points and levers requires more robust descriptors of flows of information in terms of persistence and velocity. Since information is a physical entity, applying physical descriptors such as the fundamental forces of nature may provide valuable clues. Financial-economic theory will take a great stride forward when we can discern the principles that govern state selection.

Applicability

As Mirowski noted in Chapter 3, the failure of applying equilibrium physics to economics occurred because economics was blocked from the formal structure of Hamiltonians and also because there was no law of conservation. Since neither exist in nonequilibrium systems this may not be a problem. It further suggests that nonequilibrium physics is applicable to financial economics. Nonequilibrium is not a Hamiltonian and cannot be expressed in Hilbert space, since we need generalized rather than singular functions to introduce irreversibility at the statistical level. Phase-space is defined by the coordinates of energy of momenta. Equilibrium is reached when probability becomes time-independent. This occurs only when the probability depends on total energy defined as the kinetic (due to the motion of the particles) and potential (due to interactions). When expressed in terms of variables this energy is called the Hamiltonian and remains constant over time. This is the first principle of the conservation of energy. Since equilibrium is associated with the probabilities of the Hamiltonian, we have to move to the extended function space of Mandelbrot, called fractals, for infinite resolution.

The second point is subtle. In the Newtonian world, the law of conservation says that energy cannot be destroyed but only change its form. The price we pay for a nonequilibrium world is not energy but entropy. Nonequilibrium systems produce entropy and biological effects of life counteract that. In financial economics the biological effects of life are specifically people, Schrödinger's conscious sorting demons. Obviously at this level of resolution we are speaking of global properties. People are the fudge factor in the equation detailing the transmutation of matter and energy. Their behavior in aggregate is probabilistically governed. This concept can be seen as a sort of interpretation of Tipler's *The Physics of Immortality*. Since the future of the universe and the population of Earth are codependent and reflexive, people have to be part of the description. The Gaia hypothesis in biology is a congruent concept.

In other words, there are inanimate and animate components in the universe as there are in financial economics and their relationship is symbiotic. Attempting to work on one to the exclusion of the other will never result in a compete picture. Of the two, though, heretofore the physical description lent itself to deterministic interpretations and quantification. This is the basis for Soros's objection to including only the objective or scientific component. If financial economics is the study of the rational allocation of scarce resources by individuals and the characterization of those relationships based on some principles, the conclusion is that the stability of nonequilibrium systems depends on feedback mechanisms that control the rates of the various cycles involved. This admission takes us far from known places, yet it seems to be the logical direction. As strange as these words are to write, thinking *qua* money manager, how can it be otherwise?

Biophysics of Financial Economics

Given that a nonequilibrium system has physical and biological components, we can see that markets have to (1) physically allow for flow of information and (2) facilitate humans' perception of an advantage. Point one has a physical description and point two a biological description.

In financial economics the physical infrastructure that allows for the flows includes laws, policies, and principles as well as the telephone lines. Laws prohibit banks from being closed for more than 72 hours, and the first Amendment protects free speech in the media. Policies exist such as the availability of liquidity in financial crises by central banks. Principles such as free trade are the raison d'être behind NAFTA (the North American Free Trade Agreement) and the now common wisdom against protectionism that was exemplified by the disastrous Smoot-Hawley Act. All of these may be seen as infrastructure constructs to facilitate flow. In conclusion, to remain stable, systems must remain open. Extending this principle in the information age is what will make the sharing of information a more palatable and even necessary business practice. Closed information is the information age's equivalent to protectionism.

The expectations of individuals are built on the perception of the stability of the system and their ability to see a future in order to commit capital. When that perception does not exist, "flow" stops temporarily. The effect is like voltage in electricity hitting a capacitor, where a threshold has to be reached before it can proceed. The flow is discontinuous. This is in contrast to a resistor, which is known as friction in the market (e.g., taxes, imperfect understanding, etc.). The flow is constricted but continuous. Perceptions of the future within the system continually set the threshold limit of investment. This is reflected in part in the risk premium demanded. Set high enough, the flow will stop and the market will crash. It will phase lock into paralysis. To influence perceptions, during financial crises central banks reassure investors that the infrastructure is stable by making liquidity available, in effect restoring the ability of the system to handle flow. Politicians and central banks cannot command investors to invest.

Locale

A consequence of nonequilibrium implies that there are some privileged positions from which to participate. In the deterministic world, from any given set of points all others may be determined. Thus, no position is privileged. Given the reality of indeterminism, the higher-dimensional interpretation is preferable to the lower-dimensional one. Using a 4D interpretation is more beneficial, just as the general found the hilltop preferable to the valley to direct the melee. Privilege will mandate being connected. Access to information will be via a computer rather than a physical presence as it was in the days of humans on the floor of an exchange. Privilege beyond this will depend on the state of mind of the participant—the more evolved the better. Those able to grasp the subtle truths of the inherent instability of the universe that underpins the information age will do the best. Soros is also correct when he says as reflexivity is more widely accepted, the markets will in turn become more reflexive. The acceptance is based on sound science, driven by pursuit of profit and accelerated by a networked economy. With this simple backdrop, let us explore the Theory of Reflexivity.

PART II—THEORY OF REFLEXIVITY

The Theory of Reflexivity has two broad premises: (1) Prices persist or trend and (2) participants' perception can affect the fundamentals. Both occur in a nonequilibrium environment. States or degrees of nonequilibrium must change, since the markets are dynamic and complex adaptive processes. The first point is more accessible than the latter and is proved directly by the Hurst exponent. The second point requires a more involved explanation.

First, far-from-equilibrium states occur only intermittently and are thus a transient phenomenon. Despite being a rare event in terms of the percentage of time they actually occur, far-from-equilibrium states are qualitatively quite important. Second, variables including prices qualitatively change roles because in a nonequilibrium environment all variables become, as Prigogine says, more "active." In an equilibrium state, there is a limited role that can be played by variables. As a system moves away from equilibrium, the number of potential states in which it can exist increases and is probabilistically governed. Thus, variables can play more roles. Although investors' perceptions always affect prices and fundamentals, it is only in the extreme condition of far-from-equilibrium that the effect is easily discernable to the casual observer. Third, the inherent instability of reality may be exacerbated by the limited knowledge of the participants in a financial system. Thus, one sees why Nietzsche concluded there are no facts, merely interpretations, and Soros concluded that social science was a false metaphor. Fourth, typically we look at prices, and almost every other variable, as a local event—that is, at a single point in space-time. A more realistic analysis begins with a time series or a series of prices over time. This is a nonlocal event. Seen in this way, a time series of prices or any other quantitative data can be interpreted as a frequency. And from frequencies we can build up to resonance. Processes like those in financial economics must be addressed nonlocally at the global level.

Prices

The qualitative role of prices is assumed to be passive in equilibrium-based economics in the sense they are derived or fall out of an equation. What is hard to describe in the transience between states is that not only do numerical levels change—this is easy—but that the roles of variables change! Near- and especially far-from-equilibrium conditions recognize that prices may aperiodically undergo a qualitative change. When Soros says that in far-from-equilibrium conditions the role of prices changes qualitatively, he is correct in that variables become more active. Perhaps it would be more precise to say that the resonance of a financial time series has become reinforced due to persistence and velocity. That is, an equilibrium system is governed by universal laws. In contrast, a far-from-equilibrium state is mechanism-dependent and thus its analysis is heavily dependent upon context. The upshot is one can no longer throw the same formula at everything; in fact, one cannot use a formula at all. An equilibrium state becomes a nonequilibrium state at a bifurcation point, like Feigenbaum found. In the far-from-equilibrium state long-range correlations exist. Prigogine says this is what allows a far-from-equilibrium system to "see." Hurst is evidence of these long-range correlations. Michel Dacorogna *et al.*'s 1993 paper found that the autocorrelation function for short-term absolute price changes confirmed the hyperbolic decay and revealed that volatility clusters tend to have a longer memory than found in other studies. Does this not sound strangely like Poincaré resonances?

No metric yet captures the qualitative change of prices or any other variable. It is a phenomenon repeatedly observed by Soros in *The Alchemy of*

Finance but not yet formalized. The closest corresponding concept I can find is the concept of price taker in competitive markets where no seller or buyer can influence others. Conversely, price makers exist in oligopolies and monopolies. No link is implied between price makers and far-from-equilibrium states other than the fact the qualitative role of prices is different. In fact, so inexpert is our understanding of this qualitative change that the treatment is legal, in the form of antitrust law, rather than purely economic. Much in that same way bankruptcy, Chapter 11, is a legal rather than an economic event.

Risk

Dissipation at far-from-equilibrium in terms of entropy production is at a maximum. This is what makes these states more risky. The fact that far-from-equilibrium states can spontaneously emerge or self-organize is the real reason that all the linear assumptions are misleading. Linear assumptions can approximate near-equilibrium conditions, but fail when they are needed most, as is the case with risk management. The solution is to continuously run simulations to detect the onset of far-from-equilibrium conditions as soon as possible.

Soros observes that the farther one moves to a far-from-equilibrium state, the greater the risk. Behavioral studies seem to confirm this in the sense that investors have a greater fear of losing what they have just gained—typically after a large market run-up. This concept is further reinforced by the fact that no investment truth is forever and that aperiodic cycles do exist. At some point, the trend will become antipersistent. Capital instruments also hint at this, since U.S. government debt is the least risky and in that sense closer to an equilibrium condition than is corporate fixed income or equity.

There will also be some confusion because the father of risk management, Frank Knight, differentiated between risk and uncertainty in 1920s. Risk is what can be known and quantified versus uncertainty which cannot. Obviously, this distinction still stands; however, 70 years of technology have allowed us to increase our ability to measure and thus bring some aspects of uncertainty under the umbrella of risk.

Functions

Soros has some other concepts such as the cognitive function, which is reality reflected in people's heads, and the participating function, which is the decision people make from their inherently flawed interpretations of these events. The pure physics description is probably the most direct connection to reality as it is reflected in people's heads. Given its instability though and lack of privileged position, imperfection is as inherent in human cognition as instability is inherent in the universe. People's actions of course are mitigated by their lack of omniscience. The effect of these functions, however, may be better described by the flow of correlations mentioned earlier.

Human Factor

One of the reasons any explanation may seem weird is because of our own misperceptions, which take on many forms. Tversky has documented investors' aversion to risk. People also demonstrate a perception problem when they ascribe human traits to their pets. This skewed psychology is the secret of pet food manufacturers. Dog food is marketed to you, but consumed by your dog. We also saw how our frame of reference was flawed with respect to probability and membership functions. Ascribing human traits is probably the big barrier to the larger acceptance of quantum physics because effects in quantum-land do not resemble anything on the level of resolution called low-energy physics at which we interact with the world. A table is actually mostly empty space since there is a large area between electrons; however, if you strike it with your fist, it will not seem very permeable.

Similarly, our frame of reference is flawed because we are used to thinking in an "if-then" chain of direct causality in the same incorrect way we say "probability" for things which are not probable. The "if-then" legacy of the Newtonian determinism is dead. There may be multitudinous reasons at work that affect the outcome of something as complex as the economy. This is another reason simulation will provide a more accurate description than any formula ever can. Low interest rates or credit expansion may act as an attractor in the sense that the phenomenon is widespread and understandable by most investors. This colors their thinking and begins to form the basis for a consensus. This consensus or bias in turn may develop into received wisdom or unchallenged assumptions taken as true.

Soros uses the word "value" as a point of departure. This is by and large correct; however, value as it is reflected in prices is too simple a descriptor of the sub-rosa process that gives rise to prices. Moreover, prices mean different things at different times. In times of equilibrium, admittedly a rarely achieved ideal, and near-equilibrium, prices are passively derived products of that process as classical theory would have us believe. We are price takers, in the sense the causal influence between the price maker (the market) and the price taker (the transactor) is weak. To use a simple physical analogy, influencing the relationship is like pushing a rope. Of course, the causal relationship can become stronger and resemble a stiffened rope like a lariat or even a metal rod.

Aspects of economic behavior are transient. Sometimes they will move farther out on the continuum and become far-from-equilibrium. In these states fluctuating prices qualitatively play a different role. Rather than being the result of a process, prices are part of a direct feedback mechanism. This is a rather odd concept to express and the best analogy I can think of is magnetism, which also a convenient segue from the field theory of Weyl. A field, incidentally, is a nonlinear feedback mechanism. The attraction is between prices—which is really a metaphor for a process—and the fundamentals. In an equilibrium or near-equilibrium market this attraction is weak and the feedback mechanism between them is indeterminate. The market drifts. However, the further from equilibrium the market moves, the stronger this interaction between processes becomes.

To see why, look at a valuation process where a certain consensus may emerge and serve as an attractor to reinforce opinion. For example, in the 1930s Benjamin Graham and David Dodd shifted the concept of corporate value from assets to earnings. Certainly the asset concept still applies in certain cases, but the earnings concept predominates. It is not the value of the physical asset that matters *per se* but the level and stability of the earnings stream that physical asset can generate over time. We are in the nascent stages of another shift, this time from earnings to so-called intellectual capital. Intellectual capital and physical capital have always existed in some mix but only recently has it been shown, for example in the software industry, that the ratio of intellectual to physical capital can be favored in wealth creation. Moreover, while earnings and cash flow are still important, several instances exist where they are not a robust enough descriptor of corporate value taken by themselves. This is true with a money-losing start-up, where the expectations of future value override current reality. Biotech is a good example. In other words, part of the reason nascent high-tech companies may have a value is the widely held concept that they *will* have value in the future. This is an example of reflexivity in a near-equilibrium situation. An example of a high-tech far-from-equilibrium condition may be Microsoft, where the overly positive act of valuation by investors has inflated Microsoft's currency. Participants' bias has affected the fundamentals. If the participants never believed, then the company would never get off the ground. In fact, the Latin root for credit means to believe. Greed is stronger than the discipline of value, and people are willing to believe in strong prices, which of course makes prices go up.

Betting on future results or expectations is rational in many instances. Lenders and investors regularly do this. However, taken to extremes, material achievements cannot keep pace with ever-rising future expectations.

Most investors do not set a limit on the return they wish to achieve and exit the investment when that return is achieved. Greed kicks in and the thought of selling a successful investment and leaving money on the table is unbearable. So they let it ride. In time when the values are sufficiently divorced from what is sustainable, investors, perhaps unwittingly, become speculators because they want to make money in *every market all the time.*

As Soros says, this causes "following the trend, even when following the trend is the wrong thing to do [from the rational basis of value]." The judgment of applying a bet on-the-come expectation applied to specific situation graduates to a blanket investment strategy applied by more people, who have even less discrimination and are armed only with received wisdom. This is participants' bias and it occurs because of imperfect information. It is easier and cheaper initially to pinch someone else's idea and research than to come up with your own. It also takes intestinal fortitude to believe in yourself.

How many people say to themselves, I will leave the party after three cocktails or at 11 P.M., whichever comes first? In the heat of the party, the thought of a groggy morning is remote. These are qualitative descriptors. However, in more precise language they relay the phenomenon of a transient resonance—transient in the sense that far-from-equilibrium markets, like parties, do not occur all the time. Reflexivity affects the fundamentals and says, in effect, I am having such a good time that I will change my criteria to four cocktails and a midnight curfew. Resonance describes the aggregation of opinion that can coalesce into a trend. Prices reflect this trend. The yardstick against which the trend of prices must be judged is thought to be value—which itself can be an unanchored concept. This is exactly the point of reflexivity. If enough partygoers believe in their own temporary immunity from hangovers, the party will continue. Soros gave two examples in *Soros on Soros* of international lending and the conglomerate boom. The objective of displaying this trend is nontrivial.

At this stage nonlinear pricing via the Hurst exponent can measure the partial predictability of a time series and thus characterize it. We can say something new about its aperiodic cyclic behavior. Perhaps the most valuable thing we can identify is when the time series reverses itself or become antipersistent. A more thorough analysis involves the evolution of variables that give rise to the yardstick called value against which prices may be judged. This is a nontrivial problem because of the tagging issue. Tagging a time series is trivial since we use prices. Tagging the process that gives rise to those prices is more involved since the tags have to be ground in logic. Tags are of two sorts—qualitative and quantitative.

The quantitative tags we find in the metrics or prices of other instruments that are thought to be related, such as interest rates or measures of cash flow, or some derivative combination of them which I call derivative metrics, such as the P/E ratio. The P/E ratio is a metric derived from the relationship between prices and earnings, which are primary metrics. A tertiary metric may be the P/E ratio and change in interest rates. These are all convenient in that they come from GAAP/FASB or are readily grasped—like interest rates. But there is no reason why non-GAAP/FASB variables cannot be used if these new metrics are thought to have a justifiable relationship to the process. For example, for a company that makes only cotton garments, the raw price of cotton may be relevant. One of the more unusual metrics in my experience was used by the fashion business. The metric was the number of cargo planes that left Hong Kong, since labor is fast and cheap there. Even with the cost of airfreight, producers could be competitive with a garment on a short-lived fad.

Qualitative tags are common and exist in the form of, "Because the Bundesbank raised the discount rate today, that will strengthen the mark, which as a reserve currency makes the alignment within the European Union more difficult and thus may make speculation on the pound an interesting idea." Of course, the account is fictitious but not implausibly so. The precise numerical articulation of these contemplated causal relationships is difficult and perhaps not germane. For example, within bounds, the relationships of an increased interest rate and a lower bond price or stronger currency are accepted. The most expedient solution is to use fuzzy logic, which allows us to quantify the relationship, thus converting a qualitative tag to a quantitative one.

Unfortunately, as Westerners we tend to suffer from a Type III handicap that the use of a number implies precision. If a number pops up on our computer, then there must be a precise reason for it. Nonsense! As the famous artist Matisse said, "Precision is not truth." Preserving the imprecision is often the real value in a statement. Conversely, removing the imprecision or fuzziness seems analogous to the linear mathematicians who "linearize" nonlinear equations. Their first act is remove the very thing we wish to preserve! Of course, they do so because their linear framework cannot cope with a richer nonlinear reality. In nonlinear pricing we do not suffer from the handicap that the quantification must always be precise; in fact, most often it will be fuzzy.

Information Meets Capital in Real-Time

It is now common practice for large institutional money managers to demand and receive access to models of security analysts. Institutions pay lots of commission dollars and insist they call the tune. Managers of brokerage firms can understand this argument.

This is a transfer of information to capital. Now let's extend this concept with the premise that there is a kind of value in stable long-term shareholders. Corporate managers will probably agree with this. Also assume that the trend of increasingly activist shareholders continues. Corporate governance and compensation issues have been the favored targets. Further, activist shareholders now want more information from the company and they want it more frequently. Waiting 90 days for the next filing is an eternity. Talking heads, in the form of reporters, analysts, and money managers, fill the void between filings.

Now, what if those same large institutions invoked the argument of Kelly's law of one price, which holds that sharing information is beneficial for capital? Management can say no. But in the final analysis, for whom do they work? The answer is shareholders and that is, for practical purposes, the institutions. The mechanism for instant dissemination exists. That is streaming information distributed electronically. Since the information is available to everyone at the same time, the SEC will be satisfied that the standards of fairness are not violated.

In sum, in return for being patient, CalPERS now sees the bar code data from the checkout stand at Wal-Mart at the same time Wal-Mart does or the Sabre reservations system. It is all electronic, anyway. But there is too much information. CalPERS will not add up every box of detergent sold; it will use a sample of the data to drive a simulation via nonlinear pricing. In practice, the data will be available to everyone instantly, but the management will continue to concentrate on serving their core constituency of shareholders—institutions. Finance professors will like it because the market will become even more efficient. Information meets capital in real-time.

Prediction

We cannot predict with perfect certainty, because uncertainty exists, as do thinking participants who possess imperfect knowledge. However, partial predictability exists. The simplest evidence is the serial correlation of a time series as evidenced by Hurst. In more advanced examples we use simulation to evolve multiple time series and qualitative information. A good simulation can tell us what to expect and the dynamics of how it may well happen. Even without evolution we can see with the naked eye evidence of trends, cycles, and catastrophe. Maybe the best way to "regulate" the less desirable aspect of catastrophe is not with static barriers like those used by the New York Stock Exchange, or targets like those used by central banks for currencies, but by simulation that can forewarn of it. If Soros is right—and I think that he is—the sufficient forewarning is often enough to allow a painless avoidance of the threat and one without well-meaning but obtrusive intervention, along with its myriad unintended consequences. Thus, the heavy burden placed on regulators to "do something" may be helped if they can see the problem coming. The same is true for competitors in the marketplace. The most painful time in financial economics is when the unexpected strikes. Thus, anything that can help to reduce the unexpected, such as partial prediction, should be welcomed.

Dialectics

In the equilibrium world we can make a statement in an absolute sense. In the out-of-equilibrium world we cannot do that. The reasoning comes from Leibniz's *identity of the indiscernible*. Things that cannot be differentiated are by definition the same. In the out-of-equilibrium world with no fixed backdrop, absolute statements are impossible. Therefore we must use dialectics. We can state something only in terms of something else. Here we introduce **K** or knowledge and **CC** or collective consciousness.

When we gave up static measures, we can view something only in terms of something else. If we cannot, then by definition they are the same. Viewing something in terms of something else means we need two parts to describe something; this is called dialectic reasoning. In religion it is good versus evil. In drama it is protagonist versus antagonist. In the physical world it is attraction versus repulsion. In simplest terms, we cannot state the strength or weakness of a currency in terms of itself but only as an exchange rate in terms of another currency. Although we do not quote stock prices in terms of the S&P, many investors already think of a stock's performance this way.

Extending the concept of dialectics raises some large questions. How does one discuss investors without the market or risk without returns or shorter horizons without longer ones? It is for this reason that I said earlier that it is impossible to state the desirability of an investment with also stating the corresponding investment horizon against which the desirability is being adjudged.

I agree with Soros—there is little theoretical foundation for technical analysis and what does exist is linear. As we have stated, the extremes of randomness in the form of Brownian motion and perfect predictability in the form of a straight line are poor inidicators. Unlike Soros, I think it is mathematically proven that serial correlation or partial predictability as evidenced by Hurst is now an empirical fact and that past events do have some influence, even if the state of the art for nonlinear pricing cannot tell exactly the value of each past event upon the future.

In fundamental analysis, trends and qualitative descriptors are valid only in a historical sense. However, once those descriptors (e.g., P/E, interest rate coverage, etc.) are used prospectively—we need to couple them with dynamics, which must be expressed probabilistically to reflect nonlinear effects. Projecting values without taking the market into account is assuming that the market conditions are static. This is false. Given the progress nonlinear pricing has made with quantitative assumptions from quadrant IV and qualitative descriptors it is a mistake on the reader's part to conclude that nonlinear pricing is technical analysis. How can that be once an underlying theory is posited and nonlinear quantitative and qualitative descriptors are added? At that point fundamental analysis becomes a static subset of nonlinear pricing.

Most controversial of all may be the realization that a material by-product of a healthy economy is a higher absolute level of volatility than we probably care to admit along with the occasional crash. I concur with Soros that limited regulation has a role to play. The question, as always, is one of degree. It is not a black-and-white issue but a fuzzy one. What I offer that is different is shifting the regulator's viewpoint from a historical perspective to the future. Remember, a historical science like paleontology, which attempts to describe the evolution of species based on extant records, sees the future through a rearview mirror. The tape cannot be played again. So says the eminent evolutionist John Maynard Smith:

> If one was able to replay the whole evolution of animals, starting at the bottom of the Cambrian (and, to satisfy Laplace, moving one of the individual animals two feet to the left), there is no guarantee—indeed, no likelihood—that the result would be the same. There might be no conquest of the land, no emergence of mammals, certainly no human beings.

This is also the essence of Stephen Jay Gould's important book, *Wonderful Life*. Although it recounts the story of the Burgess Shale, the title makes reference to the movie *It's a Wonderful Life*, where a depressed man, seeking to commit suicide, is taken by an angel and allowed to see the world had he not existed! After becoming a stranger in his town, he rightly concludes that whatever his worldly troubles, he meant something to his family and friends. The point to be made here is that the tape was played again. We cannot do that per se but at least we can play the tape concurrently, and playing our tape is called simulation.

We as policymakers and investors tend to favor stability and low volatility. However, too much of a good thing is bad, as Karl Marx's failed experiment with a planned economy proved. The realpolitik of proposing the acceptance of increased volatility may belong with other inadmissible thoughts, such as the benefit to have limited armed conflicts at least every 20 years if for no other reason than to keep combat experience alive in the armed forces. Certainly the idea of an army of virgins has limited appeal but what politician can admit that Grenada, Somalia, and the Gulf War were excellent live-fire exercises?

Let us conclude with a quote from Soros and see where its veracity lies. "Reflexivity is, in effect, a two-way feedback mechanism in which reality helps shape participants' thinking in an unending process in which thinking and reality may come to approach each other but can never become identical." Certainly it is feedback processes of information flows that govern self-organized criticality in open systems. In nonequilibrium the future is open, not deterministic. Nonlinear pricing as it applies to financial economics is certainly a dynamic rather than a static process. It is continuous rather than discrete. No description of a physical environment that contains biological elements can be considered complete without discussing their recursive interaction. Equilibrium is by definition not possible. People, due to either the limitations of availability of 50% information as evidenced by Heisenberg's uncertainty principle or their own inherent flawed frames, cannot reconcile reality and their reaction to it. In sum, the quote is well supported.

PART III—THEORY OF NONLINEAR PRICING

At this juncture, let's try to see the Theory of Reflexivity against the more general nonlinear pricing. Just as a working knowledge of Soros's and Prigogine's works were fundamental to the prior section, so Smolin's *The Life of the Cosmos* is fundamental here. Smolin's concepts are vast and their concision severe.

The argument that can make nonlinear pricing a theory, that is, make it in Popper's term falsifiable, is analogous to the structure of the argument Smolin used to posit the creation of universes. Of course, the analogy cannot be verbatim but in the main the thrust is compelling. Both the universe and the economy exist in far-from-equilibrium states. In the physical world equilibrium is disproved as evidenced by stars and black holes. Literally the source and sink are different temperatures and densities and preclude equilibrium. In the temporal realm this is analogous to the boom/bust sequence, with a boom corresponding to a star and its implosion resulting in a bust. This is not a variation *from* equilibrium, but rather a variation in a stable out-of-equilibrium that has the potential to induce either stasis or chaos. Not every star becomes a black hole any more than every boom becomes a bust. Often a boom dissolves or its rise is permanent. In a bust the investment horizon collapses on the timescape from a nonlocal to a local analysis. That is, horizons collapse to the next instant.

Using the analogy to biology, Smolin's point is that it is precisely because of this sequence that evolution occurs at the cosmic level. The boom/bust sequence gives rise to change and thus evolution to new economic paradigms. Boom and quasi-boom scenarios are inevitable because markets are driven by expectations that mandate change, which Smolin calls a "bounce." Counterintuitively, far from being unwelcome, the boom/bust and quasi-boom/quasi-bust sequences provide the incentive for new ideas and facilitates the skewed vision of the future that must occur to risk capital.

Here it may be helpful to cognize a two-tiered process on a timescape. On the lower level is the economy, which is an allocation mechanism that optimizes the assimilation of new ideas as evidenced by the "joining" of resonances. Superimposed upon it is the upper level, which is a consensus-driven reward mechanism called the market. It is in the proverbial long term where Buffett calls the market a weighing machine that they are in more in sync. But it is in the short term when the market is a voting machine that the greatest distortions can occur because of false expectations. Michel Dacorogna *et al.* say, "In the long intervals, market price changes are 'flatter' and have fewer relevant movements (trend changes) than in short terms intervals. . . . A market participant's response to outside events should always be viewed as relative to his intrinsic opportunity set." They go on to say that heterogeneous responses lead to a delayed secondary effect called a *relaxation time*. Like the stages of a pumping heart, this is evidence of a process at work that gives rise to change and can be characterized in biological terms. The rhythmic stages are a reflexive process at work between tiers. The information flows between the tiers, which are partially characterized by prices, are fractal, and often follow a power law that is Levy distributed.

We need to make three hypotheses: First, change occurs at each bounce. Second, like evolution the incremental change in parameters is small. Change has an element of randomness but is mostly persistent or antipersistent. Third, our observed economy is a typical member of the group. This gives the theory explanatory power. With this assumption we are freed from knowing the initial parameters of the economy and realize that it is a representative example of other unobservable economies that are highly developed. It is axiomatic that there is no incentive to change or to incur risk given an equilibrium-like status quo. In fact, the economic incentive is to maintain the status quo for the benefit of vested interests against those who would seek to become so. Smolin basically posits that the universe is poised at a critical state to maximize the number of black holes. We do not go that far, but posit rather that the economy is poised in a stable out-of-equilibrium state that maximizes the assimilation of new ideas, and the flexibility to attempt to apply capital profitably to them. Under equilibrium assumptions higher throughput could be achieved, but at the cost of stability. Under non-equilibrium the critically self-organized state is the most efficient state that can be achieved dynamically. Viewed in this way, an economy is poised at the ready for the expectations of change. Ironically, fluctuations are the price we pay for stability!

The result, in theory, is predictability, testability, freedom from initial values, and the ability to integrate biology with physics. We have a structure that allows change. The 20 parameters of the standard model in physics roughly correspond to variables we use, such as capacity utilization, interest rates, and unemployment. The idea is not the absolute level of the parameter but that for a successful economy to exist, the parameters must exist within some certain boundaries. If they exceed those boundaries they do not do so for long. For a fuller treatment of the structure of this argument see Smolin's *The Life of the Cosmos* and Bak's *How Nature Works*.

Structure of the Model

The description of a far-from-equilibrium system like an economy has two components: first, the description of the physical environment from physics, and second, the biological description of its participants, which are people. We begin by building a model on the biological side and superimpose wave operators upon it. This biologically-based simulation of the dialectic between **K** and **CC** uses simple rules to create the dynamics we observe in real economies, much like John Conway's Game of Life. The addition of wave operators removes us from the deterministic ultra-Darwinism of genetic algorithms.

However, this is only half the task. We must then link dynamics to the physical reality we seek to emulate. The limited availability of real-world data imposes a material restriction in generating the dynamics directly. However, as we see from theory, initial conditions are not necessary. Linking the dynamics with extant data from the physical description completes the model. Conceptually we do not link the physical and biological descriptions at the base level but rather at a higher level in much the same way that scaffolding is attached to a building. The scaffolding is not directly dependent on the building for the scaffolding's support but is made stronger by the linking high up in the structure. The reason we can do this is that the computer itself is a metaphor and the language of iterative nonlinear programming is not a language of substance but rather one of information, to paraphrase Smolin.

The Secret Formula

There isn't one.

Why? How many potential fathers would ever think to ask their wife for an a priori "proof" of what their planned baby is going to look like before conception? This example is so absurd as to be laughable. It is laughable only because you think you know better. Now take this same educated man, who happens to be a money manager, and send him to the office and present him with the results of a simulation to make an important portfolio or risk management decision. His knee-jerk reaction will be, "where is the proof?" or "Show me the formula." "The formula" as an a priori proof is no more sensible here in the investment world than it is at home for family planning. The only difference is he does not know better. If the biological parallel is not strong enough and knowing the reason why is going to cause his rejection of such a notion, then recall Feynman's advice from Chapter 1: "Do not keep saying to yourself, if you can possibly avoid it, 'But how can it be like that?' because you will get 'down the drain,' into a blind alley from which nobody has yet escaped. Nobody knows how it can be like that."

One may smirk and even dismiss this example as ridiculous, but do not. It is germane. It is the very stuff and substance of what distinguishes a computational proof from an analytical proof. Even though your genes and your wife's genes may be known, there is no way to tell in advance exactly what the baby will look like. You have to take your chances like every other mammal has done since the dawn of sex and have one to find out. And if you have another child, he or she may or may not resemble the sibling. Having a baby is the essence of a computational rather than an analytic solution. Babies are not determined by formula.

For a comparison, were the adaptive processes of nonlinear pricing applied to family planning, we would take your genes and your wife's and simulate with thousands of iterations in a computer and evolve a set of likely candidate children. The computational ability and the mathematics to support such an effort exist now. Your genes will be fully mapped a few years hence when the Human Genome Project is complete. Now, what is the difference between evolving a likely set of offspring and a likely set of circumstances for the portfolio? The answer, in principle, is nothing since they are both highly nonlinear processes. This is in effect what you see on William Sharpe's web site www.financialengines.com when you simulate a portfolio. Yes, this is the same Sharpe, Nobel laureate and inventor of the Capital Asset Pricing Model, using computational solutions.

Kernel of Duality

The kernel of theoretical nonlinear pricing is simple. It holds that agents capable of anticipating behave much like biological organisms. We find a niche and desire to grow. Any constraint that can be expressed can be included in this kernel. We begin with the realization that it is the individual's desire to do *something*, Schrödinger's conscious sorting demon, which is at the root of all financial economics inquiry. This desire is represented by **K** or the transactor's acquisition and assimilation of knowledge. The thing to which something is done is the market, represented by **CC** or collective consciousness. The distinction of the dialects of **K** and **CC** hinges on perception. Individually **K** is not the market, but collectively they are. We are the market.

We look at the world in terms of a dichotomous process because our research has provided us with some very important clues. From biology there is coevolution of genders and certain species. From physics, there is the relational rather than individualistic thinking as characterized by the difference between Leibniz and Newton and put forth by Weyl in the 1920s and Prigogine in the 1990s. There are also multiple levels of resolution. From mathematics and Mandelbrot comes the multiple time scales called multifracticality. From economics we have the interaction of investor and market. Lastly, from many disciplines is the concept of resonance.

K and CC

Rather than concentrate on either the transactor or the market, we focus on their interactive relationship (see Table 9.3). Traditionally, economics has focused on the market and such topics as behavioral finance has focused on the transactor. Our inspiration comes from the relational philosophy of Leibniz, who gave us the *principle of sufficient reason*. That is, in a description of the world we cannot make any choice unless there is a rational reason to do so.

Table 9.3 Relationship between Transactor and Market

Relationship	
K	**CC**
Transactor	Market
(electron)	(field)

Weyl followed this concept when he sought to preserve choice between identifying charges of electrons. He found that he could preserve this choice if the electrons were not allowed to communicate with each other but rather mediated through a field. In *The Life of the Cosmos*, Smolin writes, "A field is something that exists in each point of space. The electrical force is carried by the field in the same sense that each charge interacts only with the field in its immediate vicinity. The presence of a charge causes a change in the field nearby, and that change is then communicated throughout the entire field. Each charge feels the other only through the effect it has had on the field." Prigogine says something similar: "A field can be thought of as the super-posing of oscillations with frequencies ω_k whose wavelength k varies from the size of the system itself to the dimensions of an elementary particle." These interactions sound vaguely like a physicist's description of a market or a computer scientist's description of a network. We need some modification. Our agents are not electrons; they are people, so they cannot be maximally rational. We do not speak of an electrical force but rather a biologically directed energy caused and required by life. Perhaps this is life force or the survival instinct.

CC

The dynamics of a market are conceived as dialects of a collective conscious (**CC**) and knowledge (**K**). The market or **CC** is amorphous and intangible. It can be narrowly defined as a specific market or it can be broadly defined and overlap with other markets in the world. It may have physical attributes in the form of an exchange floor with specialists, computers, staff, and margin clerks or not, like Deutsche Termin Bourse (DTB) or NASDAQ. **CC** can also be an individual, but as no human exists in true isolation, the individual is still typified by a collective since other avenues of information gathering exist to form a composite opinion even though it is individually held. In terms of the body of math necessary to construct such as theory, it exists. It is the population physics of Prigogine.

K

The other dialect is knowledge. It is typically embodied in humans but because of the Turing principle this knowledge can be extended to machines. Arguably those machines are not on par with humans in most respects and have enjoyed success only in the limited application of program trading, where the size and speed of the orders cannot be done by humans. There is a reason for defining this dialect as knowledge, because knowledge is a *physical quantity*. For the most part, **K** has been embodied only in humans but this will change in the future. Machine **K** may never surpass man **K**, but machine **K** will continue to make demonstrable inroads.

K is endowed with self-awareness. "Consciousness" seems too strong a word since it is pregnant with too much meaning for too many disciplines. Like a bureaucracy, **K** seeks its own survival. This process mimics in many respects a biological process. **K** bids its expectations. **K** bids for stocks, bonds, or what ever it is in the market for, but these instruments are only proxies for expectations. Myriad independent **K**s bid for a central commodity in the form of a stock, where those bids are brought into unison in the form of a **CC**. The cause of false expectations is imperfect **K**, which results from a closed system or closed mind, since if **K** were known, it would be translated into expectations. **CC** in return responds with information as to how those collective bids are generally perceived. This is a feedback mechanism.

K is not always rational. **K** recognizes that we do things for biological reasons that have no basis in the rational mind, like having cocktails, getting married, and having children. If this is not so, then why do we refer to a ticking biological clock? The assumption of rationality would have us act like dispassionate and disembodied intellects. The formal study of **K** today in financial economics is behavioral economics.

Relationship

Any financial situation can be represented as the market or **CC** and a transactor, **K**, who seeks to benefit by perfecting knowledge because a relationship exists. Thus, there are really three processes to be considered. First, the process internal to the transactor (what is inside the humans' heads); second, the activity of the market or **CC**; and third, the relationship between them. (See Table 9.4.)

The relationship approach is also philosophically in sync with what we have been saying in terms of a relational approach. Like the field theory de-

Table 9.4   States of Nonequilibrium

	$K < CC$	$K = CC$	$K \geq CC$	$K > CC$
P&L	Loss	No profit	Risk-free rate Near equilibrium	Profit Far-from-equilibrium

veloped by Weyl in the 1920's neither the market nor the transactor have a meaning in financial economic terms apart from the other. It is the relationship between the market and the transactor that is important because it gives rise to profit and loss.

When we use a dichotomous process to view financial economics we can also introduce the important concept of resonance. Using the coevolution stance, the dialectics of **K** and **CC** also allows times to change at different rates. This is a fact we have seen with multifractal time. No longer are bound by a Newtonian view of having the whole world beat to the cadence of the same drummer. We can now see an event in terms of something else—in relational terms. **K** and **CC** can and often do exhibit different characteristic time scales. In fact they must to be differentiated. By definition, in the relational world those things which cannot be differentiated are the same. This is why shares of IBM are fungible. They cannot be differentiated in a legal sense or in a mathematical sense using the concepts of frequency or resonance. Our goal is not perfect resonance since nothing would happen, or anti-resonance, noise cancellation, since that would result in nothing either. What is desirable is a slight offset of the two parties or frequencies so that the difference is magnified in the feedback—magnified but regulated before it becomes damaging.

When **K**'s rate of knowledge acquisition and assimilation is greater than **CC**'s rate of change, then abnormal profits accrue to **K**. There is an informational advantage to the transactor over the market. Note, this is not the total informational advantage, but useful information as defined by the transactor. That is, information provided to one transactor may be of great benefit, while the same information provided to another may be of little or no value at all.

When **K**'s rate of knowledge growth and **CC**'s rate of change are at parity then they are said to be equal to each other or in equilibrium. The result is no profit since there is no advantage to either. Perfect equilibrium is not possible because **K** is almost never perfect. When **K** slightly positively exceeds **CC**, they are competitively set and the risk free rate of return is earned. They are said to be near equilibrium. When **K**'s rate of knowledge acquisition and assimilation is less than **CC**'s rate of change then losses result. The informational advantage lies with the market and not with the transactor.

Often the relationship between **K** and **CC** is indeterminate. However, intermittently the market will phase-lock or enter a self-reinforcing trend, like a bull or bear market. That is, it becomes critically self-organized. It is the feedback mechanism that, given sufficient conditions, amplifies **K**'s slight advantage over **CC** at near equilibrium to a position further from equilibrium. The result is often a far-from-equilibrium state.

For the movement to a far-from-equilibrium state two preconditions must exist. First, rising expectations from **K**, and second, once-favorable conditions in **CC**. The idea of "once-favorable" is important because while those favorable conditions may have been initially present, their importance declines as the feedback mechanism, which initially caused the move, takes over. That is, prices go up because of good initial conditions, **K** raises expectations, invests more money, causing prices go up. At a later point in time prices may have no real basis in value. Stocks, or any other commodity, are bought for no other reason than they go up. Although prices may continue to rise, risk is actually increasing because **K**'s ability to acquire and assimilate a change in **CC** is decreasing.

In looking at the relationship between **K** and **CC**, it is never desirable to be in true equilibrium but with a slight and varying advantage to **K**. If this was not the case, no one would ever make any money. This slight advantage can become self-reinforced to extremes and cause bull markets or in the extreme cases speculative markets. A sudden reversal can cause a crash and a more gradual decline of **CC** relative to **K**, a bear market. Complexity is the bounded degree of variety within a system. That boundary is determined by **K**'s inability to maintain its advantage over **CC**.

The relationship between the market and the transactor is post-Darwinian and by definition, relational. In terms of resolution it is a more macro view than is the market or its participants individually. From the vantage of the relationship we can also see the different time scales for **CC** and **K**. It is the relationship that is marked by self-organized criticality. Both the transactor and the market as components of the relationship are Darwinian and typically marked by incremental improvement. Their relationship is post-Darwinian, subject to far-from-equilibrium conditions like self-organized criticality or order for free, as Kauffman says.

The transactor **K** is like the genetic algorithm that continually tries to adapt against the market. Inputs are usually the same but the relationships between and among them change. The transactor's question is how to adapt with that change to a more preferred risk/reward stance). Even supply and demand are represented by a static intersection on a 2D graph, when in fact what we want to characterize are processes.

As Prigogine said, "Time precedes existence." It is not until an event occurs that a benchmark exists against which to measure it. The event is caused by a divergence of resonance, dissonance if you will, of a dichotomous process experiencing different time scales that leads to an event and the marking of time. We know this as event-driven style of investment. As the term "event-driven" is currently used, it refers to styles of investing such as risk arbitrage and bankruptcy. In fact, because time can only be measured with an event, all investment styles are event-driven.

Risk

Here we posit a general relationship. Near to equilibrium, the potential rate of change of the market is usually never so quick that it cannot be tracked by **K**, thus the low but relatively certain risk-free rate of return. As the rate of change for **K** decreases relative to **CC** or **CC** increases relative to **K**, risk is introduced. As both **K** and **CC** individually are nonlinear processes, the relationship between them can be unwieldy. The intuition here is that as a time series becomes more antipersistent it becomes riskier.

As **CC** decreases relative to **K** or **K** increases relative to **CC** higher profits can exist, but so will higher risk, because the potential for either **K** or **CC** to change or become antipersistent increases as well. It is not determined whether risk (i.e., the potential of **CC**'s rate of change to increase or **K**'s rate of knowledge acquisition and assimilation to decrease) and reward (i.e., improvement or profit) are linearly commensurate.

Probably the clearest analogy is the Real Player, which can be downloaded on the Internet from www.real.com, which allows audio and video to be Webcasted. If the Internet is overloaded (something which happens regularly) your audio or video signal will be temporarily interrupted and a small sign that says "buffering" and a red arrow will appear. It means that the signal cannot reach you on a continuous basis and is waiting until bandwidth is available to catch up. It is a temporary mismatch between sender and receiver. Buffering also happens between **CC** and **K** or **K** and **CC**. It is the cause of market imbalances and near-equilibrium states. We have to wait long enough for information to be digested by either **CC** or **K** and for **K** to regain a new attempt at equilibrium. The analogy is imperfect because the feedback mechanism back to Real Player is indirect. That is, the only feedback on the Net is to e-mail and state that constant buffering in causing problems, which one hopes will be met with increased bandwidth.

If the buffering is severe enough in the case of a war or other large catastrophes, or exists for long enough in the case of bull market, the feedback can become severe enough to affect the underlying fundamentals of expectations. This is an example of Soros's reflexivity. As the feedback mechanism continues, the danger zone increases—that is, the difference between an original expectation that was more rational than the recently raised one.

To begin the transaction process, the magnitude of information is judged by **K** and preliminary expectations are bid. The bids are often inaccurate and it takes a much longer time for the correct assessment of magnitude to be accurately assessed. This is an example of Buffett's comment that in the short run the market is a voting machine and in the long run it is a weighing machine. Time is relative to the investment horizons of the **K**'s bid. **CC**'s and **K**'s respective time frames and rates of change have a relationship but can exhibit a great deal of variation.

When no buffering exists and when **K** is growing fast enough to accurately assess the response of the market, the market is said to be an orderly market or near equilibrium. When **K** does not grow fast enough because of lack of information (e.g., no communication) such as the closing of markets on weekends in the case of the Hong Kong and Tokyo equity markets for lunch, the potential for **K** growth is diminished and the chances of disequilibrium increased. This is why U.S. banks may not be closed for more than three consecutive calendar days. Conversely, one wonders how prudent the circuit breakers that stop trading on the New York Stock Exchange really are.

Markets crash when **K** perceives that it cannot grow. The investment horizon for all investors becomes uniform and collapses to a single point— which is only the next moment. Nonlocal analysis becomes local analysis. It is flight for survival in biological terms since avoidance is perceived to be cheaper than experience. This is not too dissimilar to Peters's *Fractal Market Analysis*, which maintains that markets crash when all participants have the same or typically short perception of time. A healthy market, by definition, has participants with different time horizons. And healthiness is most accurately measured by liquidity or willingness to trade. Trading volume is an imperfect but the most practical measure of liquidity. Thus, day traders and pension funds all have their role to play. Ed has been a confrere and it is wholly accurate to say that *Fractal Market Analysis* was a foundation subliminally if not explicitly. I did not write with the specific intent to extend *Fractal Market Analysis*, but the fact that nonlinear pricing agrees with *Fractal Market Analysis*, while not intentional, is not surprising either.

The attempt for equilibrium has to do with rate of assimilation. That is, **K** grows and tracks **CC** to anticipate its next move over a specified investment horizon. If knowledge is security, then the opposite of knowledge is ignorance or, in base terms, fear. We can express these sentiments individually, but the sentiments find their ultimate manifestation collectively in the **CC**.

Process

We have stressed the word *process* because the strongest commonality between physical and intellectual goods or those that are best characterized by decreasing and increasing returns, respectively, is the process. Consider a physical object such as a painting. A physical good has an immediate and a terminal process (in the sense that it can be occupied or consumed). Intellec-

tual goods have a continuous process. Decreasing returns **CC** gradually becomes "smart enough" to limit profitability. Conversely, the economics of ideas, which are characterized by increasing returns **CC**, is never likely to catch up because **K**'s potential for new ideas is unbounded.

May's Law

Most wise investors follow the dictum of not investing in things they do not understand. I propose May's Law, which states that if the capacity to process information roughly doubles every 18 months according to Moore's Law, then the investor must keep an identical pace of understanding or risk becoming increasingly more ignorant. The math is simple. If the change in information processing scales exponentially and **K** scales only arithmetically, then that is not good. We cannot yet make a relationship for qualitatively what is understood but only the quantitative rate at which one is acquiring and assimilating it.

Resolution, Continued

One of the observations we made in the physical realm was resolution. Our simple examples were the funnel in the bathtub and the ball of string. In financial economics we often differentiate between the division, company, sector, and industry. Much of what theory has to say depends on the vantage point of the transactor, which is typically a specific portfolio or set of circumstances and seeks to make specific very general circumstances such as the market. Thus, the level of resolution to the transactor is relatively local, to the market it is nonlocal. There is a mismatch. In other words, we wish to characterize the relationship between the two from the specific in the case of the transactor to the general in the case of the market. It is the relationship between the transactor and the market that is our aim.

The difference in levels of resolution is important because of the type of analysis applied. Just like measuring the valence of water molecules will not help us to understand the funnel, applying a characterization of specificity where the phenomena are general will be misleading. It is self-organized criticality that is high-level and Darwin's evolution which is low-level, which is the lower, more concrete level. Part of the message we must convey according to the matching principle is that it is acceptable to be general where circumstances dictate. In other words, it is a waste of energy to attempt to be rigorous or specific where generality prevails. Doing so represents the triumph of hope over experience. Thus, **K** is probably better marked by a lower-level process and the market or **CC** by a higher-level process. Where they intersect will be a mixture of high- and low-level processes.

There is one last thought with respect to the theory of nonlinear pricing that I want to leave you with. Rather than give it to you straight, I am going to entertain you with a story. I am going to tell you a parable. I am also going to apologize in advance for taking the reader through yet another seemingly abstract concept—Japanese. The reading is light though and I hope you find a chuckle in it (at my expense of course). We have covered some physics, biology, computer science, and financial economics. Taken individually we have only scratched the surface of each discipline. Taken in concert, at this point the survey forms a level of interdisciplinary understanding, which exists at a rarified level. To encompass those disciplines without the benefit of 3D graphics or abstract formulas as they apply to financial economics is not trivial.

Since most of the world's financial centers are Western European or derivative from it, I assume that the population of this book's readership will fall proportionally to reflect that fact. The first thing we are going to do is amuse you with my tales in Asia, specifically Japan, because one needs a greater appreciation for the type of thinking that divides East from West. To understand what an Easterner is, first consider what makes us Westerners. I think it is specifically the common denominators of the Industrial Revolution, the Judeo-Christian ethic, and the Greco-Roman sense of beauty upon which we form our thoughts. We saw in Chapter 2, "Nonlinearity: A Retrospective," the effects of Greco-Roman influence with the demiurge, atomism, and its heirs reductionism and determinism. We will mention incidentally that at least one man has formulated a hypothesis that Westerners dominated the Industrial Revolution because we, as a meta-tribe, have a love of numeracy. That is, because we could measure, we could navigate; and because we could navigate, we could rule and trade. The Christian ethic in the form of the Ten Commandments, and I suppose the Jewish and Muslim ethics as well, since we are all share the same God, are also somewhat like our old deterministic Newtonian world. For example, "Thou shall not steal" is an absolute commandment in the sense that it makes no reference to situational ethics. This logic taken to its extreme immortalized Victor Hugo's *Les Misérables*, where Jean Valjean was imprisoned for 20 years for stealing a loaf of bread. Remember that the West's common denominators hardly affected the East and to they extent they did, they affected the East in a way radically different than they did in the West.

Religion

No doubt, religious beliefs are a sensitive topic but it is important to mention them because, like the concept of time, they are so fundamental that they are rarely considered in forming perceptions. The Industrial Revolution, the Judeo-Christian ethic, and the Greco-Roman sense of beauty are potentially Type III errors mentioned earlier, which are the inherent assumptions upon which a Western worldview is based. I am not advocating moral relativism or situational ethics. I am only noting some parallels between the worlds of science and Western religion. For example, in Japan, the appeal to an absolute authority such as the One who issued the Ten Commandments so clearly implied was a major, if not the major, impediment for the establishment of Christianity by Portuguese Jesuits. The story of feudal Japan has popularly been told by James Clavell's *Shōgun*. The concept of an allegiance to a set of absolute values belonging to a foreign power over which domestic political leaders had no control was unacceptable. I note parenthetically that it is this notion of unanchored relativism, which quantum physics introduced as a probabilistic description of the world, that makes the larger conclusions of quantum physics so repugnant to many. It led Einstein to remark that "God does not play dice."

Relational behavior has its advantages and disadvantages. On the plus side this trait of adherence to a set of relative rather than absolute values offers increased flexibility to adapt. Which is philosophically why, when world forces required it, the Japanese were competitive when their currency fell from 240 to 138 to the dollar several years ago. Conversely, having no moral anchor or ideal removed a benchmark to which the Emperor and the Navy may have appealed in an effort to reign in an increasing bellicose Army in 1937. The results of their military fanaticism still strikes fear in the hearts and minds of Asians today when talks of rearming Japan arise. For the best current exposé, see Karl van Wolferen's *The Enigma of Japanese Power*.

Ease Your Bosoms

In 1990, while grocery shopping in Tokyo, I came across a seasonal promotion of a coffee called "Ease Your Bosoms" and nearly tripped over the stocking-clerk in peals of laughter. The scene was awkward; not only was I the only foreigner in the small store, but tears of laughter ran down my face as I bought their entire supply. I then sent them to my friends. We still get a chuckle out of it today.

Living in Asia, in my case Japan, compelled me to see many things in a new light and sometimes notice that the indirect approach works better than the direct approach, or as we say in the West, the left-brained approach rather than the right-brained approach. Let me walk you through this example and see if you can catch my drift.

Obviously, the literal translation was not the correct one, even though the Japanese are notorious for adding marketing zing to their products by putting written English either on it or in the advertisement. The reason I suspect is that if English is associated with it, some sort of international presence is assumed, making the product more prestigious. For example, advertising to the youth market, especially girls, is trademarked by its cloyingly sick approach of purity and perkiness—*genki*, to use a Japanese word. Subways were plastered by one advert for "wedding halls," which look like churches but are not, that began with, "Thank you mama, fun time happy talk. . . ." Many informal clothes had nonsensical wordings like "Zap 2 four." Now, many Japanese study English, some Japanese even speak English, but from my four-year experience there, it is not as many nor are they as fluent as the Ministry of Education might claim.

Of course, native English speakers and accomplished English speakers are not so rare that one could not be found to hire to review advert copy. Nor are the Japanese incapable; quite the contrary. Maybe their usage of

English is figurative rather than literal—just like the painter whose style is impressionistic rather than realistic. I am reminded of a story of Picasso, when he was confronted on a train by a man who asked him, "Why do you not paint people as they really are?" Picasso asked the stranger if he carried a picture of his wife, which the man proudly produced. Picasso saw it and asked, "Is she really that small and that flat?" And to be fair, how many Americans would get a joke in a foreign language in their grocery store?

Since the literal translation was not correct, and I assume a coffee company can afford a translator, I wondered, what *did* they mean? "Ease Your Bosoms" seemed a bit more deliberate than "Zap 2 four." Literally, easing your bosoms is relaxing. It then occurred to me that if you are communicating with anyone other than your teacher or grandmother, mastery of any language assumes familiarity at the idiomatic or colloquial level and not just the basic stuff in the textbook. Maybe the meaning was metaphorical and that abstraction of metaphor is certainly a higher-ordered reasoning than literal. Metaphorically speaking, maybe "easing one's bosoms" is like "taking a load off one's chest," to use the vernacular. And when we take a load off of our chest we are relaxed and if a product can help me to relax, then. . . . Professional translators wrestle with this problem every day—what was said versus what was meant? It is reasonable to posit that the advertising department attempted to paraphrase idiomatic English only to result in some unintentional humor.

Grasshopper

Continuing this line of circumlocutory reasoning in Japan, at least, will lead you either straight to the bar or to the local Buddhist temple and into pondering the enigmatic and potentially spiritually enlightening Zen *koans* such as, "What is the sound of one hand clapping?" As the bars were not yet open on Saturday morning, I took the challenge at the temple, where an obliging priest was ready to do his job. Mr. All-American MBA was about to unwittingly become like "grasshopper" on the *Kung-fu* TV series.

I reverently entered the temple. Given the apparent earnestness of my supplication, as evidenced by some bowing, many refrains of *Ah so ne* and one sucking-of-wind-between-the-teeth, I was given solitary. Four hours of navel-gazing later, my legs were fully anesthetized from sitting in the lotus posture on *tatami* mats. The priest shuffled to my part of the temple and unmercifully interpreted my thousand-yard stare and tepid pulse as evidence of having reached the sublime state—rather than just being utterly confused and starved because it was now lunchtime. So pleased was he with his instructions for the spiritual progress of the Japanese-speaking-barbarian-who-wandered-in-off-the-street-early-on-Saturday-morning-without-an-appointment-and-who-failed-to-make-the-ritual-obeisance-to-the-great-Lord-Buddha-or-any-of-the-lesser *kami-sama*s. He cancelled lunch and gave me another *koan*. Grasshopper was too dumb to speak and too numb to move.

Kaze ga fukeba; okeya ga mokaro literally translated says, "When the wind blows, the cooper becomes more profitable." (See box on page 279.) For the latter half, a more modern translation might be, "a shopkeeper increases his sales." I confess, I could not take it any more. The prospect of missing dinner was more than I could bear and since I rarely miss a meal, I tipped myself over, massaged my legs awake and sneaked out of the temple. As a result, I am still chewing on this *koan* five years later. As you can see, the clues come from the kanji—the Chinese pictograms. The kanji for *kaze* or wind is a buzzing insect, like a bee, trapped in an overturned bucket. The kanji for *okeya* or cooper is a wooden bucket and a salesman. The graphical link is the buckets. The logical link, which is distinctly nonlinear, has to do with the wind causing activity, and there are more sales when the shopkeeper is active, like the wind, than when he just sits around. What capitalist would argue with that?

As for the price of enlightenment, I reckon, how can one call it a pain in the neck if one cannot even feel it? *Ah so desu.* That is wisdom.

The indirect approach humorously illustrated with these vignettes has a serious side as well. In financial economics we, especially as Westerners, tend to take a rational, logical, direct, right-sided brain approach. In fact, in his recent book *The Measure of Reality: Quantification and Western Society, 1250–1600*, Alfred W. Crosby argues that the propensity for direct measurement, rather than any innate cultural ability, led to the West's dominance through technical innovations such as the mechanical clock, double entry accounting, and modern cartography. The measurement of space and time gave Westerners the means to explore and conquer the New World. Crosby does not claim this as a complete account of the rise of Western civilization; however, his thesis is compelling. This love of direct and discrete measurement dovetailed rather nicely with the philosophical approach later set into motion by Newton 86 years later (no pun intended).

The evidence of the failure in using *only* the simpler right-brained approach to assess economic output created in the information age is obvious. From the June 9, 1997, *Fortune* we read, "The gains in efficiency and productivity from this investment are surely reflected in the economic data for manufacturers—manufacturing productivity is rising at a far-above-the-trend rate of 3.9% per year. But the statistics for the service sector are mysteriously low, leading many economists to question the quality of the data itself. 'Where we can measure productivity [in manufacturing], it is doing

風 (kaze)

Kaze ノ an important insect 虫 like a bee in an upside down bucket 几 sounds like the wind.

が ga

吹 fu
Blowing is what happens when the palanquin bearers 欠 exhale through their 口 mouth.

け ke

ば ba

A bucket is wooden staves from a tree 木 surrounding a garden. The garden is a hand ▽ with citrus fruit 干 that is busy growing and active with colors.

桶 oke

= cooper

A store is an individual thing like silkworms 垂 finally living individually in their 尸 own cocoon or house or shop.

屋 ya

が ga

も mo

か、 ka

る ro

。 o

very well,' says Allan Meltzer, an economist at Carnegie Mellon University. 'Where we can't, it isn't.' But the evidence of the real world, Meltzer maintains, proves that service productivity must be higher."

Graphics

We are discussing an approach, that of graphical interpretation and formulation of financial economics, which at this early stage of development is necessarily vague. It may not do well to hold too high the ideal of infinite precision so dear to the Western mind. For example, fuzzy logic deals with the inherent imprecision although there is nothing imprecise in the formulation of the technology. It is noted that the founder of fuzzy logic, Lotfi Zadeh, is of Persian extraction; Persia (Iran) is part of Asia and thus, the Orient. (Asia begins east of the Urals.) But Zadeh was at Berkeley when he developed fuzzy logic in 1965. More to the point, who really adopted fuzzy logic and made it their own? Orientals. Japanese, specifically, in the form of washing machines, thermostats, and rice cookers, which are available this Christmas from Williams-Sonoma for $250. Many other examples exist.

The realization and adoption of precise methods about dealing with imprecision is a mark of intelligence but it is an appreciation of a different type of associative or graphical thinking that derives from culture. The Oriental's appreciation is the cumulative effect of thousands of years of thinking in pictures. Associative processes in the brain are different graphically than they are symbolically. English, like the mathematical formula one hates to read, is symbolic and thus has to be interpreted by the brain to produce a mental image. With pictures we skip this interpretive step. If you have ever been a tourist in a country where they don't use your language or have read a story to a three-year-old, you understand the power of pictures. Graphical interpretation is logic by metaphor.

Fuzzy logic has been called a geometric and thus graphical approach to modeling nonlinear systems. Zadeh has also made a telling statement: "In the United States, there's a tradition for what is precise, for Cartesian logic. In Japan, there is more appreciation of the imprecise, of ambiguity. I've always been confident that people will come around to my way of thinking." Mandelbrot's fractals are a geometric property. His mental solutions are images of pictures, not formulas.

Probably the leading modern proponent of how to "see it in pictures" is Edward Tufte, a professor at Yale. His three books are *The Visual Display of Quantitative Information*, *Envisioning Information*, and *Visual Explanations*. They are referred to as the pictures of numbers, nouns, and verbs, respectively. In many ways these works are the West's 21st-century interpretation of the same principles of formulating information in graphical form used in kanji. It is, of course, difficult to explain relative performance of information design in the alien medium of words. Perhaps a mental image is the best response. Again, who has not been the recipient of a foreign gift that needed assembly or a financial report, and wondered, after some consideration, what is it trying to say?

Tufte comes to some other interesting aspects of information design, such as its relative cost in time and money to gather versus its benefit. I have never seen this question addressed in financial economics in other than the most cursory of methods, such as, "We do not have time to visit the management three weeks from now since we have to make a decision today." Or, "No, I don't think it's worth $70,000 a year to hire a junior analyst." Since financial economics is the information processing business, a better understanding of the design and consumption of information as well as a cost-benefit analysis of gathering and compiling it seems very logical. What analyst would not like to better judge this trade-off in one's daily business so that one can say with some confidence, "There is no more to be learned here"? In other words, the costs exceed the benefits. And what Wall Street manager would not like to know where the diminishing returns of gathering information are, so one knows better how to marshal one's hiring dollars?

Although the graphical design of information is the least discussed topic in terms of space allotted, in terms of importance it is probably equal if not superior to the performance of the algorithms themselves. We must be careful here. We are not arguing style over substance. No, if the algorithms do not make money, all the style in the world is useless. We are arguing that when the substance, in the form of a technical improvement under the hood of an automobile or, in this case, nonlinear techniques, becomes hard to know, then the litmus test for acceptance in the commercial sense is more heavily weighted on what most people do know, which is its design. Is it intuitive and appealing? If one thinks for a moment, this is how the preponderance of financial products and other services are sold. Customers do not analytically rate salesmen's ability to pick stocks and do paperwork. Customers rank their appearance, manners, and associative ability. That is, do we like them? Are they like us? After all, if the client did know and could therefore judge for oneself, he would not need that professional's service in the first place. It is for this reason that we emulate the example set forth in John Molloy's book on men's style and Dress Our Information for Success.

To conclude, good design improves acceptance. It improves performance in that it is easier to use. Good design also uses a pragmatic aesthetic of functionality guided by a cost-benefit rationale. If one needs a more concrete example of this pragmatic aesthetic, visit the Museum of Modern Art in New York, where some very well designed products are showcased.

Back to Asia.

The early adoption of fuzzy logic by Orientals is probably due to the pictographic nature of written Chinese, which was adapted by the Koreans to make Hangul, and both subsequently by the Japanese beginning in 552 A.D., and to the resultant thought processes.

Kanji

Again from Wilson's *Consilience* we see at least tangential evidence why the Chinese approach, as evidenced by their language, may be more holistic.

> ... according to Joseph Needham, the principal Western chronicler of Chinese scientific endeavors, their focus stayed on the holistic properties and on the harmonious, hierarchical relationships of entities, from starts down to mountains and flowers and sand. In this world view the entities of Nature are inseparable and perpetually changing, not discrete and constant as perceived by the Enlightenment thinkers. As a result the Chinese never hit upon the entry point of abstraction and break-apart analytic research attained by European science the seventeenth century.

Of course, this statement may shock the average Westerner's ears. We as Westerners will see some of this graphical interpretation as logic by metaphor, as time goes on, when we begin to communicate in the form of 3D graphics on the Internet. In this particular respect, we are behind our Oriental cousins by a few millennia, but with Moore's and Gilder's Laws we should catch up quickly enough. It is the concept of logic by metaphor and the ability to keep that metaphor rich and varied that will be our final challenge.

I anticipate the reaction for lack of rigor, for dealing with a high level of abstraction with metaphor and analogy. Zadeh had the same problems when he started out with fuzzy logic. It was said that fuzzy logic was just "probability." We deal with that later. Useless precision is one of the concepts we are trying to get around or lessen. This is the Westerner in you. Define it, reduce it to a formula, be rational, be objective. We have loads of precise numbers in financial economics. How accurately do the numbers reflect reality? How much better are our predictions for having them? Like corporate forecasts, perhaps we should be asking what the limits of precision are. It is not bad to have precision, but it seems much value is derived from the appearance of objectivity and the psychological and emotional comfort it offers rather than the inherent accuracy in the projections, which derive from those "hard figures."

Also, we said earlier that the information economy is becoming more intangible and as a result less susceptible to direct and discrete measurement as this system (i.e., GAAP) works now. The conflict between this statement and the fact the information is a physical quantity in quantum physics is that our systems are not sensitive enough to detect the physical quantity or quality of information. It is a current task. But for the present we are sort of on quicksand in the sense that the manufacturers of tangible discrete stuff are ebbing and cognizers of intangible amorphous stuff are growing.

Rules for Tagging

Quoting directly from Joseph De Roo, here are the two principles which govern the logic of kanji creation:

1. Graphemes and kanji evoke specific situations from which meanings and connotations are drawn.

2. The situation, rather than the meaning, is often dominant when one kanji is part of another.

There is an interesting observation to make before we proceed. The dominance of the situation in kanji sounds strangely like Leibniz's principle of sufficient reason and the gauge principle subsequently proposed by Weyl where meaning is derived from relationships. In fact, with the abolition of Newtonian physics, meaning can only be derived from within the context of a relationship with another thing. There is no meaning in isolation. It is noteworthy that the Chinese stumbled on this notion millennia ago.

There are, of course, other reasons for using kanji. The fact that the language is old, well-developed, and widely accessible contributes substantially as a basis for its inclusion as a metaphor for use in nonlinear pricing. Also, although a few kanji are context-bound, the overwhelming majority of the examples in kanji are universally human. The components or building blocks of kanji, the graphemes, total only about two hundred—not insubstantial number, but certainly nowhere close to the 50,294 kanji recorded. Lastly, kanji are graphical in nature, and graphics is the language of nonlinear pricing.

Patterns

De Roo also mentions five patterns of kanji. At this stage, the patterns remain kanji-specific but their inclusion may provide some stimulation for future adaptation to nonlinear pricing.

First, where several situations may possibly be interpreted from a kanji, the highest-ranking one is chosen. From Confucian logic, all aspects of life may be ordinally ranked.

Second, connotations may be derived: from an important plant like a tree may be derived rice, hemp, tea, and so on.

Third, when it is possible to sketch an idea, images are used to provoke a thought which may remind one of the idea; for example, the sound of bees may remind one of the wind.

Fourth, because of the practicalities of brush writing, when compound kanji were made some kanji got compressed or abridged. These are called allographs.

Fifth, an abstract idea may use an existing idea and modify it.

Letter

Ever ready to prod the spiritual aspirant, the Buddhist priest recently sent me this *koan*:

> Grasshopper-kun,
>   "What is the ROI of a computer?"
>   A fellow traveler

In his own inimical way, the priest wants me to know that, like the proverbial long arm of the law, I am within his reach wherever I am on the planet. In a way he reminds me of the artillery officers I knew in the Marine Corps who delighted in the simple fact that their 155-millimeter howitzers could, to borrow a phrase from AT&T, "reach out and touch someone." The priest's letter had about the same effect.

Nonlinear Analysis

There is no direct-logical-simple link between the sound of one hand clapping, or bosoms and coffee, or wind and sales, or return on investment and a computer, or using fundamental analysis to determine the potential impact of object-oriented programming, relational databases, or e-commerce. Intel's CEO, the ever-paranoid Andy Grove, said when asked about his ROI on e-commerce, "This is the brave new world," and rhetorically asked, "What was Columbus's ROI?"

Fortunately, he quelled his critics with the facts that he is CEO, has 80% market share, and is turning a profit. I think he would have been correct even if he had been an entrepreneur or a divisional functionary out of "Dilbert" with less than a 1% share and was a yet-to-be profitable start-up or project. It does not mean that failures won't be punished or successes rewarded; it does mean that no one knows. And since no one has the angle, you might try it yourself. It does argue for a damn-the-torpedoes approach, because after you see 80% of what you think needs to be in place already in place, you have to jump on the opportunity.

That does not mean that relationships should not be drawn or interpreted. It means only that the unenlightened keep trying to extend old solutions to solve new problems. From a human perspective it is very understandable; it is also keep us in a position of perpetual ignorance. The reason *koans* provide enlightenment is that they defy the obvious attempts to use the most fundamental link of reasoning linking them. Every attempt to use direct, absolute logic is thwarted and one must use a more abstract or relational form of thinking to address the enigma.

In physics when the laws break down and cannot explain what is observed, it is called a singularity. The above *koan* is my favorite singularity in financial economics because it highlights the intersection of two juggernauts: finance and technology. On the surface we have two options; either we admit this is a silly question, with the realization that economic necessity demands an answer or we conclude that we are asking a good question the wrong way.

Perhaps contemplating kanji as a metaphor for the process for tagging based on situations which uses building blocks in the form of graphemes, and the concept of graphics seems less radical than it did at the beginning of the chapter. Since this is an introductory work, elementary graphs corresponding to specific situations in financial economics will not be covered. The learning process is hampered sufficiently without the graphics capability of a workstation that I think the attempt is best foregone. The insight, which is the essence of the logic process used to derive these modern-day graphemes in financial economics, has been fairly dealt with, though.

It is true that the output of our work in financial economics may be reduced to terms that are familiar to conventional practitioners. And this is a realistic objective. However, at this juncture we are trying to build the insight necessary to apply nonlinear pricing. In terms of order of magnitude of difficulty, imagine trying to reduce a conventional economics textbook to an investment manual.

No exact lexicon of pictures exists in financial economics. It is something being developed. It is a sort of pattern recognition. In conventional terms, just as "cheap" stocks may be characterized by selling at less than a 10×

P/E, graphical displays of standard yardsticks of nonlinear pricing exist. The concept is the same, but the approach is more sophisticated. We have started with traditional concepts as a departure point. Conceptually, it is also interesting to note that object-oriented programming languages such as Eiffel and Smalltalk also share a thread of commonality since an object, even a small bit of interchangeable code like bit of a graph, is reusable. For example, the grapheme of a piece of rice, a prominent food in Japan, occurs thematically throughout many kanji. Rice is used to build the concept of, among other things, food, meal, restaurant. It can take on the meaning of good and individualism and country. The latter ideas are of course more abstract and are represented by a box abound a rice plant. This simple concept in various contexts can mean "alone" as in standing apart. Certainly this is the essence of a sovereign nation. The grapheme of rice is more contextual used to represent the concept of "good." In Confucian values, eating is ordinally ranked as one of the highest virtues. As we might understand that concept today that it is impossible to break bread and to enjoy a bottle of wine with an enemy, the converse of that sentiment is a very desirable thing. We also begin to see here the building blocks which Holland mentioned as well.

To rectify this I asked myself, what does a computer do? And the literal answer is, of course, only what it has been programmed to do. On a slightly more sophisticated level, a computer either speeds up a process, as in the case of adding up all the numbers in the phone book, or it reconfigures information. Assigning an economic value to either of these processes will not be easy, but of the two, the former seems easier.

CONCLUSION

Given the evidence of self-organized criticality, the nonlinearity of financial economics, and the relational and biological orientation to which financial economics must turn for its future intellectual and practical development, "theory" is perhaps too strong a word for what is attempted here. Perhaps we must be satisfied for the time being with only an incremental improvement in our understanding with explanations such as those put forth by Holland, which increase intuition with rigor. The arguments for nonequilibrium and a biologically dependent approach are compelling.

Far-from-equilibrium states are a transient phenomenon. Near-equilibrium states exist almost always and perfect equilibrium as assumed by neoclassical economics almost never. Nonlinear pricing and the Theory of Reflexivity are more sophisticated views of reality and should be welcomed by the practitioner since we recognize that there is "no permanent investment truth," to use Jim Grant's words. We admit that relationships are causally weak and articulate them with simulations based on the best thinking the world has to offer. Indeterminacy is inherent in financial economics and is certainly what an observer in the physical sciences calls (qualitatively) fuzzy, as in the population physics of Prigogine based on the extended function space of Mandelbrot's fractals. Genetic algorithms give us a better-informed description of that reality. Evolution in nonlinear pricing is the basis to extend the Theory of Reflexivity.

Soros's simulation or abduction of the dynamic interplay of events, like many of ours, takes place in the brain. The reason for an indirect approach is that deduction and induction cannot work. Abduction is the most prudent course. If social science is a false metaphor because of thinking participants, their presence seems to ensure the nonequilibrium of financial economics.

Soros's impressionistic mechanics, Holland's levers, and Kelly's tipping points are similar concepts and the result of attempting to explain or model a complex adaptive system. Therefore, they will not be found a priori in the form of a formula. The "if-then" logic that appeals to the least sophisticated mind is absent. The only difference now is that we admit its fallacy and deal with the consequences of "if-then very possibly could be." The proof is based on simulation. One will not find the lever without bearing substantive up-front costs, since the lever is a transient phenomenon and only detectable in near real-time. Of course, big market changes and the ability to do something about them remain the province of well-capitalized investors. Nonlinear pricing and the Theory of Reflexivity exist at even a smaller subset—those investors are who are well-capitalized *and* forward-thinking.

10

The Last Word—Resonance

... the secret lies in the stepping-up of the mind's vibratory rate.

—PARAMAHANSA YOGANANDA,
Autobiography of a Yogi

The question put to three very accomplished men of differing backgrounds and in different parts of the 20th century is a Type III question: Is our approach correct? In science the question may be the unification of the four basic forces—gravity, electromagnetism, and the weak and strong nuclear forces. Is it possible given the methodology in which science is asking the questions? In financial economics, the question is, are we describing and thus understanding reality more accurately?

Lee Smolin, physicist, writing in his 1996 book *The Life of the Cosmos:* It makes sense then to ask whether the properties of an elementary particle like an electron are intrinsic to it, or are in part a manifestation of the interactions between it and the other things in the world.

The debate about whether the properties of an elementary particle are absolute or arise from the relationships that tie it to the rest of the universe is very old. It goes back at least to the debates between Leibniz and Newton in the seventeenth century. But this controversy has turned out to be of more than philosophical interest, for it is central to all the important developments of twentieth century theoretical physics. Relativity, quantum theory and the gauge principle, which underlies the standard model, can each be understood to have evolved from attempts to answer this question. Furthermore, they all come down on the same side of the issue, as they are all based in one way or another on the point of view that properties of things that arise from relationships.

To understand the gauge principle we may consider the simple case of electrical charge. We all learn in school that the electron has a negative charge and the proton has a positive charge. But, really, can there be any meaning to which is the positive and which is the negative? Certainly what is important is only the relationship between the charges, which ones are the same and which ones are opposite.

Paramanhasa Yogananda, yogi and swami, writing in his 1948 book *Autobiography of a Yogi:* Modern science has, as yet, no answer; though with the advent of the Atomic Age the scope of the world-mind has been abruptly enlarged. The word "impossible" is becoming less prominent in man's vocabulary.

The Vedic scriptures declare that the physical world operates under one fundamental law of *maya*, the principle of relativity and duality. God, the Sole Life, is Absolute Unity: to appear as the separate and diverse manifestations of a creation He wears a false or unreal veil. That illusory dualistic veil is *maya*. Many great scientific discoveries of modern times have confirmed this simple pronouncement of the ancient *rishis*.

Newton's Law of Motion is a law of *maya*. "To every action there is always an equal and contrary reaction: the mutual actions of any two bodies are always equal and oppositely directed." Action and reaction are thus exactly equal. "To have a single force is impossible. There must be, and always is, a pair of forces equal but opposite."

Fundamental natural activities all betray their *mayic* origin. Electricity, for example, is a phenomenon of repulsion and attraction; its electrons and protons are electrical opposites. Another example: the atom or final particle of matter is, like the earth itself, a magnet with positive and negative poles. The entire phenomenal world is under the inexorable sway of polarity: no law of physics, chemistry, or any other science is ever found free from inherent opposite or contrasted principles.

Physical science, then, cannot formulate laws outside of *maya*: the very fabric and structure of creation. Nature herself is *maya*: natural science must perforce deal with her ineluctable quiddity. In her own domain, she is eternal and inexhaustible; future scientists can do no more than probe one aspect after another of her vast infinitude. Science thus remains in a perpetual flux, unable to reach finality; fit indeed to discover the laws of an already existing and functioning cosmos but powerless to detect the Law Framer and Sole Operator. The majestic manifestations of gravitation and electricity have become known, but what gravitation and electricity are, no mortal knoweth.

To surmount *maya* was the task assigned to the human race by the millennial prophets. To rise above the duality of creation and perceive the unity of the Creator was conceived of as man's highest goal. . . .

"The stream of knowledge," Sir James Jeans writes in *The Mysterious*

Universe, "is heading toward a non-mechanical reality; the universe begins to look more like a great thought than like a great machine."

Twentieth-century science is thus sounding like a page from the hoary Vedas.

Ilya Prigogine, Nobel laureate in chemistry, writing in his 1980 book *From Being to Becoming:* It is perhaps one of the hottest topics of our time, one in which science and philosophy merge: Can we understand the microscopic world in "isolation"? In fact, we know matter, especially its microscopic properties, only by means of measuring devices, which themselves are macroscopic objects consisting of a large number of atoms and molecules. In a way these devices extend our sense organs. The apparatus can be said to be the mediator between the world that we explore and ourselves.

THE MUSES REVISITED

As a philosopher and physicist manqué, I found this chapter to be the most fun to write. In a few pages of unbridled intellectual promiscuity, I privately muse on the interrelatedness of things and in so doing risk offending the sociological sensibilities of various tribes of scientists and businessmen. While there is a more than a reasonable chance that I am not correct, I will have succeeded if I cause even one person to think in original terms.

Earlier we gave three examples of an ideal state superimposed on a messy reality, calendrics, Euclidean geometry, and the octave. If you have savored them at all during the course of your read, then you realize that they were only metaphors for more important concepts in this book.

Calendrics = Time

In measuring the length of a year, we measure an *event* called the mean solar year. It is the time it takes the Earth to run around the Sun. As we saw, there are three ways to measure this and some disagreement but we have settled on a reasonable definition. The concept that is important to remember here is event-driven time. If you still believe that there is a *real* relationship between the Earth's orbit of the sun and why markets go up and down, then we are in bad shape. The relationship of a smoothly flowing time, neatly divided into 24-hour increments and a constant rate of diffusion as it stands is nothing more than a convenient fiction. That is all.

When events speed up so does time. When events slow down so does time.

Geometry = Graphics

In constructing geometry, Euclid gave some identifiable rules about how it should be constructed. His tools were simple and so were his results. These rules are how to create and describe graphical images in a space. The concept of a space to hold the total possible number of solutions is a common construct called solution-space. The concept of space is gaining momentum at the popular level with cyberspace. Meatspace is were we shake hands. Hilbert space is where we describe quantum physics.

In space-time we find our solutions. To construct a graphical interpretation of a solution we need some sort of rules, like fractals, whether they come from phase-space or kanji. And graphics are desirable since they transmit information more efficiently; 4D graphics are logic by metaphor.

Music = Resonance

We are not concerned with music or the octave per se, but rather what music is. In the physical world, music is vibrations and resonance moving through space. These concepts are fundamental since the time series of a financial instrument can be thought of as a frequency. Fractals are used to measure this frequency. The fact that mutlifractals exist means that the frequencies (and speed of time) are more complex than originally envisaged. Successful hedges and exploitations embrace a sort of financial harmony.

The option of the S&P 500 and the S&P 500 basket move in sympathy because they are of the same resonance. Index arbitrage keeps them in tune. To begin to describe resonance we need the ability to have multiple times, a complex solution-space, and a more sensitive measure of resonance like fractals. Genetic algorithms and other nonlinear techniques are used to detect and track those moving waves. They are also used to build an inventory of certain combinations of resonance which result in profit or reduced risk.

For pedagogical reasons I have outlined roughly my thought process for driving the concept of resonance in financial economics. Sometimes it is more valuable to know how the concept is built rather than the result of the concept itself. The scaffolding for time and graphics followed a similar pattern.

TIME DOMAIN VERSUS FREQUENCY DOMAIN

As any one who has ever seen the pendulum of a grandfather clock knows, the sound is tock-tock-tock. It typically swings at one stroke per second. What most people do not think about is that the events in the time domain can be expressed in the frequency domain via fast fourier transforms or FFTs and vice versa. The movement of a pendulum or a plucked string plotted in the time domain is a distribution, and plotted in the frequency domain it is measured in MHz. Frequencies and distributions are two ways of looking at the same thing.

The Fourier transform is based on the 1:1 correspondence between the probability distribution function of a random variable and its characteristic function. The characteristic function is the complex generalization of the moment-generating function. The moment-generating function is used to generate the moments of the distribution. The characteristic function is always extant, whereas the moment-generating function does not exist for some probability distribution functions. The characteristic function is equivalent to the inverse of the Fourier transform. Thus:

DISTRIBUTIONS = FREQUENCY   via FFTs

BROWNIAN MOTION AND THE GAUSSIAN DISTRIBUTION

Old finance theory makes great use of Brownian motion to describe a time series and Gaussian distributions to describe returns. In fact, in the following example, if a Bm is taken to its limit it is a Gaussian distribution. This linking of probability and statistics has been one of the major reasons, if not *the* reason, people are so reluctant to abandon the linear paradigm in financial economics. It fits together, it is elegant, its properties have a century or more of research behind them; but unfortunately it is also wrong.

As Prigogine tells us in *From Being to Becoming*: We can push such probability arguments still further to obtain quantitative formulations that describe how irreversible processes evolve with time. Consider, for example, the well-known random walk problem, an idealized but nevertheless successful model for Brownian motion. In the simplest example, a one-dimensional random walk, a molecule makes a one-step transition at regular time intervals (1.3). With the molecule initially at the origin, we ask for the probability of finding it at point m, after N steps. If the probability that the molecule proceeds forward or backward is assumed to be one-half, we find that

$$W(m, N) = (1/2) (N! / [1/2(N + m)]![1/2(N - m)]!$$ (1.0)

Thus, to arrive at point m after N steps, some $1/2(N + m)$ steps must be taken to the right and some $1/2(N + m)$ to the left. Equation (1.0) gives the number of such distinct sequences multiplied by the overall probability of an arbitrary sequence of N steps.

Expanding the factorials, we obtain the asymptotic formula corresponding to a Gaussian distribution:

$$W(m, N) = (2 / \pi N)^{1/2} e^{-m^2/2N}$$ (1.1)

Using the notation $D = 1/2nl^2$, in which l is the distance between two sites and n the number of displacements per unit of time, this result can be written:

$$W(x, t) = 1 / (2 (\pi Dt)^{1/2}) e^{-x^2/4Dt}$$ (1.2)

in which $x = ml$. This is the solution of the one-dimensional diffusion equation identical in form to the Fourier equation:

$$\delta T / \delta t = \kappa \, \delta^2 T / \delta x^2$$ (1.3)

but κ is replaced by D. Evidently, this is a very simple example.

The fact is that Brownian motion and Gaussian distributions are also two ways of looking at the same thing. Thus:

BROWNIAN MOTION = GAUSSIAN DISTRIBITION

Using Socratic logic (a = b and a = c, therefore a = c), can we not view Brownian motion as a frequency? The above example supports this question in the affirmative only for the narrow case when the time series is a Brownian motion or when $\mathbf{H} = 0.5$ and the returns are normally distributed. I think it is a very useful concept and one that we do not use much at all in financial economics at present.

BROWNIAN MOTION (financial time series) = FREQUENCY

Obviously, three pieces of evidence show that a financial time series is not a Brownian motion: First, we know that in about 1963 Mandelbrot showed that financial time series did not follow a Brownian motion and Fama showed that the distributions of stock returns are stably distributed, not normally distributed. Second, from the finance literature dealing with options we know that volatility smiles exist and should not. Third, from several sources, other disciplines with new concepts such as self-organized criticality have a role to play.

We can practically extend the mathematics a bit. For example, if we assume that the time series is independent, then we can also make some relationships for $H > 0.5$ or a persistent time series and the shape of an α-stable distribution with fat tails. Admittedly, no distribution shape exists for antipersistent time series. We also know that wavelets are better than FFTs since FFTs assume periodicity and stationarity. The FFT illustration is here only to show that the link between time and frequency under some ideal circumstances can be easily stated. I do not think the conceptual link goes away in other less amenable circumstances; however, the treatment becomes far more complicated.

While it is obvious some of the necessary math has yet to be invented, let us retain the concept that time series in general can be viewed as a frequency rather than in terms of a distribution. While the concept is not as easily documented in the nonlinear world as in the linear world, there are enough practical workarounds to preserve and implement it. (See Table 10.1.) Thus:

FINANCIAL TIME SERIES = FREQUENCY

At this point we move from the human scale where I have arbitrarily assigned the frequency-time relationship because this is where the investors and presumably the stock market is, and jump to 1923 and to the quantum scale.

While physicists were puzzling over light's seemingly contradictory properties, another storm was brewing in Paris. French aristocrat Louis de

Table 10.1 Linking Concepts

Scale	Physical		Temporal	
		Dimensions		
Cosmic	Length Width Height	Relativity	Time	
Human		Frequency Brownian motion	FFTs	Time Distribution
Atomic	Particles (matter and energy)	Waves (frequency)	Quantum	Probability
Subatomic			Superstring theory	

Broglie had submitted a strange PhD thesis to his physics professors at the Sorbonne. By arguments that seemed dubious to his examiners, de Broglie contended that each particle of matter was associated with a wave whose temporal and spatial frequencies f and k were given by the Planck-Einstein recipe $E = hf$ and the Compton relation $p = hk$ where E and p are the particles energy and momentum. De Broglie argued that just as Einstein showed waves of light to have particle properties, so particles of matter might have wave properties. So Nick Herbert says in *Quantum Reality: Beyond the New Physics*. Thus:

PHYSICAL THINGS = FREQUENCY   quantum mechanics

De Broglie's advisers were clearly shocked, and sent the thesis to Einstein who enthusiastically backed it. Six years later, in 1929, de Broglie won the Nobel Prize for it.

Recall Heisenberg's uncertainty principle, which says we can determine either the momentum or location of an electron but never both simultaneously. We know that the world at the quantum scale can only be described by waves. Now, these waves are not like the physical waves of water that one may consider; they are waves of *probability*.

Gribben in *In Search of Schrödinger's Cat* mentions that de Broglie's equations, these waves of probability, unusually also apply to the human scale. The catch, of course, is that the length of the waves diminishes proportionately with the mass or momentum of the object. For a baseball it is 10^{-32} centimeters and for people it is even shorter. He goes on to say these probability waves apply to things like crime waves. That means a crime wave is a thing—albeit a temporal thing, but that is okay since relativity says that temporal things and physical things are part of the same fabric of space-time. If crime waves are included, then so must financial waves be included because they are probabilistic events. We have basically reified waves or tendencies.

PHYSICAL THINGS < > TEMPORAL THINGS   relativity

It is this series of relationships—time-series to distribution > distribution to frequency > frequency to quantum probability waves > probability waves to physical things > physical things to temporal things—that lead me to speculate that time series may, for short periods of time anyway, have characteristic lengths—*resonance* if you wish. It is this resonance that I described as sweet spots using the KAOS screen. I do not yet know the precise relationship between a quantum wave and a temporal thing, but the conceptual link is provocative. It is the thought that leads me to posit that the KAOS screen is analogous, even homologous, to a stereo tuner.

TEMPORAL THINGS = FREQUENCY   physics

Continuing a thought in quantum reality, so named because particles can exchange packets of energy called quanta as certain discrete levels: That is, if an electron is in some sense a wave, then in order for a wave to "fit" into the orbit of an atom, the size of the orbit must correspond to a whole number of wavelengths. Only certain discrete levels of energy are allowed because only at certain distances from the nucleus will probability patterns join up. The idea of a thing occupying only discrete places sounds strangely like self-organization, where at some point—or some characteristic frequency—there are enough water molecules to enable a funnel to occur or enough sand gains to enable an avalanche. I wonder if can we make this conceptual leap: Do systems have sweet spots like atoms do?

QUANTA = SELF-ORGANIZATION   SWAG

Further, the intermittent or transient aspect of the financial wave seems in keeping with the necessary criteria of dynamism in financial economics analysis. To continue, at the subatomic level, the concept of resonance is prominent in string theory. And resonance has to change if we are to allow the view of a dynamic and relational universe to replace our static and defined universe. It is the elastic concept of pulsating, undulating, living universe and one that has measures relative to other things that replaces the rigid template of a static universe.

STRING THEORY

Frequency is borne out by the superstring theory in quantum physics, where strings at the *Plank Length* 10^{-33}, or by an order of magnitude 20 times smaller than an atom, vibrate to create all matter. This means that the things that make the atoms that make you are very subtle frequencies and that matter can also be expressed as pure energy.

THINGS HAVE CHARACTERISTIC FREQUENCIES - Superstring theory

Conversely we may also wonder, do things also have a characteristic time? If the subject is humans, an actuary or gerentologist can answer that. If is a hard disk drive, a quality control expert will be able to tell you the MTBF or mean time between failure. At its root though, if frequency is an event and events mark time, then does frequency suggest a characteristic time?

String theory, if you can believe it, says that at a level too small for us to presently detect—the *Plank Level* 10^{-33} centimeters, a 100 billion billion times smaller than an atom—the stuff of which the world is made is essentially little strings which vibrate. They add to and subtract from each other to form different things, presumably the ever-increasing potpourri of elementary particles which in turn form atoms and then molecules and so on. They are all composed of the same vibratory stuff, only in different characteristic lengths.

Now, that string theory is untestable at the millennium should not be the sole reason we disregard it. After all, Einstein proposed relativity before the ability existed to test it and confirmed it. Alan Gamow, the great Russian cosmologist, calculated the age of the universe many years before results confirmed it. Alan Guth, at MIT, proposed the inflationary universe theory long before space ships could test it. Maybe someday we will have the ability to test string theory, but until then it does satisfy some important hallmarks of real scientific insight: First, it is simple and symmetrical or elegant. This may seem strange to the reader but it is accepted that nature, if explained correctly, is usually simpler than we initially might suspect.

Second, string theory seems to explain or unify the fundamental force gravity with the other three, weak and strong nuclear and electromagnetic forces. Third, it does so logically using higher dimensions, 10 to be exact— the four we know about, length, breadth, height, and time, and six others that exist at the Plank level.

The basic problem with string theory, according to Kaku in *Hyperspace*, is that string theory is a bit of the 21st century discovered by accident in the 20th. The math and related bodies of knowledge required to gain real insight to the theory either do not exist or are at too nascent a stage of development to be applicable.

For example, modular operators occur frequently in string theory and this body of math happened to be the province of an exceptional character named Ramanajun, an Indian who derived the previous 100 years of European mathematics in three. He studied for a few years at Cambridge before World War I sent him home, where he died at 33.

In much of Ramanajun's work is the number 24. Mathematicians refer to it as a magic number because it keeps popping up but no one knows why. Perhaps it has to do with the formulas achieving symmetry—a critical piece of both practically and esthetically great science. Maybe symmetry is a synonym for the resonance of a certain vibration, or what I called in the KAOS chapter the characteristic length or sweet spot.

The theme of resonance is redolent of a Bach fugue. It keeps rising again and again—the fundamental stuff or strings of which the world is made, vibrating, and becoming longer and shorter. Is this the eternal golden braid referred to in Douglas Hofstadter's classic *Gödel, Escher, Bach*? Is this the central theme of the cosmos, only replayed with variations?

If power law distributions may be thought of as sort of a characteristic frequency at the system level, then from Simon, who first wrote about them in economics in 1955, we may include not only time series but systems. We certainly find this phenomenon in networks. Stephen Grossberg and Gail Carpenter for the Center of Adaptive Systems at Boston University have developed Adaptive Resonance Theory.

Lastly, Prigogine's new book, *The End of Certainty: Time, Chaos and the New Laws of Nature* speaks extensively and convincingly on the use of the concept of resonance to describe reality.

RESONANCE AND THE SCRIPTURES

I will not be the first who writes something about science at this fairly abstract level and ends up straying into another field like philosophy or religion. When one wrestles with problems of this magnitude, one naturally turns to any knowledge at hand, and since most people I assume have had Sunday school or its equivalent, this makes sense. After all, Sunday school is where I first learned about the concept "eternal."

The Vedas and the Bible also offer some insight on the fundamental claim of resonance, however tangentially. The Vedas are the hoary scriptures of India. No evidence links Ramanajun and the Hindu scriptures other than the fact that they share a common country, but it did lead me to speculate.

Yogananda tells us in his *Autobiography of a Yogi* that the Hindu scriptures speak of God as *Sat* and *Tat* and *Aum*, the cosmic *creative vibration*, or more familiarly to Western ears as God, the Father, Son, and Holy Ghost.

God the Father, is the Absolute, Unmanifested existing *beyond* vibratory creation.

> No man hath seen God at any time; the only begotten Son, which is in the bosom of the Father, he hath declared him.
>
> —John 1:18

God the Son is Christ Consciousness (Brahma or *Kutastha Chaitanya*) exiting *within* vibratory creation; this Christ consciousness is the "only begotten" or sole reflection of the Uncreated Infinite.

> God . . . created all things by Jesus Christ.
>
> —Ephesians 3:9

God the Holy Ghost or *Aum*, or the Word, is its "witness": invisible divine power which is the sole causative and activating force that upholds all of creation.

> He that hath an ear, let him hear what the Spirit saith unto the churches.
> And unto the angel of the church the Laodiceans write: These things saith the Amen, the faithful and the true witness, the beginning of the creation of God;
> —Revelations 3: 13-14

> In the beginning was the Word, and the Word was with God, and the Word was God.
> —John 1:1

Aum which reverberates through out the universe has three manifestations or *gunas* those of, creation, destruction and preservation. (Taittiriya Upanishad 1:8) Each time a man utters a word he puts into operation one of these three equalities of *Aum*. This is the lawful reason behind the injunction of all scriptures that man should speak the truth.

Aum of the Vedas became the sacred word *Hum* of the Tibetans, *Amin* of the Moslems, and *Amen* of the Egyptians, Greeks, Romans, Jews, and Christians. Its meaning in Hebrew is *sure, faithful.*

Sort of unusual, don't you think? Words, being sound pressure waves or vibrations, being God at the beginning which sort of sounds like the little vibrations of string theory with a characteristic level of the 10^{-33} centimeters. Lest we forget the electromagnetic spectrum and visible vibrations of light, of course the first thing God says in the Old Testament is:

> Let there be light.
> —Genesis 1:3

All that is seen and unseen is merely the manifestation of the cosmic creative vibration—God. The cosmic motion picture we mistake as ultimate reality on Earth is but chiaroscuro and a stepping-stone to each man's apotheosis to divine reality. The show is much larger than we think!

CONCLUSION

In reality, financial economics practitioners have been given a difficult task—such as buying and selling. The tools with which they have had to equip themselves are inadequate. In sum, the average trader or money manager's intuitive map of reality far outstrips the state of formalism for reality. Formalism is making inroads, though.

The two worlds proceed along different paths—"bond daddies" don't go to school and professors of any stripe (mathematicians, physicists, biologists, etc.) do not sit on trading desks. Their bodies of research seem to intersect only tangentially and they interface with a great deal of détente. This must change.

The film *Driving Miss Daisy*, portrays the improbable friendship between an upper-middle-class Jewish woman and the black man who worked for her in Georgia in the 1930s. In the closing scene, Miss Daisy, now in her 90s, is being visited at the old folks' home by her former chauffeur, now also in advanced age and touchingly her one true friend. Her final question is, "How are you doing?" To which he replies, "I guess we are all doing the best we know how."

I believe, perhaps naively, that we do the best we know how and if there is a better way we will do it (eventually). To close the gap between what we can state and what we can intuit, I propose that in the final analysis:

- We should not adopt **H** and the computational solutions nonlinear pricing admits only because of empirical evidence.

- We should not adopt it only because of the availability of new technology.

- We should not adopt nonlinear pricing only because of shortcomings in the old ways.

- We *should* adopt nonlinear pricing because it is the best explanation of the facts available.

We have toured some far-reaching concepts which are not traditional to the rank-and-file financial economics practitioner. Technology is doing this to us all, in every discipline. Technology is challenging our beliefs. We have taken this long tour because a big reward awaits those who successfully do their homework. None of this effort is worthwhile unless it translates into dollars and cents.

Despite its cerebral bent, this chapter has invaluable clues for Wall Street. To those money people in the know, i2 has a $1.5 billion market capitalization using primarily genetic algorithms to help companies save money in complex processes such as scheduling, assembly lines, and project management. Typically the argument to industry goes something like this: "Our software can help you save 15% of your costs." Period. Since the dollar amounts are huge and the process is long-lived, whatever the software costs, the deal still makes financial sense. Now for that success to be replicated in financial economics, we will have to determine how to make an open system like financial economics resemble a closed system like an assembly line. The key to that success and yet another new weird high-tech company that you never heard of with a market cap of $1.5 billion lies hidden in the concept of resonance.

ADIEU

The best of the smartest, richest, prettiest, most accomplished people I
have ever met share a common trait. They are secure. They are all pretty
relaxed about who they are. And as a consequence they put you at ease
too. It is the insecure who obscure. I believe, as the late physicist Richard
Feyman did when he compiled the then sum body of knowledge of
physics for the freshmen at CalTech into the opus *Feyman Lectures on
Physics*, that if you cannot explain something at the freshman level, you
do not understand it that well yourself. And he was humble enough to admit that not all parts of physics could be explained at that level. I have
tried to address some non-freshman issues at the freshman level. If you
do not understand, it is probably because I have not understood it that
well myself.

I leave you now with one thought: Risk and reward and time are border-less. Seeking techniques like some of those in this book, which are either lit-tle known or outside the traditional financial economics literature, should be a priority of all those who abjure the arrogance of certainty. Further ad-vancement lies not only in seeking increasingly more isolated answers from within the discipline, which has been popular for the last three and a half centuries, but also in seeking descriptions of phenomena from other fields which may be applied in the instant case. In that spirit, much remains to be described in light of a new interpretation.

Appendix

Survey of Nonlinear Thinking in Financial Economics

> The threatened wreckage is the greater part of economic theory.
> —JOHN HICKS,
> *in 1939 on surveying the possibility of nonequilibrium in economics*

In looking at nonlinear financial economics it is informative to survey the developments that are taking place. In keeping with the information age's ability to absorb ideas democratically, do not look for financial economics ideas *only* from people with the financial economics label on their degrees or business cards. As financial economics begins to be modeled on principles that have been articulated in physics, computer networks, and ultimately biology, the list of people with insight becomes eclectic. We will see some academics, a practitioner, a computer scientist, and an editor.

TRAIN

John Train is a cerebral, patrician, and eminently successful money manager who has also become noted for his many books on Wall Street and finance over the years.

In 1975, Train wrote *Dance of the Money Bees*, a difficult title to find today. It is the first book ever, to my knowledge, to use a biological example to describe financial phenomena. Bees forage for food, and when they return, the state of agitation of their dance before the hive indicates the status of the find. The larger the agitation the better the find. Train used this phenomenon as an analogy to describe money mangers when they are excited by a stock. Of course, fellow money managers and investors follow—they swarm like the hive. It is a wholly accurate, if unflattering, portrayal of how the real world works. Of course, it is now called swarm theory and modeled in computers.

Train's insight was more prescient than even he could have imagined. The same year *Dance of the Money Bees* was published, John Holland at the University of Michigan was siring genetic algorithm, the mathematical technique and formalism that mimics biological adaptation and which would in time give rigor to Train's intuition. Train effectively preceded the entire field of financial economics by over 20 years in using biology as a paradigm.

Train, in his investing style, is a no-nonsense sort that does not care for academic theory, derivatives, or exotica. In writing *Dance of the Money Bees*, one of the most conservative men in investing has penciled a sketch that many others, including myself, are trying to complete in color and with technologically appropriate terms. It will be interesting to note Train's reaction to the maturation of his thought. It may resemble Bohr's when he sired quantum mechanics. Bohr said, "Anyone who is not shocked by it has not understood it." The conclusion I would like to draw is that even if Train's peers do not explicitly embrace nonlinear pricing because they find the terminology off-putting, implicitly they do because nonlinearity describes the state of the world that embraces them every trading day of the year.

KELLY

If the selection of an editor strikes you as odd, perhaps that is a good thing. The information age is quite democratic in absorbing ideas, regardless of origin. Kevin Kelly is the executive editor of *Wired* magazine, the monthly chronicle of the culture of the *digerati*, or digital literati. Kelly exists at the interesting intersection of technology and financial economics. One of the consequences for traditionalists is that without exposure to this intersection they will be less capable of producing relevant research.

In 1995, Kelly came out with a captivating book, *Out of Control: The Rise of the Neo-Biological Civilization*, which is a series of vignettes illustrating the parallels between a biological system and the dynamics of interactive networks. That parallel also applies to financial economics. For example, birds exhibit self-organization when they flock. No one bird has to be the leader, since every other bird cues off of a wingman, resulting in the inverted V familiar to hunters.

Social Interaction Can Exhibit Self-Organized Criticality (SOC)

The corollary in financial behavior is a group of nervous sellers, such as highly leveraged arbitrageurs. The perceived risk of loss in merger arbitrage is high, so in the face of information that we could not rapidly assimilate or that was contradictory we would stop thinking and flock. For example, if one arbitrageur notices another selling, the first arb will assume that the other fellow knows more than he does and begin selling too—a very lemming-like quality. Selling commences with the time it takes to call the broker, quicker than the time cycle of a report or a meeting. As a result, we would flock like birds—or become critically self-organized—and buy and sell together.

The dynamics of networks are congruent to those of biological systems. Evidently we may think it is better to fail together than to succeed alone. Warren Buffett echoed similar criticisms of money managers who flock toward a consensus; they abandon independent reasoning for groupthink and, to use Buffett's term confuse "conservatism with conventionality."

Kelly later published *New Rules for the New Economy* at the web site www.wired.com/winred/5.09/newrules.html, which are summarized here since they are quite insightful and demonstrate, if nothing else, that economic theory must expand beyond its equilibrium roots to explain new phenomena. There are four main points:

1. Wealth flows from innovation, not optimization. That is, it is better to be doing a new thing imperfectly than to be doing a known task even better.

2. The ideal environment to nurture the unknown is dynamism of the network. A free flow of information in a complex state is best.

3. Harnessing the unknown means abandoning the known. Creation and destruction are two sides of the same coin. You have to know when to let go of a concept, technology, skill base, and so on and move on.

4. The cycle of find, nurture, destroy happens quicker in the information age than it did in the industrial age.

The 12 *New Rules* are:

1. The Law of Connection
Also called embracing dumb power, this law holds that as increasingly inexpensive chips—called jelly beans in the high-tech industry—become ubiquitous, they will become an essential ingredient of everything. Products

with these chips will be "smart products." They will become points of information gathering.

2. The Law of Plenitude

This law has traditionally been expressed as "Them that has gets." Mathematics has proved that while the nodes on a network increase arithmetically, the value of the network itself increases exponentially.

3. The Law of Exponential Value

Success is *nonlinear*. During their initial stages the Internet, Federal Express, and Microsoft were uninteresting for many years before a critical mass was reached, and then they took off in the mid-1980s due to the value of memberships in the Law of Plenitude. In the 1980s jelly beans began to proliferate and telecommunications charges decreased. Biology also exhibits this exponential growth, which is why the economic understanding of any high-technology society will be driven more by evolution found in biological models than by Newtonian physics. If the World Wide Web feels like a frontier, it is because we are witnessing a biological growth in technological systems.

Of course, as a corollary, failure will be nonlinear too. Failure will occur with astonishing speed.

4. The Law of Tipping Points

Significance precedes momentum. Again a biological interpretation is used. At some tipping point momentum becomes so overwhelming that success feeds on itself. What changes in the information age is that the response time is radically reduced because the threshold to achieve the tipping point is lower. Information has a lower fixed cost, a lower marginal cost, and rapid distribution. Thus, detecting events below the threshold is essential.

Major U.S. retailers ignored TV home-shopping and regarded it as insignificant in the 1980s. Instead of exploiting the subthreshold significance, they waited for it to grow. By that time, of course, it was too late to cash in.

5. The Law of Increasing Returns

This is the prime law of networking and expresses the fact that the value explodes with membership. The Law of Increasing Returns is an example of a positive feedback loop. It is similar to the industrial age notion of economies of scale. The difference is that industrial age examples like Henry Ford whose increasing efficiency producing cars in turn sold more cars, have not been dependent on Internet power, whereas information age examples, such as Silicon Valley start-ups attracting other start-ups, are.

Also, whereas in the industrial age economies of scale have been dependent on individual companies, in the information age it is several companies but one Internet. The gains may be unequal between companies, but the value of the gain resides in the greater web of relationships.

This trend can be extended into the very nature of the organization itself. The hardware and software is not the real value; more important is the ability to continuously create that value such as car pools, old colleagues, talent, legal and financial services, and so on.

The nature of the Law of Increasing Returns favors the early adopters. The parameters and conventions quickly congeal into a standard. Consumers benefit from a standard. Owners and controllers of the standard are disproportionately rewarded until the standard is replaced.

6. The Law of Inverse Pricing

Anticipate the cheap. This commodity pricing principle is caused and exemplified by the well-known Moore's Law. Gilder's Law, named after George Gilder the technotheorist, posits that the total bandwidth of communications will triple every 12 months for the next 25 years. These laws cause an asymptotic-like curve reflecting pricing that rapidly approaches but never reaches zero, and in effect become "free."

For consumers this is great. Producers and all those who hope to make a buck have to expand the idea of what the product is or does. As products slip down the curve of pricing toward free, your job in the information age is to create quicker than the product or service can become commoditized.

7. The Law of Generosity

Follow the free. As a result of laws 2 and 6, the extension of this logic says that the most valuable things are given away. Microsoft and Netscape give away their Web browsers and Qualcomm gives Eudora, the standard e-mail program, away for free. McAfee's antivirus is free. Cellular phones are given away to sell the service.

Once the value is established, all the ancillary products, updates, and services can be sold.

8. The Law of the Allegiance

Feed the Web first. The distinction of us versus them, known well to the industrial era organization man, is now known as on the Net or off. The Internet is a possibility factory. The attempt to instill order and tame the Net is the creation of standards.

A network is like a country. In both, the surest route to raising one's own prosperity is raising the system's. In the industrial age individual prosperity has been closely linked to the nation's prosperity. In the information age individual effort counts more.

There are three important differences between network and country.

1. No geographical or temporal boundaries exist on the Internet.

2. Relations in the network economy are more intense and tightly coupled.

3. Multiple overlapping networks and allegiances exist.

9. The Law of Devolution

Let go at the top. In terms of ecological behavior, the ideal is to let go of an idea, concept, or technology when it is at its top. Given an ultraconnected constitution makes the network behave ecologically. The fate of an individual firm is not only dependent on its own activities but that of its neighbors, allies, competitors, and the immediate environment.

The biological nature of this era means that the sudden disintegration of established domains will be as certain as the sudden appearance of the new. Therefore, there can be no expertise in innovation unless there is also expertise in demolishing the ensconced.

10. The Law of Displacement

The Internet wins. Many have observed the gradual displacement in our economy of materials by information. Automobiles weigh less and perform better. High-tech know-how and composites have replaced steel. This displacement will continue.

Whereas the unique dynamics of the software and computer industry were seen as special cases within a larger "real" economy of steel, oil, and so on, the dynamics of the network will replace them. Energy visionary Amory Lovins already envisions cars as chips on wheels where more high-tech materials reduce weight and thus the power required to move it. If we can have smart cars, can smart planes, tractors, and such be far behind?

Nicholas Negroponte estimates on-line commerce to reach $1 trillion by the year 2000. All transactions and objects will obey network logic.

11. The Law of Churn

Seek sustainable disequilibrium. In the industrial perspective, the economy was a machine that was to be tweaked to optimal efficiency, and once finely tuned it was to be maintained in productive harmony. Companies or industries especially productive of jobs or goods had to be protected and cherished at all costs, as if these firms were rare watches in a glass case.

The network economy resembles an ecology of organisms, interlinked and coevolving, constantly in flux, deeply tangled, ever expanding at its edges. As we know from ecology, no balance exists in nature.

Innovation is disruption; constant innovation is constant disruption. As economists such as Paul Romer and Brian Arthur begin to study the network economy, they see that it, too, operates by poising itself on the edge of constant chaos. In this chaotic churn is the life-giving renewal and growth.

The dark side is that turbulence is a hallmark of the network economy and the experiences within the companies. Lifetime employment is gone. Careers increasingly resemble networks of multiple and simultaneous commitments with a constant churn of new skills and outmoded roles.

In the coming churn, the industrial age's titans will fall. In a poetic sense, the prime task of the network economy is to destroy—company by company, industry by industry—the industrial economy. While it undoes industry at its peak, it weaves a larger web of new, more agile, more tightly linked organizations.

Effective churning will be an art. In any case, promoting stability, defending productivity, and protecting success can only prolong the misery.

12. The Law of Inefficiencies

Don't solve problems. Economists once thought that the coming age would bring supreme productivity. It has not. This is because productivity is exactly the wrong thing to care about. Only robots should worry about productivity. And, in fact, the one area of the economy that does show a rise in productivity has been the U.S. and Japanese manufacturing sectors, which have seen a 3% to 5% annual increase throughout the 1980s and into the 1990s. This is where you want to find productivity. But we do not find productivity gains in the catchall service sector; why would we? Is a Hollywood movie company that produces longer movies per dollar more productive that one that produces shorter movies?

The problem with trying to measure productivity is that it measures how well someone can do the wrong job. Any job that can be measured for productivity should probably be eliminated.

Peter Drucker has noted that in the industrial age, the task for each worker was to discover how to do one's job better, that's productivity. But in the network economy, where machines do most of the inhumane work of manufacturing, the task of each worker is to discover not "how to do the job right" but rather "what is the right job to do." In the coming era, doing exactly the right next thing is far more "productive" than doing the same thing better. But how can one measure this vital sense of exploration and discovery? It will be visible to productivity benchmarks.

In the network economy our bottleneck is not productivity; it is imagination in seizing opportunities. In the words of Peter Drucker as echoed by George Gilder, "Don't solve problems; seek opportunities." When you are solving problems you are investing in your weakness; when you are seeking opportunities you are banking on the network. The wonderful news about the network is that it plays right into human strengths. Repetition, sequels, copies, and automation all tend toward the free, while innovation, originality, and imagination all increase in value.

HOLLAND

Nobel prizes are not awarded for certain fields such as mathematics or computer science; if that is ever amended, John Holland will be on the short list. In 1994 he wrote *Hidden Order*, a very readable account of how adaptation builds complexity, and later, in 1998, he wrote *Emergence: From Chaos to Order*. Holland distills seven attributes of complex adaptive systems or *cas*, of which there are four properties and three mechanisms. An economy, like the biologically interpreted ecosystem, is a pattern in time and thus a *cas*. Defined differently, a *cas* exhibits bounded variation and changes with time.

Properties

1. Aggregation
Aggregation enters into *cas* in two senses. First, in simplest terms, aggregation is reusable classifications or stereotyping without the pejorative overtones. It is the human attempt to make the difficult simple. For example, we aggregate firms into an economy from which an emergent property like gross domestic product arises.

Aggregation in the second sense is an aspect of all *cas* and the emergent phenomena that result are the most enigmatic aspect of *cas*. Study of *cas* hinges on the ability to discern the mechanisms that enable simple aggregates to form highly adaptive aggregates. What kind of boundaries demarcate adaptive aggregates? How do the contained interactions generate behaviors that transcend the behaviors of the compound agents?

2. Nonlinearity
Nonlinearity has been discussed in some detail and merely reflects the fact that the if inputs and outputs of a system are disproportionate, then the system is nonlinear.

Financial economics is a nonlinear system, and it is for this reason that the title of this book was chosen. Non-anything is not the best choice of words from a strictly marketing point of view; however, as you have already seen, once you roll up your sleeves a bit, keeping terminology straight between the disciplines of physics, biology, computer science, mathematics, and financial economics is no mean feat.

3. Flows

Jet streams, information, and money are all flows. None are constant, and the concept spans many disciplines, such as goods flowing to and from a city. The flows are part of a pattern that changes with time and experience.

Flows have two properties—a multiplier effect and a recycling effect. The multiplier is best exemplified by the concept of the same name in economics. In fixing your house, you pay your contractor, who in turns pays the subcontractors, and so on. If there are five stages and 20% is saved at each step, the multiplier effect is five. The multiplier is a major feature of networks and flows. It is particularly evident in evolutionary changes and jeopardizes long-term predictions based on simple trends.

The recycling effect is the effect of cycles in networks. The more a cycle can trap of its resources, the more efficient the process will be. The concept of recycling resources applies to recycling old automobiles for their steel as well as resources in a rain forest.

Laszlo Birinyi, founder of Birinyi & Associates in Greenwich, Connecticut, who pioneered the concept of money flows on Wall Street, has made a business of this concept alone.

4. Diversity

Rain forests and New York City are diverse places. Much of what can be characterized by an agent depends on other agents. Each agent fills a niche, and removing it leaves a hole in the fabric of the ecosystem. The system responds by adapting with a new agent to fill the hole.

One of the central questions of *cas* is, what allows and maintains this pattern of diversity in time? Resources that are retained allow for further diversity. Agents that fail to retain resources lose their resources to those that do. It is natural selection writ large.

The recycling of resources by a diverse group of agents inhibits development with the group's resources. *Cas* will not settle to a few highly selected types that can exploit all opportunities. Perpetual novelty is the hallmark of *cas*.

MECHANISMS

1. Tagging

Tagging as it is used here is the label for transmitter and receptor. It is the flag of a team, or the header of an Internet message, or what we used to call the date-time group on a message at the Comm Center in the Marine Corps. We cannot do anything with any piece of information unless we can tag it, classify it, and organize it.

2. Internal Model

Internal gyroscopes exist. This is a complex concept and means that the agents can anticipate. Insectivorous birds learn to avoid eating the monarch butterfly because it tastes bitter. The subject is broached using selective patterns that are repeated. A bacterium moves to a chemical gradient, implicitly assuming that food is there. Wolves base their interpretations on a mental map that includes scents and the terrain. We now use computers for this internal model to fly commercial aircraft.

3. Building Blocks

There are some constituent parts from which we can build, just like Lego® building blocks. In the face of the perpetual novelty of a market, the repetitive use of core concepts may seem contradictory; however, the paradox is resolved since those blocks are continually retested for usability. The process of retesting is called adaptation. A simple example is the human face, with lips, nose, eyebrows, and so on. The building blocks are the same, yet the number of possible combinations is quite high—about 10 billion. Still, we are able to recognize people. It would be a mistake to say that once those building blocks are known we automatically know all the possible relationships, any more than if we know the axioms of geometry we know all the theorems; but it is an important step.

SEIGEL

Lester Seigel is an interesting fellow; he has a PhD in physics and is a managing director at the World Bank in Washington, DC. I first crossed paths with him at a SIAM (Society for Industrial and Applied Mathematics) conference in Philadelphia in 1993, where he presented *Towards a Nonequilibrium Theory of Stock Market Behavior*.

Lester's intuition was simple and quite insightful. When an option expires, say at the end of one year, we stop calculating the diffusion. What happens if we don't stop and the diffusion keeps diffusing? The diffusion exhibits some queer characteristics. First, and most importantly, it exhibits a relaxation process. This is an essential ingredient of a nonequilibrium or complex system.

The simple way to relate to the concept of a relaxation process is to think about your heart, which runs through a cycle of charge, contract, expand, relax. The parallel is not exact, but the fact that Seigel found a relaxation process is very important. It means that diffusion is diffusing at uneven rates. Conversely, it is also assumed at some points to contract at uneven rates. A stronger statement is that, in terms of events, time appears to flow unevenly.

To cement the concept, the only time your heart is in equilibrium is when it stops beating. The fact that it is beating regularly means it is in a far-from-equilibrium state. Your heart goes chaotic when it fibrillates or beats irregularly and cannot recover to its normal far-from-equilibrium state. This is the reason why the paramedics bring in the defibrillator to override your heart's current fibrillating and shock it back into a normal regime.

Seigel found that the relaxation process was between seven and twenty-five years. Remember, Peters [1994] found four years. Maybe other periods exist as well. It is not unreasonable to speculate that this is so. Seigel's argument is already powerful and will be brought into contemporary interpretation if the links between power law distributions and the realization process can be established. Since the Hurst exponent detects statistical long-term memory and is a measurement of diffusion, this should be of some import to Seigel's expression of his well-articulated idea.

Although von Neumann's statement that no general theory of nonequilibrium exists still stands, it is encouraging to know that progress is being made by at least one thoughtful gentleman in Washington, DC.

KAUFFMAN

If the term "the fastest draw in the West" was still in vogue, it would be used on Stu Kauffman—not only because he lives in Santa Fe, but because his mind works exceedingly fast. He recently started the consulting firm Bios Group in Santa Fe, after a stint at the Santa Fe Institute. Stu has had a peripatetic career, beginning with his training as a medical doctor, then theoretical biologist cum scientist, and finally consultant. I think his career reflects a journey, which he masterfully detailed in *At Home in the Universe: The Search for the Laws of Self Organization and Complexity*. Happily he as found his home in the universe in the sense that he has made substantial progress finding those laws; and because the prevailing view of the world is changing toward nonequilibrium, he is in a position to capitalize on his life's work.

Like it or not, it will be biology that replaces physics as the paradigm for financial economics, because only in biology with its concept of evolution do we find the most robust insight to deal with complexity. Computer scientists have made great inroads into complexity, as they have set up experiments to deal with such areas as artificial life. Financial economics will also achieve similar progress once it accepts non-equilibrium as a paradigm and computational rather than analytically based proofs. The intersection of the set of biologists who are competent in financial economics and vice versa is very finite at this point.

Several themes run through Stu's work: diversity of the economy like an ecology, the network, phase transitions, and power law distributions. Much of his interpretation of economics, though, has a grammar more suited to the background of a biologist than an economist. One of his most prescient examples, that of a network and phase transition, is produced here because it is the best I have seen.

Kauffman writes:

Scientists often gain insight into a more complex problem by thinking through a simpler toy problem. The toy problem I want to tell you about concerns "random graphs." A random graph is a set of dots, or nodes, connected at random by a set of lines, or edges. To make the toy problem concrete, we can call the dots "buttons" and the lines "threads." Imagine 10,000 buttons on a hardwood floor. Randomly choose two buttons and connect them with a thread. Now put this pair down and randomly choose two more buttons, pick them up, and connect them with a thread. As soon as you continue to do this, at first you will almost certainly pick up buttons that you have not picked up before. After a while, however, you are more likely to pick at random a pair of buttons and you find that you have already chosen one of the pair. So when you tie a thread between the two newly chosen buttons, you will find that three buttons are tied together. In short, as you continue to choose random pairs of buttons to connect with a thread, after a while the buttons start becoming interconnected into larger clusters. Every now and then, lift a button up and see how many other buttons you pick up. Some buttons may not be connected and others may be connected in pairs or triples or larger numbers.

The important features of random graphs show very regular statistical behavior as one tunes the ratio of threads to buttons. In particular, a phase transition occurs when the ratio of threads to buttons passes 0.5. At that point a "giant cluster" suddenly forms. When there are very few threads compared to the number of buttons, most buttons will be unconnected, but as this ratio of threads to buttons increases, small clusters begin to form. As the ratio of threads to buttons continues to increase, the size of these clusters of buttons tends to grow. Obviously, as clusters get larger, they begin to become cross-connected. Now the magic! As the ratio of threads to buttons passes the 0.5 mark, all of a sudden most of the clusters have become cross-connected into one giant structure. In the small system with 20 buttons, you can see this giant cluster forming when the ratio of threads to buttons is half, 10 threads to 20 buttons. If we used 10,000 buttons, the giant component would arise when there were about 5,000 threads. When the giant component forms, most of the nodes are directly or indirectly connected. If you pick up one button, the chances are high that you will pull up something like 8,000 of the 10,000 buttons. As the ratio of threads to buttons continues to increase past the halfway mark, more and more of the remaining isolated buttons and small clusters become cross-connected into a giant component. So the giant component grows larger, but its rate of growth slows as the number of remaining isolated buttons and isolated components decreases.

The rather sudden change in the size of the largest connected cluster of buttons, as the ratio of threads to buttons passes 0.5, is a toy version of the phase transition that I believe led to the origin of life.

In explaining a network, if we substitute money managers for buttons and telephone lines for thread, we quickly gain insight into how financial markets mimic the dynamics of a network; irrespective of whether the network is seen in a computer or a biological context, the behavior is the same.

OLSEN & ASSOCIATES

Richard Olsen and his associates in Zurich specialize in selling high-frequency data to the foreign exchange departments of commercial banks. They publish many high-quality papers at the www.olsen.ch web site and hold a conference on high frequency every other year.

Whereas the Hurst exponent is a detector of long-term dependence, Olsen & Associates' approach is to look at intraday or high-frequency data. Although their thrust is slightly different, their worldview is highly nonlinear. Clive Davidson wrote *Views from the Frontier: Commentary on the New World of Forecasting and Risk Management* in May 1996. It is probably the best simple exposition I have seen on the fact of nonlinearity in the markets and it is available from Olsen's web site. It is divided into five parts:

1. *The Changing Markets* cites the explosion in turnover in foreign exchange and equities markets in the past five years and, interestingly enough, suggests a delinking from news to movements in the foreign exchange markets by Charles Goodhart, Norm Sosnow professor of banking and finance at the London School of Economics.

2. *The New Sciences* cites the shortcomings of the Capital Asset Pricing Model (CAPM) and Black-Scholes with extant assumptions and highlights Robert Engle's finding the "clustering of volatility." In sum, this clustering of volatility and fractal patterns are compelling that the market is nonlinear.

3. *The New Tools* are the physics- and computer science–related aspects previously discussed, such as fuzzy logic and genetic algorithms. These tools complement humans since they sift through lots of data, whereas the human insight is better at intuitive and analytical understanding of the world, to paraphrase Christine Downton, founding partner and chief investment officer of London-based Pareto Partners, which manages $100 million in bonds using these techniques.

4. *The Risk Challenge* recognizes that with the growth of the markets and their increased diversity come new sorts of risk not embodied in traditional concepts of risk management and thus measurement arise.

5. *What's Ahead?* is a rhetorical question which portends the future will and must use many of the unfamiliar concepts mentioned in this book, such as nonlinear techniques and 3D. The markets and the technology employed therein will be very unfamiliar to today's observer a few years hence.

PETERS

As the first practitioner to publish, Edgar Peters's work is seminal.

It was the first version in 1992 of *Chaos and Order in the Capital Markets* that led me down this nonlinear path of life. I discovered that what Peters described was the very essence of the problem I had wrestled with in Tokyo for several years. The term "chaos" was alien, as I had forgotten that I had read James Gleick's book several years earlier. Much of Ed's initial appeal was that he was a fellow practitioner and thus his view was tempered by reality and clear writing. Since then Ed has written *Fractal Market Analysis* and updated the previous work to *Chaos and Order in the Capital Markets, 2nd Edition*. Both works are the modern classics that form the bridge from traditional thinking to nonlinear thinking for the practitioner.

In addition to being our tutor, Ed posits the Fractal Market Hypothesis (FMH) as a modification of the CAPM. The FMH holds that markets are fractal in their structure and thus in a far-from-equilibrium state. The far-from-equilibrium state is a sign of a healthy market since conversely an equilibrium state is by definition dormant or dead. A healthy market is characterized by at least two major points: First, investors have different time horizons over which they choose to invest. The market needs both day traders and pension funds. If the investment horizon of all investors, like the physicists say, "collapses like a wave function" to the near term, markets crash or exhibit chaos. In other words, the market exceeds the normal bounds of complexity and proceeds over the "edge of chaos" to the real thing, albeit temporarily. The second point, is investors willingness to trade or commit capital, for which volume is an *ex post* proxy. That is, practically speaking, we cannot measure investors' willingness to commit capital going forward; we can only see the result of that willingness in hindsight as it becomes recorded as volume.

DAY

Long an unsung hero in the nonlinear wars, Richard Day has pressed on at the University of Southern California, where he warmly received me and shared his thoughts with me. Unfortunately, many without the requisite background in mathematics will find Dick much more accessible than his work.

The first part of his trilogy, *Complex Dynamics in Economics: An Introduction to Dynamical Systems and Market Mechanisms*, is the most erudite work linking conventional economic thinking and nonlinear reality. It is formal, rigorous, and thorough. It also performs a valuable service, since one must realize that there is no perfect viewpoint in presenting the phenomenon of nonlinearity in financial economics. Practitioners are easily dismissed as nonrigorous and academics are too easily dismissed as irrelevant. We lean more toward the practitioner in this effort and thus, by definition of viewpoint, must sacrifice some technical accuracy for accessibility. Dick systematically makes many of the points covered here but at a level more suitable for the graduate student or the serious practitioner. His trilogy will become the standard texts when universities offer courses in nonlinear financial economics.

ORMEROD

Prior to going off on his own, Paul Ormerod was the head of economic assessment for the *Economist*—the only newspaper I read cover-to-cover. I do not always agree with it, but that is okay because it compels me to *think* why I may disagree. Ormerod's editorial pithiness shows in *The Death of Economics*. Ormerod does one of the best jobs of presenting nonlinearity to the conventional reader of macroeconomics because his terminology and examples are familiar to them. The treatment is intelligent and accessible.

Consider his discussion on unemployment rates: Conventional economics pays little attention to this interplay between profits and unemployment as the key determinant of business cycles—an interplay that is observed in the empirical data. Instead, economists use two approaches to explain the existence of such cycles. First, there are models which are built on the premises of the micro theory of competitive equilibrium. In most such models, with individuals and companies maximizing their self-interest and forming rational, correct expectations about the future, cycles can only be generated by the application of a series of random shocks to the model, for otherwise all markets clear. We are asked to believe that the cycles that have been observed in every Western economy since the beginnings of industrialization are due to the convenient evidence of a series of random shocks, rather than to cycles being inherent in the behavior of such economics.

Second are "the macro-models" in which the business cycle is not based on micro-models but rather arises from a series of equations which were adapted in the post-war period from Keynes's *General Theory*, and through which Keynes's challenge to economic orthodoxy was sterilized into Keynesianism. In its simplest form, this model divides the total amount of spending in an economy in any given period into three categories: consumption by individuals; investment by companies; and 'the rest', comprising government spending, exports, imports and so on. Cycles can be generated in this model even if the rest is assumed to grow at a steady pace, with no cycles at all.

ROMER

Since his 1983 thesis at the University of Chicago, Paul Romer has been one of the leaders in explaining the economics of ideas—that is, the economics of ideas that are subject to increasing returns. Unlike conventional economic theory and the physical goods to which it applies, ideas are different. The physical form of ideas, which is typically bits of software code, are called nonrival goods. Use of a compact disk by me does not lessen the CD's value when you take a turn. This is in contrast to rival goods, like a fish, around which most our theory is built. If you eat the fish, I cannot. Endogenous growth is the technical term that describes the extra kick we derive from reusable ideas and technological advancement in general.

Two of Romer's sources of inspiration are biology and high technology. Perhaps the reader, unaccustomed to so much discussion of these seemingly alien topics in a financial economics treatise, may derive some consolation from a man of whom MIT economist and Nobel laureate Robert Solow said, in referring to a Nobel prize, "He must be on many people's short list." Romer's favorite brainteaser sounds somewhat like an example from Chapter 3. What is the scope for discovery of new ideas? With 10^{18} seconds elapsed since the big bang, and contemplate the combinatorial possibilities of carbon, oxygen, hydrogen, and some others to combine to form a molecular refinery. Nature has done it. It is called the milk cow. How many more are possible? Atoms rearranged to form useful information on a hard drive have the same sort of mind-bending numbers. Romer's ideas are sophisticated and cogently presented; in addition, they have the good fortune to be prescient.

"Old growth theory says we have to decide how to allocate scarce resources among alternative uses," says Romer. "New growth theory says, 'Bullshit!' We're in this world; it's got some objects, sure, but it's got these ideas, too, and all that stuff about scarcity and price systems is just wrong." Who says academics are indecisive?

ARTHUR

Brian Arthur is a beacon of increasing returns in the financial economics wilderness of decreasing returns and equilibrium. This soft-spoken but revolutionary figure divides his time between Stanford University and the Santa Fe Institute, pursuing a line of reasoning that is having far-reaching effects in financial economics. Increasing returns or positive feedback refers to the fact that creation of a standard, like VHS when it defeated Betamax in the VHS market, or Microsoft's operating system, can lead to greater profits and opportunities for those who adopt the standard. It is winner-take-most strategy. If you have the idea and the deep pockets for the heavy up-front R&D and you win in the market, you tend to win in the market for as long as your technology is defensible. For example, DVD, which replaced VHS, was brought by a consortium to save the cost of a marketing war. Increasing returns have parallels in nonlinear aspects of physics as well as in learning and adaptation in biology.

Increasing returns are symptomatic of the behavior of high-tech companies and the information age in general. In contrast, decreasing returns better characterize the industrial age. Coal will be mined and sold, for example, but it never will be able to capture the entire market, because the further coal has to be shipped the less the return is for mining coal at the old location. This will lead to an optimal solution in that there is one best coal supplier. The mathematical description of the dynamics of a coal supplier achieving dominance in an area is an approach to equilibrium, since an equilibrium eventually muffles out discordant probabilities and achieves a stasis or stabilizes at a unique solution in the form of one best coal buyer. This is an example of negative feedback that leads to equilibrium, and is how neoclassical economics sees the world.

Mathematically, Arthur's insight was to return to the Fokker-Planck equations, which are probabilistic assessments of field theory. These equations are quite good at handling phase transitions and thus arbitrary growth. It is interesting to note that Fokker-Planck equations are also the same ones from which diffusion is derived—the heart of Black-Scholes. Once a product like VHS versus Betamax begins to achieve dominance in a market, it "phase locks" for some period of time. The market also finds parallels.

KRUGMAN

Paul Krugman at MIT is a rising star in the field of economics, achieving many distinctions along the way, including the John Bates Clark Medal to the most promising economist under 40. In his brief book *The Self-Organizing*

Economy, he makes two major points: First is the principle of order from instability, and second is the principle of order from random growth.

Order from instability happens when a flat or disordered structure spontaneously emerges in some sort of order. The physical example is convection, where global temperature differences self-organize into weather patterns. His economic example is the way metropolitan growth seems to self-organize as the city grows. Cities tend to have central business districts, heavy manufacturing districts, suburbs, and so on.

Order from random growth says that many natural phenomena such as earthquakes and asteroids exhibit a power law distribution. His explanation is that the growth process of these phenomena is independent of scale, but the actual growth is random. Again he returns to cities and shows that the distribution of the size of cities (by population) follows a power law distribution. Krugman's conclusion does not admit a practical goal other than possible real estate speculation, but that is okay.

The noncontroversial reason that increasing returns were ignored by most of economics in the postwar era was technical rather than ideological. Increasing returns destroys simplicity and determinism. Complexity theory may be a more accurate descriptor of reality, but it is the antitheses of simplicity. Determinism, which we have covered previously, is a more fundamental concept to science in general and to financial economics. This philosophical link from Newton to the present day is the thread which binds how we look at problems and propose solutions. A simple visual analogy of a deterministic and thus linear process is a wine corkscrew. Archimedes' Screw will pull the cork out and push it in. It is a reversible process. It is deterministic. Move from the spatial to the temporal realm. Newton's laws of motion could both predict and retrodict. So can equilibrium in economics and randomness in finance. But this is not the way the real world works. In financial economics, time series are not always random, and equilibrium is rarely the rule. The technical ability to describe the postdeterministic world is our first step in understanding it.

CONSULTANCIES

Sadly for Wall Street, the vanguard of nonlinear thinking comes from the consultants. Win Farrell at Coopers & Lybrand just wrote a book. He uses aspects of complexity theory to predict "hits"—that is, rapid consumer acceptance of tangible goods like musical recordings, toys, and books. Anderson Consulting has sponsored *The New Economy*, which *Hotwired* has serially posted on www.hotwired.com/special/ene. It is a series of terms articulating the economic aspects of information technology. But Ernest &

Young is the real leader. Christopher Meyer, director of the Center for Innovation Studies in Boston, has done two important things. First, he has formed a joint venture with Stu Kauffman called Bios Group in Santa Fe. Second, in 1998 along with Stan Davis he published *BLUR: The Speed of Change in the Information Economy*. It is a cogent overview that will be considered accessible by the conventionally trained business mind. The points Davis and Meyer make are prescient—technology is challenging our beliefs and the agents of change do not occur sequentially or linearly. They occur together and very quickly, which quite literally makes their aggregate effect a blur.

Ernest & Young's investment in Bios Group is also prescient. Although Bios Group originally had the status of a skunk works, if complexity takes off—and it will—Ernst & Young will have a great asset. The talent pool of people who really understand this stuff is very limited. In fact, most that I could find are included in this text.

To use nonlinear pricing you need three things: (1) the conceptual understanding—this expertise is typically resident in academics; (2) the context of application, which is usually resident in practitioners; and (3) the ability to execute it, which is held by certain types of programmers and computer systems people. Of course, the pairings are not sacrosanct, and Meyer is building the bridge between points 1 and 2.

While I encourage the thrust of management consultancies in raising the general awareness of nonlinear thinking, I think the application to financial economics will bear the greatest fruit—not because the practitioners in financial economics are any less dogmatic than their counterparts, the management of large companies, since they are not. But as Davis and Meyer point out, sellers' costs will become transparent to buyers, and conventional markets will begin to resemble the nonequilibrium of financial markets. Technology will change the context and thus our viewpoint about the context and subject matter.

BLUR

In echoing Drucker's information revolution by concept in *Forbes ASAP*, Davis and Meyer do a good job of explaining that the next killer application is a qualitatively different sort from what we now have. The change will be caused by the thousands of smart and networked products. Toasters that don't burn toast are a trivial example. Lets extend this concept to examples where measurement can directly impact financial results—for example, "smart" highways and automobiles where insurance can be charged per unit of risk per unit of time consumed.

This simple fact will dramatically change the three-way battle between insurance, securities, and commercial banking. Measurement will determine who has the advantage, because the ability to redefine one's own market and the other fellow's follows.

This example extends our notion of markets. Markets produce prices—the most distilled form of information available. But with smart products, we can extend qualitative techniques to develop simulations of value against which we can judge price.

Put the other way around, if one has the capability to look at prices in a market using a more logical and relativistic approach, why would one continue using linear technology to develop notions of value? There is not only a logical incongruence but a practical one as well. Networks on which finance is processed and even generated in the information era exhibit the same biological-like dynamics. In other words, they behave like organisms. As commercial applications move on-line, the dynamics of financial economics will become even more biological as well. And, as we know, biology exhibits a nonlinear behavior capable of complexity. Thus not only are our tools nonlinear, the processes which give rise to prices are becomingly increasingly nonlinear as well.

CONCLUSION

From the morass of nonlinear phenomena this appendix witnesses the rise of the primordial mixture of axioms and theories to be. Not everything to be known is known. But that is true with equilibrium-based economics 50 years on, only we have gotten used to not knowing it. Knowing the axiom does not immediately mean you will know the theorems, but it is an excellent first step, and this work is rapidly developing.

There is much more, but this is a survey not an exposition. Readers are directed to the references for a fuller treatment and to see the works of Rick Riolo at the University of Michigan, Robert Lucas at the University of Chicago, Tim Bollerslev at the University of Virginia—Charlottesville, Frank Diebold at University of Pennsylvania, David A. Hsieh at Duke, Andrew Lo at MIT and Ian Stewart and G. Keith Still at Warwick University. It is safe to say, however, that the future of financial economics is nonequilibrium and, thus, nonlinear.

GLOSSARY

Antipersistence   The tendency of a time series to reverse itself from what it has been doing as measured by **H** where **H** < 0.5. Also called pink noise.

Asset allocation   Typically a large scale money management technique designed to time the transferal of funds within a portfolio between classes of assets, as between equity and fixed income, so as to optimize the risk-reward trade-off of the portfolio.

Attractor   A way to describe the long term behavior of a dissipative system in phase space. Equilibrium and steady states correspond to fixed-point attractors, periodic cycles to limit attractors, and chaos to strange attractors.

Black noise   Noise which evidences clustering like the stock market where ß = 3. It is a statistical time series with a power spectra (squared magnitude of the Fourier transform) of > 2 , which can be represented by homogenous power laws in the form f^{-B} as a function of frequency f, thus f^{-3}. Widespread in nature and governs natural and unnatural catastrophes such as floods, droughts, and bear markets.

Brownian motion   A purely random motion or noise that is considered to be independent. In terms of **H**, Bm exists when **H** = 0.5

Brown noise   a statistical time series with a power spectra (squared magnitude of the Fourier transform) of 2, which can be represented by homogenous power laws in the form f^{-B} as a function of frequency f, thus f^{-2}. It is white noise integrated over time such as the projection of Brownian motion on to one spatial dimension. Brown noise is white noise integrated over time that is frequency-dependent where ß = 2.

Capital asset pricing model (CAPM)   An equilibrium-based asset pricing model developed independently by William Sharpe, Linter, and Mossin. The simplest version states that all assets are priced according to their relationship to the market portfolio of all risky assets determined by the securities' beta.

Category theory   A general framework for mathematics, in which any mathematical structure is described in terms of a set of objects and the relationships between them.

Churn   The creative/destructive process required to create stability. Reminiscent of Schumpeter.

Complex adaptive system (cas)   No generally recognized definition exists; however, the Santa Fe Institute posits common denominator of these systems is the question of coherence under change. It signals their intuition that general principles govern *cas* behavior, and those principles point to antecedent behavior. For example, an economic or biological system, which evolves with time and is based on simple rules that generate a complex state, is considered to be a cas. More generally, any process which changes states in time and exhibits complexity or bounded variety.

Crisp set   In fuzzy logic and approximate reasoning, usually applied to classic (Boolean) sets where membership is either [1] (totally constrained in the set) or [0] (totally excluded from the set). As an example, the crisp representation for the concept TALL might have a discrimination function $T = \{xxxxx > 6\}$ meaning that anyone with a height greater than or equal to six feet is a member of the TALL set. Crisp sets, unlike fuzzy sets, have distinct and sharply defined membership edges. Note that the vertical line connecting nonmembership with membership, unlike a fuzzy set, is dimensionless. An intrinsic property of a crisp set is the well-defined behavior of its members. In particular, crisp sets obey the geometry of Boolean and Aristotelian sets. This means that the universe of discourse for a set and its complete is always disjoint and complete. Thus the relation $XXX = X$ (also known as the law of the excluded middle) is always obeyed.

Critical system   A macroscopic system in which structure can be observed at every length scale from the atomic scale to the size of the system itself. A related property is that every part is correlated with every other part, in the sense that if any one part is perturbed the influence can be felt in any other part of the system.

Dependence   The exhibition of a relationship in time, where the previous value affects the contingent and subsequent value, also called serial correlation. As in $H > 0.5$. Dependence refers to the fact that points in a time series are related in time meaning that yesterday has an impact upon today and today has an impact upon tomorrow. Including the concept of dependence in mathematical descriptions of financial economics is intuitively desirable, because investors are not indifferent after a crash; however, the concept is a significant leap in conceptual and practical sophistication.

Determinism   A theory that certain results are fully ordained in advance. Given enough information both predictability and retrodicatability are possible given enough information. A deterministic chaos system is one that gives random-looking results, even though the results are generated from a system of equations.

Derivative   In finance, an instrument whose value is derived from an underlying instrument as a cquity option's value is derived from that of the equity or underlying instrument. Derivatives can either be listed or traded on an organized exchange like the Chicago Board Options Exchange (CBOE) or unlisted and traded directly between parties.

Drawdown   The value by which an original investment decreases. Used as a proxy for risk in lieu of volatility (in mathematics standard deviation) because in the presence of $H > 0.5$, the second moment of the distribution cannot assumed to be finite or in other words to exist.

Ergodicity   A property of a system that provides a means to study the statistical behavior of dynamical systems as the system evolves according to probability theory. It is indicative of irreversibility. The ergodic principle can help us with the long-term, nontransient behavior of systems.

Fat tails   The informal name given to distributions whose falling slopes approach but do not intersect the horizontal axis. Slopes touching the axis indicate a finite variance or second moment. Slopes which do not are infinite or undefined.

Fitness landscape   An abstract representation of the concept of the fitness of a gene, used in evolutionary theory. One imagines a abstract space where the different points correspond to different DNA sequences. The fitness landscape assigns to each point a number, which is analogous to the altitude of a landscape, which is the average number of progeny a creature with those genes would have.

Fractal   A property in geometry for which no generally accepted definition aside from Mandelbrot's (1986) exists, which is a fractal is a shape of parts similar to the whole in some way. Fractals have the generally accepted attributes of self-similarity or invariant scaling in time and noninteger dimensions.

Fractional Brownian motion   A noise characterized by an exponent other than $H = 0.5$ or randomness. It is also called a biased random process.

Fractional stable motion   *See* Stable fractional motion.

Fuzziness   The degree or quality of imprecision (or, perhaps, vagueness) intrinsic in a property, process, or concept. The measure of the fuzziness and its characteristic behavior within the domain of the process is the semantic attribute captured by a fuzzy set. Fuzziness is not ambiguity nor is it the condition of partial or total ignorance; rather, fuzziness deals with natural imprecision associated with everyday events. When we measure temperature against the idea of hot, or height against the idea of tall, of speed against the idea of fast, we are dealing with imprecise concepts. There is no sharp boundary at which a metal is precisely cold, then precisely cool, then precisely warm, and finally precisely hot. Each transition state occurs continuously and gradually, so that at some given point of measurement a metal rod may have some properties of warm as well as hot.

Fuzzy logic   A universal approximator that is a class of multivalent, generally continuous-valued logics based on the theory of fuzzy sets initially proposed by Lotfi Zadeh in 1965, but that has its roots in the multivalued logic of Lukasiewicz and Gödel. Fuzzy logic is concerned with set theoretic operations allowed on fuzzy sets, how these operations are performed and integrated, and the nature of fundamental fuzziness. Most fuzzy logics are based on the min-max or the bounded arithmetic sum rules for set implication.

Fuzzy numbers   Numbers that have fuzzy properties. Models deal with scalars by treating them as fuzzy regions through the use of hedges. A fuzzy number generally assumes the space of a Gaussian distribution with the most probable value for the space at the center of the distribution. Fuzzy numbers obey the rules for conventional arithmetic but also have some special properties (such as the ability to subsume each other or to obey the laws of fuzzy set geometry)

Fuzzy operators   The class of connecting operators, notably AND and OR, that combines antecedent fuzzy propositions to produce a composite truth value. The traditional Zadeh fuzzy operators use the min-max rules, but several other alternative operator classes exist, such as the classes described by Yager, Schweizer and Sklar, Dubois and Prade and Dombi. Fuzzy operators determine the nature of the implication and inference process and thus also establish the nature of fuzzy logic for that implimentation.

Fuzzy sets   Differs from conventional or crisp sets by allowing partial or gradual memberships. A fuzzy set has three principal properties: the range of values over which the set is mapped, called the domain and made up of monotonic real numbers in the range $[-oo, +oo]$; the degree of membership axis that measures the value's membership in the set; and the actual surface of the fuzzy set—the points that connect the degree of membership value is a consequence of its underlying domain. The fuzzy set's degree of membership value is a consequence of its intrinsic truth function. This function returns a value between [0] (not a member of the set) and [1] (a complete member of the set) depending on the evaluation of the fuzzy proposition *X is a member of a fuzzy set.* In many interpretations, fuzzy logic is concerned with the compatibility between a domain's value and the fuzzy concept. This can be expressed as *How compatible is X with fuzzy set A?*

Fuzzy Space   A region in the model that has intrinsic fuzzy properties. A fuzzy surface differs from a fuzzy set in its dynamic nature and composite characteristics. In modeling terms, we view the fuzzy sets created by set theoretic operations, as well as the consequent sets produced by the approximate reasoning mechanism, as fuzzy spaces. This distinction remains one of the semantics, enabling the model builder to draw a distinction between the sets that are created as permanent parts of the system and those that have a lifetime associated with the active model.

Gauge principle   The basic principle behind the standard model, which expresses the idea that all physical properties of elementary particles are defined in terms of interactions between them. A modern expression of Leibniz's *principle of the identity of the indiscernible.*

Gaussian distribution   A member of the stable family of distributions which has a finite mean and variance.

Gilder's Law   From Gilder, the notion that the available bandwith in telecommunications will triple every 12 months.

Hamiltonian   The energy of a dynamical system expressed in terms of its coordinates and momenta.

Heat death of the universe   The name given by 19th-century science to the belief that the whole universe is tending to equilibrium, after which all life, change, and structure would disappear.

Higgs boson   A kind of particle, so far not observed, whose existence is required by the standard model of elementary particle physics. Its existence is associated with the mechanism of spontaneous symmetry breaking.

Hilbert space   The space of functions for which the integral of the square of the functions is well defined and finite. This is the functions space that is used as the setting for the first orthodox quantum mechanics.

Hurst exponent   A nonparametric statistic developed by Harold Edwin Hurst (1900–1978) to measure the rescaled range (R/S). That is, the range of the data over a time interval (after subtracting any linear trend) divided by the sample standard deviation. H measures the persistence or long-range dependency of a point in time upon a previous point. If $H > 0.5$ or persistent, then randomness or Brownian motion does not exist. A nonparametric statistic, which can indicate statistical long-term memory called persistence.

Infinite variance   Fat tails are indicative of an infinite second moment of a distribution. Standard liner tools such as volatility and covariance depend on a finite second moment to be meaningful.

Intractable   A condition where the amount of computation required to solve a problem increases so quickly that the problem becomes impractical with current technology.

Irreversibility Paradox   The paradox arising from the fact that macroscopic systems are irreversible and microscopic systems are reversible.

Jelly beans   Increasingly inexpensive chips or microcontrollers, which are becoming ubiquitous due to their utility and cheapness.

KAM Theory   Describes the dynamical behavior of classes of nonintegrable systems. As the energy of a system is increased, chaotic behavior becomes more prevalent.

Law of the Excluded Middle   In classical set theory an element has two states respective to its membership in a set: true [1], complete membership, or false [0], complete nonmembership. This means that the intersection of set A with its complement $-A$ is the null or empty set, expressed symbolically as A, A, +X indicating that an element cannot be, at the same time, a member of a set and its complement (which by definition, says that $-A$ contains all the elements not in A). This is also the law of noncontradiction. Since fuzzy sets have partial membership characteristics we might expect that they behave differently in the presence of their complement.

Matching principle   From May, the notion that a system or system's output must be characterized by the technique that most robustly renders the properties of the system or its output.

Metric of space-time   A mathematical description of geometry of space and time, that gives the size and distance and time intervals and determines which framers of reference are inertial.

Moore's Law   From Moore, the observation that semiconductor chips double in density and thus processing capacity roughly every 18 months. Amended by Moore in 1997 to reflect an enhancement in performance.

Moore's Second Law   From Moore, the observation that fabs or semiconductor fabrication plants double in cost every generation.

Multifractal   Related to the study of a distribution of a physical or other quantities on a geometric support. Literally a fractal of a fractal.

Nash equilibrium   In economics, states in which no one can improve their situation by choosing a different strategy. No more optimal trade-off is possible.

Negentropy   The countervailing force to entropy which provides organization and whose source is disputed. JC Maxell called them "Conscious sorting demons." In FE the provider is thought to be its participants because FE as an open dissipative system produces entropy but does not typically exist at the chaotic limit but at some far-from equilibrium state.

Neoclassical economics   A theory of economics which assumes a Nash equilibrium and is therefore linear.

Neoteny   In nonlinear pricing, the selective retention of juvenile characteristics to foster creativity and adaptivity.

Newtonian   Any theory based on the basic principles of space, time, and motion used by Newton, which encompasses all physical theories developed in the 18th and 19th centuries. A deterministic description of the world given by Newton which holds that reality is predicable or deterministic.

Noah effect   The exhibition of infinite variance. Coined by Mandelbrot after Noah's biblical Flood because the Flood represents a wide swing from the norm.

Noise   A stationary process formed by stationary increments. In general, when referring to a time series the term is synonymous with motion. In mathematics, a time series or series of data points plotted in time also referred to as a motion, as in Brownian motion. *Note: In information theory, the definition of noise is more precise, where the signal-to-noise ratio refers to the relationship of information to garbage within the transmission itself.*

Nonequilibrium thermodynamics   The study of nonequilibrium systems, among them, self-organized systems.

Nonlinear   A disproportional relationship between input and output.

Nonlinear dissipative systems   An open system that can exhibit chaos and self-organization.

Nonlinear equation or process   A process in which the response or output is not directly proportional to the input. Its significance is that all linear equations can be solved, whereas most nonlinear equations are understood only through approximation. Any feedback mechanism, or process of self-organization is nonlinear.

Nonlinear pricing   Any technological trading aid that acknowledges the nonlinearities exhibited by markets to more accurately characterize the patterns of traded assets.

Normal distribution   *See* Gaussian distribution.

Occam's razor   A theory that the model with least number of assumptions and least number of components that adequately explains it and that is the simplest explanation of a phenomenon is usually the most desirable. Named after the English philosopher William of Ockham (1285?–1349?).

1 / f noise   *See* Pink noise.

Pink Noise   a statistical time series with a power spectra (squared magnitude of the Fourier transform) of 1, which can be represented by homogenous power laws in the form f^{-B} as a function of frequency f, thus f^{-1}. Pink noise is widespread in nature and is also called $1/f$ or flicker noise.

Planck length   The basic unit of mass in a quantum theory of gravity, equal to approximately 10^{-33} centimeters.

Poincaré's resonances   Coupling degrees of freedom that lead to divergent expressions due to small denominators if there is resonance between them. The resonances may prohibit the solution of the equations of motion.

Principle of sufficient reason   Leibniz's principle according to which any question that can be asked about why the world is one way rather than another must have a rational answer. Used to eliminate theories, such as Newton's absolute space and time, that allow one to ask questions that don't have such answers.

Principle of the identity of the indiscernible   A corollary of the principle of sufficient reason, according to which there can be no two things in the world that are distinct, but which share all their properties.

Quantum chromodynamics   Part of the standard model that explains how the quarks make up protons, neutrons, and other strongly interacting particles.

Quantum gravity   The hoped-for theory that would unify in one framework both quantum and gravitational physics.

Quantum mechanics   At present the basic theory of matter and motion, developed during the 1920s.

Randomness   *See* Brownian motion.

Red Queen Effect   From Alice in Wonderland, the biological phenomena illustrating competing rates of co-evolution where one party of co-evolvers must change or adapt at an increased rate (twice as fast) to maintain the original state (to stay in place) between the co-evolvers.

α-Stable family of distributions   A family of distributions of which the Gaussian distribution is a special case, with a finite mean and variance. The Cauchy, also a member, has infinite mean and variance and the stable distribution has a finite mean and infinite variance.

α-Stable distribution   A distribution within the stable family that has finite mean and infinite variance.

Stable fractional noise   If $\{X(t), t \in \mathbb{R}\}$ is a process for dealing with stationary Increments, from a stationary sequence. The sequence $\{Y_j\}$ is called a *noise*. "Fractional noises" are obtained by taking the increments of H-sssi (i.e., self-similar with index **H** and with stationary increments) processes. For example, the fractional Gaussian noise defined as: Fix $0 < H \le 1$ and $\sigma^2_0 = EX^2$ (1). The following statements are equivalent:

(i) $\{X(t), t \in T\}$ is Gaussian and H-sssi.

(ii) $\{X(t), t \in T\}$ is fractional Brownian motion with self-similarity index H.

(iii) $\{X(t), t \in T\}$ is Gaussian, has mean zero (if $H < 1$) and autocovariance function

$$R_H(t_1 1, t_2) := \text{Cov}(X(t_1), X(1t_2)) = \frac{1}{2}\{|t_1|^{2H} + |t_2|^{2H} + |t_1 - t_2|^{2H}\}\text{Var } X(1).$$

is the increment of the H-sssi Gaussian process, there are many different H-sssi α – stable processes with a given $0 < a < 2$, and each of these processes gives rise to a different fractional a – stable noise.

Strange attractors   The bounded states of a system graphed in multidimensional phasespace.

String theory   A unified theory of the interactions of elementary particles, that successfully includes gravity and Yang-Mills fields. Under intensive development since the early 1980s, it is based on the postulate that the fundamental entities in the world have a one-dimensional rather than a pointlike character.

Swarm Theory   A biological interpretation of phenomena like telephone and computer networks, financial markets, and economies in the information age proposed by Kelly, which share certain advantageous traits like adaptability, evolvability, resilience, boundlessness, and novelty and disadvantageous traits in that they cannot, be optimized, controlled, predicted, understood or hurried.

Timescape   A concept borrowed from Gregory Benson's book of the same name that is a temporal analogy of a physical landscape.

Time series   A series of recorded values, such as closing prices, linked in time. *See also* noise.

White noise   A statistical time series with a power spectra (squared magnitude of the Fourier transform) of 0, which can be represented by homogenous power laws in the form f^{-B} as a function of frequency f, thus f^{-0}. It is the audio equivalent of Brownian motion; sounds that are unrelated and sound like a hiss. The video equivalent of white noise is "snow" in television reception. White noise has a flat power spectrum where $\beta = 0$.

Yang-Mills theory   The basic theoretical structure underlying the standard model, based on the gauge principle, developed in the 1950s.

BIBLIOGRAPHY

Abbott, EA 1889 *Flatland: A Romance of Many Dimensions,* London:

Adami, C 1997 *Introduction to Artificial Life,* New York: Springer-Verlag.

Adler, R, R Feldman & M Taqqu (eds.) 1998 *A Practical Guide to Heavy Tails,* Boston: Birkhäuser.

Akgiray, V & CG Lemoureaux 1989 Estimation of Stable Law Parameters, *J Bus & Eco Stat* **7**: 85.

―――― 1988 The Stable-Law Model of Stock Returns, *J Bus & Eco Stat* **6**: 51

Altrock, C von 1995 *Fuzzy and NeuroFuzzy Applications Explained,* Englewood Cliffs, NJ: Prentice Hall.

Anderson, PW, KJ Arrow, & D Pines (eds.) 1988 *The Economy as an Evolving Complex System,* Santa Fe Institute Studies in the Science of Complexity vol. 5, Redwood City, CA: Addison-Wesley.

Anis, AA & EH Lloyd 1976 The Expected Value of the Adjusted Rescaled Hurst Range of Independent Normal Summands, *Biometrika* **63**.

Aptronix, Inc. 1993 Fuzzy Logic: From Concept to Implementation.

Aristotle, 375?B.C. *Politics Book I.*

Arnold, BC 1983 *Pareto Distributions,* Fairland, MD: International Cooperative.

Arthur, WB 1996 Increasing Returns and the Two Worlds of Business, *Harvard Business Rev* Jul–Aug.

―――― 1995 Complexity in Economic and Financial Markets, *J Complexity* **1**, April.

―――― 1994 *Increasing Returns and Path Dependence in the Economy,* Ann Arbor, MI: U Michigan Press.

―――― 1993 Pandora's Marketplace Supp to *New Scientist*: 6–8.

―――― 1992 On Learning and Adaptation in the Economy Stanford U. working paper Apr 25.

―――― 1988 Competing Technologies, Increasing Returns, and Lock-in by Historical Events, Stanford U. working paper.

―――― Inductive Reasoning and Bounded Rationality (The El Farol Problem) *Santa Fe Institute,* Complexity in Economic Theory.

Arthur, WB, JH Holland, B LeBaron, R Palmer & P Taylor 1996 Asset Pricing Under Endogenous Expectations in an Artificial Stock Market, *Santa Fe Institute,* Working Paper 96–12–093 Dec 12.

Axelrod, RM & WD Hamilton 1997 *The Complexity of Cooperation: Agent-Based*

Models of Competition and Collaboration, (Princeton Studies in Complexity), Princeton: Princeton U Press.

――――― 1985 *The Evolution of Cooperation*, New York: Basic Books.

Bachelier, L 1900 *Theory of Speculation*, Paris: Gautheir-Villars. Translated by AJ Boness and reprinted in Cootner, *loc. cit.*

Baille, RT 1996 Long Memory Processes and Fractional Integration in Econometrics, *J Economics* **73**: 5–59.

Bak, P 1997 *How Nature Works: The Science of Self-Organized Criticality*, New York: Springer-Verlag.

Bak, P & K Chen 1991 Self-Organized Criticality, *Sci Amer* Jan: 46.

Bak, P, C Tang & K Weisenfeld 1988 Self-Organized Criticality, *Phys Rev A* **38**.

Barbour, JB 1989 *Absolute or Relative Motion: A Study from a Machian Point View of the Discovery and the Structure of Dynamical Theories: The Discovery of Dynamics,* Cambridge: Cambridge.

Barclay, A 1509 *The Ship of Fools*, Translation from the original 1494 Alsatian German by Sebastian Brant an exposition of abuses within the church and precursor of the Protestant Reformation.

Bateson, G 1972 *Steps to an Ecology of Mind*, New York: Ballantine.

Bauer, R 1994 *Genetic Algorithms and Investment Strategies*, New York: Wiley.

Baum, JAC & J Singh 1994 *Evolutionary Dynamics of Organizations*, New York: Oxford.

Bernstein, P 1996 *Against the Gods: The Remarkable Story of Risk*, New York: Wiley.

――――― 1992 *Capital Ideas: The Improbable Origins of Modern Wall Street*, New York: Free Press.

Bezdeck, JC 1993 A Review of Probabilistic, Fuzzy, and Neural Models for Pattern Recognition, *J Intelligent and Fuzzy Systems* **1**: 1–25.

――――― 1981 *Pattern Recognition wit Fuzzy Objective Function Algorithms*, New York Plenum.

Bezdek, J & S Pal (eds.) 1992 *Fuzzy Models for Pattern Recognition*, New York: IEEE Press.

Bergstrom, H 1952 On Some Expansions of Stable Distributions, *Arkiv for Matematik* **2**.

Bidfarkota, PV & JH McCullogh 1997 Testing for Persistence in Stock Returns with GARCH-Stable Shocks, working paper, Ohio State U.

Black, F 1989 How We Came Up with the Option Formula, *J Portfolio Mgmt*, Winter: 4–8.

――――― 1972 Capital Market Equilibrium with Restricted Borrowing, *J Business* **45**.

Black, F, MC Jensen & M Scholes 1972 The Capital Asset Pricing Model: Some Empirical Tests in MC Jensen 1972 *Studies in the Theory of Capital Markets,* New York: Praeger.

Black, F & M Scholes 1973 The Pricing of Option and Corporate Liabilities, *J Political Eco*, May/June.

Blattberg, R & T Sargent 1971 Regression with Non-Gaussian Stable Distributions, *Econometrica* **39**: 501-10.

Blattberg, R & N Gonedes 1974 A Comparison of Student and Stable Distributions as Statistical Models of Stock Prices *J Bus* **47**: 244-80.

Bochsler, D 1991 The Investment Applications of Fuzzy Logic, Togai InfraLogic Inc.

Bohm, D & FD Peat 1987 *Science, Order and Creativity*, New York: Bantam Books.

Bohr, N 1958 *Atomic Physics and Human Knowledge*, New York: Wiley.

Boskin, MJ 1996 Prisoners of Faulty Statistics, *Wall Street J*, Dec 5.

Bowler, PJ 1989 *Evolution: The History of an Idea*, Berkeley, CA: UC Press.

Brian, D 1996 *Einstein: A Life*, New York: Wiley.

Brock, WA, DA Hsieh & B LeBaron 1992 *Nonlinear Dynamics, Chaos and Instability*, Cambridge, MA: MIT Press.

Brock, WA 1988 Applications of Nonlinear Science Statistical Inference Theory to Finance and Economics, Working Paper, March.

Brockman, J 1995 *The Third Culture*, New York: Simon & Schuster.

Broomhead, DS, JP Huke & MR Muldoon 1992 Linear Filters and Non-linear Systems, *J Royal Stat Soc* **54**.

Callan, E & D Shapero 1974 A Theory of Social Imitation, *Physics Today* **27**.

Çambel, AB 1993 *Applied Chaos Theory: A Paradigm for Complexity*, San Diego; Academic Press.

Campbell, D 1974 *Evolutionary Epistemology* in *The Philosophy of Karl Popper*, PA Schiff (ed.), Lasalle, IL: Open Court.

Campbell, JY, AW Lo & AC MacKinlay 1997 *The Econometrics of Financial Markets*, Princeton, NJ: Princeton U Press.

Carroll, L 1869 *Through the Looking Glass,* London.

────── 1864 *Alice's Adventures in Wonderland,* London:

Carse, JF 1986 *Finite and Infinite Games*, New York: Ballantine Books.

Casdagli, M 1991 Chaos and Deterministic versus Stochastic Non-linear Modelling, *J Royal Stat Soc* **54**.

Casdagli, M, DD Jardins, S Eubank, JD Farmer, J Gibson, N Hunter & J Theiler 1991 Nonlinear Modeling of Chaotic Time Series: Theory and Applications LANL working paper.

Casdagli, M & S Eubank (eds.) 1992 *Nonlinear Modeling and Forecasting*, Redwood City, CA: Addison-Wesley.

Casti, JL 1997 *Five Golden Rules: Great Theories of 20th-Century Mathematics—and Why They Matter*, New York: Wiley.

────── 1997 *Reality Rules: Picturing the World in Mathematics: The Frontier*, New York: Wiley.

────── 1996 *Would-Be Worlds: How Simulation Is Changing the Frontiers of Science*, New York: Wiley.

────── 1994 *Complexification: Explaining a Paradoxical World Through the Science of Surprise*, New York: HarperCollins.

────── 1992 *Reality Rules: Picturing the World in Mathematics: The Fundamentals*, New York: Wiley.

Castrigiano, DPL & SA Hayes 1993 *Catastrophe Theory*, Reading, MA: Addison-Wesley.

Caudill, M 1993 Neural Network Primer 3rd Edition Revised, *AI Expert*, San Francisco: Miller-Freeman.

Caudill, M & C Butler 1990 *Naturally Intelligent Systems*, Cambridge, MA: MIT Press.

Chen, P 1988 Empirical and Theoretical Evidence of Economic Chaos, *System Dynamics Rev* **4**.

Chen, P 1993a Power Spectra and Correlation Resonances, IC2 Working Paper.

Chen, P 1993b Instability, Complexity, and Time Scale in Business Cycles, IC2 Working Paper.

Cheung, Y-W 1993 Long Memory in Foreign Exchange Rates, *J Bus & Eco Stat* **11**.

Chiu, S 1994 Fuzzy Model Identification Based on Cluster Estimation, *J Intelligent & Fuzzy Systems* **2**: Sep.

Clark, P 1973 A Subordinated Stochastic Process Model with Finite Variance for Speculative Prices, *Econometrica* **41**: 135.

Cootner, P (ed.) 1964 *The Random Character of Stock Market Prices*, Cambridge, MA: MIT Press.

Copeland, TE & JF Weston 1988 *Financial Theory and Corporate Policy 3rd Edition*, Reading, MA: Addison-Wesley.

Copernicus, 1520 *Revolutions of the Spheres*.

Cottle, S, RF Murray & FE Block 1988 *Graham & Dodd's Security Analysis 5th Edition*, New York: McGraw-Hill.

Coveny, P & R Highfield 1990 *The Arrow of Time*, New York: Ballentine.

Cowan, GA, D Pines & D Meltzer 1994 *Complexity: Metaphors, Models and Reality*, Reading, MA: Addison-Wesley.

Cox, ED 1995 *Fuzzy Logic for Business and Industry*, Rockland, MA: Charles River Media.

——— 1994 *Fuzzy Systems Handbook: A Practitioners Guide to Building, Using and Maintaining Fuzzy Systems*, Cambridge, MA: AP Professional.

Cox, JC & S Ross 1976 The Valuation of Options for Alternative Stochastic Processes, *J Fin Eco* **3**.

Cox, JC & M Rubinstein 1985 *Options Markets*, Englewood Cliffs, NJ: Prentice-Hall.

Crosby, AW 1997 *The Measure of Reality: Quantification and Western Society, 1250–1600*, Cambridge: Cambridge U.

Cummins, JD & RA Derrig 1991 Fuzzy Financial Pricing of Property-Liability Insurance, working paper U Pennsylvania. Nov 22.

Cutland, NJ, PE Kopp & W Willinger 1993 Stock Price Returns and the Joseph Effect: Fractional Version of the Black-Scholes Model, U Hull *Mathematics Research Reports* **VI**, #12.

Dacorogna, MM, UA Müller, RJ Nagler, RR Olsen & OV Pictet 1993 A Geographical Model for the Daily and Weekly Seasonal Volatility in the FX Market, *J Int'l Money and Finance* **12**: 413–438.

Darwin, C 1986 *The Origin of the Species by Means of Natural Selection of the Preservation of Favored Races in the Struggle for Life*, London: Penguin Classics.

—— 1868 *The Variation of Animals and Plants under Domestication*, New York: Organe Judd.

Davidson, C 1996 *Views from the Frontier: Commentary on the New World of Forecasting and Risk Management*, Zürich: Olsen & Associates.

Davies, L (ed.) 1991 *Handbook of Genetic Algorithms*, New York: Van Nostrand Reinhold.

Davies, P 1995 *About Time*, New York: Simon & Schuster.

—— 1993 *The Mind of God: The Scientific Basis for a Rational World*, New York: Touchstone.

—— 1989 *The Cosmic Blueprint*, New York: Touchstone.

—— 1984 *God and the New Physics*, New York: Simon & Schuster.

Davies, P & D Harte 1987 Test for the Hurst Effect, *Biometrika* **74**.

Davis, P & J Gribben 1992 *The Matter Myth*, New York: Touchstone.

Davis, S & C Meyer 1998 *BLUR: The Speed of Change in the Information Economy*, Reading, MA: Addison-Wesley.

Dawkins, R 1995 *River Out of Eden*, London: Weidenfeld & Nicolson.

—— 1987 *The Blind Watchmaker: Why the Evidence of Evolution Reveals a Universe without Design*, New York: Norton.

—— 1982 *The Extended Phenotype*, New York: Freeman.

—— 1976 / 1989 *The Selfish Gene, New Edition*, New York: Oxford.

Day, R 1983 The Emergence of Chaos from Classical Economic Growth, *Quarterly J Eco* **98**.

Day, RH 1997 Complex Dynamics, Market Mediation and Stock Price Behavior, *N Amer Actuarial J* **1**: 6–24.

—— 1997 Economics, the State, and the State of Economics, Presentation Stirling U, Scotland.

—— 1996 Toward a Dynamical Economic Science, unpublished working paper.

—— 1994 *Complex Economic Dynamics*, Cambridge, MA: MIT Press.

—— 1982 Irregular Growth Cycles, *Amer. Eco Rev* **72**: 406–410.

Day, RH & P Chen 1993 *Nonlinear Dynamics & Evolutionary Economics*, New York: Oxford.

Day, RH & W Haung 1990 Bulls, Bears and Market Sheep, *J Eco Behavior and Organization* **14**: 299–329.

DeBoeck, GJ (ed.) 1994 *Trading on the Edge: Neural, Genetic and Fuzzy Systems for Chaotic Financial Markets*, New York: Wiley.

De Grooijer, JG 1989 Testing non-linearities in World Stock Market Prices, *Economics Letters* **31**.

Dembo, RS & A Freeman 1998 *Seeing Tomorrow: Rewriting the Rules of Risk*, New York: Wiley.

Denecker, M & D DeSchreye 1997 SLDNFA: an abductive procedure for abductive logic programs, *J Logic Programming* **34**: 111–167.

Dennett, DC 1995 *Darwin's Dangerous Ideas: Evolution and the Meanings of Life*, New York: Simon & Schuster.

—— 1991 *Conscience Explained*, Boston: Little, Brown.

DeRoo JR 1980 *2001 Kanji: Structure Analysis Association Method*, Tokyo: Bonjinsha.

Deutsch, D 1997 *The Fabric of Reality: The Science of Parallel Universes and Its Implications*, New York: Penguin.

Devaney, RL 1989 *An Introduction to Chaotic Dynamical Systems*, Menlo Park: Addison-Wesley.

Devlin, K 1994 *Mathematics: The Science of Patterns,* New York: Scientific American.

Dixit, AK & RS Pindyck 1994 *Investment under Uncertainty*, Princeton: Princeton U Press.

Dothan, MU 1990 *Prices in Financial Markets*, New York: Oxford.

Driebe, DJ 1998 *Fully Chaotic Maps and Broken Time Symmetry*, Boston: Kluwer.

Drucker, P 1998 The Next Information Revolution, *Forbes ASAP*, 28 Aug.

Dubois, D & H Prade 1980 *Fuzzy Sets and Systems: Theory and Applications*, New York: Academic Press.

DuMochel, WH 1983 Estimating the Stable Index α in Order to Measure Tail Thickness: A Critique, *Annal Stat* **11**.

———— 1975 Stable Distributions in Statistical Inference 2, Information from Stably Distributed Samples, *J Amer Stat Assoc* **70**.

———— 1973 Stable Distributions in Statistical Inference 1, Symmetric Stable Distributions Compared to Other Symmetric Long tailed Distributions, *J Amer Stat Assoc* **70**.

Dyson, E 1997 *Release 2.0: A Design for Living in the Digital Age*, New York: Broadway.

Eco, U 1994 *The Island of the Day Before*, New York: Harcourt Brace.

The Economist 1998 The Real Risk in Banking, Feb 28: 21–22.

The Economist 1998 Model Behavior, Feb 28: 80.

The Economist 1997 A Little Learning, Dec 13: 72.

The Economist 1997 Sexual Evolution, Dear Dr. Tatiana: Why is Sex So Much Like War? Dec 20: 118.

The Economist 1996 Chaos under a Cloud, January 13: 69–70.

The Economist 1996 Real Virtuality, May 4: 86.

The Economist 1993 Survey of the Frontiers of Finance.

Eigen, M & R Winkler 1993 *Laws of the Game: How the Principals of Nature Govern Chance*, Princeton: Princeton U Press.

Einstein, A 1961 *Relativity: The Special and the General Theory*, New York: Bonanza.

———— 1908 Über die von den molekularkinetishen Theorie der Wärme geforderte Bewegung von in ruhenden flüssigkeiten suspendierten Teilchen, *Ann. der Physik* **322**.

The Emerging Digital Economy, www.ecommerce.gov.

Euclid, 330?B.C. *Elements*.

Fama, EF 1991 Efficient Capital Markets—II, *J Fin* **46**: 1575.

———— 1970 Efficient Capital Markets, *J Bus* **25**: 383.

———— 1965 The Behavior of Stock Market Prices, *J Bus* **38**: 34–105.

———— 1963a Mandelbrot and the Stable Paretian Hypothesis, *J Business* **36**: 420–429.

———— 1963b *The Distribution of Daily Differences of Stock Prices: A Test of Mandelbrot's Stable Paretian Hypothesis*, Doctoral dissertation, U Chicago.

Fan, LT, D Neogi & M Yashima, 1991 *Elementary Introduction to Spatial and Temporal Fractals*, Berlin: Springer-Verlag.

Farmer, JD & JJ Sidorowich 1988 Exploiting Chaos to Predict the Future, LANL working paper.

Feder, J 1988 *Fractals*, New York: Plenum.

Feigenbaum, M 1983 Universal Behavior in Nonlinear Systems, *Physica 7D*.

Feller, W 1951 The Asymptotic Distribution of the Range of Sums of Independent Variables, *Ann Math Stat* **22**.

Feynman, RP et al 1964 *Lectures on Physics*, Reading, MA: Addison-Wesley.

Flandrin, P 1989 On the Spectrum of Fractional Brownian Motion, *IEEE Trans Info Theory* **35**.

Foster, D 1985 *The Philosophical Scientists*, New York: Barnes & Noble.

Forrest, S 1993 Genetic Algorithms: Principles of Natural Selection Applied to Computation, *Sci.* **261**: 872.

Fortune, 1998 The Theory of Fads, Oct 14: 49.

Friedman, BM & DI Laibson 1989 Economic Implications of Extraordinary Movements in Stock Prices, Brookings Papers on Economic Activity 2.

Gardner, M 1978 White and Brown Music, Fractal Curves and $1/f$ Fluctuations, *Sci Amer* **238**.

Gell-Mann, M 1994 *The Quark and the Jaguar: Adventures in the Simple and the Complex*, New York: Freeman.

Gianturco, MC 1997 The Terminal Investor: Online Help for Timing Your Stocks, *Forbes* Feb 24.

———— 1996 *How to Buy Technology Stocks*, Boston: Little, Brown.

Gilder, G 1997 Fiber Keeps Its Promise, *Forbes ASAP* Apr 7: 91.

———— 1990 *Microcosm: The Quantum Revolution in Economics and Technology*, New York: Touchstone.

Gim, G & T Whalen 1994 Dimensions of Knowledge: Fact, Skill, Quality or Quantity, *Proceedings of the First Int'l Joint Conference of NAFIPS/IFIS/NASA* San Antonio, Dec 18–21:447.

Ginsberg, M 1993 *Essentials of Artificial Intelligence*, San Mateo, CA: Morgan Kaufmann.

Glass, L & M Mackey 1988 *From Clocks to Chaos*, Princeton: Princeton U Press.

Glazier, SC 1995 Patents for Program Trading Strategies, *AI in Finance* Summer: 37.

Gleick, J 1992 *Genius: The Life and Times of Richard Feynman*, New York: Pantheon.

———— 1987 *Chaos: The Making of a New Science*, New York: Viking.

Goldberg, DE 1994 Genetic and Evolutionary Algorithms Come of Age, *Comm ACM* **37**: 113.

———— 1989 *Genetic Algorithms in Search, Optimization and Machine Learning*, Reading, MA: Addison-Wesley.

Goodwin, B 1994 *How the Leopard Changes Its Spots*, London: Weidenfeld & Nicolson.

Graham, B & DL Dodd 1934 *Security Analysis*, New York: McGraw-Hill.

Grandmont, J & P Malgrange 1986 Nonlinear Economic Dynamics: Introduction, *J Eco Theory* **40**.

Grandmont, J 1985 On Endogenous Competitive Business Cycles, *Econometrica* **53**.

Granger, CWJ 1964 *Spectral Analysis of Economic Time Series*, Princeton, NJ: Princeton.

Granger, CWJ & D Orr 1972 "Infinite Variance" and Research Strategy in Time Series Analysis, *J Amer Stat Assoc* **67**.

Granger, CWJ & T Teräsvirta 1993 *Modeling Nonlinear Economic Relationships*, New York: Oxford.

Grant, J 1997 *Bernard M. Baruch: The Adventures of a Wall Street Legend (Trailblazers, Rediscovering the Pioneers of Business)*, New York: Wiley.

———— 1996 *The Trouble With Prosperity: The Loss of Fear, the Rise of Speculation, and the Risk to American Savings*, New York: Times Books.

———— 1993 *Minding Mr. Market: Ten Years on Wall Street with Grant's Interest Rate Observer*, New York: Farrar Straus & Giroux.

Grassberger, P & I Procaccia 1983 Characterization of Strange Attractors, *Phys Rev Ltrs* **48**.

Greene, MT & BD Fielitz 1979 The Effects of Long Term Dependence on Risk-Return Models of Common Stocks, *Operations Research*.

————1977 Long-Term Dependence in Common Stock Returns, *J Financial Eco* **4**.

Grefenstette, JJ 1987 Genetic Algorithms and Their Applications, *Proceedings of the Second International Conference on Genetic Algorithms*, Hillsdale, NJ: Lawrence Erlbaum Assoc.

Gribben, RJ 1984 *In Search of Schrödinger's Cat,* New York: Bantam.

Grove, AS 1996 *Only the Paranoid Survive: How to Exploit the Crisis Points That Challenge Every Company and Career*, New York: Currency / Doubleday.

Gould, SJ 1989 *Wonderful Life: The Burgess Shale and the Nature of History*, New York: Norton.

———— (ed.) 1993 *The Book of Life*, New York: Norton.

Hagstrom, RG 1994 *The Warren Buffett Way: Investment Strategies of the World's Greatest Investor*, New York: Wiley.

Haken, H 1975 Cooperative Phenomena in Systems Far from Thermal Equilibrium and in Non Physical Systems, *Rev Modern Phys* **47**.

Harvey, AC 1993 *Time Series Models 2nd Edition*, Cambridge, MA: MIT Press.

Hausman, J 1997 Cellular Telephones, New Products and the CPI, *NBER* working paper #5982, Mar.

Hawking, SW 1988 *A Brief History of Time: From the Big Bang to Black Holes*, New York: Bantam.

Hawking, SW & R Penrose 1996 *The Nature of Space and Time*, Princeton: Princeton.

Heisenberg, W 1989 *Physics and Philosophy*, London: Penguin.

Heitzman, D 1997 The Market's Price Patterns: An Orderly Chaos; *Bloomberg Magazine* **6**: 41.

Herbert, N 1985 *Quantum Reality: Beyond the New Physics,* New York: Doubleday.

Hershey, RD 1996 Concern is Voiced Over the Quality of Economic Data, *New York Times* 24 Nov.

Hicks, J 1979 *Causality in Economics*, New York: Basic Books.

Hodges, SD 1995 Arbitrage in a Fractal Brownian Motion Market, FORC Working paper Warwick U, Mar.

Hodgson, GM 1993 *Economics and Evolution: Bringing Life Back into Economics*, Cambridge: Polity Press.

——— 1991/2 *Thorstein Veblen and Joseph Schumpeter on Evolutionary Economics*, ZIF Research Group, Biological Foundations of Human Capital, Bielenfeld, Germany: U Bielenfeld.

——— 1991 Economic Evolution: Intervention Contra Pangloss, *J Eco Issues* **2**: 519–33.

Hofstadter, DR 1995 *Fluid Concepts and Creative Analogies*, New York: Basic Books.

——— 1979 *Gödel, Escher, Bach: An Eternal Golden Braid*, New York: Basic Books.

Holland, JH 1998 *Emergence: From Chaos to Order*, Reading, MA: Addison-Wesley.

——— 1995 *Hidden Order: How Adaptation Builds Complexity*, Reading, MA: Addison-Wesley.

——— 1992 Genetic Algorithms, *Sci. Amer.* Jul: 114.

——— 1975 *Adaptation in Natural and Artificial Systems*, Ann Arbor, MI: U Michigan Press.

Holland, JH, KJ Holyoak, RE Nesbitt & P Martin 1987 *Induction*, Cambridge, MA: MIT Press.

Hopf, E 1948 A Mathematical Example Displaying Features of Turbulence, *Commun Pure App Math* **1**.

Hosking, JRM 1981 Fractional Differencing, *Biometrika* **68**.

Hsieh, DA 1992 Implications of Nonlinear Dynamics for Financial Risk Management, Duke U, working paper.

——— 1991 Chaos and Nonlinear Dynamics: Application to Financial Markets, *J Fin* **46**: 1839.

——— 1989 Testing for Nonlinear Dependence in Daily Foreign Exchange Rates, *J Bus* **62**.

Hsu, K & A Hsu 1991 Self-Similarity of the $1/f$ Noise Called Music, *Proceedings National Academy Sciences* **88**.

——1990 Fractal Geometry of Music, *Proceedings National Academy Sciences* **87**.

Hull, J 1993 *Options, Futures and other Derivatives Securities 2nd Edition*, Englewood Cliffs, NJ: Prentice-Hall.

Hurst, HE 1951 The Long-Term Storage Capacity of Reservoirs, *Trans. Amer. Soc. Civil. Eng.* **116**.

Institutional Investor 1996 Fischer Black Defends His Famous Pricing Model, Jan: 12.

James, W 1956 "The Dilemma of Determinism," in the *Will to Believe*, New York: Dover.

Jang, J –SR 1993 ANFIC: Adaptive-Network-Based Fuzzy Inference Systems, *IEEE Transactions on Systems, Man and Cybernetics* **23**: 665–685.

———— 1993 Fuzzy Modeling Using Generalized Neural Networks and Kalman Filter Algorithm, *Proc of the Ninth Nat'l Conference on Artificial Intelligence*, Jul: 762–767.

Jang, J –SR & C-T Sun 1995 Neuro-fuzzy modeling and control, *Proc of the IEEE*, Mar.

Johnson, G 1995 *Fire in the Mind: Science, Faith and the Search for Order*, New York: Alfred A Knopf.

Josephson, JR & SG (eds.) 1996 *Abductive Inference: Computation, Philosophy, Technology*, New York: Cambridge.

Kahneman, D, P Slovic & A Tversky (eds.) 1982 *Judgement under Uncertainty: Heuristics and Biases*, New York: Cambridge.

Kahneman D & A Tversky 1982 Psychology of Preferences, *Sci Amer* **246**.

Kakas, AC, RA Kowalski & F Toni 1993 Abductive Logic Programming, *J Logic and Computation* **2**: 719–770.

Kaku, M 1997 *Visions: How Science Will Revolutionize the 21st Century*, New York: Anchor Books.

———— 1994 *Hyperspace*, New York: Oxford.

Kaplan, LM & C-CJ Kyo 1992 Fractal Estimation from Noisy Measurements via Discrete Fractional Gaussian Noise (DFGN) and the Haar Basis USC working paper.

Katz, M & C Shapiro 1994 Systems Competition and Network Effects, *J Econ Perspectives* **8**: 29–56.

Kauffman, SA 1995 *At Home in the Universe: The Search for the Laws of Self-Organization and Complexity*, New York: Oxford.

———— 1993 *The Origins of Order: Self-Organization and Selection in Evolution*, New York: Oxford.

Kelly, JL 1956 A New Interpretation of Information Rate, *Bell Sys Tech J* **35**: 917–926.

Kelly, K 1996 The Economics of Ideas, *Wired* **4.06**, June.

———— 1994 *Out of Control: The Rise of Neo-Biological Civilization*, Reading, MA: Addison-Wesley.

Kelsey, D 1988 The Economics of Chaos or the Chaos of Economics, *Oxford Eco Papers* **40**.

Kida, S 1991 Log-Stable Distribution Intermittency or Turbulence, *J Physical Soc of Japan* **60**.

Kindleberger, CP 1978 *Manias, Panics and Crashes: A History of Financial Crises*, New York: Basic.

Klein, AD 1998 *Wallstreet.com: Fat Cat Investing at the Click of a Mouse: How Andy Klein and the Internet Can Give Everyone a Seat on the Exchange*, New York: Henry Holt.

Klein, JL 1997 *Statistical Visions in Time: A History of Time Series Analysis, 1662–1938*, Cambridge: Cambridge.

Kline, M 1972 *Mathematical Thought from Ancient to Modern Times*, Vols. 1–3, New York: Oxford.

Klir, GJ & TA Folger 1988 *Fuzzy Sets, Uncertainty and Information*, Englewood Cliffs, NJ: Prentice Hall.

Knight, K 1993 Estimation in Dynamic Liner Regression Models with Infinite Variance Errors, *Econometric Theory* 9: 570.

Kocak, H 1986 *Differential and Difference Equations Through Computer Experiments*, New York: Springer-Verlag.

Kolmogorov, AN 1941 Local Structure of Turbulence in an Incompressible Liquid for very Large Reynolds Numbers, Comptes Rendus (Doklady) *Academie des Sciences de l'URSS (N.S.)* 30. Reprinted in Friedlander, SK & L Topper 1961 *Turbulence: Classic Papers on Statistical Theory*, New York: Interscience.

Korsan, RJ 1993 Fractals and Time Series Analysis, *Mathematica J* 33.

Koselka, R 1997 Playing the Game of Life, *Forbes* 7 April: 100–108.

Kosko, B 1993 *Fuzzy Thinking: The New Science of Fuzzy Logic*, New York: Hyperion.

Kosko, B & S Isaka 1993 Fuzzy Logic *Sci Amer* July: 76–81.

Koza, JR 1994 *Genetic Programming II: Automatic Discovery of Reusable Systems (Complex Adaptive Systems)*, Cambridge, MA: MIT.

——— 1992 *Genetic Programming: On the Programming of Computers by Means of Natural Selection (Complex Adaptive Systems)*, Cambridge, MA: MIT.

Krugman, P 1996 *The Self-Organizing Economy*, Malden, MA: Blackwell.

Kuhn, TS 1970 *The Structure of Scientific Revolutions, 2nd Edition*, Chicago: U. Chicago Press.

Kuwahara, H & TA Marsh 1991 The Pricing of Japanese Equity Warrants, 21 Mar, working paper.

Langton, CG 1989 *Artificial Life*, Santa Fe Institute Studies in the Science of Complexity vol. 6, Redwood City, CA: Addison-Wesley.

Larrain, M 1991 Empirical Tests of Chaotic Behavior in a Nonlinear Interest Rate Model, *Financial Anal J* 47.

Lauterbach, B & P Schultz 1990 Pricing Warrants: An Empirical Study of the Black-Scholes Model and Its Alternatives, *J Finance* 45, Sep: 1181–1209.

LeBaron, B 1990 Some Relations Between Volatility and Serial Correlations in Stock Market Returns, Working Paper, February.

Leake, DB 1994 Using Goals and Experience to Guide Abduction, Technical Report #359, Indiana U.

——— 1993 Focusing Construction and Selection of Abductive Hypothesis, *Proceedings of the Eleventh Int'l Joint Conference on Artificial Intelligence*: 24–29.

——— 1991 Goal-Based Explanation Evaluation, *Cognitive Science* 15: 509–545.

Le Bon, G 1894 *The Crowd*, London: Ernest Benn.

Lederman, L 1993 *The God Particle: If the Universe Is the Answer What Is the Question?*, New York: Houghton Mifflin.

Lefèvre, E 1994 (1923) *Reminiscences of a Stock Operator*, New York: Wiley.

Leibnez, 1973 *The Monadology and the Leibnez Clark-Leibnez Correspondence* in

Leibnez, Philosophical Writings, London: Dent. GHR Parkinson (ed.), M Morris & CHR Parkinson (trans.)

L'Engle, M 1962 *A Wrinkle in Time* New York: Doubleday.

Leonard, A 1997 *Bots: The Origin of a New Species*, San Francisco: HardWired.

Levenson, T 1995 *Measure for Measure: A Musical History of Science*, New York: Touchstone.

Lévy, P 1937 *Théorie de l'addition des variables aléatoires*, Paris: Gauthier-Villars.

Lewin, R 1992 *Complexity: Life at the Edge of Chaos*, New York: Macmillan.

Lewontin, RC 1996 *Human Diversity*, New York: Freeman.

—— 1991 *Biology as Ideology*, New York: Harper.

—— 1974 *The Genetic Basis of Evolutionary Change*, New York: Columbia U Press.

Li, T-Y & J Yorke 1975 Period Three Implies Chaos, *Amer Math Monthly* **82**.

Li, WK & AI McLeod 1986 Fractional Time Series Modeling, *Biometrika* **73**.

Litner, J 1986 The Valuation of Risk Assets and the Selection of Risk Investments in Stock Portfolios and Capital Budgets, *Rev Eco Stat* **47**.

Lo, AW 1989 Long Term Memory in Stock Market Prices, *NBER* Working Paper 2984 Washington, DC: National Bureau Economic Research.

Lo, AW & AC Mackinlay 1988 Stock Market Prices Do Not Follow Random Walks: Evidence from a Simple Specification Test, *Rev Financial Studies* **1**.

Lorenz, E 1963 Deterministic Nonperiodic Flow, *J Atmospheric Sciences* **20**.

Lorenz, H 1989 *Nonlinear Dynamical Economics and Chaotic Motion*, Berlin: Springer-Verlag.

—— 1987 International Trade and the Possible Occurrence of Chaos, *Economics Letters* **23**.

Mackay, C 1841 *Extraordinary Popular Delusions and the Madness of Crowds*, London: Richard Bently.

MacRae, D 1997 Removing the Randomness of Risk Management, *Financial Trader* **4**: 32–34.

Maddala, GS & CR Rao (eds.) 1996 *Statistical Methods in Finance*, New York: Elsevier.

Malkiel, BG 1973 *A Random Walk Down Wall Street College Edition Revised*, New York: WW Norton.

Mamdani, EH 1977 Applications of Fuzzy Logic to Approximate Reasoning Using Linguistic Systems, *IEEE Transactions on Computers* **26**; 1182–1191.

Mandelbrot, BB 1997a *Fractals and Scaling in Finance*, New York: Springer.

—— 1997b *Fractals & Self-Affinity: R/S, 1/ f, Global Dependence, Relief & Rivers*, New York: Springer.

—— 1997c *Multifractals & 1 / f Noise*, New York: Springer.

—— 1972 *The Fractal Geometry of Nature*, New York: Freeman.

—— 1963a The Variation of Certain Speculative Prices, *J Business* **36**: 394–419.

—— 1963b New Methods in statistical Economics, *J Political Eco* **71**: 421–440.

Mandelbrot, B & JW van Ness 1968 Fractional Brownian Motions, Fractional Noises and Applications, *SIAM Review* **10**.

Margulis, L 1981 *Symbiosis in Cell Evolution*, San Francisco: Freeman.

Margulis, L & D Sagan 1986 *Microcosmos*, New York: Simon & Schuster.

Marimon, R, E McGratten & TJ Sargent 1990 Money as a Medium of Exchange in an Economy with Artificially Intelligent Agents, *J Eco Dynamics and Control* **14**: 329–373.

Markowitz, HM 1952 Portfolio Selection, *J Finance* **7**.

Markowitz, HM 1959 *Portfolio Selection: Efficient Diversification of Investments*, New York: Wiley.

Marshall, A 1848 *Principles of Economics 8th Edition*, London: Macmillan.

May, CT 1998 Complex Indicators in *Computerized Trading,* L Lederman & J Klein (eds.), New York: Random House.

———— 1995a An Introduction to Non-Traditional Pricing, *J Hedge Fund Research* **2**.

———— 1995b An Introduction to Nonlinear Pricing, *Asia Risk Manager* **1**.

———— 1995c Nonlinear Pricing: A New Investment Category, *Private Asset Management,* Sep 25: 8.

May, RM 1976 Simple Mathematical Models with Very Complicated Dynamics, *Nature* **261**.

———— 1973 *Stability and Complexity in Model Ecosystems*, Princeton: Princeton U Press.

McCulloch, JH 1998 *Linear Regressions with Stable Distributions* in *A Practical Guide to Heavy Tails* Adler, R, R Feldman & M Taqqu (eds.), Boston: Birkhäuser.

———— 1997 Measuring Tail Thickness to Estimate the Stable Index α: A Critique, *J Bus & Eco Stat* **15**: 74–81.

———— 1996 Estimation of the Bivariate Stable Spectral Representation by the Projection Method with Application to Joint Stock Returns working paper, Ohio State U, Mar 6.

———— 1996 *Financial Applications of Stable Distributions* in *Statistical Methods in Finance*, Maddala, GS & CR Rao (eds.) New York: Elsevier.

———— 1991 On the Parameterization of the Afocal Stable Distributions, *Bull London Math Soc* **28**: 651–655.

———— 1985 The Value of European Options with Log-Stable Uncertainty, Working Paper.

McCulloch, JH & DB Panton 1997 Precise Tabulation of the Maximally-Skewed Stable Distributions and Densities, *Computational State & Data Analysis* **23**: 307–320.

McCulluch, CW & W Pitts 1943 A Logical Calculus of the Ideas Imminent in Nervous Activity, *Bull. Math. Biophysics* **5**: 115.

Merton, R 1990 *Continuous-Time Finance*, Cambridge, MA: Basil Blackwell.

Michalewicz, Z 1992 *Genetic Algorithms + Data Structures = Evolutionary Programs*, New York: Springer-Verlag.

Miller, MH 1997 *Merton Miller on Derivatives*, New York: Wiley.

Mirowski, P 1996 Mandelbrot's Economics after a Quarter Century, *Fractals* **3**: 581–596.

———— 1994 A Visible Hand in the Marketplace of Ideas: Precision Measurement as Arbitrage, *Science in Context* **7**: 563–589.

———— 1990 From Mandelbrot to Chaos in Economic Theory, *Southern Eco J* **57**: 289–307.

Mitchell, M 1996 *An Introduction to Genetic Algorithms*, Cambridge, MA: MIT Press.

———— 1993 *Analogy Making as Perception*, Cambridge, MA: MIT Press.

Modigliani, F & L Modigliani 1997 Risk-Adjusted Performance, *J Portfolio Mgmt* **23**.

Moore, GA 1995 *Inside the Tornado: Marketing Strategies From Silicon Valley's Cutting Edge*, New York: HarperCollins.

Müller, UA, MM Dacorogna, RD Davé, OV Pictet, RB Olsen, & JR Ward 1993 Fractals and Intrinsic Time—A Challenge to Econometricians, XXXIXth Int. Conference Applied Econometrics Assoc., *Real Time Econometrics—Submonthly Time Series* 14–15 Oct.

Murray, JD 1989 *Mathematical Biology*, Berlin: Springer-Verlag.

Needham, J 1978 *The Shorter Science and Civilization in China: An Abridgement of Joseph Needham's Original Text* v 1, prepared by CA Ronan, New York: Cambridge U Press.

Negroponte, N 1995 *Being Digital*, New York: Random House.

Nelson, RR 1995 Recent Evolutionary Theorizing About Economic Change, *J Eco Literature* **33**: 48–90.

Nelson, RR & SG Winter 1982 *An Evolutionary Theory of Economic Change*, Cambridge, MA: Harvard.

———— 1977 In Search of a Useful Theory of Innovation, *Research Policy* **1**: 36–76.

———— 1974 Neoclassical v. Evolutionary Theories of Economic Growth: Critique and Perspectives, *Econ J* **336**: 895–905.

Nest Generation Internet Initiative, www.ccic.gov.

Newton, I 1962 *Mathematical Principles of Natural Philosophy*, Berkeley: UC Press, Trans T Otte & F Cajors.

Nieuwland, FGMC 1993 *Speculative Market Dynamics*, U Limburg.

Nicolis, G 1995 *Introduction to Nonlinear Science*, New York: Cambridge.

Nicolis, G & I Prigogine 1989 *Exploring Complexity*, San Francisco: Freeman.

Noever, D & S Baskaran 1994 Genetic Algorithms Trading on the S&P 500, *AI in Finance* **1**: 41.

Nychka, D, S Ellner, AR Gallant & D McCaffrey 1992 Finding Chaos in Noisy Systems, *J Royal Stat Soc* **54**.

O'Driscoll, GP, Jr & MJ Rizzo 1996 *The Economics of Time and Ignorance*, New York: Routledge.

Olsen *et al. see* www.olsen.com.

Ormerod, P 1994 *The Death of Economics*, St Martin's Press: New York.

Packard, N, J Crutchfield, D Farmer & R Shaw 1980 Geometry from a Time Series, *Phys Rev Lett* **45**.

Pagels, HR 1982 *The Cosmic Code: Quantum Physics as the Language of Nature*, New York: Simon & Schuster.

Panjer, HH & GE Willlmot 1992 *Insurance Risk Models*, Schaumberg, IL: Society of Actuaries.

Pareto, V 1897 *Cours d'Économie Politique*, Lausanne, Switzerland.

Peebler, RP 1996 www.lgc.com.

Peitgen, H-O 1988 *Beauty of Fractals: Images of Complex Dynamical Systems*, New York: Springer-Verlag.

Peitgen, H-O, H Jurgens, & D Saupe 1992 *Chaos and Fractals: New Frontiers of Science*, New York: Springer-Verlag.

Peng, Y & JA Roggia 1990 *Abductive Inference*, New York: Springer-Verlag.

Peters, EE 1996 *Chaos and Order in the Capital Markets 2nd Edition*, New York: Wiley.

————— 1994 *Fractal Market Analysis*, New York: Wiley.

————— 1993 The Fractal Rationale, *Graham & Company*, March.

————— 1992 R/S Analysis using Logrithmic Returns, A Technical Note, *Financial Analysts J*, November/December.

————— 1991 A Chaotic Attractor for the S&P 500, *Financial Analysts J*, March/April.

————— 1989 Fractal Structure in the Capital Markets, *Financial Analysts J*, July/August.

Peterson, I 1995 Petacrunchers: setting a course toward ultrafast computing, *Science News* **147**:232-5.

Phillips, GA 1988 *Japanese Warrants*, London: IFR Publishing.

Pierce, CS 1955 *The Architecture of Theories* in *The Monist*, reprinted in *Philosophical Writings of Pierce* J Buchler (ed.) New York: Dover.

Pinker, S 1997 *How the Mind Works*, New York: Norton.

Plain, SW 1995 Simulated Wetware, *Computer Shopper*, July: 584–586.

Poincaré, H 1958 *The Value of Science*, New York: Dover.

————— 1921 *Science and Hypothesis*, New York: Science Press.

Polkinghorne, J 1994 *The Faith of a Physicist: Reflections of a Bottom-Up Thinker*, Princeton, NJ: Princeton U Press.

Pople, H 1973 On the Mathematization of Abductive Logic, *Proc of the Int'l Joint Conference on AI*: 147–152.

Popper, KR 1986 1st Medawar Lecture, The Royal Society, unpublished.

————— 1982 *The Open Universe: An Argument for Indeterminism*, Cambridge: Routledge.

————— 1982 *Quantum Theory and the Schism in Physics,* Totowa, NJ: Rowman & Littlefield.

————— 1968 *Conjectures and Refutations: The Growth of Scientific Knowledge*, New York: Harper.

————— 1963 *The Open Society and Its Enemies*, Princeton, NJ: Princeton U Press.

————— 1959 *The Logic of Scientific Discovery*, London: Hutchinson.

Posner, RA 1992 *Sex and Reason*, Cambridge, MA: Harvard U Press.

————— 1986 *Economic Analysis of Law 3rd Edition*, Boston: Little, Brown.

Prigogine, I 1997 *The End of Certainty: Time, Chaos and the New Laws of Nature*, New York: Free Press.

————— 1980 *From Being to Becoming: Time and Complexity in the Physical Sciences*, New York: Freeman.

Prigogine, I & I Stengers 1984 *Order Out of Chaos*, New York: Bantam.

Quammen, D 1996 *The Song of the Dodo: Island Biogeography in an Age of Extinctions*, New York: Scribner.

Rachev, ST 1996 *Modeling Financial Assets with Alternative Stable Models*, New York: Wiley.

Rachev, ST & S Mittnik 1997 *Stable Modeling in Finance*, special issue of the journal *Mathematical and Computer Modeling*.

Radizicki, M 1990 Institutional Dynamics, Deterministic Chaos, and Self-Organizing Systems, *J Eco Issues* **24**.

Radman, C 1997 Where There's Heat, There's Light, *Institutional Investor*, Mar: 24.

Ramsey, JB 1996 If Nonlinear Models Cannot Forecast, What Use Are They?, *Studies in Nonlinear Dynamics and Econometrics* **1**.

———— 1996 On the Existence of Macro Variables and of Macro Relationships, *J Eco Behavior and Organization* **30**: 275–299.

Ramsey JB & Z Zhang 1996 The Analysis of Foreign Exchange Data Using Waveform Dictionaries, *J Empirical Finance* **4**: 341–372.

Ray, TS 1994 An Evolutionary Approach to Synthetic Biology: Zen and the Art of Creating Life, *Artificial Life* **1**: 179–209.

Ridley, M 1996 *The Origins of Virtue*, New York: Viking.

Riolo, RL 1992 Survival of the Fittest, *Sci Amer*: 114.

Roll, R 1969 Bias in Fitting the Sharpe Model to Time Series Data, *J Fin Quant Analysis* **4**.

Roll, R & SA Ross 1980 An Empirical Investigation of the Arbitrage Pricing Theory, *J Finance* **35**.

Romer, P 1996 In the Beginning Was the Transistor, *Forbes*, Dec 2.

———— 1995 Beyond the Knowledge Worker, *Worldlink* Jan/Feb.

———— 1994 Beyond Classical and Keynesian Macroeconomic Policy, *Policy Options* July-Aug.

———— 1993 Ideas and Things, *The Economist* Sep 11.

———— 1993 Implementing a National Technology Strategy with Self-Organizing Industry Investment Board, *Brookings Papers on Economic Activity*, Washington, DC: Brookings Institution.

———— 1991 *Increasing Returns and New Developments in the Theory of Growth* in *Equilibrium Theory and Applications*, Barnett, L et al (eds.), Cambridge: Cambridge: 83–110.

———— 1990 Endogenous Technological Change, *J Pol Eco* **98**, pt 2.

———— 1986 Increasing Returns and Long-Run Growth, *J Pol Eco* **94**, pt 2.

Rose, SP 1998 *Lifelines: Biology Beyond Determinism*, New York: Oxford.

Rose, SP, RC Lewontin & L Kamin 1984 *Not in Our Genes*, New York: Penguin.

Ross, SA 1976 The Arbitrage Theory of Capital Asset Pricing, *J Eco Theory* **13**.

Roth, HR 1993 *Leaps (Long-Term Equity Anticipation Securities: What They Are and How to Use Them for Profit and Protection)*, Homewood, IL: Irwin.

Royte, E 1996 Attack of the Microbiologists, *New York Times Sunday Magazine*, Jan 14: 21–23.

Rudd, A & HK Clasing 1982 *Modern Portfolio Theory*, Homewood, IL: Dow Jones-Irwin.

Ruelle, D 1991 *Chance and Chaos*, Princeton: Princeton U.

Ruhla, C 1992 *The Physics of Chance*, New York: Oxford.

Sagan, C 1997 (1986) *Contact*, New York: Pocket Books.

Samorodnitski, G & M Taqqu 1994 *Stable Non-Gaussian Random Process*, New York: Chapman & Hall.

Samuelson, PA 1967 Efficient Portfolio Selection for Pareto-Levy investments, *J Financial & Quantitative Analysis*, Jun.

Satchell, S & A Timmermann 1992 Daily Returns in European Stock Markets: Predictability, Non-linearity, and Transaction Costs, Working Paper, July.

Saviotti, P & JS Metcalfe 1991 *Evolutionary Theories of Economic and Technological Change*, Reading, MA: Harwood.

Scheinkman, JA & B LeBaron 1989 Nonlinear Dynamics and Stock Returns, *J Business* **62**.

Schinasi, GJ 1981 A Nonlinear Dynamic Model of Short Run Fluctuations, *Rev Eco Studies* **48**.

Schoemaker, PJ 1991 The Quest for Optimality: A Positive Heuristic of Science?, *Behavioral and Brain Sciences* **2**: 205–245.

Schroeder, M 1994 *Fractals, Chaos and Power Laws*, New York: Freeman.

Schumpeter, JA 1976 (1942) *Capitalism, Socialism and Democracy 5th Edition*, London: Allen & Unwin.

Schweizer, B & A Sklar 1963 Associative Functions and Abstract Semi-Groups, *Pub Math Debrecen* **10**: 69–81.

Schwert, GW 1990 Stock Market Volatility, *Financial Analysts J*, May/June.

Seigel, L 1993 Toward a Nonequilibrium Theory of Stock Market Behavior, *SIAM Annual Meeting*, July 12.

Senner, M 1989 *Japanese Euroderivatives*, London: Euromoney Publications.

Shaklee, GLS 1958 *Time in Economics*, Westport: Greenwood Press.

Shannon, CE & W Weaver 1963 *The Mathematical Theory of Communication*, Urbana, IL: U Illinois.

Sharpe, WF 1970 *Portfolio Theory and Capital Markets*, New York: McGraw-Hill.

———— 1964 Capital Asset Prices: A Theory of Market Equilibrium Under Conditions of Risk, *J Fin* **19**.

———— 1963 A Simplified Model of Portfolio Analysis, *Mgmt Science* **9**.

Shiller, RJ 1989 *Market Volatility*, Cambridge, MA: MIT Press.

Schrödinger, E 1945 *What Is Life?*, Cambridge: Cambridge U Press.

Simkowitz, MA & WL Beedles 1980 Asymmetric Stable Distributed Security Returns, *J Amer Stat Assoc* **75**.

Simon, HA 1955 On a Class of Skew Distribution Functions, *Biometrika*.

Slater, R 1996 *Soros*, New York: Irwin.

———— 1989 *Portraits in Silicon*, Cambridge: MIT Press.

Smith, A 1981 *Paper Money*, New York: Summit Books.

———— 1972 Supermoney, New York: Random House.

———— 1968 *The Money Game*, New York: Random House.

Smith, JM 1993 *Did Darwin Get It Right?: Essays on Games, Sex and Evolution*, New York: Penguin.

———— 1982 *Evolution and the Theory of Games*, Cambridge: Cambridge.

———— 1978 *The Evolution of Sex*, Cambridge: Cambridge U Press.

Smith, RL 1992 Estimating Dimension in Noisy Chaotic Time Series, *J Royal Stat Soc* **54**.

Smithson, M 1987 *Fuzzy Set Analysis for Behavioral and Social Sciences*, New York: Springer-Verlag.

Smolin, L 1997 *The Life of the Cosmos*, New York: Oxford.

Soros, G 1995 *Soros on Soros*, New York: Wiley.

———— 1994 *The Alchemy of Finance 2nd Edition*, New York: Wiley.

———— 1994 MIT Address, Address before the MIT Economics Department Washington, D.C. Apr 26.

Sterge, AJ 1989 On the Distribution of Financial Futures Price Changes, *Financial Analysts J*, May/June.

Stewart, I 1998 *Life's Other Secrets: The New Mathematics of the Living World*, New York: Wiley.

———— 1992 *The Problems of Mathematics*, New York: Oxford.

———— 1989 *Does God Play Dice?: The Mathematics of Chaos*, Cambridge, MA: Blackwell.

Stewart, I & M Golubitsky 1992 *Fearful Symmetry: Is God a Geometer?*, Cambridge, MA: Blackwell.

Sugeno, M 1985 *Industrial Applications of Fuzzy Control*, New York: Elsevier.

———— 1977 *Fuzzy Measures and Fuzzy Signals: A Survey* in *Fuzzy Automata and Decision Processes*, Gupta, MM, GN Sardis & BR Gaines (eds.) New York: North-Holland.

Sutherland, S 1994 *Irrationality: Why We Don't Think Straight!*, New Brunswick NJ: Rutgers U Press.

Swift, J 1725 *Gulliver's Travels*, London:

Talbot, M 1991 *The Holographic Universe*, New York: Harper Collins.

Terano, T, K Asai & M Sugeno 1991 *Fuzzy Systems Theory and Its Applications*, San Diego: Academic Press.

Thaler, RH 1993 (ed.) Advances in Behavioral Finance, New York: *Russell Sage Foundation.*

Tipler, FJ 1994 *The Physics of Immortality*, New York: Doubleday.

Tirthaji, BK 1989 *Vedic Mathematics*, Delhi: Motilal Banarsidass.

Tong, H 1990 *Non-Linear Time Series: A Dynamical System Approach*, Oxford: Oxford.

Train, J 1994 *The New Money Masters*, New York: HarperBusiness.

———— 1984 *The Money Masters*, New York: HarperBusiness.

———— 1974 *Dance of the Money Bees*, New York: HarperCollins.

Tufte, ER 1997 *Visual Explanations: Images and Quantities, Evidence and Narrative,* Cheshire, PA: Graphics Press.

———— 1992 *The Visual Display of Quantitative Information*, Cheshire, PA: Graphics Press.

—————— 1990 *Envisioning Information*, Cheshire, PA: Graphics Press.

Turing, AM 1937 On Computable Numbers, with an Application to the Entscheidungsproblem, *Proc London Math Soc*, series 2, **4**: 230–265.

Turner, AL & EJ Weigel 1990 An Analysis of Stock Market Volatility, Russell Research Commentaries, Tacoma, WA: *Frank Russell Company*.

Tversky, A 1990 The Psychology of Risk in *Quantifying the Market Risk Premium Phenomena for Investment Decision Making*, Charlottesville, VA: Institute of Chartered Financial Analysts.

Ulam, S 1974 *Sets, Numbers and Universes*, Cambridge, MA: MIT Press.

Ulrich, W (ed.) 1993 *Evolutionary Economics*, London: Edward Elgar.

Vaga, T 1991 The Coherent Market Hypothesis, *Financial Analysts J*, December/January.

Vaga, T 1994 *Profiting From Chaos*, New York: McGraw-Hill.

van Wolferen, K 1989 *The Enigma of Japanese Power*, New York: Knopf.

Volcker, P & T Gyohten 1992 *Changing Fortunes*, New York: Times Books.

Von Mises, L 1963 *Human Action 3rd Revised Edition*, New Haven: Yale U Press.

von Neumann, J 1966 *Theory of Self-Reproducing Automata* (ed.) AW Burks, Urbana: U Illinois Press.

von Neumann, J & O Morgenstern 1947 *Theory of Games and Economic Behavior*, Princeton: Princeton U Press.

Waldrop, MM 1992 *Complexity: The Emerging Science at the Edge of Order and Chaos*, New York: Simon & Schuster.

Wang, L -X 1994 *Adaptive Fuzzy Systems and Control Designs and Stability Analysis*, Englewood Cliffs, NJ: Prentice Hall.

Weigand, AS & NA Gershenfeld 1994 *Time Series Prediction: Forecasting and the Future and Understanding the Past*, Reading, MA: Addison-Wesley.

Widrow, D & D Stearns 1985 *Adaptive Signal Processing*, Englewood Cliffs, NJ: Prentice Hall.

Wilson, EO 1998 *Consilience: The Unity of Knowledge*, New York: Knopf.

Wolf, A JB Swift, HL Swinney & JA Vastano 1985 Determining Lyapunov Exponents From a Time Series, *Physica 16D* **3**, July.

Wolf, FA 1989 *Taking the Quantum Leap: The New Physics for Nonscientists*, New York: Harper & Row.

Wysocki, B 1997 For This Economist Long-Term Prosperity Hangs on Good Ideas, Jan 21.

—————— B 1996 Do Investors Confuse Price with Quality? *Wall Street J*, Dec 4.

Yager, R 1980 On a General Class of Fuzzy Connectives, *Fuzzy Sets and Systems* **4**: 235–242.

Yager, R & D Filev 1994 Generation of Fuzzy Rules by Mountain Clustering, *J Intelligent & Fuzzy Systems* **2**: 209–119.

Yogananda, P 1995 *God Talks to Arjuna: The Bhagavad Gita*, Los Angeles: Self-Realization Fellowship.

Yogananda, P 1974 *The Science of Religion*, Los Angeles: Self-Realization Fellowship.

—————— 1946 *Autobiography of a Yogi*, Los Angeles: Self-Realization Fellowship.

Yukteswar, S 1949 *The Holy Science*, Los Angeles: Self-Realization Fellowship.

Zadeh, L & J Kacprzk (ed.) 1992 *Fuzzy Logic for the Management of Uncertainty*, New York: Wiley.

Zadeh, LA 1989 Knowledge Representation in Fuzzy Logic, *IEEE Transactions on Knowledge and Data Engineering* **1**: 89–100.

———— 1988 Fuzzy Logic, *Computer* **1**: 83–93.

———— 1975 The Concept of a Linguistic Variable and Its Application to Approximate Reasoning Parts 1, 2, & 3, *Information Sciences* **8**.

———— 1973 Outline of a New Approach to the Analysis of Complex Systems and Decisions Processes, *IEEE Systems, Man and Cybernetics* **1**: 28–44.

———— 1965 Fuzzy Sets, *Information and Control* **8**: 338–353.

Zaslavsky, GM, R Sagdeev, D Usikov & A Chernikov 1991 *Weak Chaos and Quasi-Regular Patterns*, Cambridge: Cambridge U Press.

Zhang, Z, K-H Wen & P Chen 1992 Complex Spectral Analysis of Economic Dynamics and Correlation Resonances in Market Behavior, IC2 Working Paper.

Zimmerman, H-J 1991 *Fuzzy Set Theory*, Boston: Kluwer.

Zipf, GK 1949 *Human Behavior and the Principle of Least Effort*, Cambridge: Addison Wesley.

Zohar, D 1997 *Rewiring the Corporate Brain*, San Francisco: Berett-Koehler.

Zolotarev, VM 1966 On Representation of Stable Laws by Integrals in *Selected Transactions in Mathematical Statistics and Probability*, Vol. 6, Providence, RI: American Mathematical Society (Russian original 1964).

INDEX

Abbott, Edwin, 216
Abductive logic, 9, 191–192
Absolute, 30
Acceptance, 58–61
Adaptation, 9, 108, 139–140
Adaptive economy, 7
Adleman, Leonard, 176
Adler, Robert, 83
Age of the universe theory, 24
Aggregation, 310
α-stable distributions, 129
AltaVista, 139
American Stock Exchange, 136–137
Anderson, Philip, 11, 14, 42, 68, 171, 179
Anomalistic year, 37
Antipersistence, 157–158
Aperiodic cycles, 126
Appel, Kenneth, 60
Arbitrage, 9, 16, 85, 94, 96, 139, 227
Arbitrageur, 97, 202
Aristotle, 30, 32, 38, 234
Arthur, Brian, 69, 163, 247, 318–319
Assumptions, 47
Astronomy, 38–40
Asynchronous digital subscriber lines (ADSL), 138, 141
Atomism, 32, 67, 76
Autobahn, 137
Auto Regressive Integrated Moving Average (ARIMA), 75–76, 85
Avellenada, Marco, 91
Average, 7

Bachelier, Louis, 77, 80
Back testing, 155–156
Bak, Per, 53, 126, 201, 243
Barbour, Julian, 218
Barclay, A., 126
Bauer, Richard, 179

Bear market, 269
Behavior, three states of, 150
Behavioral finance, 66, 188
Belief system, 1
Bell-shaped curve distribution, 77
Bennett, Charles, 108
Bernstein, Peter, 30
Beta, 206
Bias, 178, 256
Bierstadt, Albert, 92
Biology, 41, 90, 108, 197–201
Biomathematics, 87
Bios Group, 320–321
Birkhchandani, Sushil, 190
Black, Fischer, 88
Black box, 60
Black noise, 126
Black-Scholes option pricing, 11–12, 41, 60, 64, 69, 82–83, 88, 98, 194, 220, 223–224
Blattberg, R., 82
Bloomberg, 58, 219
Blue chips, 164
Bohm, David, 47, 74
Bohr, Niels, 47–48, 163, 171, 304
Boltzman, Ludwig, 239
Bonds, convertible, 223
Bots, 139–140
Bounded rationality, 20
Brahe, Tycho, 39
Brockman, John, 68
Bronowski, Jacob, 233
Brownian motion, implications of, 9, 16, 64, 74, 77, 80, 95, 115, 121, 123, 128–130, 145–146, 157, 292–296
Bruno, Giordano, 38
Buffett, Warren, 2, 49, 97, 169, 230, 271
Bull market, 269
Burden of proof, 89
Business cycle, 96

Butterfly effect, 15
Buy/sell signals, 10

Calculus, 43–48
Calendar, 37–38, 291. *See also* Investment
    horizon; Time
CalPERS, 259
Camp, William J., 143
Campbell, John, 87
Cantor, Georg, 106
Capital, 255–259
Capital Asset Pricing Model (CAPM), 11,
    82–83, 192, 265, 316
Carpenter, Gail, 298
Causal relationships, 15, 191, 255–256
Central Limit Theorem, 77
Change, 248–249
Chaos
    butterfly effect, 15
    complexity and, 53–54
    defined, 52–53
Chen, P., 191
Chicago Board Options Exchange (CBOE),
    82, 137
Chicago Mercantile Exchange, 137
Citibank, 195
Clark, Peter, 81, 130
Clarke, Bruce, 189
Classical economic theory, 10–11, 64, 78
Classical physics, 16, 44
Clausius, Rudolf, 48, 233
Clinamen, 92
Closed-form solution, 59, 83
Coarse graining, 92
Coevolution, 103–104, 246
Cohen, Jack, 117
Collective consciousness (CC), 267–274
Completeness theorem, 106
Complexity theory, 9, 53–54, 72, 78, 91,
    179, 200, 246, 320
Compression, 218–219
Computation, 19, 56, 106–109
Computer chips, 140–145
Computer programming, 87
CONCEPTS, 2–3
Consumer price index (CPI), 191
Continuous change, 146
Conway, John, 264
Cooper, Ronald, 85
Cootner, Paul, 80
Copernicus, 38
Correlation, 6, 75
Cowes style econometrics, 85
Cox, E. D., 183

Credit Suisse, 135
Crosby, Alfred W., 279
Cryptography, 109
Currencies, floating, 4
Curve fitting, 161
Cyclic behavior, 147
Cyclical stocks, 96

Dacorogna, Michel, 253, 263
Darwin, Charles, 102
Darwinism, 197–198, 201
Davis, Dave, 179, 321
Dawkins, Richard, 54, 102, 104, 199–200
Day, Richard, 69, 191, 238, 317
De Broglie, Louis, 294–295
Deductive reasoning, 191
De la Maza, Michael, 182
Dembo, Ron, 239
De minimus risk, 222
Demiurge, 32, 35, 275
Democritus, 37–38, 92
Dependence, long-term, 85, 147
Derivatives, 223
Derivative sciences, 99–100
De Roo, Joseph, 283
Determinism, 39, 44, 67, 71, 232–233, 245
Deterministic worldview, 73
Deutsch, David, 19, 60, 86, 100–101,
    105–106, 109, 218, 234, 237–238
Deutsche Termin Boursis (DTB), 137, 267
Diffusion, 16
Digital age, 1
Dimensions, 216–217
Discounting, 3
Disequilibrium, 190, 243–244, 249–250
Dissipative system, 55
Distributions, 6–7, 127. *See also specific*
    types of distributions
Diversification, 76
Diversity, 311
Dixit, Avinash, 171, 239
Domain, time *vs.* frequency, 292
Drucker, Peter, 2–5, 309
Duality, 266
Dynamic disequilibrium, 249–250
Dynamic market, 227
Dynamics, generally, 76, 238
Dysan, Esther, 140

E-commerce, 136
Economic crisis, 8–9
Economics, 234–235. *See also specific types*
    of economic theories
Ecophysics, 20

Eddington, Sir Arthur, 48–49, 92, 233
Edge of chaos, 54
Efficient market, 80
Einstein, Albert, 12, 16, 24, 45, 48, 67, 77,
    98–99, 216, 233, 235, 275
Elliot wave, 159–160
Emergent phenomenon, 14, 16
Emergent property, 11
Emerging markets, 220
Energeticists, 76
Entropy, 48–49, 51, 55, 233, 242, 244,
    254
Epicurus, 92, 233
Epistemiology theory, 19
Equilibrium
    far-from-, 247, 252–254, 256–257, 262,
        269–270
    implications of, generally, 16, 55,
        247–248
    near-, 247–248, 253, 255
    physics, 64, 250–251
Equilibrium-based economics, 13, 41
Equity market, 190
Error types, 88–89
Euclid, 34, 37–38, 91, 237
Euclidean geometry, 35, 37, 74, 95, 121,
    125
Event-driven time, 93–94, 290–291
Everett, Hugh, 87, 162–163
Evolution, 9, 101–105, 108. See also
    Darwinism
Experimental sciences, 201–202

Fama, Eugene, 7, 80–81, 130, 133
Far-from-equilibrium, 247, 252–254,
    256–257, 262, 269–270
Farmer, Doyne, 194
Farrell, Win, 320
Fat tails, 132
Feder, Jan, 112
Federal Accounting Standards Board
    (FASB), 199, 249, 258
Feigenbaum, Mitchell, 49, 53
Feldman, Richard, 83
Feynman, Richard, 21, 28, 198, 241, 301
Fibonacci, 2
Field theory, 46, 248, 256, 267
Finance
    behavioral, 66, 188
    simple, 6–8
    three states of, 150
Financial economics
    biophysics and, 251–252
    conditions for emergence, 244

defined, 13, 100
disequilibrium, 243–244
equilibrium-based, 74
evolution model, 180
as field theory, 46
fractals, 112
historical perspective, 77–86
linearity in, 73
nonlinear technology, links to,
    188–191
science and, 63–65, 89–91
theory, generally, 13
time and, 219–221
virtual reality, 106–107
Flows, significance of, 15, 251, 311
4D graphics, 34–35, 47, 118, 144, 159, 209,
    217, 231, 291
Fourier transforms, 164, 292
Fractal(s)
    adaptive process, 138
    applications, 112
    bots, 139–140
    capital usage, 130–131
    concept, 112–116
    defined, 112–113, 213
    denominators, 121–124
    dimensions, 74
    distribution, 7, 165
    domains and spaces, 116–117
    geometry, 118
    Hurst exponent, 119–121
    implications of, generally, 69, 87
    information era, 136–138
    legal dimensions, 134
    loosely coupled sets, 144–145
    mathematics, 127–130
    microchips, 138–144
    noises, 125–127
    phase transitions, 117–119
    power laws, 125–127
    regulatory issues, 134–135
    risk measurement, 131–133
    self-similarity, 125
    timing, 135
Fractal Market Hypothesis (FMH), 316
Freeman, Andrew, 239
Free market, 19
Free trade, 103
Fundamental analysis, 185–186, 240, 261
Fuzzy logic
    approximating with, 184
    background, 183–184
    bias and, 190
    defined, 280

Fuzzy logic (*continued*)
  implications of, generally, 6, 9, 26, 72, 131, 247
  industrial applications, 184–187
  numerical models, 225

Gaia hypothesis, 101, 250
Galileo, 12
Gamow, George, 24, 297
Gauss, Carl, 218
Gaussian distribution, 6–7, 9, 71–72, 74–75, 77, 82, 129, 133–134, 292–296
Generally accepted accounting principles (GAAP), 2, 199, 249, 258, 283
Genetic algorithms
  applications, generally, 9, 26, 72, 161, 174, 185, 200, 291
  defined, 227–228
  fuzzy logic compared with, 186–187
Geometry, 34–37, 118, 291. *See also specific types of geometry*
Gerstner, Lou, 136
Gestalt, 12
Gilder, George, 141, 309
Gim, Gwangyong, 185
Gisin, Nicolas, 109
Gleick, James, 53, 82
Gödel, Kurt, 106
Goodman, George J. W., 4, 231
Goodwin, Brian, 197, 201
Gould, Stephen Jay, 198, 201, 239, 261
Granger, Clive, 82
Graphics, 280–282. *See also* 4D graphics; 3D graphics; 2D graphics
Gribben, John, 295
Grossberg, Stephen, 298
Gross national product (GNP), 92
Grove, Andy, 36–37, 284–285
Grover's algorithm, 109
Gutenberg-Richter Law, 125

Haken, Wolfgang, 60
Hard science, 201, 206
Hardware, 177–178
Harnett, William Michael, 92
Hassam, Childe, 92
Heisenberg, Werner, 10, 48–49, 183–184, 262
Herbert, Nick, 295
Hicks, John, 79
Hinduism, unity of science and religion, 22
Historical sciences, 201–202
Historical volatility, 223–224

History, of nonlinear pricing, 156–157
Hofstadter, Douglas, 297
Holism, 16, 40–43
Holland, John, 6, 69, 131, 174, 179, 181, 248–249, 287, 310
Howery, Philip, 85
Hsieh, David, 81
Hurst, H. E., 119
Hurst exponent
  antipersistence, 157–158
  applications, generally, 2, 10–11, 58, 71–72, 74, 95, 112, 147, 149–150, 237, 242, 257
  assumption, 152–153, 164–165
  day trading, 158
  example, 151–152
  frequency of sampling data, 158
  hyper-time, 162–164
  intellectual capital, 169–170
  lookback, determination of, 165–167
  modern finance, 171
  persistence, 157–158
  price, 167–169
  quality, 167–169
  radio analogy, 160–161
  randomness, 157–158
  risk, 170–171, 221–223
  technical analysis, compared with, 159–160
  turning a position, 158–159
  variables, 154–157
Hyper-time, 162–164

IBM, 224–225
ID representation, 217
If-then logic, 287
Implied volatility, 224
Indeterminism, 85, 234
Inductive reasoning, 58, 61–62
Inductivism, 59, 105
Inferential reasoning, 192–194
Information age, 1, 3
Information management, 5
Initial public offerings (IPOs), 59, 61–62, 136
Instrumentalists, 13
Integrated Services Digital Network, 137
Intel
  Janus, 143
  MMX technology, 217
  x86 processor, 141
Intellectual capital, 169–170, 199

Interdisciplinary approach, 63
Internal models, 312
Internet, 137–138, 141, 271
Intuition, 98, 102, 166, 207
Investment horizon, 23, 98, 158, 272
Ito, Kyoshi, 219

James, William, 235
Japanese reasoning, 275–280
Joseph effect, 126

Kaku, Michio, 74, 297
KAM theory, 241
Kanji, 282–283, 285–286
KAOS function, 56–58
KAOS screen, 11, 96, 207, 216, 235,
    295
Kauffman, Stu, 42, 127, 197, 201, 238,
    313–315, 320
Kelly, John, Jr., 131
Kelly, Kevin, 11, 140, 178–179, 248, 259,
    287, 304
Kepler, Johannes, 39
Keynes, John Maynard, 1–2, 28, 134,
    221
Keynesian economics, 79
Knight, Frank, 254
Knowledge (K), 105–106, 108,
    267–274
Knuth, Donald, 16
Koan, 285
Kosko, Bart, 183
Krugman, Paul, 70, 81, 96, 126, 247,
    319–320
Kuhn, Thomas, 24

Langton, Chris, 54, 201
Laplace, Pierre-Simon, 44
Laplacian determinism, 44, 233
Leibniz, Gottfried, 21, 38, 43–48, 171, 260,
    266
Leonard, Andrew, 139
LeRoy, Steven, 80
Levenson, Thomas, 33
Leveraged buyout (LBO), 59
Levy, Paul, 77, 80–83
Levy-Pareto distribution, 165
Lewontin, Richard, 197, 201
Life/evolution, 101–105, 108
Linear mathematicians, 84–85
Linear programming, 78
Liquidity, 242, 251
Lo, Andrew, 64, 87, 130
Locality, 199, 252

Logic, *see specific types of logic*
Lookback
    denominator, 156
    determination of, 165–167
    period, 154–155
Lorenz, Edward, 69
Low energy, 92

McCulloch, C. W., 186
McCune, William, 144
Mackinlay, Craig, 64, 87, 130
McLuhan, Marshall, 136
Mandelbrot, Benoît, 69, 71–72, 80–81, 83,
    97, 112–113, 120, 125–127, 130, 133,
    145, 266, 287
Mantissa, 39
Market dynamics, 3, 106
Markov dependence, 80
Marshall, Alfred, 197
Matching principle, 61, 230
Mathematicians, 84–85
Mathematics, 75, 122, 213–216
Maxwell, James Clerk, 76
May, Sir Robert, 53
May's Law, 273
Mean, generally
    defined, 7
    solar year, 93
    -variance portfolio, 69, 83
Meatspace, 116, 291
Meltzer, Allan, 280
Memory builders, 29–30
Merrill Lynch, 195
Merton, Robert, 71–72, 89,
    219
Meyer, Christopher, 320–321
Microsoft, ActiveX, 217
Miller, Merton, 69
Misleading information, 70–71
Mispricing, 124
Mitchell, Melanie, 179
Modeling, mathematical, 217
Modern Portfolio Theory (MPT), 11
Modern science, 12
Modigliani, Franco, 226
Moments, 7
Monte Carlo simulations, 47
Moore, Gordon, 18
Moore's Law, 17, 58, 140–141,
    238
Morgan, JP, 131–132, 135
Morris, Michael, 217
Motion, types of, 127
Muller, U. A., 81, 114, 240

Multifractal(s)
   applications, generally, 116, 135
   time, 223
Multifracticality, 246–247, 266
Music, 33–34, 291

NASDAQ (National Association of
   Securities Dealers Automated
   Quotations), 136–137, 267
Nash equilibrium, 64
Natural philosophy, 90
Natural selection, 200
Near-to-equilibrium, 247–248, 253, 255
Negatively skewed, 132
Negentropy, 242
Negroponte, Nicholas, 140
Neoclassical economic theory, 2, 16, 41, 67,
   76, 78, 85, 190
Neural nets, 164, 186
New reality, 100
Newton, Sir Isaac, 4, 38, 43–48, 67, 266
Newtonian physics, 20, 40, 91, 100,
   234–236, 283
Newtonian worldview, 73
New York Stock Exchange, 136, 269
Noah effect, 126
Noise, 127
Nonequilibrium, 55–56, 92, 242, 250,
   268–269
Noninteger dimension, of fractals, 113
Nonlinear, defined, 26
Nonlinear analysis, 284–286
Nonlinearity, generally
   history of, 31–32
   implications of, generally, 310–311
   simple, 38–40
   in 20th-century financial economics
      early 1900s, 77
      1930s, 78–79
      1940s, 79
      1960s, 80
      1970s, 80–82
      1980s, 82–83
      1990s, 83–86
Nonlinear mathematicians, 84–85
Nonlinear pricing theory, generally
   defined, 9
   duality, 266
   graphics, 280–282
   Japanese reasoning, 275–280
   K and CC, generally, 266–268
   kanji, 282–283
   May's Law, 273
   model, structure of, 264

nonlinear analysis, 284–286
   patterns, 283–284
   process, 272–273
   relationship, 268–270
   religion, 275–276
   resolution, 274–275
   risk, 271–272
   secret formula, 265
   tagging rules, 283
Nonlinear simulations, 2
Nonlinear technology
   abductive logic, 191–192
   analysis, local vs. nonlocal, 187–188
   bio-computing, 175–177
   creative applications, 182
   example of, 178
   financial applications, 179–180
   financial economics, links to, 188–191
   fuzzy logic, 182–187
   genetic algorithms, 174–175
   hardware, 177–178
   human factor, 195–196
   industrial applications, 178–179
   inferential reasoning, 192–194
   nonlinear shifts, 181
   secrecy and, 194–195
   slide rule analogy, 180–181
Nonrandomness, 178
Normal distribution, 77, 133

Observation, 72–73, 105
O'Driscoll, Gerald, 94, 190
Oil industry, 27
Olsen, Richard, 194, 315–316
Omega Point, 237
On-line trading, 136
Open Society, 232–234
OptiMark, 3, 136
Options, 223–225
Order, 70
Organic chemistry, 100
Ormerod, Paul, 70, 317
Orr, D., 82
Oscillators, 240
Out-of-equilibrium, 263–264
Over, Christopher, 177
Over-fitting, 175

Paley, William, 54
Paradigm
   nonlinear, 5
   shift, 11, 39, 73–74
Parallel theorem, 91–92, 237
Pareto, Vilfredo, 77, 80, 126–127, 165

Pareto distribution, 84, 127, 165
Pareto-Levy, 72, 127
Partial differential equations (PDEs), 83
Partial predictability, 150, 165, 178, 257
Patents, 195
Patterns, 283–284
Peak around the mean, 132
Peebler, Robert, 27
Pentium processors, 143
P/E ratio, 258, 286
Perfect predictability, 150
Permanency, 97
Persistence, 157–158, 248
Peters, Ed, 11, 32, 77, 83, 125, 129–130, 160, 188, 221, 231, 245, 272, 316
Peto, John Frederick, 92
Peynaud, Emile, 18
Phase shift, 159
Phase-space, 117–118
Philosophy, 232–234
Physics
    envy, 41
    expanded, 235–239
    Newtonian, *see* Newtonian physics
Pierce, Charles Sanders, 192
Pindyck, Robert, 171, 239
Pinker, Steven, 102, 104
Pink noise (1/f), 126
Pitts, W., 186
Planck, Max, 48
Plane geometry, 211
Plato, 32
Playfair, William, 36
Poincaré, Henri, 240, 242, 253
Poincaré resonance, 97
Politics, 234
Polkinghorne, John, 22
Popper, Karl, 105, 108, 233–234, 238–239
Portfolio theory, 64. *See also* Modern Portfolio Theory (MPT)
Posner, Richard A., 102, 104
Power Laws, 127
Predator-prey model, 53
Predictability, 190
Predictable phenomena, 49–51
Predictions, 13, 39, 44, 200
Price, 167–169
Prigogine, Ilya, 49, 76, 86, 91, 93, 95, 115, 171, 229, 233, 235, 240–241, 262, 266–267, 270, 287, 290, 292, 298
Principle of sufficient reason, 46

Probability
    applications, generally, 60, 86, 95, 98–99, 131
    theory, 64
Problem-solving, 105, 108
Process, 168, 272–273
Production cycle, 96
Product release cycle, 96
Profit and loss (P&L), 154, 157, 166
Proof, 58–61
Prowse, Michael, 188
Ptolemy's theory of planetary orbits, 73–74
Pythagoras, 33

QED, 59–60
Quadrant I/Quadrant II/Quadrant III/Quadrant IV, 128–130
Qualitative tags, 258
Quality, 167–169
Quantitative analysis, 83
Quantitative tags, 257
Quantum computing, 17–18
Quantum mechanics, 49
Quantum physics, 4, 16, 19, 108–109
Quantum theory, 67, 101, 109

Radio analogy, 160–161
Ramanajun, 22, 297–298
Randomness, 9, 48, 150, 157–158, 219, 238, 263
Random shocks, 71
Ray, Thomas, 103–104, 201
Real estate investment trusts (REITs), 102
Real Player, 271
Real time, 95
Real-time modeling, 93
Red Queen effect, 104
Reductionism, 15, 17, 40–43, 67, 198
Reductionist approach, 14
Reflexivity theory
    dialectics, 260–262
    functions, 254–255
    human factor, 255–258
    implications of, generally, 11–12, 102, 133, 231
    information meets capital, 258–259
    prediction, 259–260
    premises, generally, 252–253
    prices, 253–254
    risk, 254
Regression (R^2), 6, 75–76, 184
Relational approach, 30, 47, 234, 246
Relational logic, 45
Relationship, 268–270

Relativism, 275
Relativity theory, 48, 67, 212, 218
Religion, 275–276
Rescaled range (R/S) analysis, 120–121
Resolution, 244–246, 274–275
Resonance
    Brownian motion, 292–296
    domain, time *vs.* frequency, 292
    event-driven time, 290–291
    Gaussian distribution, 292–296
    geometry, 291
    implications of, generally, 95–98, 161,
        239–242, 246
    music, 291
    scriptures and, 298–299
    string theory, 296–298
Resor, Stanley B., 82
Retrodict, 44
Return on investment (ROI), 61, 106
Riemann geometry, 214
Risk
    arbitrage, 94, 227
    Hurst exponent, 221–223
    management, 13, 76, 81, 107, 124, 130,
        169, 224, 254
    measurement of, 271–272
    statement of, 170–171
    time and, 65, 212–213, 221, 225–228
Risk-aversion, 182, 225
RiskMetrics™, 131–132, 134
Risk-return profile, 168
Risk-reward performance, 25–26, 226
Rivest, Ronald, 176
Rizzo, Mario, 94, 190
Romer, Paul, 238, 247, 318
Rose, Steven, 197, 201
RSA, 109
Rutherford, Ernest, 41

S&P Index, components of, 6, 202–207
Sagan, Carl, 217
Samorodnitsky, Gennady, 83
Samuelson, Paul, 78, 80
Sargent, Thomas, 80–81
Scholes, Myron, 89. *See also* Black-Scholes
        option pricing
Schrodinger, Erwin, 163, 241, 250
Schroeder, Manfred, 126–127, 130
Science
    children's, 213–216
    derivatives, 99–100
    in financial economics, 63–65
    historical *vs.* experimental, 201–202
    implications of, generally, 89–91

    modern, 12
    unity with religion, 22
Scriptures, 298–299
Secrecy, 194–195, 265
Securities and Exchange Act of 1933, 2
Securities and Exchange Commission
        (SEC), 136–137
Seigel, Lester, 91, 312–313
Sclf-affinity, 113
Self-organized criticality (SOC), 14–15,
        103, 198, 201–202, 237, 240, 262,
        305–310
Self-referential analysis, 133
Self-similarity, in fractals, 113
Semipredictable phenomena, 49–51
Shamir, Avi, 176
Shiller, Robert, 82
Shor, Peter, 109
Shor's algorithm, 61, 109
Sidereal year, 37
Simon, Herbert A., 81, 127
Sims, Christopher, 82
Slide rule, 180–181
Small-cap investing, 164
Smith, Adam, 4, 15, 36, 40, 42, 231–232
Smith, John Maynard, 261
Smolin, Lee, 23, 38, 46, 86, 140, 262–264,
        267, 288–289
Socratic logic, 293
Soft science, 201, 206
Solar year, 37, 93
Solutions, computations, 247
Soros, George, 10, 68, 94, 102, 105, 133,
        229, 231–232, 234, 239, 244–245, 247,
        251, 254–255, 257, 259–260, 262, 287
Space-time physics, 45, 213, 216, 221, 235,
        291
Specialization, 207
Spinoza, 233
Stable distributions, 75, 82–83, 85, 165
Stable Family of Distributions, 77
Standard deviation, 7
Stars, nonlinearity and, 38–40
Static disequilibrium, 249–250
Steady state, 222
Stewart, Ian, 87, 117
Still, G Keith, 322
Stochastic model, 71
Strike prices, 223–224
String theory, 296–298
Supercomputers, 144, 161
SWAPs, 83, 223
Swarm theory, 231
Systems, 54–56

Tagging, 249, 257, 283, 311
Taqqu, Murad, 83
Taxonomy, 42
Technical analysis, 159–160, 185–186
Technological advances, impact of, 99, 134, 141–145, 238
Technology gap, 9
Tesseract, 210–211
Thales, 30, 32, 171
Theory, generally, 72–73. *See also specific theories*
Theory of relativity, 12, 24, 67
Thermodynamics, 48, 67, 85
Thinking outside the box, 209
Thorne, Kip, 217
3D graphics, 37, 141–142, 144, 216, 282
Time
    data and, 225
    distributions and assumptions in, 128
    event-driven, 290–291
    horizon, 97
    implications of, generally, 81, 92–95, 211–212, 218
    perception, 65–66
    resonance and, 239–242
    risk and, 225–228
    series, 85, 147, 224, 241
Time's arrow, 92
Tipler, Frank, 22, 101, 237, 250
Trading limits, 16
Train, John, 179, 231, 303–304
Transitions, 54
Tufte, Edward, 280–281
Turing, A. M., 106–108
Turing machine, 176, 186
Tversky, Amos, 166, 188–189, 255
Twachtman, John Henry, 92
2D graphics, 216
Type I/Type II/Type III errors, 88, 90, 101, 275

Uncertainty principle, 10, 48, 67, 183–184, 262

Underlying assumptions, 9
Universality, quantitative, 49
UNIX, 138
Unpredictable phenomena, 49–50, 52

Vaga, Tonis, 11
Valuation, 3
Value analysis, 240
Value investing, 165
Varadhan, Ragu, 91
Velocity, 248
Virtual reality, 106–107
Vision, 68–70
Volatility, implications of, 6–7, 76, 124, 216, 222
von Mises, Ludwig, 188
von Neumann, John, 55, 69
V statistic, 121

Wave operators, 197
Wealth creation, 97
Welch, Ivo, 190
Weltanschauung, 12
Weyl, Herman, 46, 103, 248, 256, 266–267, 269
Whalen, Thomas, 185
Wheeler, John Archibald, 47
Wiener, Norbert, 219
Wilson, EO, 78, 282
World, states of, 49
Worldview, 72–73
Wriston, Walter, 9
Wysocki, Bernard, 189

Yield-management, 2
Yogananda, Paramanhasa, 289–290, 298

Zadeh, Lotfi, 280, 282
Zipf's law, 125
Zolotarev, V., 82